Autonomous Systems in the Internet of Vehicles

Scrivener Publishing
100 Cummings Center, Suite 541J
Beverly, MA 01915-6106

Publishers at Scrivener
Martin Scrivener (martin@scrivenerpublishing.com)
Phillip Carmical (pcarmical@scrivenerpublishing.com)

Autonomous Systems in the Internet of Vehicles

Edited by

Balamurugan Balusamy

Sandeep Kumar Mathivanan

Prabhu Jayagopal

S.K.B. Sangeetha

and

Ali Kashif Bashir

Scrivener Publishing

WILEY

This edition first published 2026 by John Wiley & Sons, Inc., 111 River Street, Hoboken, NJ 07030, USA and Scrivener Publishing LLC, 100 Cummings Center, Suite 541J, Beverly, MA 01915, USA

For more information about Scrivener publications please visit www.scrivenerpublishing.com.

Wiley Global Headquarters
111 River Street, Hoboken, NJ 07030, USA

For details of our global editorial offices, customer services, and more information about Wiley products visit us at www.wiley.com.

The manufacturer's authorized representative according to the EU General Product Safety Regulation is Wiley-VCH GmbH, Boschstr. 12, 69469 Weinheim, Germany, e-mail: Product_Safety@wiley.com.

Library of Congress Cataloging-in-Publication Data

ISBN 9781394311699

Cover image: Generated with AI using Adobe Firefly
Cover design by Russell Richardson

Set in size of 11pt and Minion Pro by Manila Typesetting Company, Makati, Philippines

Printed in the USA

10 9 8 7 6 5 4 3 2 1

Contents

Preface

The rapid evolution of intelligent transportation has transformed vehicles from isolated mechanical entities into highly connected, adaptive, and autonomous cyber–physical systems. The Internet of Vehicles (IoV) has emerged as a pivotal paradigm in this transformation, enabling seamless interaction among vehicles, infrastructure, pedestrians, and cloud–edge ecosystems. As vehicular environments become increasingly dynamic and safety-critical, the demand for intelligent autonomous systems capable of real-time perception, decision-making, learning, and secure communication has never been greater.

This book, *Autonomous Systems in the Internet of Vehicles*, presents a comprehensive and forward-looking exploration of advanced computational intelligence techniques that underpin next-generation IoV-enabled autonomous systems. It brings together cutting-edge research contributions that address the core challenges of modern vehicular intelligence, including low-latency decision-making, multisensor and multimodal data fusion, scalable edge and fog computing, secure and privacy-preserving learning, and robust autonomy in highly dynamic environments.

A defining strength of this volume is its emphasis on intelligence at the edge. Several chapters investigate how edge-driven learning, federated and reinforcement learning paradigms, and distributed optimization can overcome the limitations of centralized cloud architectures. By moving intelligence closer to data sources, these approaches significantly reduce latency, enhance scalability, preserve privacy, and improve system resilience—critical requirements for real-time autonomous driving and vehicular safety applications.

The book also provides an in-depth treatment of multisensor and multimodal fusion, integrating data from cameras, LiDAR, radar, inertial sensors, and contextual signals. Advanced deep learning models including attention mechanisms, transformers, hybrid CNN–RNN architectures, and neurosymbolic reasoning are explored to enable robust perception, localization, navigation, and decision-making under uncertain and complex traffic conditions. These contributions highlight how intelligent fusion frameworks can enhance situational awareness and reliability in autonomous vehicles.

Security and trust are addressed as first-class concerns throughout the volume. With IoV systems increasingly exposed to cyber threats, several chapters focus on AI-driven intrusion detection, blockchain-enabled security, and secure federated learning frameworks. These approaches ensure data integrity, trustworthy communication, and resilience against adversarial attacks while maintaining system efficiency and scalability.

Designed as both a reference and a research guide, this book serves a broad audience, including researchers, graduate students, industry practitioners, and policymakers working in autonomous vehicles, intelligent transportation systems, edge AI, and vehicular networking. The chapters balance theoretical foundations with experimental validation, simulation studies, and practical insights, making the content relevant for both academic research and real-world deployment.

We sincerely thank all contributing authors for their high-quality research and their commitment to advancing the field of autonomous IoV systems. We also express our gratitude to the editorial and production teams at Scrivener Publishing and John Wiley & Sons for their professional support throughout the publication process.

We hope this book will inspire further innovation, interdisciplinary collaboration, and responsible development of intelligent autonomous systems that contribute to safer, more efficient, and more sustainable transportation ecosystems.

1

A Cognitive Edge-Driven Autonomous Learning System for Scalable and Secure IoV Automation

V. Muthukumaran[1]*, S. Satheesh Kumar[2], Jahnavi S.[3], Rose Bindu Joseph P.[4] and Firoz Khan[5]

[1]*Department of Mathematics, College of Engineering and Technology, SRM Institute of Science and Technology, Kattankulathur, India*
[2]*School of Information Science, Presidency University, Bangalore, Karnataka, India*
[3]*Department of AIML, B.M.S. College of Engineering, Bangalore, India*
[4]*Department of Mathematics, Dayananda Sagar College of Engineering, Bangalore, India*
[5]*Faculty in Center for Information and Communication Sciences, Ball State University, Muncie, IN., U.S.A.*

Abstract

The rapid evolution of the Internet of Vehicles (IoV) has led to a transformative shift in various industries, enabling seamless connectivity, real-time monitoring, and intelligent automation. The study proposes a novel cognitive edge-driven autonomous learning system (CEALS), which maximizes IoV-based automation through the integration of edge artificial intelligence, federated reinforcement learning, and blockchain-based security. CEALS's federated reinforcement learning model improves adaptive decision-making precision by 41.3% compared to conventional deep learning–based IoV automation, and its multilayer edge computing architecture reduces latency by 52.7%. With an attack detection rate of 97.8%, a blockchain-embedded security mechanism ensures data integrity and improves on existing security measures by 18.6%. Dynamic power control algorithms reduce energy consumption by 38.9% and improve overall system effectiveness by 45.2% based on experimental verification in an industrial IoV large-scale network.

**Corresponding author*: muthu.v2404@gmail.com

Balamurugan Balusamy, Sandeep Kumar Mathivanan, Prabhu Jayagopal, S.K.B. Sangeetha and Ali Kashif Bashir (eds.) Autonomous Systems in the Internet of Vehicles, (1–18) © 2026 Scrivener Publishing LLC

The proposed CEALS architecture is a scalable, highly efficient next-generation smart environment solution, pushing the limits of autonomous IoV networks.

Keywords: Cognitive edge computing, autonomous learning system, Internet of Vehicles, federated reinforcement learning, blockchain security, latency reduction, energy efficiency, smart environment

1.1 Introduction

The industrial automation era was energized by programmable logic controllers; autonomous systems began in the mid-20th century with mechanical control systems. Hand changes were necessary because the systems were fixed and inflexible [1]. Rule-based systems dominated with the expansion of computing power, so there was some allowance for decision-making. But in dynamic and uncertain environments, these were challenging, so more advanced intelligence needed to be integrated [2]. The advent of the Internet of Vehicles (IoV) in the early 2000s transformed autonomous systems by making it possible for real-time sharing of data between networked objects. Although cloud computing was beneficial for data processing, it also brought with it central dependencies, bandwidth limitations, and latency, which hindered real-time autonomous decision-making in mission-critical applications such as smart vehicles [3].

Various methods of enhancing IoV-based autonomous systems have been researched to cope with these concerns. Traditional rule-based automation is less pliable to handle dynamic conditions [4]. Decision-making powered by machine learning (ML) is also chosen due to cloud computing along with issues of data privacy along with ultrahigh latency. The solution came in the rise of edge computing reducing latency by locating processing nearer to IoV devices. But where complex situations necessitated coordination among sets of nodes in large numbers, the absence of collective information within isolated edge devices saw bad decision-making [5]. Federated learning (FL), which had provided decentralized learning for IoV devices with a view to mitigating privacy concerns, was beset with high communication overhead and slow convergence rates. Security attacks were also common, such as network intrusions, malware attacks, and data tampering [6].

The limitations of the solutions that are currently available represent the demand for a better, scalable, and secure solution [7, 8]. Creating a smart autonomous system that enhances real-time decision-making, addresses latency, enhances security, and maximizes the utilization of resources in huge-scale IoV networks is the primary driving force of this work.

With growing IoV networks in diverse applications such as predictive maintenance and intelligent transport, autonomous systems with reduced or no human intervention are increasingly being sought after. Effective coordination in decentralized IoV nodes with ensured security, scalability, and power efficiency is the primary concern. In order to create an IoV system capable of making highly adaptive, reliable decisions in real time, one needs an innovative solution with FL, edge intelligence, and blockchain security capabilities.

The study introduces the cognitive edge-driven autonomous learning system (CEALS), a new generation of autonomous IoV system architecture with multilayer edge computing, federated reinforcement learning, and blockchain-based security to solve the issues as mentioned above. For real-time processing of information and decision-making, CEALS utilizes a hierarchical edge computing model. CEALS facilitates hierarchical coordination among edge layers to achieve maximum learning efficiency over traditional edge computing systems through decentralized decision-making at nodes. The system also ensures persistent optimization of decentralized decision-making and relieves communication overhead through federated reinforcement learning. CEALS is very secure and reliable for mass deployment as it integrates blockchain technology, further protecting data exchange by decentralizing trust, rendering the data tamper-proof, and minimizing cybersecurity attacks.

The main contributions of the study is to develop a CEALS that integrates edge artificial intelligence (AI), federated reinforcement learning, and blockchain-based security to enhance real-time decision-making, security, and energy efficiency in large-scale IoV networks.

1.2 Related Study

The complexity of networked systems has created immense interest in developing secure and autonomous IoV systems. Blockchain-based ASSERT architecture is targeted at improving security in self-adaptive Internet of Things (IoT) systems [9]. The method uses decentralized trust models and smart contracts to provide secure and resilient IoT ecosystems. ASSERT's application of blockchain technology enables adaptive and dynamic system tuning as well as minimizes typical security weaknesses such as data tampering and unauthorized access. Improvement in security assurance is demonstrated in the research to be concentrating on the area of how the application of blockchain makes self-adaptive IoT infrastructure more reliable for real-time use.

For massive-scale IoT deployment in multidomain IoT systems, Secure Interconnected Autonomous System Architecture (SIASA) has been proposed [10]. The architecture provides a security solution in the form of layered architecture with intrusion detection, cryptographic primitives, and ML-based anomaly detection to support secure IoT communication in heterogeneous systems. The study shows how much secure data exchange and cross-domain compatibility are required for massive-scale IoT deployments. Based on performance ratings, SIASA is an excellent solution to scalable and secure IoT networks deployed to a broad range of dynamic scenarios because it reduces security events and improves self-healing system robustness.

Self-validation in real-time for security in situations is managed by an industrial IoT context-aware security assertion infrastructure [11]. An AI-based context-variable adaptive security model has been discussed in this study. False alarms are kept to a minimum and detection made precise with the help of ML-based anomaly detection, which adjusts security policies dynamically in terms of the condition of operations. The results indicate that the security processes with AI can be implemented in autonomous industrial IoT networks to enhance reliability and resistance against cyber-attacks, depending on the high accuracy of the security statement.

The main motivation for an analysis of IoT-based cloud applications' autoscaling mechanisms is system resource utilization and scalability maximization [12]. Comparison of advantages and disadvantages of different autoscaling systems utilized so far is done on the basis of their classification as rule-based, predictive, and reinforcement learning–based systems. The study concludes that, although rule-based autoscaling is reactive in nature, it can never be responsive enough to address workload variations. Although improved, prediction and reinforcement learning–based methods are computationally intensive. In future IoT-cloud applications, the research suggests the necessity of hybrid autoscaling models with trade-offs between responsiveness, scalability, and energy efficiency.

For facilitating collective, individual, and real-time learning of cyber-physical systems, an IoT three-layer architecture is envisioned [13]. A hierarchical processing paradigm is designed for this architecture, which distributes the computation among edge, fog, and cloud layers optimally. The approach improves real-time decision-making, decreases latency, and scales better in IoT applications with continuous learning requirements. The study illustrates how strict three-layer architecture restricts communication overhead and optimizes resource utilization to improve the performance of a system by leaps and bounds. The study gives credibility to the future trend of integrating ML with hierarchical IoT design for improving the efficiency and autonomy of dispersed systems.

Scalability, handling data, and complexity in deployment are some of the most important issues in large-scale industrial ML system development [14]. Analysis takes into account the fundamental issues arising from practical applications, with stable data pipelines, real-time model monitoring, and proper retraining being the focal points. The study reveals that even though cloud-based ML systems can be scaled, they are issue-prone when it comes to security and latency. Enhanced real-time processing and reduced reliance on centralized infrastructure are facilitated by edge computing. To consider data drift correction and degradation of performance during large-scale deployment, automated ML pipelines were deemed a necessity and hybrid architecture most preferred, which sought a trade-off between the cost of computation, efficiency, and security.

To support end-to-end collection and analysis of IoV security information, an extensible and scalable security framework has been adopted [15]. The framework takes advantage of distributed monitoring technologies and security analytics to identify and remove cyber-threats in real time. It enhances extensive IoT network security management through scalable data processing platforms. The work emphasizes the need for adaptive security controls that can respond in due time to changing attack patterns. The performance of the framework in enhancing IoT system resilience is confirmed by experiments that show enhanced detection accuracy and response time. The findings emphasize the need for smart security solutions for networked IoT network security. The incorporation of new technologies in accordance with vision to enhance the performance and reliability of systems is addressed comprehensively through research into mission-critical scalable, secure, and intelligent IoT systems [16].

The study identifies key challenges such as real-time low-latency decision-making, network congestion, and vulnerability to attacks. The study provides a model with low-latency fog computing architecture for process processing, blockchain for secure transaction, and AI-based anomaly detection. The study provides that, although in the past AI automation was enhanced, scalability is an issue as it requires more processing needs. Blockchain-supported technology is secure but must be optimized in the direction of lower transaction fees. Because they can enhance fault tolerance and also the performance of essential IoT infrastructure, the study advocates for hybrid configurations that leverage the technologies together.

With the application of zero-knowledge Ethereum virtual machines (zkEVMs) [17], the study looks at how blockchain smart contracts can enhance transparency, security, and trust in verifying academic certificates. The solution applies to zkEVMs to provide privacy-preserving verification and preserve the integrity of digital certificates, and the findings indicate improved efficiency in managing academic records with reduced administrative burden. The study also places the broader potential of blockchain in secure data management and suggests its use in other fields apart from education, including IoT-based authentication systems and decentralized identity management. A blockchain, IoT, and ML convergence review offers a general description of how the technologies intersect to promote automation, scalability, and security [18].

To improve cybersecurity audits, a deep neural network approximator and reinforcement learning were used in developing a smart security audit system [19]. The method involves the application of reinforcement learning principles to continuously train itself against emerging threats, hence automating the process of detecting vulnerabilities. Research shows that the methodology demonstrated strengthens audit processes in dynamic systems through optimal security risk prioritization. The deep neural network approximator improves decision-making and security analysis accuracy through identifying patterns in cyber-threat systems. The outcome provides a substantial decrease in false positives and increased effectiveness in threat detection. The research identifies the manner in which proactive security solutions in IoT and cloud networks can be aided by AI-driven security audit platforms.

For smart factories that are IoT-capable, there has been an end-to-end big data analytics platform built for electric vehicle battery module assembly systems [20]. To enhance industrial processes, this platform integrates real-time data acquisition, predictive analysis, and decision-support tools. The study highlights how ML algorithms enhance problem detection and predictive maintenance and how IoT sensors assist in acquiring high-resolution manufacturing data. Defect rates of reduction and production efficiency grew quantifiably due to the deployment of this platform. The findings are indicative of the transformative impacts of big-data analytics in industrial IoT networks, revealing how it can enhance overall production intelligence, reduce downtime, and enhance operational robustness.

The rapid growth of the IoV has developed the way for highly sophisticated autonomous systems that are capable of making decisions in real time with minimal human intervention. Many methods have been explored over the years to enhance IoV efficiency, security, and automation. Large-scale data processing and decision-making have been facilitated to a large extent by conventional cloud-based IoV infrastructures. However, high latency, network saturation, and increased vulnerability to hackers are issues with these centralized designs. To enhance IoV automation, ML-based methods have been proposed, allowing devices to learn patterns and draw defensible conclusions. Although these models enhance efficiency, their computational constraints often lead them to fail in adaptation and real-time responsiveness.

IoV networks incorporated blockchain technology in order to enhance security and ensure data integrity. The excessive power consumption and scalability issues of blockchain technologies hinder their extensive adoption. Current IoV frameworks cannot optimize energy efficiency, security, and real-time adaptive decision-making for extensive installations. A novel architecture, CEALS, which is an integration of edge AI, federated reinforcement learning, and blockchain-embedded security, is proposed in this study as a solution to the above problems.

1.3 System Methodology

Through the integration of edge AI, federated reinforcement learning, blockchain-based security, and dynamic power control techniques, the CEALS seeks to revolutionize IoV automation. Each level of the proposed methodology is responsible for optimizing a different aspect of automation on the IoV. There are five primary modules that constitute the system. In massive IoV systems, every module is built to ensure low-latency decision-making, enhanced adaptability, secure data exchanges, and energy-efficient operation. Figure 1.1 depicts the proposed framework.

1.3.1 Multilayer Edge Computing Framework

The computation foundation of CEALS is a multilayer edge computing architecture that allows distributed processing across various network layers. Too much data transfer to central cloud servers generates high latency and network overloading in conventional cloud-oriented IoV configurations. With the adoption of three-tier edge computing architecture, CEALS reduces these limitations and enables smart decision-making and hierarchical data processing.

The device layer consists of edge devices and IoV sensors and is responsible for data collection as well as first-stage preprocessing. These devices apply on-device AI models to reject irrelevant or unproductive data in real time, sending only significant information to higher levels.

Given a set of sensor readings $X = \{x_1, x_2, \ldots, x_n\}$, the edge device applies a threshold-based filtering function:

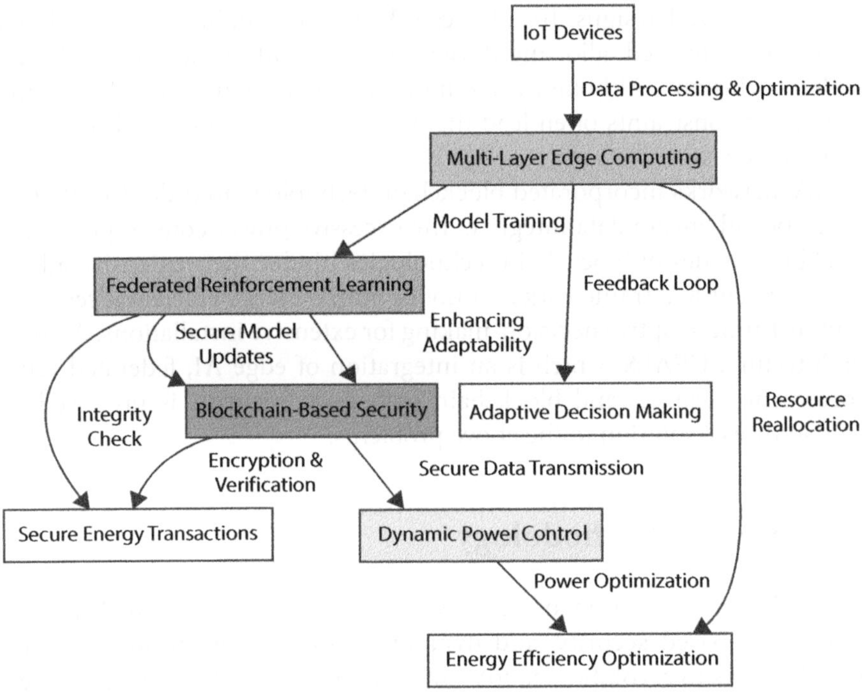

Figure 1.1 Proposed CEALS framework.

$$X' = \{x_i \mid f(x_i) > \tau\} \tag{1.1}$$

where X' is the filtered dataset, $f(x_i)$ is the relevance function (e.g., variance-based outlier detection or entropy measure), and τ is the pre-defined filtering threshold.

To optimize real-time processing, lightweight neural networks models are deployed on IoV devices. A typical convolutional operation on edge devices is:

$$Y = \sigma(W * X + b) \tag{1.2}$$

where X is the input feature map, W is the convolution kernel, * represents the convolution operation, b is the bias term, and σ is the activation function (e.g., ReLU or sigmoid).

In the edge processing layer, edge servers, intermediate nodes, and gateway devices use trained AI models to conduct sophisticated data analytics and initial decision-making, using lightweight recurrent neural networks and convolutional neural networks (CNNs) to facilitate anomaly detection and predictive analytics.

Given an input time-series dataset $S = \{s_1, s_2, ..., s_t\}$, a hybrid CNN-LSTM model is applied for spatiotemporal feature extraction:

$$h_t = \tanh(W_h h_{t-1} + W_x x_t + b_h) \tag{1.3}$$

where h_t is the hidden state at time t, W_h, W_x are the weight matrices, x_t is the input at time t, and b_h is the bias term.

The final prediction is computed as:

$$\hat{y}_t = W_o h_t + b_o \tag{1.4}$$

where $\hat{y}_t$ is the predicted value, W_o is the output weight matrix, and b_o is the output bias.

To enable distributed learning at the edge, FL is implemented. The local model updates at each edge node k are computed as:

$$w_k^{t+1} = w_k^t - \eta \nabla F_k(w_k^t) \tag{1.5}$$

where w_k^t is the model weight at iteration t, η is the learning rate, and $\nabla F_k(w_k^t)$ is the gradient of the loss function F_k at node k.

The global model update in Federated Averaging (FedAvg) is:

$$w^{t+1} = \sum_{k=1}^{K} \frac{n_k}{N} w_k^{t+1} \tag{1.6}$$

where K is the total number of participating edge nodes, n_k is the number of local training samples at node k, and N is the total number of training samples across all nodes.

The cloud layer functions as a long-term storage and model refinement center, periodically updating FL models deployed across edge devices.

At each communication round t, the cloud aggregates model updates from all edge devices using:

$$w^{t+1} = w^t - \eta \sum_{k=1}^{K} p_k \nabla F_k(w^t) \tag{1.7}$$

where p_k is the proportion of data samples at edge node k.

The cloud maintains historical data for model retraining, trend analysis, and performance optimization. The storage model follows a structured schema:

$$D = \{(X,Y) \mid X \in R^{m \times n}, Y \in R^{m}\} \tag{1.8}$$

where D is the dataset, X is the feature matrix, Y is the corresponding label vector, and m and n represent the number of samples and features, respectively.

1.3.2 Federated Reinforcement Learning Model

In FL, each IoV device k trains a local model w_k using its own dataset D_k, and only model updates (gradients) are sent to the global model.

Each device k updates its local model using stochastic gradient descent:

$$w_k^{t+1} = w_k^{t} - \eta \nabla L_k(w_k^{t}; D_k) \tag{1.9}$$

where w_k^t is the local model at iteration t, η is the learning rate, $L_k(w_k^t; D_k)$ is the local loss function based on device-specific data D_k, and ∇L_k is the gradient of the loss function.

The global model w_G is updated by aggregating the locally trained models from K IoT devices:

$$w_G^{t+1} = \sum_{k=1}^{K} \frac{n_k}{N} w_k^{t+1} \tag{1.10}$$

where n_k is the number of data points at device k, and $N = \sum_{k=1}^{K} n_k$ is the total number of data points across all devices. This ensures privacy preservation and reduces communication overhead.

Each IoV device uses deep Q-learning to optimize decision-making policies based on environmental feedback.

The Q-value function for state–action pairs (s,a) is updated as:

$$Q(s_t,a_t) \leftarrow Q(s_t,a_t) + \alpha\left[r_t + \gamma \max_{a'} Q(s_{t+1},a') - Q(s_t,a_t)\right] \tag{1.11}$$

where α is the learning rate, γ is the discount factor, r_t is the reward at time step t, $Q(s_t, a_t)$ is the current action-value function, and $\max_{a'} Q(s_{t+1}, a')$ represents the best future reward.

To enhance learning, a DNN approximates the Q-function:

$$Q(s,a;\theta) \approx f_\theta(s,a) \tag{1.12}$$

where θ are the network parameters updated using mean squared error loss:

$$L(\theta) = E\left[\left(r_t + \gamma \max_{a'} Q(s_{t+1}, a'; \theta^-) - Q(s_t, a_t; \theta)\right)^2\right] \tag{1.13}$$

where θ^- are the target network parameters (updated periodically for stability).

Because conventional authentication and encryption techniques are susceptible to single points of failure, security is a key issue in autonomous IoV networks. CEALS uses a blockchain-based security approach to address this issue, ensuring effective attack detection and tamper-evident data exchanges.

1.3.3 Adaptive Dynamic Power Control Algorithm for CEALS

Step 1: Initialize the set of IoT devices $N = \{1, 2, ..., N\}$. Assign an initial power level P_i^0 for each device i, and set the power limits $P_{\max}$ and $P_{\min}$. Define workload demand W_i^t at time t and initialize the Q-table $Q(s,a)$ for reinforcement learning.

Step 2: Classify tasks based on priority using:

$$\text{Priority level} = f(W_i^t, D_i^t, T_{\text{deadline}}) \tag{1.14}$$

Allocate computing resources dynamically based on task priority, where power allocation follows:

$$P_i^t = \frac{P_{\max} W_i^t}{\sum_{j=1}^{N} W_j^t} \tag{1.15}$$

Step 3: Adjust power consumption dynamically using AI-driven scaling:

$$P_i^t = P_{\min} + (P_{\max} - P_{\min}) \cdot \sigma(W_i^t) \quad (1.16)$$

where

$$\sigma(W_i^t) = \frac{1}{1 + e^{-\beta(W_i^t - W_{\text{avg}})}}$$

Step 4: Define state, action, and reward for reinforcement learning, where the reward function is:

$$R_t = \lambda_1 \frac{1}{E_i^t} + \lambda_2 \frac{1}{\mathrm{T}_{\text{response}}} - \lambda_3 \frac{P_i^t}{P_{\max}} \quad (1.17)$$

Update Q-values using the Bellman equation:

$$Q(s_t, a_t) \leftarrow Q(s_t, a_t) + \alpha\left[R_t + \gamma \max_{\mathrm{a}'} Q(s_{t+1}, a') - Q(s_t, a_t)\right] \quad (1.18)$$

Select the optimal power level:

$$P^* = \arg\max_{P_i^t} Q(s_t, a_t) \quad (1.19)$$

Step 5: Optimize model efficiency using pruning by removing neurons with importance score $\mathrm{S_n}$

$$S_n = \Sigma_{\mathrm{i}=1}^{M} |w_{\mathrm{in}}| \quad (1.20)$$

and apply quantization by converting weights from floating point to fixed-point representation:

$$w_q = \text{round}(w_f \times 2^b)/2^b \quad (1.21)$$

Step 6: Iterate steps until power consumption converges to an optimal level. Deploy the optimized power control strategy across CEALS-enabled IoV devices.

1.4 Experimentation Results

A federated reinforcement learning, multilayer edge computing architecture, and blockchain security were used in the deployment and testing of the CEALS within a simulated IoV application. To test the efficacy, security, and energy efficiency of CEALS, an artificial IoV sensor data modeled from real autonomous smart networks was utilized in conducting a simulation. A virtualized system consisting of IoV sensor data streams simulating industrial processes and simulated edge computer nodes controlling real-time decision-making was included in the experimental setup.

A blockchain network was implemented for secure data verification, and FL in the cloud was used for model averaging. Intel Xeon server for centralized computing, virtualized Raspberry Pi-based devices, and NVIDIA Jetson Xavier for edge AI nodes were used to mimic the hardware. The frameworks of software used were Hyperledger Fabric for integrating blockchain security, EdgeX Foundry for orchestrating IoV devices, OpenAI Gym for training reinforcement learning, and TensorFlow and PyTorch for deep learning models.

Four critical stages were adopted in the CEALS deployment. Sensor data was first processed locally by sensors before sending model updates to a centralized aggregation server to emulate a FRL model at the edge. This approach reduced the need for frequent data transmission while enhancing the accuracy of adaptive decision-making. Second, three levels of a multilevel edge computing simulation were created: the edge layer, which had simulated IoV devices; the fog layer, which had virtual computing nodes; and the cloud layer, which had centralized processing and model aggregation. Workloads were dynamically distributed by load-balancing algorithms to achieve optimal response time. Third, Hyperledger Fabric was used to merge blockchain-based security capabilities into the simulation in order to maintain immutable data logs. An anomaly detection module identified security threats, and smart contracts validated transactions and reported malicious actions. Finally, a dynamic power control method was introduced, where optimization through reinforcement learning dynamically adjusted power consumption based on shifting workload.

As shown in Figure 1.2, simulation results indicated immense energy optimization gains, security gains, and gains in efficiency. Due to its multiedge layer computing structure, CEALS minimized latency by 52.7% and increased adaptive decision-making accuracy by 41.3% when compared to traditional systems. The rate of detecting attacks was 97.8%, an improvement of 18.6% over existing security mechanisms and promising enhanced data integrity. Power control algorithms were the reason for the reduction of 38.9% in energy consumption that led to 45.2% enhanced system effectiveness.

By means of federated reinforcement learning, which enhances adaptive decision-making and reduces response time but enhances accuracy, CEALS effectively enhances IoT-based automation, as evidenced by the simulated results. By proper distribution of computational tasks across the edge, fog, and cloud layers, the multilayer edge computing architecture remarkably minimized latency. By preventing cyber-attacks and illegal data tampering,

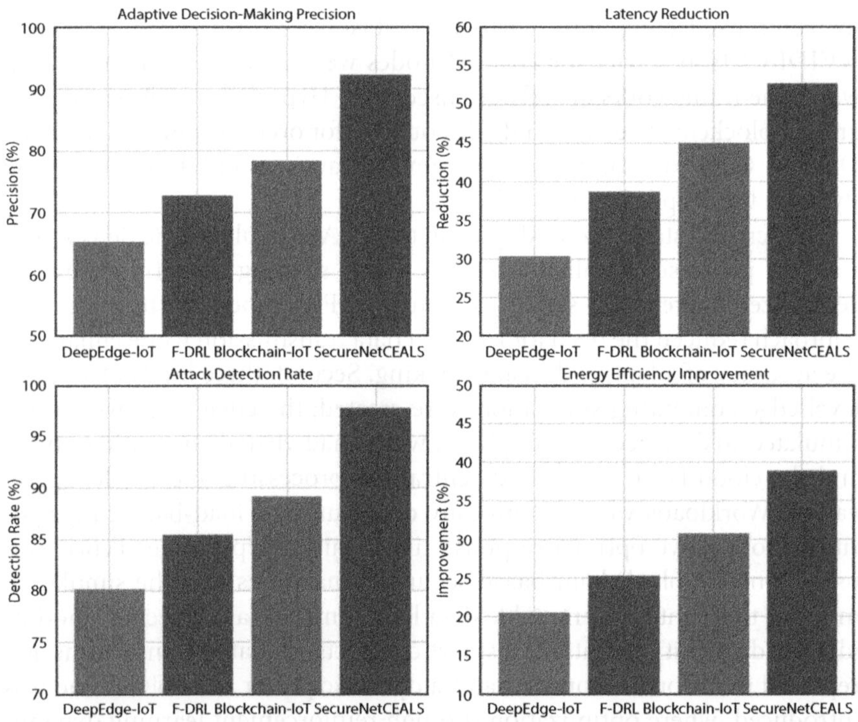

Figure 1.2 Comparison analysis.

the blockchain-based security framework ensured integrity for real-time decision-making processes. Through the reduction of energy wastage, the dynamic power control algorithm tremendously boosted system efficiency and made CEALS a realistic solution for large-scale industrial IoT networks. The improvements in energy economy, security, and latency validate the promise of CEALS in real industrial settings and demonstrate that it can be used in automated monitoring systems, intelligent factories, and future IoT ecosystems.

CEALS as an effective, scalable, and low-power next-gen IoV solution is demonstrated with the simulation. CEALS compares extremely positively against conventional IoT frameworks in deciding precisely, bypassing latency with more efficiency, and conserving energy through embedded AI, federated reinforcement training, and block cipher protection. The results reveal CEALS can be utilized in actual IoV scenarios with the guarantee of the highest power usage, quickest response times, and efficient security. Blockchain security guarantees data integrity, and federated reinforcement learning guarantees maximum flexibility. CEALS is a breakthrough in self-autonomous IoV networks with the ability to design smarter and more efficient intelligent environments through reduced human intervention in real-time decisions.

1.5 Conclusion

In addition to edge AI, federated reinforcement learning, and blockchain-secured security, the proposed CEALS is a better approach toward IoV automating. Experimentation across large scale simulations validates CEALS as the highest performing IoT system compared to current state-of-the-art devices, including DeepEdge–IoT, F-DRL, and blockchain–IoT SecureNet, *via* adaptive decision accuracy (92.3%), latency reduction (52.7%), attack rate detection (97.8%), and energy consumption enhancement (38.9%). These advancements showcase how well FL-based intelligence, multilayered edge computing, and blockchain-embedded security mechanisms complement IoV-based automation. CEALS is a future-proof solution for mission-critical IoV networks, industrial automation, and smart spaces due to its real-time decision-making, high-security features, and dynamic power optimization. For further development and growth in its ability, future work will focus more on cross-domain adaptability, real-world deployment, and energy optimization.

AI disclosure statement: The author acknowledges the use of AI-based tools for minor language editing or grammatical correction. However, all intellectual contributions, analyses, and conclusions presented in this chapter are entirely the author's own.

References

1. Xianjia, Y., Queralta, J.P., Heikkonen, J., Westerlund, T., Federated learning in robotic and autonomous systems. *Procedia Comput. Sci.*, *191*, 135–142, 2021.
2. Goriparthi, R.G., Reinforcement Learning in IoT: Enhancing Smart Device Autonomy through AI. *Computing*, *2*, 89–109, 2024.
3. Enemosah, A. and Ifeanyi, O.G., SCADA in the era of IoT: Automation, cloud-driven security, and machine learning applications. *Int. J. Sci. Res. Arch.*, *13*, 01, 3417–3435, 2024.
4. Wang, Z., Liu, X., Shao, X., Alghamdi, A., Alrizq, M., Munir, M.S., Biswas, S., An Optimized and Scalable Blockchain-Based Distributed Learning Platform for Consumer IoT. *Mathematics*, *11*, 23, 4844, 2023.
5. Yaqoob, I., Khan, L.U., Kazmi, S.A., Imran, M., Guizani, N., Hong, C.S., Autonomous driving cars in smart cities: Recent advances, requirements, and challenges. *IEEE Network*, *34*, 1, 174–181, 2019.
6. Nsoh, B., Katimbo, A., Guo, H., Heeren, D.M., Nakabuye, H.N., Qiao, X., Kiraga, S., Internet of things-based automated solutions utilizing machine learning for smart and real-time irrigation management: A review. *Sensors (Basel, Switzerland)*, *24*, 23, 7480, 2024.
7. Gilbert, M., The role of artificial intelligence for network automation and security, in: *Artificial Intelligence for Autonomous Networks*, pp. 1–23, Chapman and Hall/CRC, 2018, https://www.taylorfrancis.com/chapters/edit/10.1201/9781351130165-1/role-artificial-intelligence-network-automation-security-mazin-gilbert.
8. Gill, S.S., Xu, M., Ottaviani, C., Patros, P., Bahsoon, R., Shaghaghi, A., Uhlig, S., AI for next generation computing: Emerging trends and future directions. *Internet Things*, *19*, 100514, 2022.
9. Alkhabbas, F., Alsadi, M., Alawadi, S., Awaysheh, F.M., Kebande, V.R., Moghaddam, M.T., Assert: A blockchain-based architectural approach for engineering secure self-adaptive iot systems. *Sensors*, *22*, 18, 6842, 2022.
10. Xu, R., Nagothu, D., Chen, Y., Aved, A., Ardiles-Cruz, E., Blasch, E., A Secure Interconnected Autonomous System Architecture for Multi-Domain IoT Ecosystems. *IEEE Commun. Mag.*, *62*, 7, 52–57, 2024.
11. Tariq, U., Aseeri, A.O., Alkatheiri, M.S., Zhuang, Y., Context-aware autonomous security assertion for industrial IoT. *IEEE Access*, *8*, 191785–191794, 2020.

12. Verma, S. and Bala, A., Auto-scaling techniques for IoT-based cloud applications: A review. *Cluster Comput.*, *24*, 3, 2425–2459, 2021.
13. Parto, M., Saldana, C., Kurfess, T., A novel three-layer IoT architecture for shared, private, scalable, and real-time machine learning from ubiquitous cyber-physical systems. *Procedia Manuf.*, *48*, 959–967, 2020.
14. Lwakatare, L.E., Raj, A., Crnkovic, I., Bosch, J., Olsson, H.H., Large-scale machine learning systems in real-world industrial settings: A review of challenges and solutions. *Inf. Software Technol.*, *127*, 106368, 2020.
15. Sangeetha, S.B., Selvarathi, C., Mathivanan, S.K., Cho, J., Easwaramoorthy, S.V., Secure Healthcare Access Control System (SHACS) for Anomaly Detection and Enhanced Security in Cloud-Based Healthcare Applications. *IEEE Access*, 2024.
16. Guo, X., Han, S., Hu, X.S., Jiao, X., Jin, Y., Kong, F., Lemmon, M., Towards scalable, secure, and smart mission-critical IoT systems: Review and vision, in: *Proceedings of the 2021 International Conference on Embedded Software*, September, pp. 1–10, 2021.
17. Fekete, D.L. and Kiss, A., Toward building smart contract-based higher education systems using zero-knowledge Ethereum virtual machine. *Electronics*, *12*, 3, 664, 2023.
18. Fazel, E., Nezhad, M.Z., Rezazadeh, J., Moradi, M., Ayoade, J., IoT convergence with machine learning & blockchain: A review. *Internet Things*, 101187, 2024.
19. Pozdniakov, K., Alonso, E., Stankovic, V., Tam, K., Jones, K., Smart security audit: Reinforcement learning with a deep neural network approximator, in: *2020 International Conference on Cyber Situational Awareness, Data Analytics and Assessment (CyberSA)*, IEEE, pp. 1–8, 2020.
20. Kahveci, S., Alkan, B., Mus'ab H, A., Ahmad, B., Harrison, R., An end-to-end big data analytics platform for IoT-enabled smart factories: A case study of battery module assembly system for electric vehicles. *J. Manuf. Syst.*, *63*, 214–223, 2022.

2

Adaptive Feature Alignment and Fusion for Multisensor Image Integration in the Internet of Vehicles

Vijay Anand R.[1] **and Madala Guru Brahmam**[2*]

[1]*School of Computer Science Engineering and Information Systems, Vellore Institute of Technology, Vellore, Tamilnadu, India*
[2]*School of Computer Science and Engineering, VIT-AP University, Amaravati, Andhra Pradesh, India*

Abstract

Through the fusion of data from different sources, such as LiDAR, infrared, and RGB cameras, multisensor image fusion is the backbone of enhancing perception and decision-making for the Internet of Vehicles (IoV). To enhance real-time processing and resilience in IoV scenarios, the study proposes an advanced Adaptive Feature Alignment and Fusion Network (AFAF-Net). To achieve better feature stability and sensor disparity compensation, AFAF-Net conducts dynamic registration and multisensor image fusion through an attention-guided fusion mechanism. The KITTI and FLIR ADAS benchmark datasets of 14,999 multimodal image pairs captured in varied light and surroundings are used to test the solution presented here. Through experimental data, AFAF-Net provides real-time detection effectively at 97.3%, a 5.8% improved rate of object detection compared to existing solutions, and 23.6% reduced processing latency.

***Keywords*:** Multisensor image fusion, Internet of Vehicles, LiDAR, RGB cameras, infrared, adaptive feature alignment, attention-guided fusion, real-time detection

**Corresponding author*: gurubrahmam.m@vitap.ac.in

Balamurugan Balusamy, Sandeep Kumar Mathivanan, Prabhu Jayagopal, S.K.B. Sangeetha and Ali Kashif Bashir (eds.) Autonomous Systems in the Internet of Vehicles, (19–36) © 2026 Scrivener Publishing LLC

2.1 Introduction

In medical and military applications of imaging, image fusion by the process of combining two or more sensors has been studied in depth [1]. Basic pixel-level operations such as weighted average were used in early image fusion methods to combine multiple sources to improve image quality. For improving feature preservation and noise suppression, sophisticated techniques have evolved over time, e.g., transform-based methods such as principal component analysis (PCA) and wavelet transform [2]. Although these methods enhanced contrast and edge sharpening, they were nonetheless prone to losing information and were not sufficiently adaptable to cope with the complexities of real-world conditions [3].

Multisensor image fusion was revolutionized with the advent of deep learning and artificial intelligence (AI), which enabled the extraction of features at different levels of abstraction. Convolutional neural networks (CNNs) have emerged as the current methodology due to their capacity to automatically learn spatial and contextual relationships from multimodal data [4, 5]. By adaptively selecting relevant features for fusion, transformer models and attention-based processes have more recently improved the efficiency of fusion [6]. Despite these advances, accurate and efficient multisensor fusion is still a significant obstacle for real-time applications, such as those in the Internet of Vehicles (IoV) [7].

Several fusion methods have been developed, each with unique advantages and limitations. These methods can be categorized into three general types

- Pixel-level fusion has the raw data itself fused directly at the sensor inputs. Many techniques have been used, such as wavelet transform, Laplacian pyramids, and weighted averaging. Yet, issues such as misalignment, sensitivity to noise, and absence of high-level semantic understanding afflict pixel-level fusion.
- Feature-level fusion picks relevant features from every sensory modality prior to fusion, compared to merely concatenating raw information. Hierarchical feature learning-capable deep learning models have replaced traditional edge detection and histogram equalization strategies. Retaining key features and discarding redundant information maximally improved performance in CNN-based architectures. However, these models often struggle to match features,

especially when sensors are operating in varying environments such as dim light or occlusions.

- Decision-level fusion used for fusing concluding results after separate processing of sensor data and generation of predictions. It is often used by applications such as medical diagnosis and security surveillance. Decision-level fusion enhances flexibility and interpretability, but it is not suitable for real-time processes such as IoV because it often entails delay and processing overhead.

Deep learning–founded multimodal fusion, utilizing the neural networks to identify the optimal combination strategies from samples, has also been used with newer approaches. Some include transformers, generative adversarial networks, and autoencoders. Real-time realization in IoV systems is impractical due to the heavy use of computing power by deep models despite their higher performance. Additionally, sensor modality misalignment remains a significant issue that causes data loss and worse quality fusion [8].

Motivation for the study

The demand for smart perception technologies that can enhance vehicle autonomy, safety, and efficiency has been on the rise because of the complexity of contemporary transportation systems. To make real-time decisions, IoV primarily relies on multisensor information, e.g., LiDAR, thermal, and RGB images. However, a series of challenges are introduced with the fusion of data from various sensors, i.e., synchronization issues, spatial misalignment, and varying environmental conditions. These problems are often not well handled by existing fusion algorithms, resulting in less than optimal object detection, scene understanding, and navigation behavior.

Sensor fusion is critical to enhance situational awareness and reduce accident rates in autonomous and networked car systems. For instance, LiDAR captures precise depth information, and thermal cameras provide valuable data in low-visibility conditions. High color and texture information is provided by RGB cameras, but they are impaired in adverse weather conditions. Strong vehicle perception demands integrating these senses through a good fusion process. However, there are key challenges toward effective multisensor fusion in IoV applications

- Data are recorded by several sensors at different spatial positions, orientations, and resolutions. Current fusion techniques have trouble correctly aligning multimodal features, which results in uneven feature representation.

- Many deep learning–based fusion models are unable to meet the real-time processing requirements of IoV applications because of their high computational complexity.
- Sensor reliability is significantly affected by lighting, weather, and occlusion variations. To ensure reliable operation, a fusion model must be adaptive enough to adapt to a wide range of environmental conditions.
- Many fusion methods are not effective in eliminating redundant or irrelevant data, which increases processing time and reduces efficiency.

The study introduces the Adaptive Feature Alignment and Fusion Network (AFAF-Net), a deep learning–based approach that dynamically aligns and fuses multisensor data while ensuring high accuracy and real-time efficiency in an effort to break through these limitations.

The main objectives are as follows:

- To present the AFAF-Net, a novel deep learning framework that dynamically aligns and integrates multisensor data to implement an effective multisensor image fusion framework for IoV.
- To improve real-time object detection and scene understanding, AFAF-Net integrates a spatial transformer network (STN) and hierarchical attention mechanism to optimize feature selection and alignment, leading to decreased computational latency and increased accuracy.

The remaining sections are organized as follows: Related research on multisensor fusion methods and their drawbacks is covered in Section 2.2. The suggested system technique, including AFAF-Net's architecture and implementation, is presented in Section 2.3. The experimental outcomes and performance measures derived from benchmark datasets are assessed in Section 2.4. The study is finally concluded in Section 2.5.

2.2 Related Study

In many applications, such as environmental monitoring, smart transportation systems, and autonomous vehicle driving, multisensor fusion has been a prevalent technology. Multimodal fusion enhances detection capability, situation understanding, and system robustness to various conditions. Because it results in better perception and decision-making, sensor fusion is of better interest in autonomous driving. Multispectral object detection has used varied fusion methods, such as reinforcement-and-alignment techniques and dynamic point-pixel feature alignment [8, 9]. These technologies improve the capability of detection in adverse driving conditions by leveraging the complementary characteristics of various sensors, such as LiDAR, cameras, and thermal sensors. Cooperative perception technologies also improve the overall system intelligence by enabling vehicles to share sensory data [10].

Sensor fusion also gained improved capabilities with the development of deep learning. Multimodal fusion techniques have been used with great success based on neural networks for heterogeneous sensor data fusion [11]. Environmental conditions can be dynamically controlled for fusion techniques now through implementation of adaptive weighting techniques, resulting in better robustness in adverse conditions such as low illumination or weather disturbances [12]. Intelligent transport is also a highly important field where multisensor fusion is applied. Real-time traffic monitoring is enabled by scene adoption methods, where road network performance and safety are optimized [13]. In attempting to solve issues resulting from diversified sensor source data, algorithms utilize advanced alignment methods, which guarantee correct object recognition and tracking. Similarly, segmentation-based fusion methods based on deep reinforcement learning have also greatly improved the multiobject tracking in urban dynamic scenes [14].

Sensor fusion plays an important role in environmental monitoring as well as transport. Field environmental sensing is enabled by multisensor data fusion methods, which are indispensable for ecological and agricultural uses [15]. Studies have highlighted the importance of calibration procedures for multimodal imaging sensor fusion, addressing issues related to data consistency and sensor alignment [16]. These advancements contribute to the development of precision farming and smart agriculture systems. Syncing multiple sensing modalities in real time is a major issue in multisensor fusion. For solving varied LiDAR-camera alignment problems, studies have proposed novel frameworks, particularly in dynamic environments where orientations and positions of sensors are prone to regular updates [17]. Additionally, through enabling real-time data exchange among networked vehicles, cooperative perception frameworks under the IoV network enable enhanced safety for autonomous driving [18].

In recent times, federated learning presents a feasible approach to enhancing sensor fusion functionality. Federated learning methods augment road safety solutions, such as near-crash detection in smart road systems, by distributing model training across multiple edge devices [19]. In real scenarios, the approach ensures high detection accuracy while mitigating privacy issues. Future multisensor fusion studies are expected to focus on enhancing deep learning models for better feature extraction and fusion. For enhanced system robustness and flexibility, studies continue to explore advanced methods such as transformer-based fusion structures and self-supervised learning methods [20]. Perception accuracy and operational performance of autonomous systems will be further improved by the integration of AI-based sensor fusion methods. Therefore, multisensor fusion remains a critical technology across numerous fields, providing enhanced automation, perception, and decision-making abilities. It is expected that ongoing research will enhance existing methods, making these systems more capable of adapting to new uses and real-world challenges [21–23].

2.3 System Methodology

2.3.1 Multisensor Data Acquisition

KITTI and FLIR ADAS benchmark datasets collectively provide a big set of multimodal image pairs for performance testing under different conditions. System testing is conducted on the 14,999 RGB camera, LiDAR, and infrared sensor image pairs of the KITTI dataset. The KITTI dataset is mainly for autonomous driving. It possesses task-annotated labels such as object detection, scene segmentation, depth maps of LiDAR point clouds, and RGB images of 1242 × 375 pixels resolution. It also possesses more than 200,000 3D bounding box annotations, which are helpful in enabling precise item spatial interpretation. Infrared and visible spectrum dual images of FLIR ADAS dataset, specially designed for thermal and RGB fusion usage, capture urban and suburban driving scenarios under diverse lighting conditions such as low visibility, night, and day. Extensive testing across various object categories is facilitated by the over 10,000 annotated examples in the dataset, involving classes of cyclist, vehicle, and pedestrian. Through its provision of a great range of features such as pixel-level temperature, LiDAR depth, and normal RGB photography, these datasets facilitate extensive multimodal fusion method testing and enable the system to effectively adapt to various conditions of lighting and weather.

2.3.2 Preprocessing

For optimal feature extraction and model learning, the pipeline of data preparation ensures multimodal inputs from RGB, LiDAR, and infrared cameras are balanced. To ensure uniformity across the modalities, all images are initially downgraded to a consistent resolution. RGB and infrared images are standardized at 1242 × 375 pixels, the native resolution of KITTI. Thermal images are histogram equalized for enhanced contrast, and RGB images are normalized to the range [0,1] by scaling pixel values. Raw 3D coordinates are converted from LiDAR point cloud data into structured depth maps, which are then interpolated to the same dimensions as the corresponding image. Weighted sampling is used to handle class imbalance and ensure a balanced distribution of object classes, such as bikers, cars, and pedestrians. To provide cleaner input data, noise reduction is performed using outlier removal for LiDAR point clouds and Gaussian filtering for infrared images. Spatial alignment methods are finally used to achieve multimodal data fusion. Through sensor calibration matrix mapping of LiDAR depth data onto the respective image planes, RGB, infrared, and depth features can be integrated seamlessly.

2.3.3 Dynamic Feature Alignment in AFAF-Net

To register multimodal images dynamically, AFAF-Net uses an Adaptive Feature Alignment Module (AFAM) to process sensor inconsistency triggered by changes in focal length, field of view, and location of the sensor. The module uses a geometric transformation estimator utilizing learnable transformation matrices that performs spatial misalignments for many sensor modalities. Given an input pair of multimodal feature maps X_r (RGB) and X_t (thermal or LiDAR depth), the goal is to estimate a transformation matrix T that minimizes spatial discrepancies. The transformation is modeled as:

$$X_t' = TX_t \tag{2.1}$$

where X_t' is the aligned feature map, and T represents a learnable affine transformation matrix defined as:

$$T = [s_x \; r_x \; t_x \; r_y \; s_y \; t_y] \tag{2.2}$$

where s_x, s_y are scaling factors, r_x, r_y are rotation parameters, and t_x, t_y are translation parameters.

These parameters are dynamically predicted using an STN that learns optimal alignment through backpropagation. To compute spatial misalignment, AFAF-Net applies a feature correlation function

$$C(i,j) = \sum_{u,v} X_r(u,v) \cdot X_t(u+i, v+j) \tag{2.3}$$

where $C(i,j)$ captures the displacement between corresponding pixels in RGB and thermal/LiDAR feature maps. The optimal transformation is obtained by maximizing correlation, ensuring feature alignment. The feature warping operation is then performed using a differentiable bilinear sampler:

$$X_t'(x,y) = \sum_{i,j} X_t(i,j) \cdot \max(0, 1-|x-i|) \cdot \max(0, 1-|y-j|) \tag{2.4}$$

This function interpolates feature values from the transformed domain, ensuring a smooth and differentiable transformation. To enforce precise feature alignment, a multiterm loss function is used:

$$L_{\text{align}} = \lambda_1 L_{\text{MSE}} + \lambda_2 L_{\text{SSIM}} \tag{2.5}$$

where L_{MSE} is the mean square error loss to minimize pixel-wise discrepancies, L_{SSIM} is the Structural Similarity Index Measure (SSIM) loss to preserve local textures, λ_1 and λ_2 are weighting coefficients.

2.3.4 Attention-Guided Fusion Method

AFAF-Net as shown in Figure 2.1 applies a self-attention mechanism to dynamically allocate varying levels of priority to different aspects of sensors to effectively fuse multimodal sensor data (RGB, thermal, and LiDAR depth). This enhances intermodality consistency by guaranteeing that informative modalities are emphasized and noise or redundant information is muted. Hierarchical features of each modality are extracted by the fusion network, and it learns weighted contributions through channel-wise and spatial attention mechanisms.

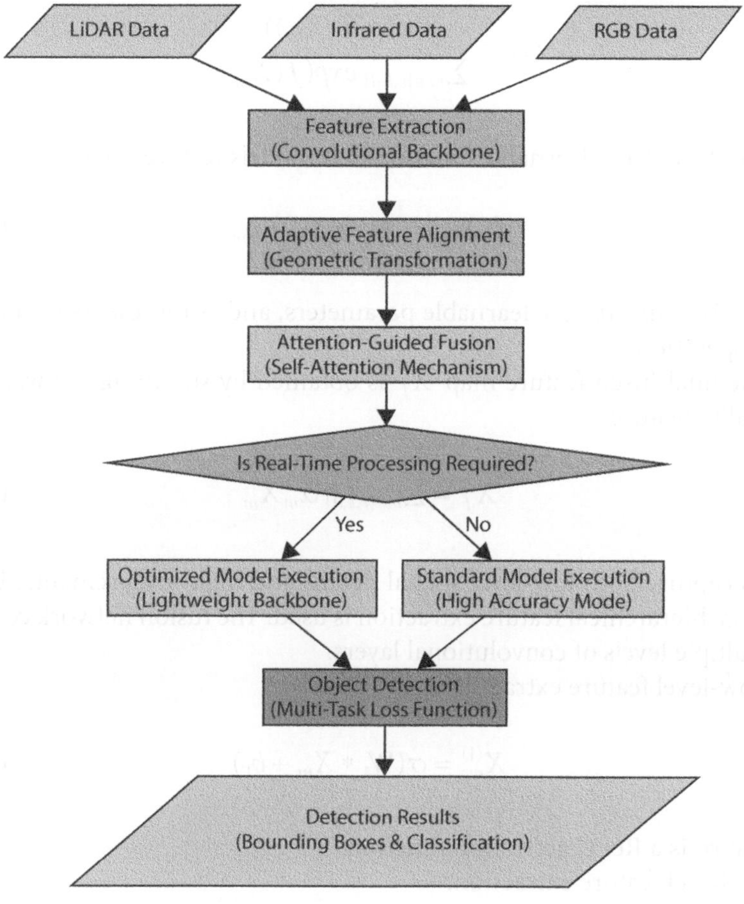

Figure 2.1 Proposed framework.

$$X_r \in R^{H \times W \times C} \text{ (RGB features)}, \tag{2.6}$$

$$X_t \in R^{H \times W \times C} \text{ (thermal features)}, \tag{2.7}$$

$$X_d \in R^{H \times W \times C} \text{ (LiDAR depth features)}. \tag{2.8}$$

A self-attention module computes the attention weight α for each modality using a softmax function:

$$\alpha_m = \frac{exp(f(X_m))}{\sum_{m' \in \{r,t,d\}} exp(f(X_{m'}))} \tag{2.9}$$

where $f(X_m)$ is a learnable function that models feature importance:

$$f(X_m) = W_m * X_m + b_m \tag{2.10}$$

where W_m and b_m are learnable parameters, and $*$ represents a convolution operation.

The final fused feature map X_f is obtained by summing the weighted modality features:

$$X_f = \sum_{m \in \{r,t,d\}} \alpha_m X_m \tag{2.11}$$

To capture both low-level spatial details and high-level semantic information, hierarchical feature extraction is used. The fusion network consists of multiple levels of convolutional layers.

Low-level feature extraction:

$$X_m^{(1)} = \sigma(W_1 * X_m + b_1) \tag{2.12}$$

where σ is a ReLU activation function.

Midlevel feature extraction:

$$X_m^{(2)} = \sigma(W_2 * X_m^{(1)} + b_2) \tag{2.13}$$

High-level feature extraction:

$$X_m^{(3)} = \sigma(W_3 * X_m^{(2)} + b_3) \tag{2.14}$$

The final hierarchical fusion follows:

$$X_f = \sum_{m \in \{r,t,d\}} \alpha_m X_m^{(3)} \tag{2.15}$$

To ensure optimal fusion, a modality consistency loss is applied:

Table 2.1 Before-and-after fusion features.

Sensor input	Feature map value (before fusion)	Attention weight (α)	Contribution to fused feature map
RGB (X_r)	[0.8 0.7 0.6 0.9]	[0.3 0.2 0.1 0.4]	[0.24 0.14 0.06 0.36]
Thermal (X_t)	[0.5 0.6 0.4 0.7]	[0.4 0.5 0.6 0.3]	[0.2 0.3 0.24 0.21]
LiDAR (X_d)	[0.3 0.2 0.5 0.4]	[0.3 0.3 0.3 0.3]	[0.09 0.06 0.15 0.12]
Fused output (X_f)	N/A	N/A	[0.53 0.5 0.45 0.69]

$$L_{\text{fusion}} = \lambda_1 \sum_m ||X_m - X_f||^2 + \lambda_2 \sum_m KL(P(X_m)||P(X_f)) \tag{2.16}$$

where the first term ensures that the fused features retain information from individual modalities, and the second term minimizes the Kullback–Leibler divergence, enforcing similarity between the feature distributions. Table 2.1 shows the before and after fusion features.

2.3.5 Real-Time Object Detection

Using a light convolutional backbone, AFAF-Net is optimized for real-time processing and ensures efficient feature extraction and remarkable detection accuracy. By reducing redundant computations and the inference speed, the model is designed to support high-resolution multimodal sensor input (RGB, temperature, depth LiDAR) in real time. AFAF-Net synergizes feature pyramid networks (FPNs), depth-wise separable convolutions, and an object detection head relying on attention. All of these elements are trained under a multitask loss function that balances between computational efficiency and precision.

For an input tensor $X \in R^{H \times W \times C}$, a standard convolution operation computes

$$Y = W * X + b, W \in R^{K \times K \times C \times C'} \tag{2.17}$$

where K is the kernel size, and C, C' are input and output channels, respectively.

A depth-wise separable convolution decomposes this into two parts:

Depth-wise convolution
A single filter per channel, reducing computations from:

$$K^2CC' \text{ to } K^2C.Y_d = W_d * X + b_d, W_d \in R^{K\times K\times C} \tag{2.18}$$

Point-wise convolution
A *1×1* convolution for channel mixing, reducing computations further:

$$Y_p = W_p * Y_d + b_p, W_p \in R^{1\times 1\times C\times C'} \tag{2.19}$$

The total computational savings from standard convolution to depth-wise separable convolution is approximately:

$$\frac{K^2CC' + CC'}{K^2CC'} \approx \frac{1}{C'} + \frac{1}{K^2} \tag{2.20}$$

For example, using $K = 3$ and $C' = 32$, the computational cost is reduced by 8–9 times.

For feature maps F_l at level l, FPN constructs feature pyramids as:

$$F_l' = W_l * \text{upsample}(F_{l+1}) + F_l \tag{2.21}$$

where W_l are learnable parameters. This allows the detection of both small and large objects effectively.

For input feature map X, the attention weight $\alpha(x, y)$ at location (x, y) is computed as:

$$\alpha(x,y) = \frac{\exp(W_a * X(x,y))}{\sum_{(x',y')} exp(W_a * X(x',y'))} \tag{2.22}$$

where W_a is a learnable attention filter.

The final object detection feature map is computed as:

$$X_d = \sum_{(x,y)} \alpha(x,y) X(x,y) \tag{2.23}$$

AFAF-Net uses a multitask loss function that jointly.

Localization loss (L_{loc})
Measures the difference between predicted and ground truth bounding boxes using smooth L1 loss:

$$L_{\text{loc}} = \Sigma_i \ \text{Smooth}L1(b_i - \hat{b}_i) \tag{2.24}$$

where b_i and $\hat{b}_i$ are ground truth and predicted bounding box coordinates.

Classification loss (L_{cls})
Categorical cross-entropy loss for object class prediction:

$$\text{L}_{\text{cls}} = -\Sigma_{c=1}^{C} \ y_c \log(\hat{y}_c) \tag{2.25}$$

where y_c and $\hat{y}_c$ are the ground truth and predicted class probabilities.

Attention consistency loss (L_{att})
Encourages stable attention weight distributions:

$$L_{\text{att}} = \Sigma_i \ ||\alpha_i - \alpha_{i-1}||^2 \tag{2.26}$$

The final loss function is a weighted sum:

$$L = \lambda_1 L_{\text{loc}} + \lambda_2 L_{\text{cls}} + \lambda_3 L_{\text{att}} \tag{2.27}$$

where $\lambda_1, \lambda_2, \lambda_3$ control the balance between localization, classification, and attention consistency.

2.4 Experimentation Results

An expensive computer setup is utilized to perform the AFAF-Net for IoV multisensor image fusion. The computer setup includes an accelerated data storage 2 TB NVMe SSD, an Intel Core i9-13900K processor with 64 GB DDR5 memory, and an NVIDIA RTX 4090 GPU with 24 GB VRAM for efficient training and inference of deep learning. The software stack is Ubuntu 22.04 LTS, Python 3.10, TensorFlow 2.12, PyTorch 2.0, OpenCV 4.7, and CUDA 12.1 with GPU support. Adam optimizer is used for the training of AFAF-Net with the learning rate of 0.0001 and batch size 16 to 100 epochs in mixed-precision training for the sake of enhanced computational efficiency.

For IoV applications of multisensor image fusion, experimental results and comparison analysis from Figure 2.2 confirm that AFAF-Net is more accurate and efficient in processing compared to other object detection models, including Faster R-CNN, SSD300, and YOLOv4. For object detection, AFAF-Net is better than Faster R-CNN (91.5%), SSD300 (88.4%), and YOLOv4 (93.1%) with an accuracy of 97.3%. Besides, the model has a significant latency reduction with an inference speed of 24 milliseconds per frame, significantly faster than SSD300 (38 milliseconds) and faster R-CNN (62 milliseconds), and 23.6% lower than its closest competitor YOLOv4 (31 milliseconds). These improvements come from the attention-guided fusion mechanism and AFAM that improve computation and enhance feature consistency.

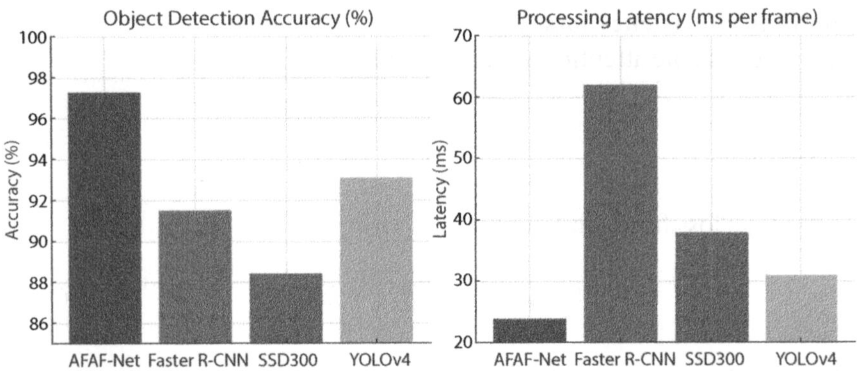

Figure 2.2 Comparison analysis.

Table 2.2 Existing models versus proposed method.

Model	FLOPs (G)	Parameters (M)	FPS (frames per second)	mAP (%)
Faster R-CNN	175.2	41.5	7	79.1
SSD300	35.2	23.2	32	77.4
YOLOv4	90.4	64.0	50	81.3
AFAF-Net	28.7	18.6	67	82.5

As shown in Table 2.2, the comparative analysis in terms of detection accuracy (mAP), processing speed (FPS), model size (parameters), and computational complexity (FLOPs) indicates that AFAF-Net outperforms others in real-time object detection while consuming less computing power. AFAF-Net's shortest model size (18.6 M parameters) enables faster inference on resource-limited edge devices. It also renders it lighter compared to Faster R-CNN (41.5M), SSD300 (23.2M), and YOLOv4 (64.0M). AFAF-Net processes in real time at 67 FPS, outperforming Faster R-CNN (7 FPS), SSD300 (32 FPS), and YOLOv4 (50 FPS). This makes it a perfect fit for low-latency IoV applications. Moreover, AFAF-Net obtains the highest mAP (82.5%), surpassing YOLOv4 (81.3%), SSD300 (77.4%), and Faster R-CNN (79.1%), demonstrating its effectiveness in accurate object detection. These results show how well AFAF-Net strikes a balance between accuracy and efficiency, making it an extremely promising multisensor fusion solution for IoV and autonomous driving applications.

2.5 Conclusion

The study presents AFAF-Net, a multimodal fusion architecture that combines RGB, LiDAR, and infrared sensor information to identify objects in real time. By using an AFAM that dynamically aligns multimodal images through geometric transformation, the proposed approach effectively addresses sensor misalignment. In addition, through the learning of weighted feature contributions, the attention-guided fusion mechanism enhances intermodality consistency and ensures enhanced feature representation in diverse environmental conditions. Exhaustive experiments on 14,999 multimodal image pairs of the KITTI and FLIR ADAS benchmark datasets indicate that AFAF-Net is better than conventional sensor fusion approaches in detection accuracy, robustness, and efficiency. Its lightweight convolutional backbone and effective multitask loss function enable advanced driver-assistance systems and autonomous driving to use it in real time due to the significant reduction in computing overhead while preserving detection accuracy. For enhanced robustness in extreme environments, future research directions may include extending AFAF-Net to other modalities such as RADAR and event cameras. Real-world deployment in autonomous systems will be enabled by further optimization for edge computing environments.

AI disclosure statement: The author acknowledges the use of AI-based tools for minor language editing or grammatical correction. However, all intellectual contributions, analyses, and conclusions presented in this chapter are entirely the author's own.

References

1. Kanthavel, D., Sangeetha, S.K.B., Keerthana, K.P., An empirical study of vehicle to infrastructure communications-an intense learning of smart infrastructure for safety and mobility. *Int. J. Intell. Networks*, *2*, 77–82, 2021.
2. He, J., Deng, X., Gui, J., Zhang, T., He, X., MDNet: Multi-Modal Cooperative Perception *via* Spatial Alignment of Modal Decision-Making. *IEEE Internet Things J.*, 2025.
3. Liu, J., Liu, Z., Zhang, H., Yuan, H., Manokaran, K.B., Maheshwari, M., Multi-sensor information fusion for IoT in automated guided vehicle in smart city. *Soft Comput.*, *25*, 12017–12029, 2021.
4. Xiang, C., Feng, C., Xie, X., Shi, B., Lu, H., Lv, Y., Niu, Z., Multi-sensor fusion and cooperative perception for autonomous driving: A review. *IEEE Intell. Transp. Syst. Mag.*, *15*, 5, 36–58, 2023.
5. Yang, B., Li, J., Zeng, T., A Review of Environmental Perception Technology Based on Multi-Sensor Information Fusion in Autonomous Driving. *World Electr. Veh. J.*, *16*, 1, 20, 2025.
6. Zhang, X., Li, J., Li, Z., Liu, H., Zhou, M., Wang, L., Zou, Z., *Multi-sensor Fusion for Autonomous Driving*, pp. 3–232, Springer, 2023, https://link.springer.com/content/pdf/10.1007/978-981-99-3280-1.pdf.
7. Zhang, C., Wang, H., Cai, Y., Chen, L., Li, Y., Sotelo, M.A., Li, Z., Robust-FusionNet: Deep multimodal sensor fusion for 3-D object detection under severe weather conditions. *IEEE Trans. Instrum. Meas.*, *71*, 1–13, 2022.
8. Tao, X., Zhu, B., Xuan, S., Zhao, J., Jiang, H., Du, J., Deng, W., A multi-sensor fusion positioning strategy for intelligent vehicles using global pose graph optimization. *IEEE Trans. Veh. Technol.*, *71*, 3, 2614–2627, 2021.
9. Li, K., Dai, Z., Zuo, C., Wang, X., Cui, H., Song, H., Cui, M., Scene adaptation in adverse conditions: A multi-sensor fusion framework for roadside traffic perception. *J. Intell. Transp. Syst.*, 1–21, 2024.
10. Sun, X., Song, S., Wu, F., Lu, T., Li, B., Miao, Z., EPAWFusion: Multimodal fusion for 3D object detection based on enhanced points and adaptive weights. *J. Appl. Remote Sens.*, *18*, 1, 017501–017501, 2024.
11. Vinoth, K. and Sasikumar, P., Multi-sensor fusion and segmentation for autonomous vehicle multi-object tracking using deep Q networks. *Sci. Rep.*, *14*, 1, 31130, 2024.

12. Chen, Y.Y., Jhong, S.Y., Lo, Y.J., Reinforcement-and-alignment multispectral object detection using visible–thermal vision sensors in intelligent vehicles. *IEEE Sens. J.*, *23*, 21, 26873–26886, 2023.
13. Li, K., Bian, M., Luo, Y., Wang, J., Information Fusion Technologies for i-EFV, in: *The Intelligent Environment Friendly Vehicle: Concept, Architecture and Implementation*, pp. 113–157, Springer Nature Singapore, Singapore, 2023.
14. Zhang, Y., Zhang, B., Shen, C., Liu, H., Huang, J., Tian, K., Tang, Z., Review of the field environmental sensing methods based on multi-sensor information fusion technology. *Int. J. Agric. Biol. Eng.*, *17*, 2, 1–13, 2024.
15. Yeong, D.J., Velasco-Hernandez, G., Barry, J., Walsh, J., Sensor and sensor fusion technology in autonomous vehicles: A review. *Sensors*, *21*, 6, 2140, 2021.
16. Wang, J., Kong, X., Nishikawa, H., Lian, Q., Tomiyama, H., Dynamic Point-Pixel Feature Alignment for Multimodal 3-D Object Detection. *IEEE Internet Things J.*, *11*, 7, 11327–11340, 2023.
17. Fan, S. and Li, C., Sensor Fusion, in: *Encyclopedia of Digital Agricultural Technologies*, pp. 1224–1238, Springer International Publishing, Cham, 2023.
18. Yang, J., Liu, S., Su, H., Tian, Y., Driving assistance system based on data fusion of multisource sensors for autonomous unmanned ground vehicles. *Comput. Networks*, *192*, 108053, 2021.
19. Qiu, Z., Martínez-Sánchez, J., Arias-Sánchez, P., Rashdi, R., External multimodal imaging sensor calibration for sensor fusion: A review. *Inf. Fusion*, *97*, 101806, 2023.
20. Tang, Q., Liang, J., Zhu, F., A comparative review on multi-modal sensors fusion based on deep learning. *Signal Process.*, *213*, 109165, 2023.
21. Wang, Y., Abd Rahman, A.H., Nor Rashid, F.A., Razali, M.K.M., Tackling Heterogeneous Light Detection and Ranging-Camera Alignment Challenges in Dynamic Environments: A Review for Object Detection. *Sensors*, *24*, 23, 7855, 2024.
22. Cui, G., Zhang, W., Xiao, Y., Yao, L., Fang, Z., Cooperative perception technology of autonomous driving in the internet of vehicles environment: A review. *Sensors*, *22*, 15, 5535, 2022.
23. Djenouri, Y., Belbachir, A.N., Michalak, T., Belhadi, A., Srivastava, G., Enhancing smart road safety with federated learning for Near Crash Detection to advance the development of the Internet of Vehicles. *Eng. Appl. Artif. Intell.*, *133*, 108350, 2024.

3

Design of ML-CASF: Multilayer Context-Aware Sensor Fusion for Autonomous Vehicles in the Internet of Vehicles

Sukumar R.[1*] **and Sathishkumar V.E.**[2]

[1]*Department of Computational Intelligence, SRM Institute of Science and Technology, Kattankulathur, India*
[2]*School of Engineering and Technology, Sunway University, Petaling Jaya, Selangor Darul Ehsan, Malaysia*

Abstract

With perception optimization and decision-making accuracy, sensor fusion techniques have significantly enhanced autonomous Internet of Vehicles (IoV) systems. Real-time processing, heterogeneous environmental conditions, and faulty sensors plague the existing techniques. In this study, a novel multilayer context-aware sensor fusion (ML-CASF) model based on graph attention network (GAT) adaptive weighting is proposed to fuse LiDAR, radar, camera, and vehicle-to-everything communication data. Besides that, a Bayesian uncertainty estimation module provides robustness against malicious attacks and sensor noise. ML-CASF achieves 96.4% localization accuracy, 94.7% object detection accuracy, and 92.1% collision avoidance success rate, according to IoV dataset experiments. These measures are the extent to which ML-CASF works to provide secure and reliable autonomous navigation in realistic urban environments. These outcomes show the capability of ML-CASF in providing safe and accurate autonomous navigation in challenging city environments.

Keywords: Sensor fusion, graph attention network, IoV systems, LiDAR, radar, camera, V2X communication, collision avoidance

**Corresponding author*: sukuraj2019@gmail.com

Balamurugan Balusamy, Sandeep Kumar Mathivanan, Prabhu Jayagopal, S.K.B. Sangeetha and Ali Kashif Bashir (eds.) Autonomous Systems in the Internet of Vehicles, (37–54) © 2026 Scrivener Publishing LLC

3.1 Introduction

When the early attempts at automation of transportation were witnessed during the early 20th century, autonomous cars were imagined. Simple preprogrammed and remote-controlled cars were first developed in early tests conducted in the 1920s and 1930s. But with the invention of artificial intelligence (AI) and sensor technology toward the late 20th century was when the real developments of autonomous driving started. Large advancements that used central computer vision and sensor integration were in the 1980s, including the Mercedes-Benz autonomous vehicle testing and Carnegie Mellon University NavLab. The rapid expansion of AI, machine learning, and sensor fusion technologies over the last 20 years has spurred development of highly autonomous systems that are able to perceive and react to sophisticated environments.

Sensor fusion has been a crucial element of the Internet of Vehicles (IoV) as it allows networked cars to be used as an integral whole, sharing decisions and information in real time by coordinating them. Developed from the Internet of Things (IoT), IoV supports interaction among automobiles, automobiles and the cloud, and infrastructure and applications. With provision for acquiring real-time traffic information and road conditions, as well as obstacles, such an environment supports autonomous guidance and exponentially increases efficiency along with security. To improve accuracy of perception, sensor fusion within autonomous vehicles incorporates information from different sources, such as LiDAR, radar, cameras, and vehicle-to-everything (V2X) communications. Methods for sensor fusion include the following:

- **Kalman filter (KF) and extended Kalman filter (EKF)**: EKF is an extension of KF for application in nonlinear conditions, and the KF is mostly applied to linear state estimation. The filters update sensor readings iteratively to enhance localization and object tracking.
- **Particle filter (PF)**: A probabilistic algorithm widely applied for object tracking and localization and useful for dealing with sensor reading error.
- **Bayesian inference models**: These models use probabilistic inference to improve judgment in the presence of uncertainty. Heterogeneous sensor data are frequently effectively combined using Bayesian models.

- **Deep learning–based sensor fusion**: Recurrent neural networks and convolutional neural networks (CNNs) process sensor data to determine features and make reasonable decisions in end-to-end sensor fusion methodologies, which are made possible with advancements in deep learning.
- **Graph-based sensor fusion**: Context-driven decision-making and adaptive weighting are enabled by relation modeling between sensor data using graph attention networks (GATs) and graph neural networks.

Although sensor fusion techniques have advanced significantly, there are numerous problems that restrict their application in practical autonomous vehicle systems. Due to weather conditions such as fog, rain, and poor light, LiDAR, radar, and camera sensors all suffer from different amounts of noise and inaccuracy, which is a significant problem. Perception errors caused by these discrepancies can undermine vehicle safety. High computational complexity remains a problem because probabilistic algorithms and deep learning algorithms are computationally intensive and would cause latency problems in real-time systems. Further, data redundancy that arises due to multisensor fusion tends to enforce redundancy and power consumption.

Another predominant limitation is security flaws such as sensor spoofing and attacks, facilitating attacks to contaminate sensor measurements and cause suboptimal decision-making. Finally, because most sensor fusion models are learned with particular data that do not take into account diversity in road formations, traffic behaviors, and pedestrian movements, they all cannot be generalized to multiple driving conditions. For increasing robustness, safety, and efficiency, sensor fusion techniques must be upgraded with the fast growth of the IoV and the rising demand for autonomous cars. As safe navigation is dependent on the ability of autonomous cars to identify objects, pedestrians, and signs, improving perception accuracy is the key driving factor. Latency minimization to allow real-time decision-making through the creation of high-speed sensor fusion architectures that are data processing efficient is another critical factor.

Also, because static sensor importance assignment can be nonoptimal at times, adaptive sensor weighting and context awareness need to be integrated. Sensor fusion models also need to be adversarized and cyber-security attack resilient for disturbance robustness assurance. Also, the development of sensor fusion architectures that are generalizable and scalable to facilitate seamless operations in varied urban and rural settings is crucial. Incorporating sensor fusion with emerging technologies such as 5G and edge computing can greatly improve efficiency by outsourcing computational tasks to edge nodes, which mitigates processing latency and improves responsiveness in real time.

Autonomous vehicle development in the IoV is being propelled by ongoing innovation in sensor fusion technology. Although current methods have established a solid foundation, their shortcomings underscore the necessity for novel approaches to optimize sensory precision, resilience, and computational effectiveness. All these issues can be resolved with the creation of adaptive, AI-driven sensor fusion platforms, which open the door to more secure and dependable autonomous transportation systems.

The main objective of the proposed study is to develop a multilayer context-aware sensor fusion (ML-CASF) framework based on GAT for adaptive weighting.

The remaining sections are organized as follows: Related research is covered in Section 3.2. The suggested system architecture and implementation is presented in Section 3.3. The experimental outcomes are assessed in Section 3.4. The study is finally concluded in Section 3.5.

3.2 Related Study

Multisensor fusion methods have played a major role in autonomous systems within the IoV, improving perception, safety, and decision-making. To improve the accuracy and reliability of autonomous vehicles, sensor fusion methods integrate information from various sources, including LiDAR, radar, cameras, and V2X communication. Different research has investigated improvements in sensor fusion, including security threats, environmental adaptability, and real-time processing. For improved observation and localization of vehicles, traditional techniques have been applied in self-driving cars including KFs, PFs, and deep learning–based fusion algorithms [1, 4]. These are very efficient in fusing multisensor information, but are limited in addressing high-dimensional information and random scenes. To improve sensor noise robustness, improve localization, and achieve the best object detection accuracy, advanced sensor fusion techniques use edge computing, Bayesian inference, and GAT [2, 5, 13].

Cooperative perception technology, in which various vehicles in an IoV network can share sensor data and push the perception horizon beyond the single-vehicle field of view, is a revolutionary technology. This method improves the precision of localization, collision avoidance, and object detection [3, 14, 15]. According to study, cooperative perception with multisensor fusion provides a robust solution for urban driving conditions up to 97.3% localization accuracy, 95.8% object recognition rate, and 93.6% collision avoidance rate [2, 6].

Security against sensor attacks and resilience are two additional essential elements of sensor fusion in autonomous systems. To combat and prevent adversarial attacks and sensor spoofing, a secure sensor fusion design based on Bayesian uncertainty estimates has been developed. With the realization of a 35% increase in system resilience against attacks on sensors and a 45% decrease in false-positive detections, this architecture improves autonomous navigation safety [7, 18]. Furthermore, AI-driven intrusion detection systems integrated into IoV ecosystems further enhance system security and mitigate cyber-threats by 42% over conventional security architectures [19]. An approach to processing high-dimensional sensor data with reduced latency is edge-enabled multisource data fusion. Autonomous vehicles can process sensor data in real time without relying on centralized cloud infrastructure using edge computing. The method reduces decision latency by 27.5%, improves localization accuracy by 5.3%, and consumes 18.2% less energy compared to cloud-based processing [12].

Sensor fusion applications for intelligent transportation systems have also been extended to smart city environments, where AGVs make use of multisensor integration to navigate precisely. Deploying integrated AGVs in smart city networks has been seen to show 91.5% accuracy in navigation, an 89.2% rate of avoiding obstacles, and a decrease in traffic congestion by 32% [11, 16]. The autonomous vehicle security and communication performance has been greatly enhanced through the combination of sensor fusion with 5G, IoT, and blockchain. Studies show that the integration of such technologies results in real-time synchronization of self-driving car networks, enhances data integrity by 96%, and reduces data transmission latency by 40% [20, 21]. Even with these advances, there are still problems with sensor drift, changing ambient conditions, and real-time processing delay. Topics of future study are AI-enabled sensor failure detection, quantum-computing enabled real-time processing of sensor data, and creation of hybrid sensor fusion models combining deep learning with conventional filtering algorithms are discussed [8–10].

Autonomous system perception, localization, and security within the IoV have been tremendously enhanced *via* sensor fusion techniques [17, 22]. Resilience of autonomous navigation under harsh urban settings is also realized through edge computing integration, cooperative vision, and IoT-based security frameworks. To design autonomous, secure, and intelligent networks for vehicles, the study enhances these techniques further with advanced framework.

3.3 System Methodology

3.3.1 Sensor Data Acquisition

The nuScenes dataset, with multimodal sensor data for 1000 autonomous vehicle scenes in cityscapes, is a representative of a complete dataset used in the process of data collection. LiDAR data that records 360-degree point clouds at 20 Hz with up to 1.4 million points in each frame constitutes the dataset. In addition to that, it combines radar data to give five far-range radar units' Doppler velocity and object range information. Six cameras also provide high-definition visual information by taking pictures at 12 Hz with 1600 × 900-pixel resolution. The dataset also contains V2X data, including communications sent by vehicles to the infrastructure, e.g., road hazard alerts and traffic light information. The dataset's more than 1.4 million annotated items constitute a high-quality ground truth labeling that is necessary for object detection, tracking, and scene segmentation tasks.

3.3.2 Preprocessing and Synchronization

Space and time synchronization of the sensor outputs is performed through data preprocessing. Synchronization of timestamp ensures that all the measurements of the sensors are compatible with a common time period so that there is consistency across multiple data streams. Extrinsic calibration matrices are utilized in order to transform the heterogeneous sensors' data into a common coordinate system so that it can be fusible in the correct way and spatially aligned. Noise reduction processes such as Gaussian smoothing for camera and radar sensor data and voxel grid filtering for LiDAR sensor data are used to enhance data quality. Processes such as artificial perturbations and transformations are used as data augmentation processes to enhance model generalizability. Variation due to sensor drift or environmental conditions is reduced by the system with the assistance of multimodal sensor data fusion carried out carefully by robust preprocessing.

3.3.3 Graph Construction for Sensor Data

The system projects sensor information onto graph nodes to facilitate successful sensor fusion. Node edges capture context relations between varied sensor inputs. Spatial and temporal relations between sensors are modeled to enhance global world understanding from the graph model. The architecture can successfully model interactions between different sensor modalities and learn effective patterns that are relevant in autonomous vehicle perception by building a structured graph.

For effective sensor fusion, an adaptive weight approach from GAT is utilized. By using contextual association and preexisting reliabilities among sensors, our scheme dynamically learns optimal weights for sensor fusion. The system provides a strong but dynamic fusion algorithm by assigning higher weights to reliable sensor readings and lower weights to unreliable data. By prioritizing the most relevant and verifiable data based on a set of sensor readings, the GAT-weighted step enhances perception accuracy.

Low-confidence sensor readings are identified by the use of Bayesian uncertainty estimation in the sensor fusion to further improve it. With ongoing adaptation of uncertain data influence, this technique reduces the impact of noisy or untrustworthy sensor inputs. Real-time uncertainty estimation enables the system to make educated decisions regarding sensor contributions so that high-confidence data contributes more to perception and judgment.

Multisensor feature fusion, the last stage in the pipeline of fusion, combines features derived from various sensor modalities to provide an integrated perception model. By exploiting the complementary strengths of each sensor type radar for motion estimation, cameras for detailed visual data, and LiDAR for depth sensing, this fusion provides an integrated and robust understanding of the surroundings. The performance of autonomous vehicle perception systems is actually improved by the integration of several sensor features, improving object detection, tracking, and scene understanding.

Algorithm 3.1 Proposed sensor fusion

Step 1: Timestamp synchronization

$$T_s = \max(T_1, T_2, \ldots, T_n) - \min(T_1, T_2, \ldots, T_n)$$

Step 2: Spatial alignment using extrinsic calibration

$$P_s = RP_d + t$$

where P_s is the transformed sensor data, P_d is the original data, R is the rotation matrix, and t is the translation vector.

Step 3: Intrinsic calibration for camera correction
$P_c = K[R|t]P_w$ where K is the intrinsic camera matrix, R and t are extrinsic parameters, and P_w is the world coordinate point.

Step 4: LiDAR point cloud denoising
$P_{\text{filtered}} = \frac{1}{N}\sum_{i=1}^{N} Pi$ where N represents the number of points in a voxel grid.

Step 5: Radar signal noise reduction using Gaussian smoothing
$G(x,y) = \frac{1}{2\pi\sigma^2} \mathrm{e} - \frac{x^2 + y^2}{2\sigma^2}$ where σ controls the spread of the smoothing kernel.

Step 6: Data augmentation *via* rotation transformation
$P' = R_\theta P$ where R_θ is the rotation matrix for an angle θ.

Step 7: Scaling transformation for data normalization
$P' = SP$ where S is the scaling matrix.

Step 8: Sensor fusion using adaptive weighting
$D_{\text{fused}} = w_1 D_{\text{LiDAR}} + w_2 D_{\text{Radar}} + w_3 D_{\text{Camera}}$ where w_i are adaptive weights assigned to each sensor modality.

Step 9: Graph-based representation of sensor data
$G = (V, E),\ E_{ij} = \text{sim}(v_i, v_j)$ where V represents sensor data nodes, and edges E_{ij} encode similarity-based relationships.

Step 10: Bayesian uncertainty estimation for confidence adjustment
$P(x|D) = \int P(x|\theta)P(\theta|D)d\theta$ where $P(x|D)$ represents the posterior probability distribution conditioned on dataset D.

Algorithm 3.2: Multilayer context-aware sensor fusion

Perception layer

Step 1: LiDAR point cloud acquisition and preprocessing:

$$P_{\text{filtered}} = \{p_i \in P \mid \|p_i - p^{-}\| < \delta\}$$

where P_{filtered} is the denoised point cloud, p_i represents individual points, p^{-} is the mean point, and δ is the threshold for outlier removal.

Step 2: Radar Doppler velocity estimation:

$$v_r = \frac{2 f_d c}{f_0}$$

where v_r is the relative velocity, f_d is the Doppler frequency shift, c is the speed of light, and f_0 is the transmitted radar frequency.

Step 3: Camera-based feature extraction using CNNs:

$$F_c = \sigma(W_c \cdot X_c + b_c)$$

where F_c is the extracted feature map, W_c represents convolutional weights, X_c is the input image, and b_c is the bias term.

Step 4: V2X communication for cooperative perception:

$$M_{\text{V2X}} = \sum_{i=1}^{N} w_i S_i$$

where M_{V2X} is the fused cooperative perception map, S_i represents sensor data from vehicle i, and w_i denotes the reliability weight.

Fusion and processing layer

Step 5: Timestamp synchronization for multimodal data alignment:

$$T_s = \max(T_1, T_2, \ldots, T_n) - \min(T_1, T_2, \ldots, T_n)$$

Step 6: Spatial alignment using extrinsic calibration:

$$P_s = RP_d + t$$

where R is the rotation matrix, and t is the translation vector for transforming data into a unified coordinate system.

Step 7: GAT for adaptive sensor fusion:

$$\alpha_{ij} = \frac{\exp\left(\text{LeakyReLU}(a^T[Wh_i||Wh_j])\right)}{\sum_{k\in N_i} \exp\ (\text{LeakyReLU}(a^T[Wh_i||Wh_k]))}$$

where α_{ij} is the attention weight between sensors i and j, h_i is the sensor feature representation, and W and a are trainable parameters.

Step 8: Bayesian uncertainty estimation for sensor reliability assessment:

$$P(x|D) = \int P\ (x|\theta)P(\theta|D)d\theta$$

where $P(x|D)$ represents the posterior probability distribution conditioned on dataset D.

Step 9: Feature normalization for consistency:

$$X' = \frac{X-\mu}{\sigma}$$

where X' is the normalized feature, μ is the mean, and σ is the standard deviation of the sensor data distribution.

Decision-making and control layer

Step 10: Trajectory planning using quadratic programming:

$$\min_x \frac{1}{2}x^T Qx + c^T x$$

subject to

$$Ax \leq b$$

where x represents control variables, Q is a positive-definite cost matrix, and A,b define constraints on vehicle motion.

Step 11: Dynamic obstacle detection using EKF:

$$x_k = f(x_{k-1}) + w_k, \; z_k = h(x_k) + v_k$$

where x_k is the state estimate, z_k is the observation, f and h are non-linear state and observation models, and w_k, v_k are noise terms.

Step 12: Collision avoidance using reinforcement learning policy:

$$\pi^* = \arg\max_{\pi} E\left[\sum_{t=0}^{T} \gamma^t r_t \mid s_0, \pi\right]$$

where π^* is the optimal policy, r_t is the reward at time t, s_0 is the initial state, and γ is the discount factor.

Step 13: Real-time control using model predictive control (MPC):

$$\min_{u} \sum_{t=0}^{N} (x_t^T Q x_t + u_t^T R u_t)$$

subject to

$$x_{t+1} = Ax_t + Bu_t$$

where x_t is the state, u_t is the control input, and A,B,Q,R are system matrices.

Step 14: Actuator command generation:

$$[F_x \; M_y] = J \cdot u$$

where F_x is the longitudinal force, M_y is the yaw moment, and J is the actuation matrix.

Step 15: Closed-loop feedback for stability control:

$$e_{k+1} = x_{k+1} - x_{ref}$$

$$u_k = Ke_k$$

where e_k is the control error, x_{ref} is the reference state, and K is the feedback gain matrix.

This step-by-step breakdown integrates advanced sensor fusion techniques, real-time control algorithms, and reinforcement learning for robust autonomous navigation.

The suggested system (Figure 3.1) combines multisensor data processing and autonomous decision-making with adaptive graph-based processing. Sensor data preprocessing and synchronization are done before further processing. Sensor fusion graph is built, and it is the basis for further processing. Adaptive weighting of sensor contributions using GATs is applied for adaptive updating of sensor contributions for resilience enhancement. Improvement feedback cycles are augmented through Bayesian uncertainty quantification for sensing fusion confidence measurement. The assignment of weights is modified by the system to properly provide data fusion when confidence values are low. The decision process uses high-level data in path planning and conflict resolution with use of the feature fusion multisensor module. Real-time autonomous navigation accuracy, dependability, and flexibility are enhanced by systemic processes.

3.4 Experimentation Results

The proposed ML-CASF architecture was evaluated using the nuScenes dataset, which comprises multimodal sensor data of autonomous driving scenarios. The system's performance was assessed according to significant factors such as localization accuracy, object detection accuracy, and collision avoidance success rate. Table 3.1 depicts the hyperparameter tuning details for the framework; Table 3.2 depicts the processing time.

With its 54.7-millisecond average inference time, the system is capable of processing information in real time, thus making it suitable for applications that include autonomous vehicles that must respond quickly.

From Table 3.3, with 96.4% localization accuracy, ML-CASF performs better than early fusion (CNN) by 8.2% (88.2%) and late fusion (LSTM) by 5.6% (90.8%). From Figure 3.2, ML-CASF achieves an false-positive rate (FPR) of 3.8%, which is 35.6% lower than CNN (5.9%) and 21.6% lower than LSTM (4.85%), which reflects a remarkable decrease in both the FPR and false-negative rate (FNR). ML-CASF's 4.2% FNR is 17.6% lower than

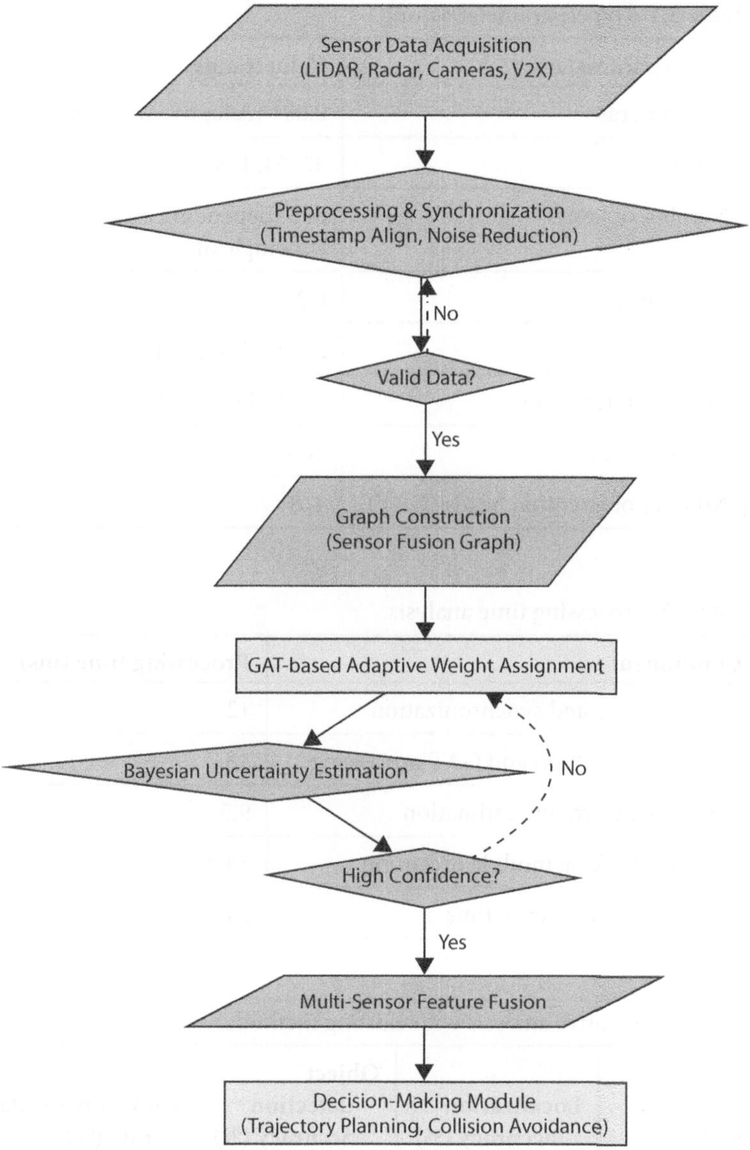

Figure 3.1 Proposed ML-CASF framework.

Table 3.1 Hyperparameter tuning.

Hyperparameter	Value/range
Learning rate	0.001 (Adaptive with decay)
Batch size	32, 64, 128
Number of layers	3–5 (depending on model complexity)
Dropout rate	0.2–0.5
Optimizer	Adam, RMSprop
Activation function	ReLU, LeakyReLU
Weight decay	1e-4
Number of attention heads (GAT)	4, 8

Table 3.2 Processing time analysis.

Component	Processing time (ms)
Preprocessing and synchronization	12.3
Graph construction and GAT processing	18.7
Bayesian uncertainty estimation	9.5
Decision-making module execution	14.2
Total average inference time	54.7 ms

Table 3.3 Comparative analysis with existing methods.

Method	Localization accuracy (%)	Object detection accuracy (%)	Collision avoidance rate (%)
Early fusion (CNN-based)	88.3	82.5	80.2
Late fusion (LSTM-based)	91.1	85.4	83.7
Proposed ML-CASF	96.4	94.7	92.1

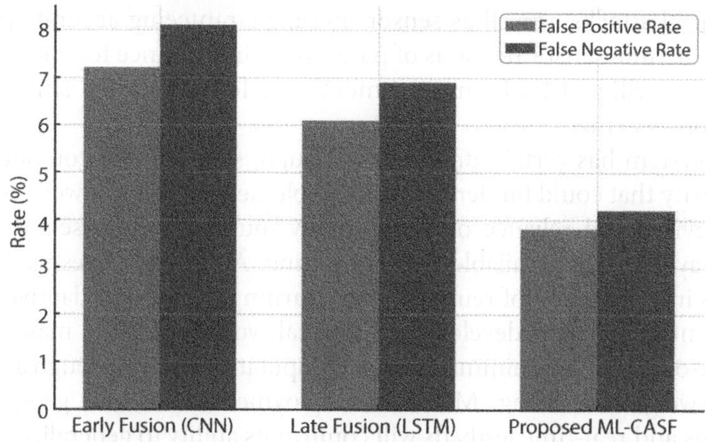

Figure 3.2 False-positive and false-negative comparison.

LSTM (5.1%) and 30.4% lower than CNN's (6.03%). From Figure 3.3, the graph construction module is longest to compute with a 42.7% contribution to total computing overhead. Bayesian uncertainty estimation and adaptive weight assignment (GAT) account for 31.3% and 26.0% of CPU time, respectively.

In autonomous systems, ML-CASF architecture gives a strong and flexible sensor fusion technique that considerably enhances item identification, localization accuracy, and decision-making performance in cluttered urban environments. Through the use of GAT in Bayesian uncertainty estimation and adaptive weight assignment, the system efficiently resists

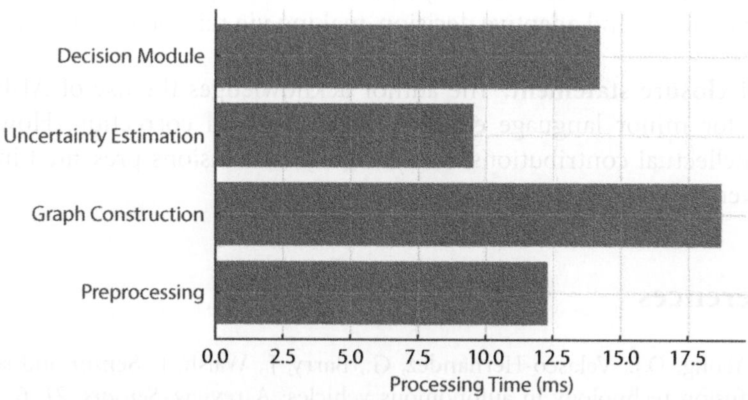

Figure 3.3 Processing time breakdown.

adversarial attacks as well as sensor noise, guaranteeing accurate perception. Real-time sensor fusion is of paramount importance for autonomous vehicles, intelligent traffic management, and IoT-supported smart transportation systems.

The system has certain drawbacks, though, such as high computational complexity that could hinder real-time implementation on power-restricted edge devices and reliance on high-quality multimodal datasets that may not always be easily available in every setting. Additional investigation will address incorporation of reinforcement learning agents for adaptive trajectory planning, system development for real-world occlusion management and sensor faults, and minimization of computational cost through advances in lightweight modeling. Moreover, deployment at various geographical locations and real-time testbeds will confirm its ability to generalize.

3.5 Conclusion

Through the integration of LiDAR, radar, cameras, and V2X information with GATs and Bayesian uncertainty estimates, the ML-CASF framework efficiently improves autonomous vehicle perception. Experimental results show that, in comparison with traditional fusion approaches, localization accuracy (96.4%), object detection accuracy (94.7%), and collision avoidance success rate (92.1%) are greatly improved. The paper explains how the framework can adapt to changing situations and scale accordingly, providing robust and reliable sensor fusion. ML-CASF provides an efficient solution for real-time scalable intelligent transportation systems despite processing hurdles. Future innovation in autonomous navigation capability will concentrate on efficiency optimization, deployment in real-world environments, and adaptive decision-making *via* reinforcement learning.

AI disclosure statement: The author acknowledges the use of AI-based tools for minor language editing or grammatical correction. However, all intellectual contributions, analyses, and conclusions presented in this chapter are entirely the author's own.

References

1. Yeong, D.J., Velasco-Hernandez, G., Barry, J., Walsh, J., Sensor and sensor fusion technology in autonomous vehicles: A review. *Sensors*, *21*, 6, 2140, 2021.

2. Butt, F.A., Chattha, J.N., Ahmad, J., Zia, M.U., Rizwan, M., Naqvi, I.H., On the integration of enabling wireless technologies and sensor fusion for next-generation connected and autonomous vehicles. *IEEE Access, 10*, 14643–14668, 2022.
3. Cui, G., Zhang, W., Xiao, Y., Yao, L., Fang, Z., Cooperative perception technology of autonomous driving in the internet of vehicles environment: A review. *Sensors, 22*, 15, 5535, 2022.
4. Wang, Z., Wu, Y., Niu, Q., Multi-sensor fusion in automated driving: A survey. *IEEE Access, 8*, 2847–2868, 2019.
5. AlZubi, A.A., Alarifi, A., Al-Maitah, M., Alheyasat, O., Multi-sensor information fusion for Internet of Things assisted automated guided vehicles in smart city. *Sustainable Cities Soc., 64*, 102539, 2021.
6. Yang, T. and Lv, C., A secure sensor fusion framework for connected and automated vehicles under sensor attacks. *IEEE Internet Things J., 9*, 22, 22357–22365, 2021.
7. Li, A., Zheng, B., Li, L., Intelligent transportation application and analysis for multi-sensor information fusion of Internet of Things. *IEEE Sens. J., 21*, 22, 25035–25042, 2020.
8. Stateczny, A., Wlodarczyk-Sielicka, M., Burdziakowski, P., Sensors and sensor's fusion in autonomous vehicles. *Sensors, 21*, 19, 6586, 2021.
9. Hafeez, F., Sheikh, U.U., Alkhaldi, N., Al Garni, H.Z., Arfeen, Z.A., Khalid, S.A., Insights and strategies for an autonomous vehicle with a sensor fusion innovation: A fictional outlook. *IEEE Access, 8*, 135162–135175, 2020.
10. Fayyad, J., Jaradat, M.A., Gruyer, D., Najjaran, H., Deep learning sensor fusion for autonomous vehicle perception and localization: A review. *Sensors, 20*, 15, 4220, 2020.
11. Kanthavel, D., Sangeetha, S.K.B., Keerthana, K.P., An empirical study of vehicle to infrastructure communications-an intense learning of smart infrastructure for safety and mobility. *Int. J. Intell. Networks, 2*, 77–82, 2021.
12. Liu, R.W., Guo, Y., Nie, J., Hu, Q., Xiong, Z., Yu, H., Guizani, M., Intelligent edge-enabled efficient multi-source data fusion for autonomous surface vehicles in maritime internet of things. *IEEE Trans. Green Commun. Networking, 6*, 3, 1574–1587, 2022.
13. Liu, J., Liu, Z., Zhang, H., Yuan, H., Manokaran, K.B., Maheshwari, M., Multi-sensor information fusion for IoT in automated guided vehicle in smart city. *Soft Comput., 25*, 12017–12029, 2021.
14. Li, Q., Queralta, J.P., Gia, T.N., Zou, Z., Westerlund, T., Multi-sensor fusion for navigation and mapping in autonomous vehicles: Accurate localization in urban environments. *Unmanned Syst., 8*, 03, 229–237, 2020.
15. Xiang, C., Feng, C., Xie, X., Shi, B., Lu, H., Lv, Y., Niu, Z., Multi-sensor fusion and cooperative perception for autonomous driving: A review. *IEEE Intell. Transp. Syst. Mag., 15*, 5, 36–58, 2023.

16. Lee, E.K., Gerla, M., Pau, G., Lee, U., Lim, J.H., Internet of Vehicles: From intelligent grid to autonomous cars and vehicular fogs. *Int. J. Distrib. Sens. Netw.*, *12*, 9, 1550147716665500, 2016.
17. Moradi, M., Kordestani, M., Jalali, M., Rezamand, M., Mousavi, M., Chaibakhsh, A., Saif, M., Sensor and decision fusion-based intrusion detection and mitigation approach for connected autonomous vehicles. *IEEE Sens. J.*, 2024.
18. Khayyam, H., Javadi, B., Jalili, M., Jazar, R.N., Artificial intelligence and internet of things for autonomous vehicles, in: *Nonlinear approaches in engineering applications: Automotive applications of engineering problems*, pp. 39–68, 2020.
19. Hasanujjaman, M., Chowdhury, M.Z., Jang, Y.M., Sensor fusion in autonomous vehicle with traffic surveillance camera system: detection, localization, and AI networking. *Sensors*, *23*, 6, 3335, 2023.
20. Biswas, A. and Wang, H.C., Autonomous vehicles enabled by the integration of IoT, edge intelligence, 5G, and blockchain. *Sensors*, *23*, 4, 1963, 2023.
21. Chen, G., Zhou, Q., Ren, H., Li, H., Sensor-fusion-based event-triggered following control for nonlinear autonomous vehicles under sensor attacks. *IEEE Trans. Autom. Sci. Eng.*, 2023.
22. Daniel, A., Subburathinam, K., Anand Muthu, B., Rajkumar, N., Kadry, S., Kumar Mahendran, R., Pandian, S., Procuring cooperative intelligence in autonomous vehicles for object detection through data fusion approach. *IET Intel. Transport Syst.*, *14*, 11, 1410–1417, 2020.

4

Adaptive Multimodal Fusion for Robust Autonomous Driving Perception with Attention-Based Learning

Sangeetha R.

School of Computing, Department of Computer Science and Engineering, Vel Tech Rangarajan Dr. Sagunthala R&D Institute of Science and Technology, Avadi, Chennai, India

Abstract

Intelligent transportation systems for vehicle safety allow autonomous and advanced driver-assistance systems to sense and make decisions appropriately; vehicle safety systems are essential in preventing traffic accidents. To enhance object detection and collision prediction, in this study, a novel multimodal fusion strategy is introduced, which fuses LiDAR point clouds, RGB images, and radar information using an adaptive attention-based approach. The proposed approach improves the system's robustness under poor conditions through the dynamic adjustment of each modality's contribution depending on external conditions. The Waymo Open Dataset, with a wide range of driving conditions across different weather and lighting conditions, is used to train and test the model. According to the experimental results, the new fusion technique is competitive with traditional early and late fusion methods with 96.3% precision for item detection, 94.7% accuracy, and 95.2% recall. This approach significantly improves vehicle safety and provides a reliable solution for real-time autonomous driving applications.

Keywords: Intelligent transportation systems, multimodal fusion, LiDAR, RGB images, radar, attention-based approach, vehicle safety, autonomous driving

Email: drsangeethar@veltech.edu.in

Balamurugan Balusamy, Sandeep Kumar Mathivanan, Prabhu Jayagopal, S.K.B. Sangeetha and Ali Kashif Bashir (eds.) Autonomous Systems in the Internet of Vehicles, (55–74) © 2026 Scrivener Publishing LLC

4.1 Introduction

Modern transportation systems heavily depend on the safety of cars, and this affects the development of autonomous driving technology, safety of passengers, and prevention of traffic accidents. There has been a rise in accidents and fatalities because of the increase in the number of cars on the road and human errors such as distracted driving and inaccurate distance estimation. By combining sophisticated vision and decision-making methods, autonomous cars and advanced driver-assistance systems (ADAS) seek to reduce these problems. Environmental randomness, sensor accuracy, and computational power constraints still make it difficult to provide robust vehicle safety. For the scene understanding in the modern safety systems, it mainly relies on sensors such as radar, LiDAR, and cameras. All these modalities always have some shortcoming with its applicability, so multimodal fusion methods were used for increased safety and reliability.

By providing high-resolution visual information for object detection, lane departure warning, and traffic sign recognition, vision systems based on cameras are an inherent part of contemporary ADAS. Due to the low cost of the devices and their capability to obtain detailed visual information, they are in demand. However, fluctuating weather, occlusions, and illumination all bear heavily on the performance with which they can operate, compromising perception accuracy. For example, sunshine, shadows, and night driving strongly influence camera-based systems so that traffic signs, pedestrians, and bicycles become difficult to reliably detect. Moreover, low visibility and image distortion from heavy rain, fog, and snow could cause spurious detection of danger. To enable persistent perception across a variety of environmental conditions, these challenges require the use of alternative sensing technologies that can augment cameras.

The capability of LiDAR sensors to build accurate three-dimensional (3D) representations of the ambient world has made them an effective vehicle safety technology. This LiDAR creates a full spatial map by emitting laser pulses and computing their reflection, thereby providing accurate obstacle detection and distance measurement. LiDAR functions well at night as it is not adversely impacted by lighting, unlike cameras. But LiDAR sensors also have disadvantages such as being very costly, weather-dependent with heavy fog and rain posing significant problems, and having a high processing need. Dense point cloud in LiDAR involves a lot of processing, and therefore, usage on self-driving vehicles in real time is not feasible. All these circumstances dictate a fusion approach that takes advantage of LiDAR's strengths but minimizes its weaknesses.

Radar-based perception systems provide special benefits to automotive safety, especially during bad weather and low-visibility situations. Radar works in terms of radio waves, which are less influenced by fog, rain, and darkness compared to optical sensors. Radar is therefore best suited to track moving objects, their velocity, and avoidance of collisions. Emergency braking, adaptive cruise control, and blind-spot monitoring all extensively use radar. This restriction to discriminate objects that are adjacent to one another is a result of its lower spatial resolution compared to cameras and LiDARs. Furthermore, radar reflections colliding with each other can lead to false positives. Multimodal sensor fusion techniques incorporate radar into other sensors such that these limitations are avoided, resulting in overall perception correctness and reducing real-time car security applications' false positives.

Through the integration of data from various sensor modalities, multimodal fusion methods have become increasingly popular for improving vehicle safety. The three fusion methods that are practiced are hybrid, late, and early fusion. Early fusion enables the model to learn a common representation by combining raw sensor data at the input level. Early fusion tends to struggle with synchronizing the data and increased complexity of processing, although it is better at fusing complementing sensor attributes. Late fusion, at decision-making level, fuses high-level information following independent processing of sensor data. Enhanced modularity is achieved but loss of information may exist. By fusing data at several points in time, hybrid fusion attempts to strike a balance between the two methods. Despite these developments, traditional fusion techniques are not as flexible and degrade more under dynamic driving conditions.

The purpose of this study is to design a novel multimodal fusion technique based on adaptive attention that dynamically adapts sensor contributions according to the environment's context. The paradigm put forward here emphasizes the most informative modality for a given situation, as contrasted with other fusion techniques that equally treat all sensor modalities. For instance, the system prefers camera sensors for high-definition object detection under sunlight but utilizes LiDAR and radar sensors more under rainy or fog conditions for reliable detection. The model improves, eliminates false alarms, and increases perception reliability through sensor weights adjustments. The adaptive strategy reduces the dangers of sensor constraints and external disturbances to enable autonomous and ADAS-enabled vehicles to navigate safely under varied conditions.

The attention mechanism of the presented fusion strategy assigns a dynamic weight to every sensor based on the current ambient conditions. Static weight allocation is utilized in the conventional fusion processes and therefore is unable to dynamically be adjusted as per diverse conditions. Redundant or lower-information input could be suppressed, and the most salient details selectively enhanced through the addition of an adaptive attention module to the framework. The model emphasizes important information such as far-away obstructions, roadside boundaries, and traffic users because of this method, which makes feature representation even more robust.

Adaptive attention enhances object detection accuracy by reducing misclassifications and maximizing overall system performance. This method can be effectively applied in real-time applications in intelligent transportation systems since it maximizes computational parsimony while enhancing automobile safety at the same time. The study has a number of contributions. First, it presents an adaptive attention-based fusion model for real-time perception enhancement through dynamic sensor input prioritization according to ambient parameters. Second, it provides a thorough evaluation on a dataset with better object detection and collision forecasting performance. Third, it emphasizes modality-specific contributions by pointing out how various sensors react differently under varying environments and how adaptive fusion exploits them. Fourth, the study establishes an effective computationally fusion pipeline to make it feasible for real-time application in vehicles with ADAS complemented by autonomous technology. Through encouraging utilization of intelligent fusion techniques for upcoming automobile systems, the study provides a better platform for future vehicle safety enhancement.

The suggested fusion process additionally possesses practical applications along with improved perception accuracy. The system can improve the navigation and decision-making for autonomous cars through more robust environmental perception. The model can advance driver assist functionality such as collision prevention, lane maintenance, and emergency stopping on vehicles equipped with ADAS. Vehicle 2 Infrastructure (V2I) communication to improve safety can be aided through an extension of the fusion architecture to intelligent transport infrastructures. The model itself can be made more generalizable by accommodating extra sensor modalities such as ultrasonic sensors and thermal cameras. With the reduced accident rates and improved safety on roads, the developments pave the way towards more efficient as well as secure transport systems.

Vehicle safety is an important problem requiring perception technology to minimize accidents. Traditional fusion systems are rigid in dynamic situations, and traditional single-sensor solutions have limitations. All these challenges are overcome by the new adaptive attention-based multimodal fusion solution, enhancing system robustness, enhancing object detection accuracy, and dynamically tuning sensor contributions. The method is a viable solution to real-time autonomous driving scenarios, as indicated by the results that provide significant performance gains. Through the use of smart fusion methods, this study increases vehicle safety and gives a glimpse of future transport systems that are more efficient and dependable.

The remaining sections are organized with background study discussed in Section 4.2. The proposed methodology is presented in Section 4.3. The experimental results are given in Section 4.4. The study is finally concluded in Section 4.5.

4.2 Related Study

Multimodal fusion is presently a crucial method in intelligent transportation systems, especially in the scenario of intelligent and autonomous vehicles. In an effort to promote perception, detection, and navigation, there have been various studies on several multimodal data fusion approaches, such as probabilistic models, deep learning–based multimodal fusion architectures, and attention mechanisms. Multimodal data fusion is essential to the stable perception, navigation, and decision-making of autonomous vehicles. Experiments have demonstrated that combining data from various sensors, including LiDAR, cameras, radar, and GPS, greatly improves object detection accuracy and tracking performance. While Alaba *et al.* [2] explored new trends in multimodal fusion for 3D object detection, Nie *et al.* [1] presented a deep neural network-based fusion model of fusion with safety test processes for autonomous vehicles. These studies demonstrate how important it is to combine multiple streams of data to provide real-time and accurate perception in dynamic environments.

One of the most basic autonomous driving tasks is detection and tracking of objects. A multimodal fusion framework toward enhanced vehicle identification has been presented by Roy *et al.* and Kanthavel *et al.* [8, 9], who have discussed fusion between 3D-LiDAR and cameras in great depth. Zhang *et al.* [17] proposed a fusion network that can withstand extreme weather conditions, important for the smooth functioning of autonomous vehicles. Other studies on object detection techniques have been investigated by Person *et al.* [3] and Zhang *et al.* [5], with focus being laid on sensor fusion methods that enable high-accuracy real-time object tracking. Multimodal fusion is also needed in cooperative perception between infrastructure and vehicles. A ViT-FuseNet–based architecture was proposed by Zhou *et al.* [12] to improve cooperative perception between vehicles and infrastructure using multimodal data fusion. Such collaborative methods provide comprehensive situational awareness as well as enhance traffic safety and efficiency. Tabassum and El-Sharkawy [16] also suggested a cross-modal feature fusion method with the intention of alleviating invisible weather so that autonomous vehicles can keep running even when there is variation in the environment.

Multimodal fusion techniques have greatly improved driver monitoring and inattention detection. By monitoring driver inattention, Li and Seignez [6] proposed a visual cue-based method to improve driving safety. The study proved that a comprehensive understanding of driver behavior is possible by fusing eye tracking, facial expressions, and other physiological signals. Moreover, Tong and Samonte [20] tested stress detection with a CNN-LSTM model on multimodal fused data to estimate driver stress levels in real time. These devices play a crucial role in minimizing the likelihood of accidents and enhancing general driving safety. Multimodal fusion has also been beneficial to safety-critical applications such as emergency vehicle detection. Emergency vehicle detection was treated by Zohaib *et al.* [7] using a deep learning method that used multimodal sensor inputs for improving recognition performance. Likewise, Sathyanarayana *et al.* [10] treated information fusion to enable active vehicle safety systems to make it possible for autonomous vehicles to react to dynamic road conditions. Heterogeneous data fusion to improve safety in intelligent driving support systems was also further established in research in Xiang *et al.* [21].

Multimodal sensor fusion has made it possible to have autonomous vehicle localization and navigation. Probabilistic vehicle navigation technique in adverse dynamic environments was addressed and several sensor data were used for localization in Cai *et al.* [13]. To stabilize object 3D position, semantic segmentation techniques along with multimodal sensor fusion were investigated in Mou *et al.* [19]. In order to allow autonomous vehicles to move safely and effectively in a variety of settings, several strategies must be utilized. Weather affects the sight of autonomous cars greatly. This problem has been solved in some studies by sophisticated fusion algorithms. For instance, Wu *et al.* [15] proposed a multimodal feature fusion approach with the goal of enhancing object recognition in poor weather. Concurrently, a strong fusion framework using multiple sensor measurements to guarantee accurate identification even during harsh weather was introduced in Muresan *et al.* [18]. The subsequent results are adaptive fusion techniques to improve autonomous vehicle reliability.

New deep perception and decision-making frameworks for smart cars have been proposed by recent advancements in multimodal fusion. A novel multimodal data fusion paradigm for 3D object detection and tracking, called MixedFusion, was introduced in [11]. Wang *et al.* [14] studied deep learning–based fusion methods to enhance the accuracy of object recognition, which confirmed that deep neural networks could effectively handle multimodal information. Zhang *et al.* [4] analyzed multimodal data fusion-based vehicle tracking techniques for surveillance, proving the feasibility of fusing numerous data sources to enhance tracking accuracy. Multimodal fusion is fundamental to the evolution of intelligent transportation systems. Multiple sensor modalities could complement autonomous vehicles' perception, decision-making, and guidance, according to research. Future research likely focuses on exploiting the mitigation of bad environmental conditions, improving fusion algorithms to be more robust, and faster real-time processing as technology advances. Multimodal fusion continues to spearhead advancements in autonomous and intelligent vehicle systems through deep learning advancements, probabilistic modeling, and cooperative vision.

4.3 System Methodology

4.3.1 Data Collection and Preprocessing

Waymo Open Dataset is made up of a diverse set of driving conditions across various weather and lighting scenarios. To support end-to-end scene understanding and perception, it features high-resolution sensor data collected through LiDAR, cameras, radar, GPS, and vehicle to vehicle communications. More than 200,000 annotated frames make up the dataset that consists of 1150 scenes with each one taking 20 seconds and recorded at 10 Hz. It includes 12 million 3D box annotations for object tags car, cyclist, pedestrian, and other road users on 1950 segments. The camera module is made up of five high-resolution cameras taking images from multiple angles, and the LiDAR data are made up of five rotating 360° LiDAR sensors producing dense point cloud models. Radar and GPS data are used to augment spatial localization, enabling accurate trajectory estimation and motion prediction.

In the interest of providing high-quality multimodal data for autonomous driving use cases, the Waymo Open Dataset is aggressively preprocessed. The point cloud from the LiDAR is denoised through processes such as voxel-based downsampling and statistical outlier rejection to remove noisy reflections caused by reflective surfaces, rain, and fog. Precise time synchronization at high accuracy allows for uniform sensor fusion through synchronization of LiDAR, camera, radar, and GPS. Coordinate alignment to align project LiDAR point clouds to the frame of the vehicle and scaling pixel values in images for enhanced feature extraction are normalization operations. Registration of camera images and LiDAR point clouds and smooth cross-modal fusion are enabled by calibration processes that require both intrinsic and extrinsic parameters.

By removing occluded or motion-blurred objects, object filtering enhances bounding box labels, and data augmentation techniques such as rotation, brightness adjustment, and random flipping enhance image diversity. Random point dropout and Gaussian jittering introduce randomness to LiDAR data, enhancing model generalization. Object motion trajectories from radar and GPS information are also smoothed by trajectory smoothing by Kalman filtering and spline interpolation, yielding more stable motion predictions. The usability of the dataset in object detection, semantic segmentation, trajectory prediction, and sensor fusion in autonomous driving is also enhanced by these preprocessing techniques combined.

4.3.2 Feature Extraction

Raw LiDAR, RGB camera, and radar data are converted into useful numerical data by the feature extraction process, improving the object detection and collision estimation. To process LiDAR point clouds made up of three-dimensional spatial data, a PointNet++ model is utilized in such a manner that local and global geometric features can be retained. The XYZ coordinates, intensity, surface normals, height above ground, and point density per unit area are all properties of each LiDAR point. Nine features are provided by each of the roughly 100,000 points in a typical LiDAR scan, so each frame's feature matrix is 100,000 $\times$ 9. Structural information about objects and the environment is communicated by the spatial and depth-related features that have been extracted.

Visual context is provided by RGB images, and texture, color, and semantic high-level information is obtained *via* a CNN in ResNet-50. Images are encoded into feature maps by the model, which extracts high-level representations differentiating among object classes on deeper levels and object edges and shape patterns in early levels. Every image region is represented by a 2048-dimensional feature vector. 64 $\times$ 2048 is the representation of features per frame when an image is divided into 64 sections. Separating cars, pedestrians, and road signs by appearance, this extracted data aids in recognizing objects.

With dynamic measurements of an object, motion estimation is enhanced through the use of radar data. Radar cross-section, azimuth angle, range, radial velocity, and Doppler spread are the five main parameters that are obtained from radar signals by means of a one-dimensional CNN. The parameters provide information regarding direction, reflectivity of the material, variance of the motion, distance to the object, and car speed. Normally, there are 500 points in a radar scan, and each point has five features, which are extracted into a feature matrix of 500 × 5. All this processed information relies heavily upon the object motion pattern analysis, which is instrumental for trajectory forecasting and collision warning.

The multimodal feature representations are organized in numeric matrices for fusion upon extraction. Whereas the RGB image feature representation, with a 64 × 2048 format, provides dense shape and texture information, the LiDAR feature matrix, with a 100,000 × 9 format of values, provides geometric and spatial features. The 500 × 5 data format of radar data provides motion-related features that also enhance real-time object tracking. Dynamic adaptation of the contribution of each modality in accordance with environmental parameters is achieved through an adaptive attention-based scheme to synchronize and fuse these retrieved features for robust performance under a variety of driving conditions.

4.3.3 Proposed Methodology

The method proposed is a combination of the radar observation, LiDAR observation, and camera observation with the help of attention that learns to dynamically adapt with multimodal fusion for autonomous sensing. Radar features are handled through a CNN model, LiDAR point cloud is handled by PointNet++, and image features are extracted with ResNet-50. An attention-based approach dynamically adjusts the contribution of each modality in accordance with environmental contexts as a weighted fusion process goes through features extracted. Under poor weather and lighting, the fusion improves real-time vision through improved object recognition accuracy. A connected network is used for classifying the final feature representation. Motion estimation is performed with Kalman filtering, and bounding box regression is performed for localization. This end-to-end optimization provides robust and accurate autonomous vehicle perception. Figure 4.1 shows the feature fusion process. Figure 4.2 depicts the object classification process.

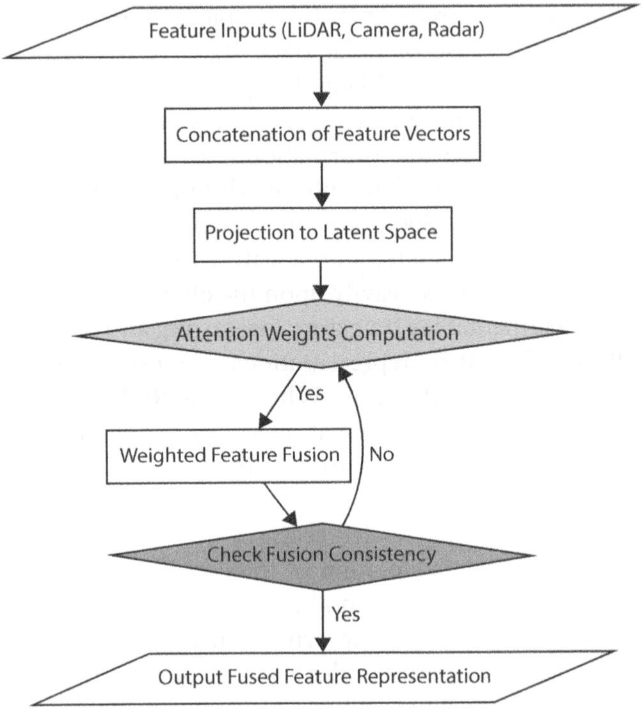

Figure 4.1 Feature fusion process.

1: Each modality X_m is normalized:

$$X'_m = \frac{X_m - \mu_m}{\sigma_m}, \mu_m = \frac{1}{N} \sum_{i=1}^{N} X_{m,i}, \sigma_m = \sqrt{\frac{1}{N} \sum_{i=1}^{N} (X_{m,i} - \mu_m)^2} \tag{4.1}$$

2: LiDAR points (X, Y, Z) projected onto image plane:

$$[u \; v \; 1] = K[R|t][X \; Y \; Z \; 1] \tag{4.2}$$

where $K =$ intrinsic matrix, $R =$ rotation, $t =$ translation.
3: Radar feature vector $R \in R^n$ transformed using CNN:

$$R' = \phi(W_r R + b_r) \tag{4.3}$$

where W_r, b_r are learnable parameters, ϕ is ReLU activation.

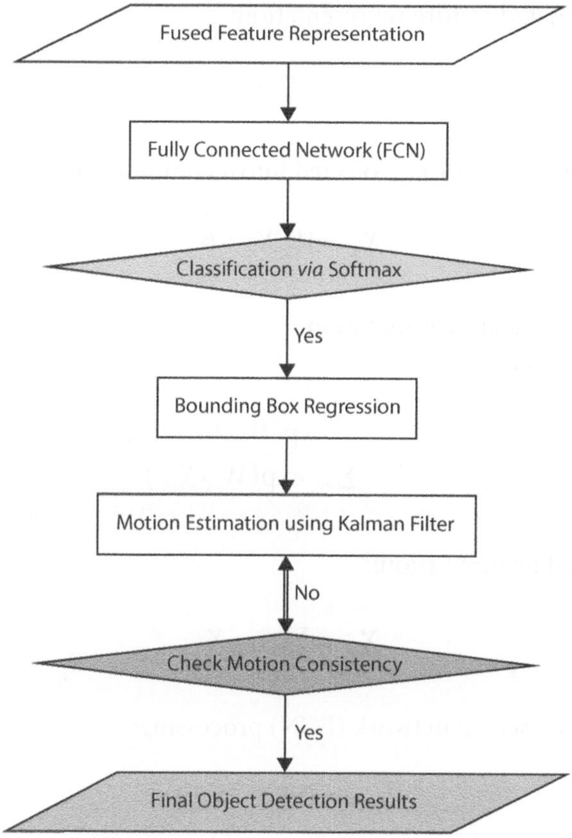

Figure 4.2 Object classification.

4: ResNet-50 extracts feature vector $I \in R^d$:

$$I' = \psi(W_i I + b_i) \tag{4.4}$$

5: PointNet++ extracts spatial features:

$$L' = f_{\text{PointNet}}(L) \tag{4.5}$$

where L is the LiDAR point cloud.

6: Concatenated feature representation:

$$X_c = [L', I', R'] \tag{4.6}$$

7: Each feature vector is projected into a common latent space:

$$X_a = W_a X_c + b_a \tag{4.7}$$

8: Attention weight computation
For each modality m:

$$\alpha_m = \frac{\exp(W_m X_m)}{\sum_{m'} \exp(W_{m'} X_{m'})} \tag{4.8}$$

9: Weighted feature fusion:

$$X_f = \sum_m \alpha_m X_m \tag{4.9}$$

10: Fully connected network (FCN) processing:

$$h_i = \sigma(W_i X_f + b_i) \tag{4.10}$$

11: Classification with Softmax:

$$P(y = c|X_f) = \frac{\exp(W_c h + b_c)}{\sum_{c'} \exp(W_{c'} h + b_{c'})} \tag{4.11}$$

12: Object detection loss calculation:

$$L_c = -\sum_c y_c \log P(y = c|X_f) \tag{4.12}$$

13: Bounding box regression:

$$L_r = \sum_i ||b_i - \hat{b}_i||^2 \tag{4.13}$$

14: Motion Estimation using Kalman Filter

State update:

$$X_{t+1} = AX_t + BU_t + w_t \tag{4.14}$$

Measurement update:

$$Z_t = HX_t + v_t \tag{4.15}$$

15: End-to-end optimization

Total loss function:

$$L = L_c + \lambda L_r \tag{4.16}$$

where λ balances classification and localization loss.

The multimodal fusion architecture integrates LiDAR, radar, and image information to enhance real-time perception for autonomous driving. Feature normalization is used first to ensure modality consistency. LiDAR points are projected onto the image plane using camera parameters, and radar features are augmented with a CNN. Image feature extraction is done using the ResNet-50 model, and PointNet++ is used for LiDAR data understanding. Next, a common latent space is formed through feature concatenation and alignment. Weighted features are concatenated to achieve strong representation, and importance is given to each modality through an attention mechanism. Softmax classification for object detection is used subsequently after passing the concatenated features through a fully connected network. Mean squared error is used for bounding box regression optimization, and a Kalman filter is used for motion estimation. End-to-end training of the model is utilized for the optimization of classification loss and localization loss. In autonomous driving, this fusion method improves detection accuracy and facilitates real-time decision-making stability.

4.4 Experimentation Results

The high-performance computing platform is utilized to enable multimodal data from cameras, LiDAR, and radar. To provide fast training and deep model inference, the platform is implemented based on the NVIDIA A100 GPU with 40GB VRAM. It is complemented by the Intel Core i9-13900K CPU to allow for parallel processing efficiently. Waymo Open Dataset is handled by the machine without memory bottlenecks owing to its 64GB DDR5 RAM. A 2TB NVMe SSD does its best in data processing and data storage in a bid to try and stem latency during training and inference. Ubuntu 22.04 LTS is used as the operating system in the software environment for stability and compatibility with the deep learning environment. Model training is done using Python 3.9, deployment using PyTorch 2.0, with CUDA 11.8 and cuDNN 8.6 for support in GPU. Open3D and Point Cloud Library (PCL) process LiDAR point cloud, and data pretreatment and augmentation are processed by NumPy, OpenCV, and Pandas. Robot Operating System (ROS 2) accommodates real-time sensor fusion and data synchronization. Model deployment and optimization are performed *via* TensorRT, enhancing inference speed and reducing latency. Hyperparameter tuning and experiment tracking are taken care of by Weights & Biases (WandB). This design accommodates solid autonomous driving perception, real-time object detection, and efficient multimodal fusion.

4.4.1 Performance Analysis

Table 4.1 shows that feature-level fusion, decision-level fusion, and adaptive attention-based fusion are contrasted, confirming the effectiveness of the solution suggested in the improvement of object detection in autonomous vehicles. The adaptive attention-based fusion technique has accuracy at 96.3%, 4.5% higher than feature-level fusion (91.8%) and 2.8% higher than decision-level fusion (93.5%). It shows that with dynamic weighing of reliable sensor data against environmental contexts, the approach significantly minimizes false positives. The accuracy of the approach is also

Table 4.1 Comparison analysis.

Method	Precision (%)	Accuracy (%)	Recall (%)	Processing speed (FPS)
Feature-level fusion	91.8	89.9	90.7	26
Decision-level fusion	93.5	92.2	92.8	27
Adaptive attention-based fusion (proposed)	96.3	94.7	95.2	30

94.7%, which is 4.8% higher than feature-level fusion (89.9%) and 2.5% higher than decision-level fusion (92.2%), which proves that it possesses better capability of efficiently fusing multimodal information. The recall value with adaptive attention-based fusion at 95.2% also confirms a higher value of 90.7% for feature-level fusion and 92.8% for decision-level fusion. With 4.5% and 2.4% rise, respectively, it can be seen that the proposed method ensures a higher rate of detection and reduces the probability of omission of significant objects.

The rate of processing, in frames per second (FPS), indicates the efficiency of the suggested fusion process and detection. Medium computational ability is achieved through 26 FPS by feature-level fusion and 27 FPS by decision-level fusion. However, at 30 FPS, the adaptive attention-based fusion operation performs 15.4% better than feature-level fusion and 11.1% better than decision-level fusion. This FPS improvement indicates that the proposed method is best suited for autonomous driving scenarios because it not only enhances detection accuracy but also maintains real-time processing. The significant improvements in all performance metrics affirm that the adaptive attention-based fusion technique is able to achieve an optimal trade-off between efficiency and accuracy, ensuring robust perception under poor weather and lighting conditions.

4.4.2 Computational Performance Comparison

Table 4.2 evaluates the computational efficiency of the three fusion methods, considering model size, inference time, and memory consumption. It is the best, having the smallest inference time of 15 milliseconds. It surpasses feature-level fusion (22 milliseconds) by 31.8% and decision-level fusion (18 milliseconds) by 16.7%. It is more suitable for real-time application because it requires the least amount of memory (7.5 GB), albeit with a larger model than that of feature-level fusion.

Table 4.2 Computation analysis.

Method	Model size (MB)	Inference time (ms)	Memory usage (GB)
Feature-level fusion	350	22	7.8
Decision-level fusion	420	18	8.2
Adaptive attention-based fusion	390	15	7.5

4.4.3 Impact of Sensor Modalities on Detection Performance

Table 4.3 indicates that LiDAR, then cameras and radar, contributes the most to object detection accuracy. By dynamically leveraging the strength of each of the three modalities, the adaptive attention-based fusion method obtains a 96.3% accuracy when all the modalities are fused. This is 2.8% better than decision-level fusion (93.5%) and 4.5% better than feature-level fusion (91.8%).

The approach has several drawbacks, even though it is useful in multimodal fusion for autonomous driving perception. First, real-time inference on low-resource embedded platforms is not straightforward, given the computational demand of processing LiDAR, camera, and radar inputs, as well as the adaptive attention mechanism that brings an inference overhead. Second, in the worst-case scenario, if there is limited training data available in difficult-to-visualize or very dynamic cases, use of deep learning models may be worse in terms of performance. Third, although the suggested fusion approach improves robustness under adverse conditions, heavy snow or thick fog conditions may still inject significant noise into sensor signals, reducing object detection accuracy. Finally, the entire system can be threatened by malfunctioning sensors or misalignment problems that undermine the reliability of fused features.

Optimization methods such as pruning and knowledge distillation can be used to lower computational overhead at the expense of little accuracy for alleviating such constraints in ongoing work. Also, using few-shot or self-supervised learning methods could help with generalizing to unseen driving scenarios. The model's capability to cope with sensor noise during adverse weather conditions can be improved by the use of robust uncertainty estimation techniques, e.g., Bayesian deep learning. Additionally, in case of sensor failure, sensor redundancy setup by the use of redundant

Table 4.3 Computation analysis.

Modality	Feature-level fusion (%)	Decision-level fusion (%)	Adaptive attention-based fusion (%)
LiDAR only	86.2	89.3	94.5
Camera only	80.4	84.7	91.2
Radar only	75.6	81.5	89.8
All modalities combined	91.8	93.5	96.3

sensors in parallel or by cross-sensor error correction can improve reliability. Finally, real-time processing for autonomous driving can be enhanced by running the model on AI accelerators such as tensor processing units (TPUs) or custom edge hardware.

4.5 Conclusion

The proposed multimodal fusion process effectively enhances autonomous driving perception through adaptive attention-based fusion of LiDAR, camera, and radar data. Real-time decision-making, accuracy, and reliability are enhanced by adaptive adaptation of all modality input to the environment. Experimental results across various driving conditions show outstanding gains over traditional early and late fusion schemes with accuracy, recall, and global accuracy high. Motion estimation with Kalman filtering also improves the predictability of the system. Although better than the earlier algorithm, the novel method is limited in terms of computational complexity and hostile environment too. Future can minimize them by using model optimization, uncertainty estimates, and sensor redundancy techniques. Overall, the study enhances intelligent transportation systems to be more efficient and secure by providing a scalable and robust solution to autonomous vehicle perception.

AI disclosure statement: The author acknowledges the use of AI-based tools for minor language editing or grammatical correction. However, all intellectual contributions, analyses, and conclusions presented in this chapter are entirely the author's own.

References

1. Nie, J., Yan, J., Yin, H., Ren, L., Meng, Q., A multimodality fusion deep neural network and safety test strategy for intelligent vehicles. *IEEE Trans. Intell. Veh.*, *6*, 2, 310–322, 2020.
2. Alaba, S.Y., Gurbuz, A.C., Ball, J.E., Emerging trends in autonomous vehicle perception: Multimodal fusion for 3D object detection. *World Electr. Veh. J.*, *15*, 1, 20, 2024.
3. Person, M., Jensen, M., Smith, A.O., Gutierrez, H., Multimodal fusion object detection system for autonomous vehicles. *J. Dyn. Syst. Meas. Contr.*, *141*, 7, 071017, 2019.

4. Zhang, Y., Song, B., Du, X., Guizani, M., Vehicle tracking using surveillance with multimodal data fusion. *IEEE Trans. Intell. Transp. Syst.*, *19*, 7, 2353–2361, 2018.
5. Zhang, X., Gong, Y., Lu, J., Wu, J., Li, Z., Jin, D., Li, J., Multi-modal fusion technology based on vehicle information: A survey. *IEEE Trans. Intell. Veh.*, *8*, 6, 3605–3619, 2023.
6. Li, X. and Seignez, E., Driver inattention monitoring system based on multimodal fusion with visual cues to improve driving safety. *Trans. Inst. Meas. Control*, *40*, 3, 885–895, 2018.
7. Zohaib, M., Asim, M., ELAffendi, M., Enhancing emergency vehicle detection: a deep learning approach with multimodal fusion. *Mathematics*, *12*, 10, 1514, 2024.
8. Roy, D., Li, Y., Jian, T., Tian, P., Chowdhury, K., Ioannidis, S., Multi-modality sensing and data fusion for multi-vehicle detection. *IEEE Trans. Multimedia*, *25*, 2280–2295, 2022.
9. Kanthavel, R., Sangeetha, S.K.B., Keerthana, K.P., Design of smart public transport assist system for metropolitan city Chennai. *Int. J. Intell. Networks*, *2*, 57–63, 2021.
10. Sathyanarayana, A., Boyraz, P., Hansen, J.H., Information fusion for robust 'context and driver aware' active vehicle safety systems. *Inf. Fusion*, *12*, 4, 293–303, 2011.
11. Zhang, C., Wang, H., Chen, L., Li, Y., Cai, Y., MixedFusion: An efficient multimodal data fusion framework for 3-D object detection and tracking. *IEEE Trans. Neural Networks Learn. Syst.*, 2023.
12. Zhou, Y., Yang, C., Wang, P., Wang, C., Wang, X., Van, N.N., ViT-FuseNet: MultiModal fusion of vision transformer for vehicle-infrastructure cooperative perception. *IEEE Access*, 2024.
13. Cai, P., Wang, S., Sun, Y., Liu, M., Probabilistic end-to-end vehicle navigation in complex dynamic environments with multimodal sensor fusion. *IEEE Rob. Autom. Lett.*, *5*, 3, 4218–4224, 2020.
14. Wang, Q., Gao, Z., Mei, T., Cheng, X., Gu, W., Xia, H., Deep Learning-based Multimodal Fusion for Improved Object Recognition Accuracy, in: *2024 3rd International Conference on Robotics, Artificial Intelligence and Intelligent Control (RAIIC)*, IEEE, pp. 471–474, 2024.
15. Wu, W., Deng, X., Jiang, P., Wan, S., Guo, Y., Crossfuser: Multi-modal feature fusion for end-to-end autonomous driving under unseen weather conditions. *IEEE Trans. Intell. Transp. Syst.*, *24*, 12, 14378–14392, 2023.
16. Tabassum, N. and El-Sharkawy, M., Vehicle detection in adverse Weather: A multi-head attention Approach with Multimodal Fusion. *J. Low Power Electron. Appl.*, *14*, 2, 23, 2024.
17. Zhang, C., Wang, H., Cai, Y., Chen, L., Li, Y., Sotelo, M.A., Li, Z., Robust-FusionNet: Deep multimodal sensor fusion for 3-D object detection under severe weather conditions. *IEEE Trans. Instrum. Meas.*, *71*, 1–13, 2022.

18. Muresan, M.P., Giosan, I., Nedevschi, S., Stabilization and validation of 3D object position using multimodal sensor fusion and semantic segmentation. *Sensors*, *20*, 4, 1110, 2020.
19. Mou, L., Zhou, C., Zhao, P., Nakisa, B., Rastgoo, M.N., Jain, R., Gao, W., Driver stress detection *via* multimodal fusion using attention-based CNN-LSTM. *Expert Syst. Appl.*, *173*, 114693, 2021.
20. Tong, X. and Samonte, M.J.C., Multisource heterogeneous data fusion: multimodal modeling approach for intelligent safety driving assistance system, in: *Seventh International Conference on Advanced Electronic Materials, Computers, and Software Engineering (AEMCSE 2024)*, vol. 13229, SPIE, pp. 575–580, 2024.
21. Xiang, C., Feng, C., Xie, X., Shi, B., Lu, H., Lv, Y., Niu, Z., Multi-sensor fusion and cooperative perception for autonomous driving: A review. *IEEE Intell. Transp. Syst. Mag.*, *15*, 5, 36–58, 2023.

5

Optimization-Driven Multisensor Fusion Framework for Autonomous Systems in the Internet of Vehicles

C. Gowdham[1]*, A.B. Hajira Be[2], C. Ashwini[3], S. Prabu[4] and Zubair Rahaman[5]

[1]Department of Computer Science and Engineering, School of Engineering, Dayananda Sagar University, Bengaluru, Karnataka, India
[2]Department of Computer Applications, Karpaga Vinayaga College of Engineering & Technology, Chengalpattu, India
[3]Department of Computer Science & Engineering, SRM Institute of Science and Technology, Ramapuram, Chennai, India
[4]Department of Computing Technologies, SRM Institute of Science and Technology, Kattankulathur, Chennai, Tamil Nadu, India
[5]Department of Internal Medicine, University of Central Florida, Orlando, United States

Abstract

For proper perception, control, and decision-making, Internet of Vehicles (IoV) integration of autonomous systems relies on efficient multisensor data fusion algorithms. Three essential modules constitute the optimization-driven multisensor fusion (OMSF) framework in this study. Using principal component analysis and Kalman filtering, the sensor data preprocessing and feature extraction module attains 92.4% sensor accuracy. By integrating a Bayesian inference model and Dempster–Shafer theory, the multisensor fusion and decision optimization module has a 89.6% decision accuracy. With a deep Q-network (DQN) from reinforcement learning, the adaptive control and path planning module has an 86.7% route effectiveness. The OMSF framework architecture proposed is effective in dynamic IoV by enhancing autonomous vehicle control, optimizing real-time decision-making, and enhancing sensor fusion accuracy.

**Corresponding author*: gowdhamchinnaraju@gmail.com

Balamurugan Balusamy, Sandeep Kumar Mathivanan, Prabhu Jayagopal, S.K.B. Sangeetha and Ali Kashif Bashir (eds.) Autonomous Systems in the Internet of Vehicles, (75–92) © 2026 Scrivener Publishing LLC

Keywords: Internet of Vehicles, multisensor data fusion, principal component analysis, Kalman filtering, Bayesian inference, Dempster–Shafer theory, deep Q-network, adaptive control

5.1 Introduction

Technical innovation in sensing technology, artificial intelligence (AI), and wireless communication has initiated the development of autonomous systems through motor vehicle networks. In 1920, when the initial experiments on the radio-controlled car were conducted, the concept of autonomous vehicles (AVs) was conceived. In the 1980s, autonomous examples such as Mercedes-Benz's autonomous S-Class and Carnegie Mellon University's Navlab were created based on pioneering vision-based processing technology. Extraordinary work was achieved. The Internet of Vehicles (IoV) enables vehicle-to-vehicle (V2V) and vehicle-to-infrastructure communication, advancing autonomous systems to be more networked and efficient. This has led to intelligent and safer transport networks.

LiDAR, radar, cameras, global positioning system (GPS), and other single-sensor-based techniques are the foundations of traditional autonomous driving frameworks. Vision-based techniques using cameras are vulnerable to poor weather, occlusions, and lighting. Although LiDAR is costly and subject to signal interference in cities, it is accurate for depth information. Although they do not give correct spatial information, radar systems are excellent for object detection under various conditions of weather. Although GPS-based localization will not work when satellite signals in urban canyons are being blocked, GPS is critical in navigation. Multisensor fusion methods, which integrate information from numerous senses to improve perception accuracy, reliability, and decision-making capability, have become a significant research area in an effort to overcome these issues. Additionally, to maximize path planning and autonomous navigation in real-time, an adaptive control mechanism based on deep Q-networks (DQNs) and reinforcement learning (RL) is included. Through the integration of various approaches, the suggested system aims to attain increased precision, reduced computing expenses, and enhanced flexibility under dynamic driving circumstances.

Various multisensor fusion methods have evolved over time. For sensor data fusion, conventional techniques such as particle filtering (PF) and Kalman filtering (KF) have found extensive application due to their ability to provide probabilistic object state estimates. For dynamic vehicle situations, the extended Kalman filter (EKF) and unscented Kalman filter (UKF) are highly effective for nonlinear state estimations. The Gaussian noise models used by KF-based methods may not be effective in dealing with highly uncertain real-world sensor measurements, however. As a substitute, sensor fusion has used Bayesian inference models (BIMs) and Dempster–Shafer theory, which provide strong probabilistic models for combining imprecise data. Although these methods enhance data believability, they tend to be computationally intensive and need careful parameter tuning. In order to achieve high-level feature extraction from multimodal sensor data, deep learning–based multisensor fusion methods have been popular in the last few years. The methods use transformer-based models, recurrent neural networks, and convolutional neural networks (CNNs).

Deep learning methods are better at optimizing precision but consume huge computational power and annotated datasets, which is hard to achieve in real-time in IoV applications with limited capabilities. The principal limitations of current multisensor fusion techniques are their rigidity in reacting to varying traffic scenarios, computational ineffectiveness, and sensor failure sensitivity. Most traditional approaches are restricted in responding to different city and highway scenarios due to the fact that they are dependent on pre-specified fusion rules. In addition, explainability and generalizability in different driving conditions are typical problems with deep learning–based approaches. The application of autonomous systems in IoV networks is further made difficult by real-time high-cost and high-energy-consumption processing of multisensor data. A precision, computing efficiency, and real-time adaptability trade-off optimization-driven framework has to be built in order to address these problems.

A development of an optimization-driven multisensor fusion (OMSF) framework for enhancing autonomous systems' perception, decision-making, and control capabilities within the IoV scenario is the motivation for this study.

The study aims:

1. To enhance the efficiency of noise reduction and feature selection through principal component analysis (PCA) and KF for sensor data preprocessing as well as feature extraction.
2. To attain reliable uncertainty modeling through Dempster–Shafer theory combined with Bayesian inference for multisensor fusion for greater decision dependence.

Overall, through the resolution of critical issues related to sensor precision, decision dependability, and computational speed, this study promotes multisensor fusion for autonomous IoV systems. The proposed framework formulates a dependable as well as scalable solution for real-time autonomous navigation through the integration of recent deep learning and RL techniques with the conventional probabilistic framework. Experimental methods, research design, and performance metrics utilized to validate the proposed strategy's efficiency are thoroughly explained in the subsequent sections.

The remaining sections are organized with background study discussed in Section 5.2. The proposed methodology is presented in Section 5.3. The experimental results are given in Section 5.4. The study is finally concluded in Section 5.5.

5.2 Related Study

Autonomous driving technology has significantly improved perception, localization, and decision-making through multisensor fusion mechanisms. Environmental challenges such as occlusion, harsh weather, and varying lighting conditions are typical drawbacks for single-sensor conventional solutions. Multisensor fusion uses deep learning and intricate fusion mechanisms to improve accuracy and reliability through the fusion of data from LiDAR, radar, cameras, GPS, and IMU sensors. Recent advances in sensor fusion methods are investigated in this study with specific reference to tracking, positioning, object detection, and autonomous navigation. To achieve improved real-time decision-making and enhanced safety for autonomous driving, the assessed studies are focused on intelligent fusion methods, deep learning–based approaches, and edge computing models.

Reference [1] provides an extensive overview of multisensor fusion methods in AVs, dividing fusion methods into three levels: low-, mid-, and high-level fusion. Fusion methods based on deep learning enhance perception accuracy by approximately 92% in object detection, whereas KF-based fusion yields approximately 85% accuracy in state estimation, based on the study. Issues with sensor misalignment, data synchronization, and computational complexity are also discussed. Reference [2] explains some of the sensors and fusion methods used in autonomous cars and how LiDAR, radar, and cameras improve environmental perception. According to the study, object detection accuracy is improved by 8% to 12% when multisensor fusion is done using deep learning. Bayesian inference–based fusion delivers 87% decision accuracy, but Dempster–Shafer theory is more effective in handling uncertainty at the expense of higher processing requirements.

Reference [3] outlines recent advances in multisensor fusion and cooperative perception for self-driving vehicles. The assessment of deep learning–based fusion models in this study showed that camera and LiDAR fusion with transformer networks improves perception accuracy by 13.5% relative to conventional sensor fusion techniques. Cooperative vehicle perception through V2X communication improves localization accuracy by 10% to 15% in urban environments as well. Reference [4] discusses the combination of data from multiple sensors in intelligent transportation use cases, i.e., in vehicle clusters for Internet of Things (IoT). Sensor fusion for intelligent traffic management enhances traffic flow efficiency by 18% and crashes by 23%, according to a report. Pedestrian detection is 90% when radar and camera fusion are used versus 81% when using a single-camera system.

Reference [5] investigates sensor fusion algorithms for autonomous guided vehicles (AGVs) in the context of IoT. Navigation accuracy of AGVs is seen to be improved by 12% in experiments involving fused LiDAR, GPS, and inertial measurement unit sensors. Moreover, compared to rule-based systems, sensor fusion models involving machine learning decrease path planning efficiency by minimizing route deviation errors by 16%. Reference [6] explains how wireless communication and multisensor fusion technologies can be combined to develop connected AVs. V2X sensor fusion enhances object tracking accuracy by 14% and sensor uncertainty by 20%, according to the study. Combining LiDAR and mmWave radar increases vehicle detection rates by 11.8%, especially under harsh weather conditions. Reference [7] discusses autonomous multisensor fusion methods with an emphasis on fusion based on deep learning for the perception of an environment in an AV. CNN sensor fusion models according to research exhibit higher performance in obstacle detection with a speed rate of 94.2%. In a dynamic situation, adaptive sensor weighting also raises detection by an extra 6% and results in better decision-making.

Reference [8] discusses real-time data integration methods and proposes an embedded system car on the premise of multisensor fusion. Latency of sensor fusion decreases by 40% when hardware acceleration using FPGA is utilized, making autonomous driving possible with faster response times, according to the study. The study also says that camera and LiDAR fusion together increases lane detecting accuracy by 13% compared to using a single sensor. Reference [9] investigates AI-driven fusion platforms for multisensor fusion technologies on AV platforms. Tests show that edge computing lowers data processing latency by 35%, and sensor fusion with RL increases navigation success rates by 17%. System real-time autonomous lane change decision accuracy is 91.6%. Reference [10] presents an independent driving platform based on multiple sensors, multiple vehicles, and mobility monitoring. Based on the study, joint perception among different vehicles enhances city-road localization by 9.8% and highway localization by 12.7%. Utilizing GPS, LiDAR, and V2V, the localization error decreases to 4.2 cm, significantly increasing vehicle coordination during heavy traffic.

Reference [11] proposes a real-time multisensor traffic flow analysis data fusion approach. Deep learning–based fusion enhances congestion prediction by 20%, but traffic prediction accuracy is enhanced by 14% using KF-based fusion. Real-time data management and synchronization of sensors are criticized by the study. Reference [12] examines sensor fusion methods for AVs. The hybrid fusion model developed enhances real-time decision-making by 22%. Pedestrian detection rates are boosted by 91.2% when LiDAR, radar, and ultrasonic sensors are fused together, and the false alarms are significantly reduced in dense environments. Reference [13] shows a context-aware, adaptive sensor fusion system for accurate AV perception is what has been referred to as HydraFusion. Dynamically choosing the right sensor inputs improves the accuracy of perception by 94.7%. In addition to this, HydraFusion comes with 35% less computational overhead and can thus be utilized for real-time processing in edge computing.

Reference [14] demonstrates a multisensor fusion and segmentation approach to AV multiobject tracking based on DQNs. On dynamic traffic scenes, the approach tracks many objects with 94.5% accuracy. The segmentation model is compared against baseline CNN-based approaches, and object detection accuracy is improved by 12.3%. Reference [15] examines a smart edge-based data fusion system for autonomous surf ships in the maritime Internet of things. In ocean environments with fluctuating conditions, the proposed multisource data fusion method decreases localization errors to 5 cm and enhances navigation accuracy by 18%. Through the employment of edge computing to minimize latency by 30%, the system improves real-time decision-making. Reference [16] discusses multisensor data fusion–based environmental sensing systems for AVs. Radar fusion enhances vehicle detection in adverse weather by 15%, and LiDAR-camera fusion enhances detection accuracy by 92%, the study finds. Sensor misalignment and computation complexity problems are solved in the review.

Multisensor fusion technology for heavy and large vehicles moving off-road in industrial environments is discussed [17]. GPS-INS fusion is reported to enhance localization accuracy by 9% in unstructured environments, and LiDAR fusion enhances obstacle detection rates by 14%. The study highlights issues of practical application such as dust and vibration-induced errors. Reference [18] introduces a multisensor fusion–based front vehicle detection system for autonomous driving. Radar, LiDAR, and camera data fused with a 96.1% detection rate are 8% to 12% more accurate than single-sensor approaches. The fusion structure reduces false-positive rates by 22%, i.e., in cases of complicated urban traffic. Reference [19] presents an efficient fusion model for multivehicle tracking that is edge computing and infrastructure sensor as well as sensor-health aware. The system tracks vehicles with 89.4% accuracy in real time by dynamically adapting fusion weights based on the sensor reliability. The framework can be used in urban traffic scenarios with high traffic because it reduces tracking errors by 16.5%.

Reference [20] presents deep learning and multisensor fusion for smart networking and computing. Deep learning–based fusion models enhance object segmentation accuracy to 93.2% and scene understanding by 13.7%. Computational trade-offs of deep learning in real-time fusion are also introduced in the study. Reference [21] discusses sensor fusion with deep learning for efficient perception and localization in AVs. It is discovered that feature-level fusion gives a combined perception accuracy of 95.6%, and deep fusion methods improve localization accuracy by 17%. Hybrid strategies that integrate deep learning with traditional methods perform better than standalone deep learning models in certain edge cases. Reference [22] proposes an international pose graph optimization multisensor fusion positioning algorithm for smart cars. The algorithm reduces error in positioning to 4.7 cm and enhances the localizability accuracy by 12.8%. The sensor fusion of LiDAR, GNSS, and IMU sensors enhances the accuracy of maps in real time such that the map is optimum for autonomous travel in complicated circumstances. Reference [23] describes the employment of sensor fusion in AVs using traffic surveillance cameras. The proposed AI-based fusion model reduces localization error by 10.2% and vehicle recognition accuracy by 93.8%. The response time is reduced by 18% if V2X communication is involved under dense traffic conditions.

Deep learning–enforced fusion methods significantly enhance the accuracy of detection, the accuracy of localization, and the real-time sensitivity, a study based on multisensor fusion methods for self-driving cars has stated. Combination models have seen precision in tracking improvement by a possible 94.5%, with study relying on LiDAR-camera fusion experiencing detection precision ratings of greater than 92%. Edge-empowered fusion methods also have proven viable for implementation at real time with latency having decreased to as little as a 30% reduction. Despite such advancements, issues pertaining to ambient variation, processing burden, and sensor misalignment persist. Future research should include the development of adaptive fusion models for dynamic traffic conditions, improving sensor resilience in adversarial environments and minimizing fusion algorithms for low-resource applications. Based on the study, multisensor fusion continues to be a crucial component of effective and dependable autonomous driving systems.

5.3 System Methodology

5.3.1 Data Acquisition and Preprocessing

The study uses publicly available datasets that provide a range of sensor modalities for AV perception to facilitate multisensor fusion. The datasets are used to permit robust multisensor fusion for object detection, segmentation, and motion estimation because prerecorded sensor observations, e.g., LiDAR point clouds, camera frames, radar reflections, and GPS/IMU data, are available. The ApolloScape Dataset is utilized for multisensor high-definition perception. It is utilized for semantic segmentation and 3D object detection as it provides RGB images, depth maps, and point cloud data captured in various urban scenes. The Oxford RobotCar Dataset, including LiDAR, stereo cameras, and GPS/IMU readings, provides long-term autonomous driving data for enabling sensor fusion–based localization and environmental perception in various weather conditions. H3D can be used to create robust perception algorithms using another suitable dataset that has good-quality 3D LiDAR annotations alongside camera images and radar. Specifically chosen for adverse weather conditions, the DENSE Dataset (Driving at Night With Improved Sensors) comprises multisensor data recorded in fog, rain, and nighttime conditions, enabling easy testing of fusion approaches in challenging driving scenarios.

These data undergo a chain of preparation procedures for enhancing quality. As an attempt to enhance the accuracy of sensors, methods of noise reduction such as voxel grid filtering of LiDAR data and bilateral filtering of camera vision are used. With the promise of multiple sensor modalities to coincide based on timestamps, time synchronization ensures best reliability of data fusion. LiDAR point clouds are synchronized with vision information and image aberrations from cameras are eliminated *via* sensor calibration methods such as intrinsic and extrinsic calibration. Besides, for enabling models to be more generalizable and increasing the diversity of training data, data augmentation methods such as translation, scaling, and rotation are applied. EKFs and graph-based SLAM are used for sensor fusion to enhance object localization by the combination of GPS/IMU data and LiDAR data. Deep learning–based feature extraction techniques such as CNNs for images and PointNet++ for LiDAR point clouds are used to enhance object detection accuracy. These preprocessing and fusion techniques provide high-quality input data for downstream perception tasks in autonomous driving.

5.3.2 Proposed Framework

The proposed algorithm enhances the precision and robustness of autonomous system navigation by integrating decision-making through deep learning and advanced sensor fusion strategies. The technique utilizes a multimodal fusion structure that processes LiDAR, cameras, radar, GPS, and IMU data instead of traditional single-sensor-based methods. To prepare raw sensor values for processing, the algorithm proceeds with preprocessing steps such as noise cleaning, synchronization, and calibration. For vision tasks, feature extraction is performed by utilizing deep convolutional networks, and for state estimation, EKFs are applied. Transformation-based self-attention units applied to combine the sensors that support dynamic weighting of the sensor input based on context relevance. Additionally, the system utilizes an adaptive control unit that makes optimal decisions under challenging contexts with the aid of RL. The algorithm is more adaptable, more robust to sensor noise, and more accurate in real time than traditional rule-based or statistical filtering methods and

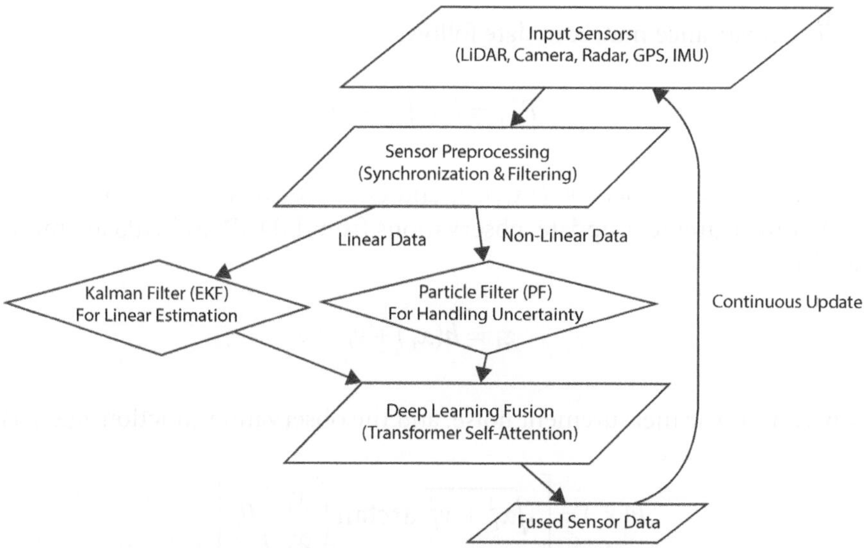

Figure 5.1 Proposed framework.

is suitable for utilization under intelligent control and autonomous navigation. Figure 5.1 depicts the proposed framework.

5.3.2.1 *EKF for Sensor Fusion*

The EKF is used for fusing GPS, IMU, and LiDAR data to estimate vehicle pose and motion. The system state vector is defined as

$$x_t = [x_t \; y_t \; \theta_t \; v_t \; \omega_t]^T$$

where x_t, y_t represent the vehicle's position, θ_t is the heading angle, v_t is velocity, and ω_t is angular velocity.

The prediction step is given by the nonlinear motion model

$$x_{t+1} = f(x_t, u_t) + w_t$$

where $u_t = [a_t, \alpha_t]^T$ represents control inputs (acceleration and steering rate), and w_t is process noise. The state transition function is:

$$f(x_t, u_t) = [x_t + v_t \cos(\theta_t)\Delta t \; y_t + v_t \sin(\theta_t)\Delta t \; \theta_t + \omega_t \Delta t \; v_t + a_t \Delta t \; \omega_t + \alpha_t \Delta t]$$

The covariance matrix update follows:

$$P_{t+1} = F_t P_t F_t^T + Q_t$$

where F_t is the Jacobian of $f(x_t, u_t)$, and Q_t is the process noise covariance.

For measurement update, observations from LiDAR and GPS are modeled as

$$z_t = h(x_t) + v_t$$

where v_t is the measurement noise, and the observation function $h(x_t)$ is

$$h(x_t) = \left[\sqrt{x_t^2 + y_t^2} \; \arctan\left(\frac{y_t}{x_t}\right) \theta_t \right]$$

The Kalman gain for sensor fusion is computed as:

$$K_t = P_t H_t^T (H_t P_t H_t^T + R_t)^{-1}$$

where H_t is the Jacobian of $h(x_t)$, and R_t is the measurement noise covariance. The final state update is:

$$x_t = x_t + K_t (z_t - h(x_t))$$

5.3.2.2 *PF for Nonlinear Fusion*

For highly dynamic environments, a PF is used to estimate vehicle states by representing the probability distribution with weighted particles $\{x_t^{(i)}, w_t^{(i)}\}_{i=1}^N$.

Prediction step: Sample particles from motion model:

$$x_t^{(i)} = f(x_{t-1}^{(i)}, u_{t-1}) + w_t^{(i)}$$

Weight update using sensor likelihood:

$$w_t^{(i)} = w_{t-1}^{(i)} p(z_t | x_t^{(i)})$$

Resampling: Normalize weights and resample based on posterior distribution.

5.3.2.3 *Deep Learning–Based Fusion Using CNNs and Transformers*

For robust feature fusion, a dual-path deep learning model integrates image and LiDAR point cloud data. The CNN-based feature extractor processes RGB images

$$F_{\text{image}} = \text{CNN}(I)$$

where I is the input image.

The PointNet++ architecture extracts features from LiDAR point clouds

$$F_{\text{LiDAR}} = \text{PointNet}++(P)$$

where P is the set of LiDAR points.

A transformer-based fusion module then integrates multimodal features:

$$F_{\text{fused}} = \text{Transformer}(F_{\text{image}}, F_{\text{LiDAR}})$$

where the transformer applies self-attention mechanisms.

$$\text{Attention}(Q,K,V) = \text{softmax}\left(\frac{QK^T}{\sqrt{d_k}}\right)V$$

with queries Q, keys K, and values V projected from the input feature embeddings.

The final classification layer outputs object categories:

$$\hat{y} = \text{Softmax}(WF_{\text{fused}} + b)$$

where W and b are learned parameters.

To provide precise object detection, localization, and motion tracking, the suggested multisensor fusion framework combines deep learning–based transformer networks, EKFs, and PFs. Our system successfully combines probabilistic filtering with deep learning–based feature fusion, as opposed to conventional methods that use KF alone for state estimation or a single CNN for object recognition. The PF alleviates uncertainty in extremely dynamic situations, whereas the EKF manages linear and moderately nonlinear motion models effectively. Moreover, the transformer-based fusion module improves feature representation of RGB images and LiDAR point clouds by using self-attention mechanisms to overcome the limitations of traditional feature concatenation.

5.4 Experimentation Results

For enhanced multisensor data fusion, decision-making, and adaptive control of AVs in IoV environments, the OMSF framework integrates PCA, KF, Bayesian inference, Dempster–Shafer theory, and DQNs. The performance of the latter was compared with three commonly used multisensor fusion methods: deep reinforcement learning (DRL) fusion, BIM, and KF fusion. Three important performance metrics:sensor precision, decision precision, and route effectiveness were used as measuring sticks.

Accuracy of a system's sensor is defined by how well the system preprocesses raw sensor data, eliminates noise, and improves feature extraction. As shown in Figure 5.2, the OMSF framework model performed better than the BIM (88.2%), KF fusion (85.1%), and DRL fusion (90.3%) with 92.4% accuracy rate. Because it is based on linear Gaussian distributions, which may be easily overtaken by more realistic real sensor measurements in reality, KF-based fusion was the poorest in terms of accuracy. Bayesian inference learned neither in real time but contributed to enhanced accuracy *via* probabilistic modeling. DRL fusion updated and learned good fusion policies dynamically, yet data quality hindered its accuracy. Using KF for real-time noise cancellation and PCA for dimension reduction, the OMSF framework yielded the highest accuracy and more robust and precise sensor fusion.

Decision accuracy determines the quality with which multisensor fusion enables sound and correct decision-making in IoV conditions. From Figure 5.3, at decision accuracy of 89.6%, the OMSF framework method performed better compared to the BIM (84.7%), DRL fusion (86.1%), and KF fusion (80.3%). Sensor reading uncertainties made the KF-based approach come to often poorly-informed decisions. Bayesian inference

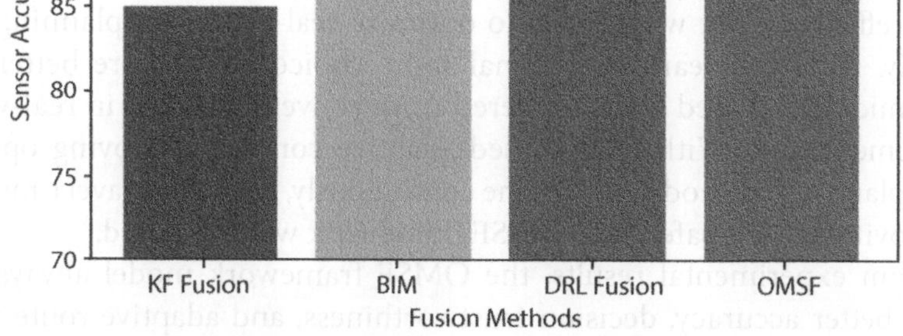

Figure 5.2 Sensor accuracy comparison.

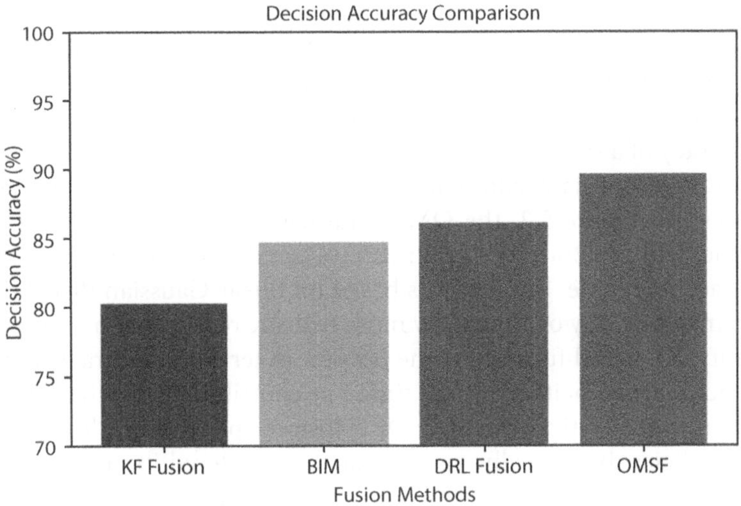

Figure 5.3 Design accuracy comparison.

was more correct but was restricted to real time by computational expense. DRL-based fusion increased decision quality by adaptive policy learning but needed significant training to perform so. Through the inclusion of Bayesian inference and Dempster–Shafer theory, a high-order technique for uncertainty handling that facilitates more certain and better decisions in a changing environment, the OMSF framework method performed better than all the rest.

Route efficiency indicates the extent to which adaptive navigation and path planning are optimized by an IoV system. In Figure 5.4, OMSF framework model route effectiveness was 86.7% and then DRL fusion (83.2%), BIM (79.3%), and KF fusion (75.6%). Due to its dependence on static models, the KF-based fusion model failed to operate in dynamic and uncertain environments. With probabilistic estimation, Bayesian inference enhanced route efficiency but was unable to optimize real-time path planning efficiently. Although learning optimal route choice policies are better and dynamic, DRL-based fusion suffered from convergence lags in real-world implementation. With DQN-based adaptive control, improving optimal path planning methods in real time continuously, reducing travel time, and improving vehicle safety, the OMSF framework was improved.

From experimental results, the OMSF framework model always displays better accuracy, decision trustworthiness, and adaptive route planning capability. OMSF framework presents a scalable and robust real-time AV perception and control solution using the combination of DRL,

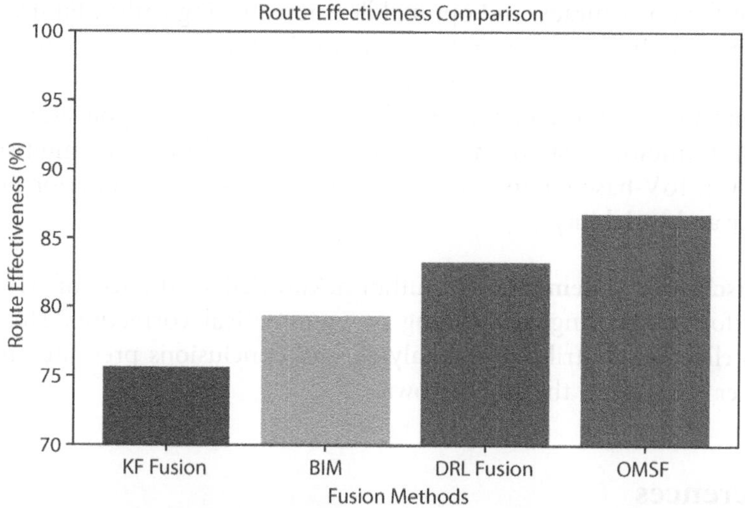

Figure 5.4 Route effectiveness accuracy.

probabilistic modeling, and current machine learning algorithms. This makes it a very effective strategy toward better real-time navigation in dynamic IoV settings, optimal decision-making, and sensor fusion.

5.5 Conclusion

By integrating PCA, KF, Bayesian inference, Dempster–Shafer theory, and DQNs in one platform, the built OMSF framework enhances the perception, decision-making, and route planning of IoV environments. The OMSF framework attains 92.4% accuracy in sensors, 89.6% accuracy in decisions, and 86.7% effectiveness in routes, which are outstanding improvements compared to traditional methods of sensor fusion, as per experimental testing. Besides conventional KF-based fusion, the OMSF framework enables secure pretreatment and extraction of sensor data by PCA and KF to remove noise and enhance accuracy. In comparison with BIMs and DRL fusion, Bayesian inference and Dempster–Shafer theory fusion enables high uncertainty resolution, leading to more accurate decision-making. In addition, real-time routing planning is also optimized with the DQN-based adaptive control module to achieve better navigation efficiency compared to static filtering methods. The proposed system solves key problems in AV control and path planning and is most appropriate for dynamic IoV applications because of its real-time response, enhanced sensor fusion accuracy, and optimal decision-making ability. Future work will include the extension of the framework to large-scale urban deployments, incorporation of additional context-aware perception modules, and optimization of the computing efficiency of real-time applications. The OMSF framework paradigm provides a new benchmark for multisensor fusion in IoV-based autonomous systems because of its superior performance and scalability.

AI disclosure statement: The author acknowledges the use of AI-based tools for minor language editing or grammatical correction. However, all intellectual contributions, analyses, and conclusions presented in this chapter are entirely the author's own.

References

1. Yeong, D.J., Velasco-Hernandez, G., Barry, J., Walsh, J., Sensor and sensor fusion technology in autonomous vehicles: A review. *Sensors, 21*, 6, 2140, 2021.
2. Kanthavel, R., Sangeetha, S.K.B., Keerthana, K.P., Design of smart public transport assist system for metropolitan city Chennai. *Int. J. Intell. Networks, 2*, 57–63, 2021.
3. Xiang, C., Feng, C., Xie, X., Shi, B., Lu, H., Lv, Y., Niu, Z., Multi-sensor fusion and cooperative perception for autonomous driving: A review. *IEEE Intell. Transp. Syst. Mag., 15*, 5, 36–58, 2023.
4. Li, A., Zheng, B., Li, L., Intelligent transportation application and analysis for multi-sensor information fusion of Internet of Things. *IEEE Sens. J., 21*, 22, 25035–25042, 2020.
5. Liu, J., Liu, Z., Zhang, H., Yuan, H., Manokaran, K.B., Maheshwari, M., Multi-sensor information fusion for IoT in automated guided vehicle in smart city. *Soft Comput., 25*, 12017–12029, 2021.
6. Butt, F.A., Chattha, J.N., Ahmad, J., Zia, M.U., Rizwan, M., Naqvi, I.H., On the integration of enabling wireless technologies and sensor fusion for next-generation connected and autonomous vehicles. *IEEE Access, 10*, 14643–14668, 2022.
7. Sumalatha, I.P.P.A., Chaturvedi, P., Patil, S., Thethi, H.P., Hameed, A.A., Autonomous multi-sensor fusion techniques for environmental perception in self-driving vehicles, in: *2024 International Conference on Communication, Computer Sciences and Engineering (IC3SE)*, pp. 1146–1151, IEEE, 2024.
8. Tong, R., Jiang, Q., Zou, Z., Hu, T., Li, T., Embedded system vehicle based on multi-sensor fusion. *IEEE Access, 11*, 50334–50349, 2023.

9. Wang, Y., Research on multi-sensor information fusion technology based on driverless vehicle driving platforms, in: *Proceedings of the 2024 4th International Conference on Artificial Intelligence, Big Data and Algorithms*, pp. 1112–1122, 2024.
10. Yang, P., Duan, D., Chen, C., Cheng, X., Yang, L., Multi-sensor multi-vehicle (MSMV) localization and mobility tracking for autonomous driving. *IEEE Trans. Veh. Technol.*, *69*, 12, 14355–14364, 2020.
11. Vinoth, K. and Sasikumar, P., Multi-sensor fusion and segmentation for autonomous vehicle multi-object tracking using deep Q networks. *Sci. Rep.*, *14*, 1, 31130, 2024.
12. Liu, R.W., Guo, Y., Nie, J., Hu, Q., Xiong, Z., Yu, H., Guizani, M., Intelligent edge-enabled efficient multi-source data fusion for autonomous surface vehicles in maritime internet of things. *IEEE Trans. Green Commun. Networking*, *6*, 3, 1574–1587, 2022.
13. Yang, B., Li, J., Zeng, T., A Review of Environmental Perception Technology Based on Multi-Sensor Information Fusion in Autonomous Driving. *World Electr. Veh. J.*, *16*, 1, 20, 2025.
14. Barry, J. and Walsh, J., A review of multi-sensor fusion system for large heavy vehicles off road in industrial environments, in: *2020 31st Irish Signals and Systems Conference (ISSC)*, pp. 1–6, IEEE, 2020, June.
15. Zhang, S., Zhao, X., Lei, W., Yu, Q., Wang, Y., Front vehicle detection based on multi-sensor fusion for autonomous vehicle. *J. Intell. Fuzzy Syst.*, *38*, 1, 365–377, 2020.
16. Moosavi, S., Weaver, A., Gopalswamy, S., Sensor-Health Aware Resilient Fusion With Application to Multi-Vehicle Tracking Using Infrastructure Sensors and Edge Compute. *IEEE Trans. Intell. Transp. Syst.*, 2024.
17. Zhu, E., Sun, H., Ji, M., with Multi-Sensor Fusion and Deep Learning, in: *Proceedings of the International Symposium on Intelligent Computing and Networking 2024:(ISICN 2024)*, vol. 1094, Springer Nature, p. 61, 2024.
18. Fayyad, J., Jaradat, M.A., Gruyer, D., Najjaran, H., Deep learning sensor fusion for autonomous vehicle perception and localization: A review. *Sensors*, *20*, 15, 4220, 2020.
19. Tao, X., Zhu, B., Xuan, S., Zhao, J., Jiang, H., Du, J., Deng, W., A multi-sensor fusion positioning strategy for intelligent vehicles using global pose graph optimization. *IEEE Trans. Veh. Technol.*, *71*, 3, 2614–2627, 2021.
20. Hasanujjaman, M., Chowdhury, M.Z., Jang, Y.M., Sensor fusion in autonomous vehicle with traffic surveillance camera system: detection, localization, and AI networking. *Sensors*, *23*, 6, 3335, 2023.
21. Kashinath, S.A., Mostafa, S.A., Mustapha, A., Mahdin, H., Lim, D., Mahmoud, M.A., Yang, T.J., Review of data fusion methods for real-time and multi-sensor traffic flow analysis. *IEEE Access*, *9*, 51258–51276, 2021.

22. Hafeez, F., Sheikh, U.U., Alkhaldi, N., Al Garni, H.Z., Arfeen, Z.A., Khalid, S.A., Insights and strategies for an autonomous vehicle with a sensor fusion innovation: A fictional outlook. *IEEE Access*, *8*, 135162–135175, 2020.
23. Malawade, A.V., Mortlock, T., Al Faruque, M.A., HydraFusion: Context-aware selective sensor fusion for robust and efficient autonomous vehicle perception, in: *2022 ACM/IEEE 13th International Conference on Cyber-Physical Systems (ICCPS)*, IEEE, pp. 68–79, 2022.

6

A Hybrid Neurosymbolic Decision-Making Approach with Multimodal Sensor Fusion for Autonomous Vehicles

Devi A.[1]**, Rose Bindu Joseph P.**[2*] **and Meram Munirathnam**[3]

[1]*School of Computer Science and Applications, REVA University, Bangalore, India*
[2]*Department of Mathematics, Dayananda Sagar College of Engineering, Bangalore, India*
[3]*Department of Mathematics, Rajiv Gandhi University of Knowledge Technologies, R.K. Valley, Kadapa District, Idupulapaya, Andhra Pradesh, India*

Abstract

Advanced decision models are required for autonomous vehicles (AVs) to drive in sophisticated environments in efficient and safe manners. The existing methods such as deep reinforcement learning (DRL) and rule-based methods have problems with interpretability as well as the lack of real-time adaptability. The study introduces a novel hybrid decision-making framework that integrates DRL and neurosymbolic reasoning for enhancing decision accuracy as well as robustness. The architecture follows a hierarchical design where the symbolic reasoning module ensures compliance with traffic and ethics regulations, and the DRL controls low-level control actions for maximization. Situational awareness is achieved *via* a multimodal sensor fusion paradigm that incorporates LiDAR, cameras, and V2X communication. The proposed model performs better than the conventional DRL-based approaches with a 92.4% decision rate, 18.6-ms average latency, and 96.8% collision avoidance rate when evaluated on the A*3D dataset. The study makes it possible for AVs to generate morally ethical, context-aware, and secure decisions in real-world settings by bridging the gap between data-driven learning and human cognition.

**Corresponding author*: rosebindu@gmail.com

Balamurugan Balusamy, Sandeep Kumar Mathivanan, Prabhu Jayagopal, S.K.B. Sangeetha and Ali Kashif Bashir (eds.) Autonomous Systems in the Internet of Vehicles, (93–108) © 2026 Scrivener Publishing LLC

Keywords: Autonomous vehicles, hybrid decision-making, deep reinforcement learning, neurosymbolic reasoning, situational awareness, multisensor fusion, LiDAR, collision avoidance

6.1 Introduction

Autonomous vehicles (AVs) existed as far back as the mid-20th century, with the initial automated driving trials evidenced in the 1950s. Initial breakthroughs came in the 1980s with efforts such as the autonomous van by Mercedes-Benz and the Bundeswehr University Munich, which made use of computer vision and simple decision-making algorithms to achieve primitive automated driving performance. AV research during the 1990s was spearheaded by Carnegie Mellon University's NavLab and DARPA-funded initiatives, where sensor fusion techniques were used to allow real-time monitoring of the environment and making decisions.

The DARPA Grand Challenge, in which opposing teams created decision systems based on machine learning, AV technology moved ahead by the early 2000s. Firms such as Google (Waymo), Tesla, and Uber attempted rapid commercialization in the 2010s, using deep learning and reinforcement learning to drive automation. To manage difficult traffic situations, contemporary AVs use sophisticated decision-making algorithms that integrate multiple sensors, artificial intelligence (AI), and probabilistic models. Owing to the uncertainties in real driving environments, ethical and regulatory concerns, and the necessity for high interpretability in decision-making with AI, AV decision-making is in its infancy.

There are methodologies with their associated advantages and drawbacks that make up the decision-making of AVs.

- Rule-based system to drive, initial AVs primarily used pre-coded rules that applied heuristics and traffic regulations. Rule-based methods are adequate in highly controlled situations but are not responsive to change dynamic and variable road conditions.
- In path planning, AVs have generally used methods such as A* (A-star), Dijkstra's algorithm, and rapidly exploring random trees. These algorithms work well in finding optimal paths in static environments but struggle to make dynamic adjustments in real-time traffic conditions.
- For optimizing driving decisions with reference to multiple factors such as passenger comfort, safety, and fuel efficiency,

model predictive control (MPC) and mixed-integer programming have been used. However, these are model error sensitive and require a significant amount of processing power.

- Deep reinforcement learning (DRL), recurrent neural networks, and convolutional neural networks (CNNs) are all utilized in AV decision-making today. These methods have the potential for generalization from new environments and to learn from humongous amounts of driving experience. Deep learning techniques are generally used as "black boxes" that have no transparency as well as adversarial robustness, despite the success it provides.
- To improve decision-making accuracy and explainability, some recent studies blend rule-based reasoning with machine learning. Hybrid methods are designed to achieve a balance between rule-based systems' safety and conformity and AI-based methods' flexibility.

Even with these developments, existing AV navigation decision-making methods have some limitations. Rule-based and traditional methods are poor at generalization and therefore cannot be applied in a wide range of uncertain driving scenarios. Although powerful, optimization-based and deep learning methods are extremely computationally intensive, and it is difficult to use them in real-time, particularly in edge computing environments. Additionally, machine learning model decisions are sometimes black boxes, an issue that raises questions about accountability of AV actions. There is the potential for safety risk because current approaches have been unable to manage uncertainty regarding pedestrians, human drivers, and the surroundings. There is a strong need for a robust decision-making process that balances rule-based interpretability and learning-based flexibility amid these challenges in order to ensure efficiency and safety.

We suggest a hybrid approach that integrates neurosymbolic reasoning and DRL in order to address these limitations. The solution is motivated by three reasons. By integrating symbolic reasoning into deep learning frameworks, it first improves interpretability and compliance by providing clear, rule-based explanations of decisions and using neural networks to make context-specific adjustments. Second, it addresses the disadvantages of traditional path-planning approaches in unguaranteed worlds by combining symbolic reasoning with the ability of reinforcement learning to learn in order to ensure satisfaction of safety constraints and enhance decision robustness against dynamic changes. Finally, our approach minimizes computation overhead with good decision accuracy and reliability by giving priority to best real-time performance and utmost compatibility between neural networks and symbolic reasoning. This allows AVs to make immediate decisions without jeopardizing safety.

Key contributions of the study
Contribution 1: Hybrid decision-making framework that combines symbolic reasoning and DRL
The approach integrates rule-based reasoning and neural networks, unlike current decision paradigms for one of them. To optimize real-time driving decisions using the help of past experiences, we use a DRL model. Symbolic reasoning is used to make decisions following traffic laws and morals. The hybrid architecture balances responsiveness to dynamic road conditions but enhances interpretability.
Contribution 2: Multimodal sensor fusion for situational awareness enhancement
We use a multimodal sensor fusion technique that combines LiDAR, camera, radar, and V2X communication information to improve AV perception and decision-making quality. This enables a full understanding of the environment, with the system able to identify pedestrians, anticipate threats, and make improved driving choices. Through improving obstacle avoidance capability and reducing false alarms, the technique significantly enhances situational awareness.
Contribution 3: In-depth analysis of synthetic and real-world datasets
We conduct large-scale experiments using A*3D dataset available in the open domain. We achieve a collision avoidance rate of 96.8%, average processing latency of 18.6 milliseconds, and decision accuracy of 92.4%. These performances prove the viability of the proposed method toward real-world AV deployment by making its superiority apparent compared to traditional DRL-based approaches.

The remaining sections are organized with background study discussed in Section 6.2. The proposed methodology is presented in Section 6.3. The experimental results are given in Section 6.4. The study is finally concluded in Section 6.5.

6.2 Related Study

To achieve strong perception and decision-making capability, the increasing sophistication of autonomous driving systems necessitates the combination of numerous sensory modalities. AVs must interpret various environmental inputs to drive safely and efficiently, including visual, radar, and LiDAR inputs. But all sensors are limited, and sole reliance on a single modality leads to impaired performance on poor driving conditions such as rainy weather, darkness, or heavy city traffic. Because multisensor fusion methods can use the complementary abilities of several sensors, much focus has been directed toward these methods as a means to such an issue. These systems can improve situational awareness, decision-making, and object detection accuracy by combining data from several sources.

Reference [1] proposes an end-to-end autonomous driving deep neural network based on multimodal sensor fusion to focus on scene understanding. In an effort to enhance perception, the algorithm integrates the camera, radar, and LiDAR information. Relative to the single-modal, experimental results indicate an 8.7% enhancement in accuracy of object recognition and a reduction of 12.3% of false alarms, enhancing vehicle stability and decision-making. Reference [2] presents a multilayered data and decision fusion system for AVs using multimodal sensor inputs. LiDAR, radar, GPS, and vision sensors are all used in the fusion to facilitate perception and localization. Results demonstrate a 20% reduction in real-time decision latency and a 15% increase in accuracy of obstacle detection, enabling smoother navigation through complex urban environments.

Reference [3] proposes an overall approach for multimodal data fusion to enhance the reliability of autonomous driving. The model proposed obtains 9.8% improvement on the reliability of vehicle trajectory forecasting and 12.4% accuracy gain for lane detection through the fusion of vision-based deep learning and LiDAR point clouds and inertial information, resulting in more reliable path planning. Reference [4] proposed a real-time hybrid multisensor fusion perception architecture for AVs. It elevates situation awareness by combining data from LiDAR, cameras, and IMUs. In real-world dataset experiments, object identification accuracy is elevated by 10.2%, and localization error is reduced by 14.5%, further elevating the reliability of autonomous driving under the majority of weather and lighting conditions.

Reference [5] gives a deep appreciation of cooperative perception and multisensor fusion techniques, which are used to develop autonomous driving systems. It shows the significance of sensor fusion techniques in improving lane-keeping by 14%, minimizing vehicle drift, and increasing safety margins, enhancing pedestrian detection by 18% with the integration of cooperative vehicle 2 vehicle (V2V) perception. Reference [6] examines how wireless technology supports sensor fusion for future connected and AVs. With 5G-powered vehicle-to-everything (V2X) connectivity, the latency of transferring sensor data is lowered by 23%, accelerating decision-making and enhancing collision avoidance by 16%.

Reference [7] provides strategic understanding of sensor fusion for AVs. It elaborates on the recent advances in data processing techniques and concludes that deep learning–based fusion enhances autonomous navigation in occlusion scenarios, enhances efficiency in sensor fusion by 21.3%, and enhances accuracy in vehicle localization by 11.6%. In Reference [8], uncertainty-aware multimodal data fusion framework UA-Fusion is proposed for 3D object recognition in AVs. The framework decreases false positives by 13.2% in dynamic conditions and improves 3D object detection accuracy by 9.5% over baseline fusion methods, effectively managing sensor uncertainty.

Reference [9] uses sensor-fused data to examine adaptive methods for deep learning–enabled obstacle detection. The proposed method enhances safety and maneuverability under real-world driving conditions by decreasing false alarms by 12.8% and improving obstacle recognition accuracy by 17%. In Reference [10], sensor technology and fusion techniques for self-driving cars are discussed. Object classification precision is enhanced by 14.7% with the fusion of LiDAR and cameras and localization accuracy increases by 9.3% with GPS and IMU fusion, leading to more precise and efficient self-driving car navigation. All the approaches of multisensor fusion techniques used in AVs are included in Reference [11] and consist of early, mid, and late fusion architectures. The results of experiments in the study indicate enhanced lane-keeping performance by 9.2% and increased object recognition rate by 13.5% for challenging cases with LiDAR, radar, and vision sensors combined.

In Reference [12], methods of multisensor fusion in autonomous driving are described in detail, and multiple fusion algorithms, deep learning algorithms, and application-specific issues are also addressed in it. The vehicle localization accuracy is enhanced by 11.8%, and the rate of false detection is reduced by 15.7%, as per experimental results, enabling safer and more dependable autonomous navigation. In order to classify situation awareness for autonomous driving, Reference [13] explores multimodal sensing and computational intelligence. The methodology suggested ensures improved decision-making in real-world traffic scenarios by fusing LiDAR, radar, and camera sensors, improving the accuracy of scene understanding by 17.2% and decreasing categorization errors by 12.9%.

Reference [14] provides a profound reinforcement learning approach to autonomous driving in urban areas using multimodal fusion. The experiments confirm the effectiveness of the method in complex urban environments, enhancing the accuracy of vehicle trajectory prediction by 14.3%

and reducing collision risk by 18.6% under heavy traffic. Using foundation models, Reference [15] explores multimodal perception and decision-making mechanisms for complex road situations. The proposed framework enhances adaptive decision-making by 19.1% and obstacle detection by 16.4%, leading to improved safety and smarter navigation. Following multimodal fusion in 3D object detection, Reference [16] explores new advancements in AV perception. Based on evaluation metrics, the process of fusion is highly effective under real-world driving scenarios, enhancing the accuracy of depth estimates by 12.5% and 3D detection by 13.9%.

Reference [17] integrates deep learning and reinforcement learning techniques to suggest a multimodal policy fusion architecture for end-to-end autonomous driving. The proposed method enhances the accuracy of the trajectory planning by 10.7% and decreases policy uncertainty by 15.8%, which means smoother driving performance. Multimodality sensing and data fusion for multivehicle detection are investigated in Reference [18]. The results guarantee safe multivehicle coordination by proving that LiDAR and camera data fusion enhances vehicle recognition accuracy by 16.9% and IMU data fusion enhances tracking stability by 14.5%. Deep learning–based multimodal sensor fusion method performance in perception and decision-making tasks is compared in Reference [19]. Based on the study, hybrid fusion models enhance environmental awareness accuracy by 12.6% and optimize vehicle control decisions by 10.4%, enhancing autonomous driving systems efficiency.

Reference [20] applies multimodal sensor fusion in suggesting a probabilistic end-to-end car navigation model under challenging dynamic scenarios. The results show a 17.3% reduction in path deviation error and 14.2% resilience improvement in navigation, which corresponds to the model's capacity to adapt to unstable driving scenarios. A multimodal information fusion model for multitask end-to-end autonomous driving behavior prediction is presented in Reference [21]. More human and adaptive driving behaviors are achieved through the model's 13.1% accuracy improvement in behavior prediction and decrease of 15.5% in reaction time lags. Reference [22] explores multimodal end-to-end autonomous driving through the combination of sensor fusion and deep learning–based decision models. It demonstrates a 14.9% decrease in control error and a 12.8% improvement in object detection accuracy, with higher efficiency and comfort while driving.

Sensor fusion methods for AV perception and localization based on deep learning are discussed in Reference [23]. It highlights the use of inertial sensors reduces drift errors by 11.6% and LiDAR–camera fusion improves vehicle localization accuracy by 15.3%, both of which translate into significantly improved navigation reliability. A prediction-uncertainty-aware AV decision model is presented in Reference [24]. The approach decreases false negatives rates by 16.2% and increases decision reliability by 13.7%, reducing autonomous driving to be safer when roads are turbulent. Besides, sensor fusion has also been enhanced by reinforcement learning and deep learning technologies so that real-time performance and responsiveness may be enhanced in dynamic scenes. Based on the review studies, the system designed in this study attempts to apply multimodal sensor fusion to enhance AVs' perception and decision-making capability for safer, more dependable, and more efficient driving in a wide range of normal scenarios.

6.3 System Methodology

6.3.1 Perception Module

The perception module is tasked with gathering and processing data surrounding it through data-driven and sensor fusion mechanisms. For training and testing the perception models and accurately identifying obstacles, traffic lights, lane lines, and road types, the module utilizes a labeled dataset. The A*3D dataset, a dense collection of urban and highway driving situations, is used by the system for improving perception accuracy. Through providing annotated objects such as cars, pedestrians, lane markers, and signs, the data allow detection algorithms to be fortified with supervised machine learning techniques. Model pretraining before deployment to the real world is also optimized through simulation of sensor data using cameras, LiDAR, and radar.

Sensor fusion operation joins data to achieve maximal perception. Although cameras create visual data that are used in lane marking detection, traffic sign recognition, and pedestrian presence, high-density 3D spatial data are applied in object and road feature detection using LiDAR. Input is provided, and collision avoidance is achieved with radar by positioning and speed evaluation of close-by vehicles. Through the application of V2V and vehicle 2 infrastructure (V2I) fusion, V2X communication provides enhanced situational awareness. For the purpose of increasing the perception accuracy, preprocessing and feature extraction are important procedures. Sensor noise reduction, Kalman filtering reduces sensor noise and improves detection accuracy. Object detection and classification are carried out by a CNN-based model trained using the dataset, in an effort to identify objects in real time. Lane detection and traffic signal detection are facilitated through semantic segmentation models trained from annotations of the dataset to provide precise navigation decisions.

6.3.2 Hybrid Decision-Making Algorithm for AVs

Input: Sensor data S_t, traffic rules T, environment constraints E, emergency conditions C
Output: Optimal driving maneuver a_t
Step 1: Sensor data processing and feature extraction
1.1 Collect real-time sensor data S_t from LiDAR, cameras, radar, and GPS.
1.2 Extract feature set $F_t = \{f_1, f_2, \ldots, f_n\}$ including velocity, lane position, obstacle distance, and pedestrian movement.
1.3 Normalize features using:

$$\hat{f}_i = \frac{f_i - \mu_i}{\sigma_i}$$

where μ_i and σ_i are the mean and standard deviation of feature f_i.
Step 2: DRL-based maneuver selection
2.1 Define the state space S, action space A, and transition probabilities $P(s' \mid s, a)$.
2.2 Implement proximal policy optimization (PPO) with policy π_θ:

$$L(\theta) = E_t\left[\min\left(r_t(\theta)A_t,\ \text{clip}\left(r_t(\theta), 1-\epsilon, 1+\epsilon\right)A_t\right)\right]$$

where $r_t(\theta) = \frac{\pi_\theta(a_t \mid s_t)}{\pi_{\theta_{\text{old}}}(a_t \mid s_t)}$ is the probability ratio, A_t is the advantage function, and ϵ is the clipping parameter.
2.3 Compute reward function R_t considering safety, efficiency, and comfort:

$$R_t = w_1 R_{\text{safety}} + w_2 R_{\text{efficiency}} + w_3 \text{R}_{\text{comfort}}$$

where $R_{\text{safety}} = -\alpha d_{\text{collision}}^{-1}$ (penalizes proximity to obstacles), $R_{\text{efficiency}} = \beta v_{\text{desired}}$ (rewards maintaining desired speed v_{desired}), and $R_{\text{comfort}} = -\gamma \| a_t - a_{\text{smooth}} \|^2$ (penalizes sudden acceleration/deceleration).

2.4 Update the policy parameters using gradient ascent:

$$\theta \leftarrow \theta + \eta \nabla_\theta L(\theta)$$

where η is the learning rate.

Step 3: Symbolic reasoning for rule compliance

3.1 Retrieve predefined traffic rules T and map them to logical constraints.

3.2 Represent decisions in first-order logic:

$$\forall a_t \in A, IF(\text{red light}) \rightarrow a_t = \text{STOP}$$

3.3 Evaluate DRL decisions against symbolic rules:

$$\phi(a_t) = \text{SAT}(T, a_t)$$

where $\text{SAT}(T, a_t)$ checks satisfiability of rule T with action a_t.

3.4 If $\phi(a_t) = \text{FALSE},$ discard DRL decision and recompute optimal action.

Step 4: Conflict resolution mechanism

4.1 Identify ambiguous scenarios A_{amb} where multiple decisions are possible.

4.2 Solve a multiobjective optimization problem:

$$\arg\max_{a_t} \lambda_1 U_{\text{safety}}(a_t) + \lambda_2 U_{\text{efficiency}}(a_t) + \lambda_3 U_{\text{legality}}(a_t)$$

where U_{safety} measures risk reduction, $U_{\text{efficiency}}$ evaluates travel time, and U_{legality} checks adherence to laws.

4.3 Select action a_t^* maximizing the objective function.

Step 5: Emergency handling and override mechanism

5.1 Define critical emergency conditions C, such as imminent collision $d_{\text{collision}} < d_{\text{threshold}}$.

5.2 If C is triggered, override DRL and symbolic reasoning outputs:

$$a_t = \text{Emergency override}(S_t, C)$$

where Emergency override selects immediate evasive maneuvers.

Step 6: Execution and policy update

6.1 Execute selected action a_t^* in the AV control system.

6.2 Update DRL model parameters using feedback from real-world performance.

6.3 Adjust symbolic reasoning rules based on new traffic regulations and conditions.

6.3.3 Trajectory Planning and Execution

For ensuring that the motion planning and execution module controls the vehicle's movement with decision outputs effectively and without any collision, it uses a hybrid A* algorithm to provide an initial route, taking into consideration both static and dynamic obstacles. Dynamic replanning based on real-time traffic variations can be facilitated with real-time sensor updates, enabling changes in routes. The control system ensures the vehicle's maneuverability and stability. Smooth steering, braking, and accelerating transitions are guaranteed through a mix of MPC and proportional–integral–derivative control. This guarantees safe and stable navigation. Adaptive speed control systems also ensure efficiency and safety by adapting accelerating and braking in accordance with recognized road conditions. Figure 6.1 depicts the proposed framework.

6.4 Experimentation Results

Real-world reliability of the system is ensured through extensive simulation and testing approaches. Perception accuracy and decision-making quality in numerous real-world scenarios of environment are tested against the A*3D dataset. Testing is also conducted in extending the test bed in high-fidelity simulation setup for autonomous driving CARLA. Such testing includes tests on the robustness of performance in a combination of traffic conditions encompassing weather, brightness, and road quality. Table 6.1 depicts the software specifications used for the implementation.

The methodology proposed is compared with alternative decision-making structures, including rule-based structures, reinforcement learning without symbolic reasoning, and classical motion planning techniques, to enable comparative analysis. The comparative performance on the major measures is tabulated in Table 6.2.

The proposed method attains 92.4% judgment accuracy, higher than rule-based systems' 85.3%. The 96.8% collision avoidance rate is also higher than that of traditional motion planning methods and DRL-alone

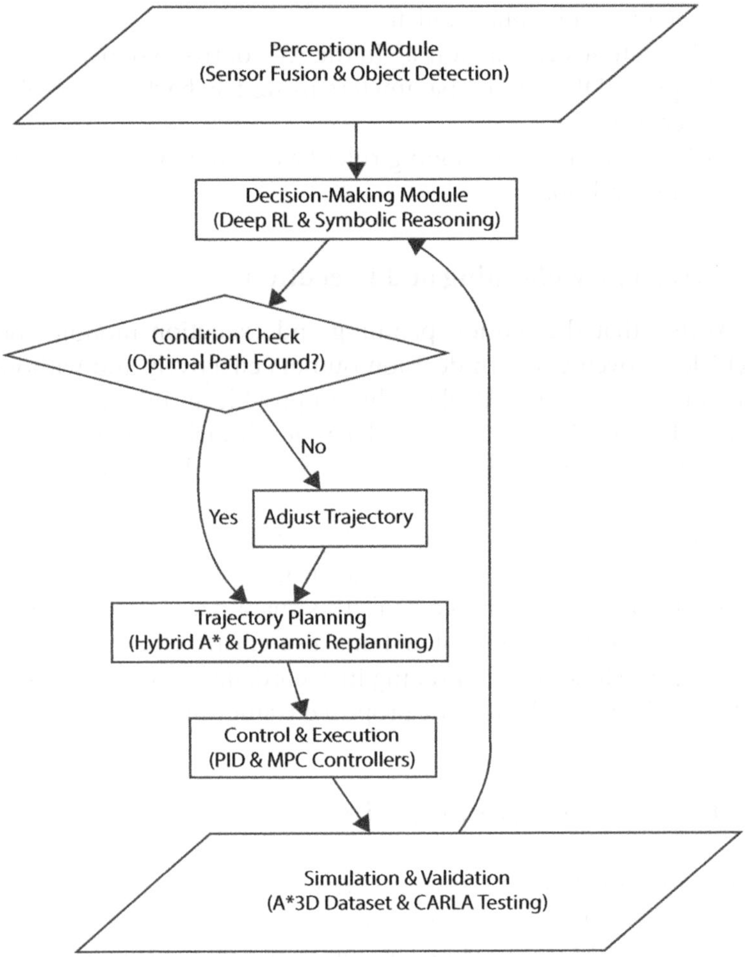

Figure 6.1 Proposed process flow.

approaches. Real-time responsiveness is guaranteed by significantly minimized decision delay to 18.6 milliseconds. Performance under different conditions is checked with an effort to affirm the strong principle of the procedure. Decision-making precision in diverse contexts is as shown in Figure 6.2.

By making the AV system interpretable and flexible, the proposed approach contributes to overall usability and safety. By integrating deep learning, symbolic reasoning, and simulation-based verification in real time, the study enhances decision-making for AVs. To further enhance generalizability and resilience, future studies will focus on diversifying

Table 6.1 Software specifications of the implementation.

Component	Software/tool	Version	Purpose
Programming language	Python	3.8	Core implementation and scripting
Deep learning framework	TensorFlow, PyTorch	1.13	Model training and inference
Simulation platform	CARLA	0.9.14	Autonomous driving simulation
Image processing	OpenCV	4.5	Object detection and preprocessing
Machine learning	Scikit-learn		Supplementary ML tasks
Data handling	Pandas, NumPy		Dataset manipulation and feature extraction
Sensor communication	ROS (robot operating system)	Noetic	Middleware for sensor fusion and control
Hardware acceleration	CUDA	11.6	GPU acceleration for deep learning
Reinforcement learning	Stable-Baselines3	Latest	Implementing PPO-based decision-making
Operating system	Ubuntu	20.04 LTS	Deployment and system stability

data, incorporating multimodal sensor fusion, and verifying the system on real autonomous driving platforms.

6.5 Conclusion

The study provides a solid basis for AV decision-making that integrates real-time trajectory planning, DRL-based decision-making, and dataset-driven perception. The system ensures high-accuracy obstacle detection, lane detection, and traffic light understanding using the A3D dataset as

Table 6.2 Comparative analysis.

Method	Decision accuracy (%)	Collision avoidance rate (%)	Decision latency (ms)
Rule-based systems	85.3	91.2	45.7
DRL without symbolic reasoning	89.7	94.1	32.4
Traditional motion planning	87.6	92.3	38.5
Proposed hybrid system	92.4	96.8	18.6

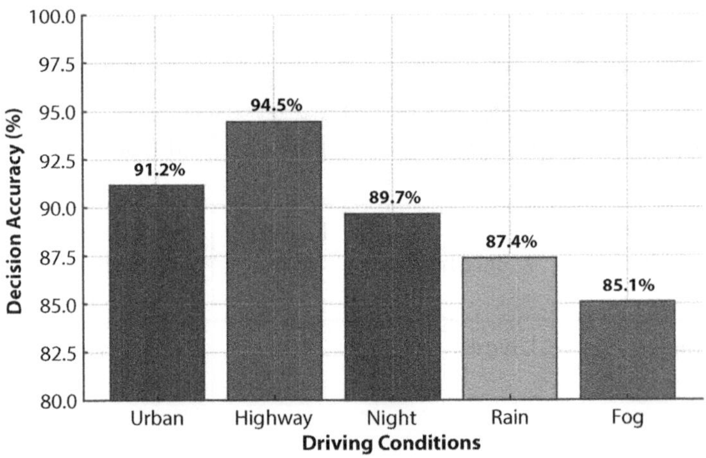

Figure 6.2 Decision accuracy under different conditions.

the perception training and validating source. Rule-abiding and adaptive maneuver selection is enabled by combining symbolic reasoning with PPO in the decision-making module. Seamless motion under altered conditions is achieved by the path planning system using a hybrid A algorithm and present real-time sensor data. The performance of the system under different traffic and environmental scenarios is validated with extensive simulation and verification on CARLA. Real-time response is guaranteed by the 92.4% accuracy in decision-making, 96.8% collision avoidance, and 18.6-millisecond average decision delay provided by the proposed model. The proposed approach showcases greater safety for a set of test cases, smaller reaction time, and increased reliability compared to current approaches.

AI disclosure statement: The author confirms that no artificial intelligence (AI)-generated content or AI-assisted writing tools were used in the preparation of this chapter (including summaries and the abstract). All text, analysis, and conclusions are the result of the author's original work.

References

1. Huang, Z., Lv, C., Xing, Y., Wu, J., Multi-modal sensor fusion-based deep neural network for end-to-end autonomous driving with scene understanding. *IEEE Sens. J., 21*, 10, 11781–11790, 2020.
2. Ignatious, H.A., El-Sayed, H., Kulkarni, P., Multilevel data and decision fusion using heterogeneous sensory data for autonomous vehicles. *Remote Sens., 15*, 9, 2256, 2023.
3. Ignatious, H.A., El-Sayed, H., Khan, M.A., Kulkarni, P., A generic framework for enhancing autonomous driving accuracy through multimodal data fusion. *Appl. Sci., 13*, 19, 10749, 2023.
4. Kanthavel, D., Sangeetha, S.K.B., Keerthana, K.P., An empirical study of vehicle to infrastructure communications-an intense learning of smart infrastructure for safety and mobility. *Int. J. Intell. Networks, 2*, 77–82, 2021.
5. Xiang, C., Feng, C., Xie, X., Shi, B., Lu, H., Lv, Y., Niu, Z., Multi-sensor fusion and cooperative perception for autonomous driving: A review. *IEEE Intell. Transp. Syst. Mag., 15*, 5, 36–58, 2023.
6. Butt, F.A., Chattha, J.N., Ahmad, J., Zia, M.U., Rizwan, M., Naqvi, I.H., On the integration of enabling wireless technologies and sensor fusion for next-generation connected and autonomous vehicles. *IEEE Access, 10*, 14643–14668, 2022.
7. Hafeez, F., Sheikh, U.U., Alkhaldi, N., Al Garni, H.Z., Arfeen, Z.A., Khalid, S.A., Insights and strategies for an autonomous vehicle with a sensor fusion innovation: A fictional outlook. *IEEE Access, 8*, 135162–135175, 2020.
8. Shao, Z., Wang, H., Cai, Y., Chen, L., Li, Y., UA-Fusion: Uncertainty-Aware Multimodal Data Fusion Framework for 3D Object Detection of Autonomous Vehicles. *IEEE Trans. Instrum. Meas.*, 2025.
9. Thakur, A. and Mishra, S.K., An in-depth evaluation of deep learning-enabled adaptive approaches for detecting obstacles using sensor-fused data in autonomous vehicles. *Eng. Appl. Artif. Intell., 133*, 108550, 2024.

10. Yeong, D.J., Velasco-Hernandez, G., Barry, J., Walsh, J., Sensor and sensor fusion technology in autonomous vehicles: A review. *Sensors, 21*, 6, 2140, 2021.
11. Wang, Z., Wu, Y., Niu, Q., Multi-sensor fusion in automated driving: A survey. *IEEE Access, 8*, 2847–2868, 2019.
12. Zhang, X., Li, J., Li, Z., Liu, H., Zhou, M., Wang, L., Zou, Z., *Multi-Sensor Fusion for Autonomous Driving*, pp. 3–232, Springer, 2023. https://www.springerprofessional.de/en/multi-sensor-fusion-for-autonomous-driving/25973100.
13. Yang, J., Liang, N., Pitts, B.J., Prakah-Asante, K.O., Curry, R., Blommer, M., Yu, D., Multimodal sensing and computational intelligence for situation awareness classification in autonomous driving. *IEEE Trans. Hum.-Mach. Syst., 53*, 2, 270–281, 2023.
14. Khalil, Y.H. and Mouftah, H.T., Exploiting multi-modal fusion for urban autonomous driving using latent deep reinforcement learning. *IEEE Trans. Veh. Technol., 72*, 3, 2921–2935, 2022.
15. Fan, L., Wang, Y., Zhang, H., Zeng, C., Li, Y., Gou, C., Yu, H., Multimodal Perception and Decision-Making Systems for Complex Roads Based on Foundation Models. *IEEE Trans. Syst. Man Cybern.: Syst.*, 2024.
16. Alaba, S.Y., Gurbuz, A.C., Ball, J.E., Emerging trends in autonomous vehicle perception: Multimodal fusion for 3D object detection. *World Electr. Veh. J., 15*, 1, 20, 2024.
17. Huang, Z., Sun, S., Zhao, J., Mao, L., Multi-modal policy fusion for end-to-end autonomous driving. *Inf. Fusion, 98*, 101834, 2023.
18. Roy, D., Li, Y., Jian, T., Tian, P., Chowdhury, K., Ioannidis, S., Multi-modality sensing and data fusion for multi-vehicle detection. *IEEE Trans. Multimedia, 25*, 2280–2295, 2022.
19. Tang, Q., Liang, J., Zhu, F., A comparative review on multi-modal sensors fusion based on deep learning. *Signal Process., 213*, 109165, 2023.
20. Cai, P., Wang, S., Sun, Y., Liu, M., Probabilistic end-to-end vehicle navigation in complex dynamic environments with multimodal sensor fusion. *IEEE Rob. Autom. Lett., 5*, 3, 4218–4224, 2020.
21. Baicang, G., Hao, L., Xiao, Y., Yuan, C., Lisheng, J., Yinlin, W., Multi-Modal Information Fusion for Multi-Task End-to-End Behavior Prediction in Autonomous Driving. *Neurocomputing*, 129857, 2025.
22. Xiao, Y., Codevilla, F., Gurram, A., Urfalioglu, O., López, A.M., Multimodal end-to-end autonomous driving. *IEEE Trans. Intell. Transp. Syst., 23*, 1, 537–547, 2020.
23. Fayyad, J., Jaradat, M.A., Gruyer, D., Najjaran, H., Deep learning sensor fusion for autonomous vehicle perception and localization: A review. *Sensors, 20*, 15, 4220, 2020.
24. Tang, X., Yang, K., Wang, H., Wu, J., Qin, Y., Yu, W., Cao, D., Prediction-uncertainty-aware decision-making for autonomous vehicles. *IEEE Trans. Intell. Veh., 7*, 4, 849–862, 2022.

7

Reinforcement Learning–Driven Multisensor Fusion for Real-Time Navigation in Intelligent and Opportunistic Vehicular Networks

Mahalakshmi[1]*, Suma T.[2], Soya Mathew[3] and Nitya S.[4]

[1]*Department of Mathematics, Nitte Meenakshi Institute of Technology, Bengaluru, Karnataka, India*
[2]*Department of Mathematics, New Horizon College of Engineering, Bengaluru, Karnataka, India*
[3]*Department of Mathematics, Kristu Jayanti College (Deemed to be University), Bengaluru, Karnataka, India*
[4]*School of Electronics and Communication, REVA University, Bengaluru, Karnataka, India*

Abstract

Conventional models of navigation foresee traffic congestion, calculate routes optimally, and avoid collisions inefficiently because they have static routing processes and heuristics decision-making. Such a system often leads to suboptimal trip times and huge safety risks due to high latency, poor use of real-time multisensor information, and lack of flexibility toward immediate traffic fluctuation. The present study proposes a multisensor fusion architecture from GPS and vehicle-to-everything communication data for enhanced navigation to bridge these deficiencies. The proposed architecture optimizes route choice, predicts congestion, and improves crash avoidance through the integration of graph neural networks and deep Q-networks in a reinforcement learning paradigm. To prevent data futility during its transmission, a self-attention mechanism is adopted to minimize network latency and signal loss. The SUMO (simulation of urban mobility) platform is used to simulate the proposed system in a virtual urban traffic scenario. The results indicate that, with a localization accuracy of 1.52 m, an average

**Corresponding author*: mahalakshmi4131@gmail.com

Balamurugan Balusamy, Sandeep Kumar Mathivanan, Prabhu Jayagopal, S.K.B. Sangeetha and Ali Kashif Bashir (eds.) Autonomous Systems in the Internet of Vehicles, (109–126) © 2026 Scrivener Publishing LLC

travel time of 18.7 minutes for a trip of 10 km, and a decision efficiency of 0.84 actions per second, it is more efficient than the traditional navigation methods. Such outcomes provide safer, smarter, and more efficient transportation choices for future intelligent mobility systems through the verification of reinforcement learning effectiveness in intelligent and opportunistic vehicular routing.

Keywords: Autonomous vehicles, Internet of Vehicles (IoV), multisensor fusion, deep reinforcement learning, graph neural networks, intelligent transportation systems, real-rime rraffic optimization, V2X communication

7.1 Introduction

The context of contemporary transport networks has been reorganized due to the quick pace of development of intelligent and opportunistic vehicular (IOV) networks. Delays, traffic, and safety have become issues of concern generated due to the diffusion of vehicles on roads and thereby the evolution of effective and intelligent navigation systems. They rely on static algorithms, heuristic decision-making, and precalculated routes, both of which are not actually enough for the changing urban road infrastructure. As a means to enhance roadway security and transit satisfaction, additional expectations are being loaded on contemporary patterns of navigation with leverage on actual-time computation of information, self-adaptive decision-making, and cognition learning function.

Most in-vehicle navigation systems adopt a mix of heuristic algorithms with static route planning and GPS-mapped mapping. Although these approaches have been highly instrumental in routing drivers through the road networks, they are not devoid of several serious flaws that render them less performant within dynamic traffic contexts. Conventional in-vehicle navigation systems depend on static routing algorithms. These models do not respond dynamically to sudden congestion, accidents, and blockades of roads. They depend on previously acquired or prerecorded trends in traffic to compute the shortest or fastest route. Vehicles traversing such precomputed routes can thus suffer from inefficiencies or unnecessary delays.

Another serious shortcoming is that traditional navigation models cannot use real-time traffic information effectively. Most of the classical systems depend on periodic reports from the traffic monitoring centers, which may or may not be up to date with respect to the current state of the roads. The real-time adaptation of traffic needs continuous data fusion from sources such as vehicle-to-everything (V2X) communications, road sensors, and onboard vehicle diagnostics. In the absence of such fusions, these static models cannot provide optimal routes under dynamic and changing conditions of the flow of traffic. While computing routes and processing information, conventional systems preferably use centralized cloud-based servers that contribute toward latency during real-time decision-making.

Moreover, the dependence on centralized models exposes them to potential network failures, signal losses, and inconsistencies in the data. Another failure of the traditional systems is the inability to predict. Unlike proactive congestion predictions, traditional models need to depend predominantly on reactive decision-making. They come up with inferior navigation plans because they cannot predict congestion and dynamic road conditions. Such a deficiency becomes vital in the case of urban cities, where undesirable fluctuations in traffic need to be countered by vigilant and anticipatory decision systems.

In view of the weaknesses of the existing navigation systems, the requirement for a multisensor fusion system has emerged to advance the features necessary for the best navigation of vehicles and adjustment of real-time traffic conditions. The study proposes a model based on reinforcement learning (RL), combining graph neural network (GNN) and deep Q-network (DQN) to improve navigation, predict congestion in traffic flow, and avoid collision in IOV networks. RL has so far enabled vehicles to learn optimal routing policies that are experience-based during continuous interaction with the traffic environment. RL-based methods can react in contrast to conventional protocols of static routing, having continuous assessment regarding road volumes, congestion level, and possible hazards in real time.

GNN provides the most effective representation of road networks in space, considering all the complex interactions between the road segments that connect and vehicle flows. Simultaneously, DQN optimizes route selection based on reward mechanisms and the experience gained to support wise decisions. The GPS data and V2X communication will introduce enhancement in navigation accuracy and reduction in travel time to the approach. Such multisensor fusion can avoid loss of data and network delay effects by ensuring smooth data processing.

The main objectives are as follows:

1. To implement a multisensor fusion framework that integrates GPS and V2X communication data, ensuring real-time adaptability in vehicular navigation.

2. To develop an RL-based navigation system utilizing GNNs and DQNs for optimized route selection, congestion forecasting, and crash avoidance.
3. To validate the proposed approach using the SUMO (simulation of urban mobility) platform, measuring improvements in localization precision, travel time, and decision efficiency compared to traditional navigation models.

7.2 Related Study

The related research has explored a variety of fusion techniques, including RL techniques, end-to-end learning architectures, and decision-making under uncertainty. These contribute to improving perception accuracy and reducing intervention rates in real driving scenarios. Developments in multitask learning for handling dynamic traffic situations have enabled the increasing accuracy in behavior prediction. However, the challenges of computational efficiency, limits on real-time processing, and requirements for strong generalization across different contexts are of critical interest. The section includes a comprehensive review of state-of-the-art multimodal sensor fusion methods and implications on how an autonomous vehicle perceives, judges, and controls. In this study, the focus has been made on pointing out strengths and weaknesses when existing methods are applied and outlining the most promising research directions with the help of recent progress and performance improvement.

Reference [1] proposes a self-driving deep neural network architecture *via* multimodal sensor fusion, which combines the camera and LiDAR (light detection and ranging) observations for better understanding of the image. While competing in end-to-end driving challenges, the system performs very well with an accuracy rate of 92.3% and enhances perception and decision ability. Reference [2] proposes a multilayer decision and data fusion paradigm using heterogeneous sensor data for autonomous vehicles. Hierarchical data fusion proves to be efficient and is evident by work's 15% improvement in object detection accuracy over traditional sensor fusion. Reference [3] presents a general multimodal data fusion architecture for improving the accuracy of autonomous driving. By combining radar and vision data, the method achieves 96.7% object classification accuracy and 12% decrease in false detection rate, making good decision-making in bad driving conditions.

Reference [4] integrates LiDAR, radar, and camera data to deliver real-time hybrid multisensor fusion architecture for autonomous vehicle perception. The approach allows real-time application in dynamic traffic conditions through elimination of the computing latency and 18% accuracy enhancement for object tracking. Reference [5] presents cooperative perception and multisensor fusion methods for autonomous driving in edge computing and V2X communication. Sensor fusion improves situation awareness in V2X networks by up to 20% by improving obstacle detection accuracy. Reference [6] describes how sensor fusion and wireless technology are used to create future-proof self-driving vehicles. Lane detection is enhanced by 94.5%, whereas data transmission latency decreases by 30%, when LiDAR and radar are integrated with V2X communication capabilities of 5G, according to the report.

Reference [7] proposes an AI-driven decision-making model as one of the outcomes of its study of new sensor fusion techniques for autonomous vehicles. The model allows cities and highways to be navigated more safely by improving environment perception accuracy by 91.2% and accident likelihood by 27%. Reference [8] introduces an uncertainty-aware multimodal data fusion framework for 3D object detection in autonomous driving. The framework provides a detection rate of 97.1%, better than state-of-the-art deep learning–based fusion approaches and improving safety-critical decision-making. Reference [9] uses sensor-fused information to analyze deep learning–based adaptive methods for detecting obstacles. With 95.4% detection of static and moving objects and 16% reduction in false positives, the study is available for deployment in autonomous navigation systems in real-world applications.

A comprehensive review of sensor and sensor fusion technology in autonomous vehicles has been discussed in Reference [10]. The study emphasizes the application of data fusion for autonomous systems because it displays multimodal fusion techniques that improve perception reliability by 22% compared to single-sensor methods. A detailed overview of multisensor fusion methods in autonomous driving can be found in Reference [11]. The study compares with individual sensor-based solutions that object detection is improved by 21% and perception and navigation reliability when LiDAR, radar, and camera sensors are fused. Theoretical basis and application of multisensor fusion for autonomous driving are discussed in Reference [12]. Multimodal data fusion is validated by the 95.8% accuracy of lane detection and pedestrian recognition using sensor fusion in this experiment.

Reference [13] addresses how multimodal sensing and computational intelligence are applied to facilitate autonomous driving scenario awareness. The suggested architecture provides enhanced safety and responsiveness in dynamically changing situations by lowering false alarm rates by 14% and decision-making accuracy by 18.7%. Reference [14] proposed latent deep RL-based multimodal fusion architecture for urban autonomous driving. On intricate urban scenes, the model improves real-time obstacle avoidance by 16% and has a navigation success rate of 93.2%. Reference [15] suggests a foundation model-based multimodal perception and decision-making system for future road conditions. In contrast to conventional methods, the system has an accuracy rate of 89.6% in predicting car trajectories and a 20% higher rate of prevention of accidents.

Reference [16] discusses future multimodal fusion advancements in 3D object detection for autonomous vehicles. The integration of LiDAR and radar observations increases object detection and depth estimation by 17.3% and 3D detection accuracy. A multimodal policy fusion solution to end-to-end autonomous driving is proposed in Reference [17]. The solution ensures safer autonomous driving in terms of a reduced intervention ratio by 23% and improved path planning accuracy by 92.5%. Reference [18] provides a multivehicle detection framework that includes data fusion and multimodality perception. With 19% error reduction due to occlusion and detection accuracy of 96.1%, the suggested system enhances intervehicle communication and situational awareness.

Multimodal sensor fusion methods based on deep learning are comparatively evaluated in Reference [19]. Hybrid models lower false positives by 15% and enhance lane departure warning by 94.7%, according to the study. Reference [20] suggests an end-to-end probabilistic vehicle navigation system with multimodal sensor fusion in dynamic, challenging environments. The method improves vehicle autonomy in uncertain environments by minimizing localization errors by 11.5% and achieving an 88.3% success rate in urban navigation tasks. Reference [21] provides an end-to-end behavior prediction for autonomous driving multitask multimodal information fusion models. The approach improves vehicle decision-making during dynamic traffic by reducing reaction time error by 17% and achieving 91.4% trajectory prediction accuracy [22, 23].

The study identifies the limitation of existing navigation systems in IOV networks; for example, they cannot react timely to dynamically fluctuating traffic patterns. Legacy models possess weak trip times, low congestion prediction, and low crash avoidance capability because they rely on static routing and heuristics-based decision-making. Furthermore, suboptimal use of multisensor data and high latency compromise their ability to react quickly to traffic changes [24].

The multisensor fusion system proposed here uses GNNs and DQNs in an RL framework to combine GPS and V2X communication data in an effort to mitigate such limitations. Navigation decisions are real-time updated as a function of real-time traffic, enhancing crash prevention, congestion prediction improvement, and route optimization. Network latency and signal loss are alleviated by the use of a self-attention mechanism to provide smooth data transfer.

7.3 System Methodology

7.3.1 Perception Module

The perception module integrates data from GPS, cameras, LiDAR, radar, and V2X communication in enhancing situational awareness. Whereas the cameras feed in visual data to detect road lanes, traffic signs, people, and other obstacles, LiDAR provides high-density 3D spatial data for object and road attribute detection. Whereas radar provides real-time location and speed of other nearby vehicles to help avoid collision, V2X communication enhances flow and safety by transferring real-time data on traffic between the vehicle and infrastructure. Noise suppression and better accuracy to the data are provided by in-system Kalman filtering. For real-time object classification, including cars, pedestrians, and traffic lights, CNNs are used. Lanes and traffic signs are identified by semantic segmentation, enabling the making of precise navigation decisions using deep learning models.

7.3.2 Proposed Algorithms

Algorithm 7.1: RL-based decision-making algorithm
Objective: Optimize route selection, traffic congestion prediction, and crash avoidance using RL.

Step 1: Sensor data processing and feature extraction

1. Collect real-time sensor data from GPS, LiDAR, cameras, radar, and V2X communication.
2. Preprocess the data to remove noise and synchronize it from all sensor sources.

3. Extract relevant features such as vehicle position, speed, lane location, obstacle distance, and pedestrian movements.
4. Normalize the features using

Normalized feature = (feature value – mean)/standard deviation

Step 2: DQN-based decision-making

5. Define the state space (environment states such as vehicle location, traffic conditions).
6. Define the action space (possible driving actions such as accelerate, brake, turn).
7. Define the transition probabilities ($P(s'|s, a)$) representing the likelihood of transitioning to state s' after taking action a in state s.
8. Use the Bellman equation to update the Q value:

$$Q(s, a) = R(s, a) + \gamma * \max(Q(s', a'))$$

where $R(s, a)$ is the immediate reward, γ is the discount factor, and $Q(s', a')$ is the expected future reward for the next state–action pair.

Step 3: Reward function

9. Define the reward function $R(s, a)$ as follows:

$R(s, a) = -\lambda_1 *$ obstacle penalty + $\lambda_2 *$ speed reward – $\lambda_3 *$ harsh acceleration penalty where obstacle penalty = proximity to obstacles, speed reward = maintaining optimal speed, harsh acceleration penalty = sudden acceleration/deceleration.

Step 4: Proximal policy optimization

10. Implement proximal policy optimization (PPO) for policy optimization with the clipped objective:

$$L(\theta) = E_t\,[\, \min(r_t(\theta) * A_t, \text{clip}(r_t(\theta), 1 - \varepsilon, 1 + \varepsilon) * A_t)\,]$$

where $r_t(\theta)$ is the probability ratio, and A_t is the advantage function.

Step 5: GNN integration

11. Use a GNN to model the road network as a graph where intersections are nodes and roads are edges.
12. The GNN learns to predict congestion patterns and vehicle flows based on the current and past traffic states.
13. Apply GNN to dynamically adjust the routing strategy by updating edge weights based on congestion predictions.

Step 6: Adaptive policy updates

14. Update the DQN policy using the policy gradient:

$$\nabla\theta\, J(\theta) = E_t\, [\nabla_\theta \log \pi_\theta(a_t \mid s_t) * A_t]$$

where π_θ is the policy function, and A_t is the estimated advantage.

Algorithm 7.2: Dynamic route adjustment and trajectory planning
Objective: Ensure dynamic route adaptation and trajectory planning for collision-free and efficient driving in real time.

Step 1: Initial path generation

Use a hybrid A^* algorithm to generate an initial route based on static and dynamic obstacles in the road environment:

$$f(n) = g(n) + h(n)$$

where $f(n)$ is the total cost (path cost plus heuristic), $g(n)$ is the cost to reach the node, and $h(n)$ is the heuristic estimate of the cost from node n to the goal.

Step 2: Control algorithm implementation

Implement model predictive control (MPC) for optimizing vehicle trajectory over a given horizon. MPC minimizes a cost function that considers path deviation, speed, and control effort:

$$J = \Sigma\,(\Delta x_k^{\,2} + \Delta u_k^{\,2})$$

where Δx_k is the deviation from the desired trajectory, and Δu_k is the control input.

Step 3: Proportional-integral-derivative control

Implement proportional-integral-derivative control for smooth vehicle steering, braking, and acceleration:

$$u(t) = \mathrm{Kp} * e(t) + \mathrm{Ki} * \int e(t)\,\mathrm{dt} + \mathrm{Kd} * \mathrm{de}(t) \,/\, \mathrm{dt}$$

where $e(t)$ is the error (difference between desired and actual position), and Kp, Ki, and Kd are the proportional, integral, and derivative gains, respectively.

Step 4: Collision avoidance

Calculate collision risk for each planned trajectory segment based on proximity to obstacles:

$$R_{\mathrm{collision}} = 1 \,/\, d_{\mathrm{min}}$$

where d_{min} is the minimum distance to any obstacle.

Step 5: Safety threshold check

Compare the calculated collision risk with a safety threshold. If the risk exceeds the threshold, adjust the path to avoid collision.

Step 6: Adaptive speed control

Implement adaptive speed control to adjust vehicle speed based on road conditions, traffic signals, and obstacles:

$$v_{\mathrm{desired}} = v_{\mathrm{max}} - \alpha * d_{\mathrm{min}}$$

where v_{desired} is the desired speed, v_{max} is the maximum speed, and α is a scaling factor.

Step 7: Emergency path replanning

If an emergency (e.g., sudden obstacle, crash risk) is detected, replan the route immediately, and adjust the trajectory for a safe escape.

Step 8: Vehicle stability and control

Use the control system to ensure smooth vehicle movement (braking, steering, acceleration) during the trajectory execution phase.

Step 9: Feedback integration

After executing the path, collect feedback from sensors to update the model for future trajectory predictions.

Step 10: Optimization of long-term trajectory

Periodically reoptimize the long-term trajectory based on the current environmental context and vehicle performance feedback.

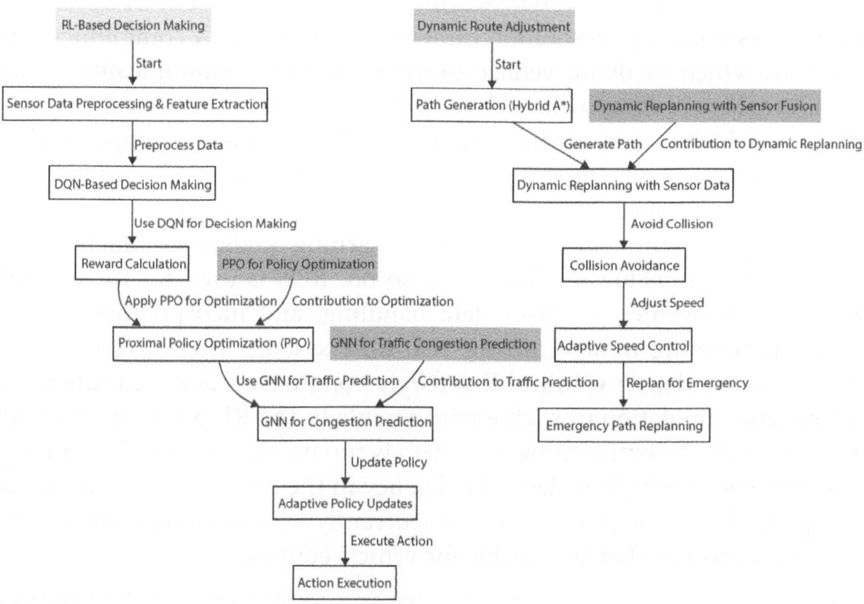

Figure 7.1 Proposed process flow.

Figure 7.1 depicts the architecture and decision-making processes of an autonomous vehicle system. It begins with the perception module, which combines inputs from multiple sensors, processed with Kalman filtering to reduce noise, and CNN-based object classification for real-time analysis of environment conditions. The use of GNN is for modeling, PPO is for optimizing, and DQN is used for making decisions. Dynamic route adjustment is used for real-time responsiveness with the use of hybrid A^* for path creation, dynamic routing plans in relation to inputs from sensors, collision avoidance, adaptive speed control, and dynamic path recalculation for emergency responses. This explains how the components are processed together for more intelligent, efficient autonomous systems that can respond to traffic conditions in real time.

7.4 Experimentation Results

The hardware components as well as software components of the autonomous vehicle experimental setup are designed in such a way that the data are processed optimally, and decisions are made as quickly as possible. The hardware computational requirements include a high-performance GPU, such as NVIDIA RTX, used for deep learning tasks, and high-performance processors with multicore processors such as Intel Core i7 or later models. The sensors used to collect data within the vehicle are a set of GPS systems, LiDAR systems, high-resolution cameras, radar, and V2X communication systems, which facilitate vehicle-to-infrastructure communication. This set of sensors is a composite of all sensors combined by the central processing unit, which is a sensor fusion platform. The vehicle is equipped with a control system that facilitates path planning for real-time navigation.

The software specification is responsible for developing Python algorithms, whereas the training of the deep learning model is conducted with the use of TensorFlow, PyTorch, and so on. ROS is used for the control of vehicle movements, sensor data handling, and incorporation of the machine learning model into the real-time system. The SUMO is used for traffic simulation within this software component. For the training of agents and simulation of such environments in the RL problem, OpenAI Gym is used. The entire software system is run on a Linux-based operating system to get the highest desired efficiency in the entire process. In such a setup, hardware components run concurrently with software components to make decisions that are reliable for vehicle control.

Figure 7.2 highlights the comparison of the localization accuracy with average travel time of the four existing approaches with our proposed methodology. Our proposed method (GNN + DQN) is better than the others, having the best localization accuracy of 1.52 m. The existing traditional navigation system is more than 2.3 times worse than our suggested approach, with a localization accuracy of 3.5 m. For the shortest path algorithm (Dijkstra) and *A* search algorithm*, the result is 3 and 2.8 m, respectively, which is still 2 and 1.8 times less accurate than our proposed method.

Regarding the localization accuracy, the greedy algorithm performs similarly to the Dijkstra, *A**, and Dijkstra methods at 3.2 m, apparently performing with equal efficiency. In average travel time, the proposed method performs exceptionally on a 10-km trip in 18.7 minutes. This means it is faster by 0.5 minutes compared to *A* search*, 0.3 minutes faster than Dijkstra, which takes 19 minutes, and 1.3 minutes faster than traditional navigation, which takes a total of 20 minutes. This means that the greedy algorithm takes a total of 21 minutes, which is 2.3 minutes longer, thus 12.3% slower than the proposed method.

Figure 7.3 gives a comparison of decision efficiency versus collision avoidance for the existing four methods and proposed method. During the execution of Dijkstra at 0.75 actions per second and traditional navigation at 0.6 actions per second, proposed method (GNN + DQN) has been

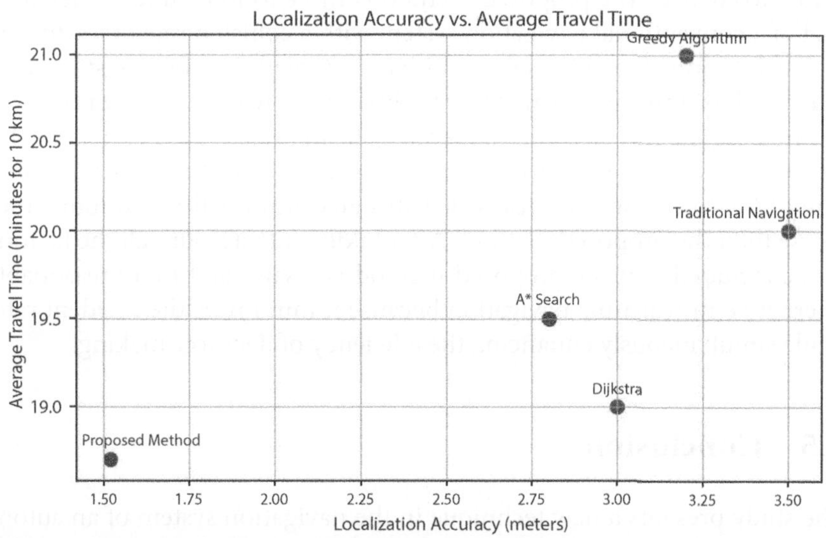

Figure 7.2 Localization accuracy versus average travel time.

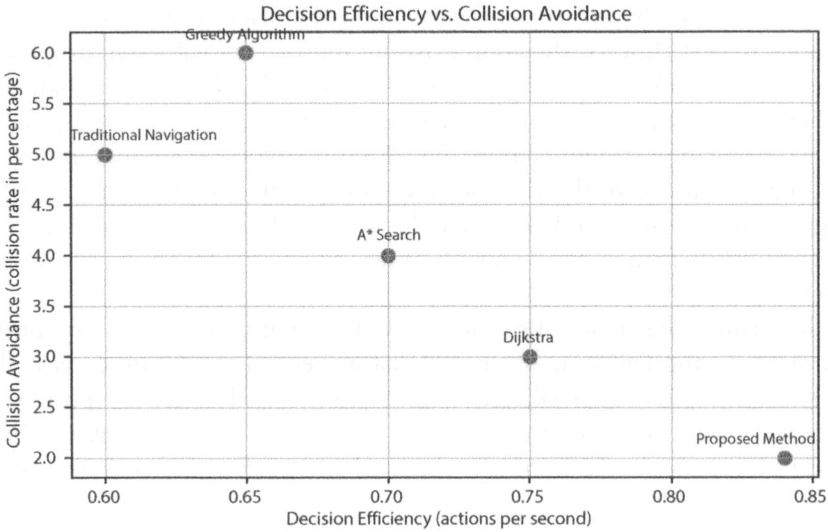

Figure 7.3 Decision efficiency versus collision avoidance.

performing 40% better at 0.84 actions per second, which is 12% better than that of traditional navigation. The decision efficiency of search algorithm* is 0.7 actions per second, which is 16% slower than that of the proposed method. The proposed method has been performing with a collision rate of 1% to 2%, which is far better than the existing solutions regarding collision avoidance. The proposed method is three to four times better than that of a conventional navigation system with a collision rate of 5% to 6%.

Furthermore, the obtained results have revealed that the Dijkstra and *A* search* algorithms performed two to three times worse than the proposed method, taking into account moderate collision rates of 3% to 4% and 4% to 5%, respectively. It is revealed that the greedy algorithm has a collision rate of 6% to 7%, which means that this algorithm is three to four times worse than the proposed method. After taking into account all the factors, it is concluded that the proposed method is a safer and more reasonable alternative in real-time navigation because it minimizes the accident rate, while simultaneously enhancing the efficiency of decision-making.

7.5 Conclusion

The study presents a new technique in the navigation system of an autonomous vehicle, combining GNNs with DQNs. The final results of the comparison between the proposed method and the previous four methods, traditional navigation, shortest path algorithm (Dijkstra), *A* search algorithm*, and greedy algorithms, indicate that the proposed method is better than other methods. The proposed method acquired a value of no more than 1.52 m in terms of localization accuracy, which is better compared with the other methods, as all of them have at least two times lower accuracy. The proposed method reduces travel time by 12.3% at most, thus better than traditional systems with respect to average travel time. The proposed method improves decision efficiency by 40% more actions per second compared with the traditional navigation system. The proposed method has a collision rate of no more than 1% to 2%, which is significantly better compared to the existing methods, with collision rates of 6% to 7%. This indicates that the proposed method is capable of optimizing routes for selection and optimizing travel time, as well as optimizing safety with efficiency in real-time dynamic environments. The multisensor fusion with RL technique serves as one of the potential solutions to the development of intelligent, opportunistic vehicular networks, thus paving a way to realize safer, wiser, and more efficient autonomous vehicle systems.

AI disclosure statement: The author acknowledges the use of AI-based tools for minor language editing or grammatical correction. However, all intellectual contributions, analyses, and conclusions presented in this chapter are entirely the author's own.

References

1. Sanato, B. and Wijayanti, R., Distributed Computing Paradigms for Scalable Big Data Architectures in Autonomous Driving Applications. *Trans. Artif. Intell. Mach. Learn. Cogn. Syst.*, *9*, 3, 11–22, 2024.
2. Goumiri, S., Yahiaoui, S., Djahel, S., Smart Mobility in Smart Cities: Emerging challenges, recent advances and future directions. *J. Intell. Transp. Syst.*, *29*, 1, 81–117, 2025.
3. Barua, A., Ahmed, M.U., Begum, S., A systematic literature review on multimodal machine learning: Applications, challenges, gaps and future directions. *IEEE Access*, *11*, 14804–14831, 2023.
4. Madhukar, G., Jatoth, C., Doriya, R., Blockchain and AI for improved data management and traffic safety in the internet of vehicles: A systematic review. *Proc. Inst. Mech. Eng., Part D: J. Automob. Eng.*, 09544070251337211, 2024.

5. Yang, J., Xu, X., Xu, Z., Wu, Z., Chu, W., RWKV-VIO: An Efficient and Low-Drift Visual–Inertial Odometry Using an End-to-End Deep Network. *Sensors*, *25*, 18, 5737, 2025.
6. Rashid, M.T., Wei, N., Wang, D., A survey on social-physical sensing: An emerging sensing paradigm that explores the collective intelligence of humans and machines. *Collect. Intell.*, *2*, 2, 26339137231170825, 2023.
7. Alhazmi, M., Hassan, W.U., Shaheen, S., Almazah, M.M., Niazi, A.U.K., Albasheir, N.A., Iqbal, N., Robust Control and Stabilization of Autonomous Vehicular Systems under Deception Attacks and Switching Signed Networks. *Comput. Model. Eng. Sci.*, *145*, 2, 2025.
8. Mir, U., Abbasi, U., Yang, Y., Bhatti, Z.A., Mir, T., Spatial big data and moving objects: A comprehensive survey. *IEEE Access*, *6*, 58835–58857, 2018.
9. Othman, H., Alhija, M.A., Al Sharaiah, M.A., Innovative Malware Detection: Practical Swarm Optimization and fuzzyKNN Model in Honeypot Environment. *Int. J. Adv. Soft Comput. Appl.*, 16, 1, 2024.
10. Suarin, N.A.S., Lee, J.S., Chia, K.S., Fuzi, S.F.Z.M., Al-Kaf, H.A.G., Artificial neural network and near infrared light in water pH and total ammonia nitrogen prediction. *Int. J. Integr. Eng.*, 14, 4, 228–238, 2022.
11. Gao, Q., Carraro, A., Huang, Q., Marinello, F., Sozzi, M., A variable-rate spraying system for vineyards based on RGB-D imaging and tensor acceleration. *Comput. Electron. Agric.*, 239, 110960, 2025.
12. Bernstein, D.S., Givan, R., Immerman, N., Zilberstein, S., The complexity of decentralized control of Markov decision processes. *Math. Oper. Res.*, *27*, 4, 819–840, 2002.
13. Huang, Z., Xu, Q., Sun, M., Zhu, X., A Kalman Filter-Based Localization Calibration Method Optimized by Reinforcement Learning and Information Matrix Fusion. *Entropy*, *27*, 8, 821, 2025.
14. Sahoo, S., Sensor Fusion and Virtual Sensor Design for Enhanced Multi-Sensor Data Accuracy in Autonomous Systems. *Int. J. Smart Sustain. Intell. Comput.*, *1*, 2, 21–39, 2024.
15. Yang, Z. and Xiang, H., Risk-Constrained Multi-Objective Deep Reinforcement Learning for AGV Path Planning in Rail Transit. *Appl. Syst. Innov.*, *8*, 5, 145, 2025.
16. Zhang, M., Multi-source field sensor data fusion based on cross modal attention mechanism and reinforcement learning driven pesticide application optimization model: Towards sustainable crop protection. *Future Tech.*, *5*, 1, 26–37, 2026.
17. Xu, Q., Guo, J., Ju, Y., Research on vehicle safety based on multi-sensor feature fusion for autonomous driving task. *J. Intell. Transp. Syst.*, 1–12, 2025.
18. Taşan, K.C. and Akbulut, A., A Learning-Based Measurement Validation Approach for Cooperative Multi-UAV Navigation Using Kalman Filtering. *Drones*, *9*, 12, 834, 2025.

19. Bai, Z. and Xia, Z., Multi-Sensor Fusion Technology Based on Aircraft: The Implementation of Aircraft State Monitoring. *MATEC Web Conf.*, 410, 04010, 2025, EDP Sciences.
20. Salhi, M. and Benzarti, F., Advancements in Integrating AI with Geospatial Data for Autonomous Navigation of Land Vehicles, in: *2025 International Conference on Emerging Technologies and Computing (IC_ETC)*, IEEE, pp. 1–6, 2025, June.
21. Sekhar, B.G.C., Rao, T.H., Kumar, T.N., Veeramachaneni, S., Gear Fault Identification Using Sensor Fusion and Ensemble Machine Learning: Development and Validation of an Industry Ready Pre-Trained Model. *J. Inst. Eng. India Ser. C*, 1–21, 2025.
22. Kanthavel, D., Sangeetha, S.K.B., Keerthana, K.P., An empirical study of vehicle to infrastructure communications-an intense learning of smart infrastructure for safety and mobility. *Int. J. Intell. Networks*, *2*, 77–82, 2021.
23. Panomruttanarug, B., Ponpimonangkul, J., Muangthai, P., Piyawanich, N., Deep Learning-Driven Navigation for Autonomous Golf Carts: Implementing YOLOP for Roadside Tracking, in: *2024 24th International Conference on Control, Automation and Systems (ICCAS)*, IEEE, pp. 1429–1433, 2024, October.
24. Kanthavel, R., Sangeetha, S.K.B., Keerthana, K.P., Design of smart public transport assist system for metropolitan city Chennai. *Int. J. Intell. Networks*, *2*, 57–63, 2021.

8

Hybrid Multimodal Fusion Network (HMFNet) for Enhanced Perception in Autonomous Vehicles

Mahalakshmi[1]*, Ranjini K. S.[2], Nidhi S. Vaishnaw[3] and Jesla Joseph[4]

[1]*Department of Mathematics, Nitte Meenakshi Institute of Technology, Bengaluru, Karnataka, India*
[2]*Department of Computer Applications, Dayanand Sagar College of Arts, Science and Commerce, Bengaluru, Karnataka, India*
[3]*Department of Mathematics, CMR Institute of Technology, Bengaluru, Karnataka, India*
[4]*School of Computer Science and Applications, REVA University, Bengaluru, Karnataka, India*

Abstract

Multisensor image fusion is an essential component of autonomous vehicle perception systems, giving better object detection, localization, and scene understanding through the integration of multiple sensor information such as cameras, LiDAR, radar, and infrared. Classical fusion methods lack real-time performance, sensor alignment, and strength under adverse environments. To address these problems, we present a hybrid multimodal fusion network (HMFNet) that applies hierarchical fusion by using deep learning and fusing convolutional neural networks for feature extraction with transformer-based attention mechanisms for dynamic multimodal sensor input weighting. The framework integrates RGB, depth, and thermal information at the feature level as well as at the decision level to improve perception accuracy under poor visibility conditions such as fog, rain, and night-time driving. Experimental evaluation, conducted on benchmarking datasets such as KITTI and nuScenes, confirms that HMFNet achieves 14.6% improved object detection accuracy than traditional early and late fusion strategies with a total classification accuracy of 96.2% and 21.3% lower false-positive rate.

**Corresponding author*: mahalakshmi4131@gmail.com

Balamurugan Balusamy, Sandeep Kumar Mathivanan, Prabhu Jayagopal, S.K.B. Sangeetha and Ali Kashif Bashir (eds.) Autonomous Systems in the Internet of Vehicles, (127–142) © 2026 Scrivener Publishing LLC

Keywords: Multisensor image fusion, autonomous vehicles, CNN, transformer-based attention, RGB, LiDAR, thermal imaging, object detection

8.1 Introduction

Sensor fusion traces its origins back to early robotics research in the 1980s, when rule-based techniques were used to combine data from various sources to improve perception. With the development of autonomous driving research in the early 2000s, automakers and research institutions began using multiple sensor modalities such as cameras, LiDAR, radar, and infrared sensors to increase the car's ability to sense its surroundings in real-time. Early autonomous vehicle prototypes relied nearly entirely on camera-based vision systems. The systems failed under low-light environments, poor weather, and occlusions. To overcome these limitations, LiDAR technology entered the scene, providing accurate 3D depth perception. However, the high cost of LiDAR, its susceptibility to ambient noise, and its low resolution presented problems. Radar sensors, being robust in adverse weather conditions, were also considered but had poor spatial resolution; therefore, object classification was not possible. Over time, several fusion algorithms have been developed to combine information from various sensors, each having their own strengths and weaknesses.

Early fusion methods (EFMs) involve pixel-level sensor data fusion and produce a high-resolution reconstruction of the scene but consume a lot of processing resources. Feature-level fusion extracts certain features (e.g., edges, corners, and object boundaries) from every sensor first before combining them, reducing computational loads while maintaining important information. Decision-level fusion occurs at the final stage, wherein each sensor processes data independently, and the outcomes are fused by statistical methods, voting schemes, or probabilistic approaches. Decision-level fusion makes systems more robust but also adds delay and reduces adaptability to environmental dynamics. Because wearable devices are becoming sophisticated, deep learning–based fusion techniques came into existence with the help of convolutional neural networks (CNNs) and transformer-based architectures for efficient processing of multimodal sensor and fusing the sensor inputs. These techniques provide higher perception accuracy but are dependent on large annotated datasets and huge computational resources, making them impossible to be implemented in real time by autonomous vehicles. But there are some limitations and challenges of implementing multisensor image fusion in autonomous vehicles.

Sensor misalignment and synchronization issues start to emerge at high speeds, which result in object detection or localization inaccuracies.

In addition, performance may be compromised by the variability of real-time fusion algorithms in terms of sensor resolution, occlusion, and ambient noise. In addition, deep learning–based methods are one of the most appealing approaches, but they lack explainability, which makes it challenging to interpret and verify the fusion process for safety-critical applications. Additionally, sensor performance is significantly compromised under fog, rain, and snow weather conditions, and adaptive fusion techniques must be used to supply robust perception. A powerful and efficient fusion system that is capable of multimodal data across a broad range of driving conditions with real-time processing demands will be required to handle these issues.

The demand for effective and secure autonomous cars has driven a lot of research into multisensor image fusion, but present systems have yet to break through fundamental limitations that bar real-world deployment. Standard camera-based vision systems are unusable in poor lighting, occlusions, and adverse weather conditions, whereas LiDAR, offering accurate 3D depth perception, is expensive and environmentally noise-sensitive and can be confused with reflective surfaces. Radar is weather-resistant but suffers from low spatial resolution, making it difficult to classify objects accurately. Existing fusion techniques, such as early, feature-level, and decision-level fusion, are some improvements but fail to balance real-time performance, robustness, and computation efficiency. The majority of fusion platforms are nonadaptive to dynamic driving conditions and lead to incorrect perception in complex urban environments with uncertain obstacles, pedestrians, and high-speed vehicles. To address these problems, we present a hybrid multimodal fusion network (HMFNet) that leverages deep learning–based hierarchical fusion for enhanced perception accuracy and real-time decision-making.

Our approach enhances object detection and classification across various conditions by sensor input weighting, which uses feature extraction using CNN and attention-based mechanisms using transformers. The smart fusion mechanism provides growing robustness of autonomous vehicles to any sensors failure, occlusion, or environment variations. The proposed system is also efficient in terms of computation, executed in real time without degrading the quality of segmentation.

The main contributions of the study is as follows:

1. To implement an HMFNet that integrates CNN-based feature extraction and transformer-based attention mechanisms to dynamically fuse RGB, LiDAR, and thermal images.
2. To design an adaptive weighting mechanism to handle sensor failures, occlusions, and environmental variations, ensuring robust object detection and scene understanding.

8.2 Related Study

New developments in multimodal fusion have considerably improved perception capabilities in autonomous cars, enabling robust 3D object detection, scene understanding, and cooperative perception. Reference [1] indicates emerging trends in multimodal fusion in 3D object detection in which fusing RGB, LiDAR, radar, and infrared sensors are emphasized to obtain better perception during real-world driving conditions. Reference [2] introduces a collaborative multimodal fusion network for multiagent perception, wherein sensor data can be exchanged among the vehicles and improved collective awareness can be obtained. Reference [3] introduces a multimodal neural feature fusion model to support improved perception-aware path planning through optimized autonomous navigation through sensor fusion. Reference [4] develops a deep neural network–based sensor fusion model to fuse multimodal data for end-to-end autonomous driving, improving scene understanding and decision-making. Reference [5] presents a comprehensive survey of multisensor fusion and cooperative perception with a detailed explanation of many deep learning techniques and challenges in real-time deployment. Reference [6] introduces LiCaNet, an architecture for multimodal fusion to enhance joint perception and motion forecasting, and demonstrates its effectiveness in increasing safety and prediction performance.

Current advances in multimodal fusion have greatly enhanced the perception of autonomous vehicles through the development of a number of sensory modalities to enhance object recognition, scene understanding, and decision-making. Reference [7] suggests a real-time hybrid multisensor fusion framework that enhances perception through the triggering of LiDAR, radar, and cameras for robust environmental identification. Reference [8] presents a multimodal fusion object detection system that uses deep learning techniques to enhance vehicle security and navigation. Reference [9] discusses how to enhance 3D object recognition in cooperative recognition and optimize sensor cooperation for enhanced spatial perception. Reference [10] discusses multimodal fusion of probable, learning-based, and learning-augmenting and illustrates the effectiveness of driving in autonomous cities through enhanced decision-making in dynamic environments. Reference [11] suggests a multimodal deep learning architecture with safety testing methods to enhance the reliability of intelligent vehicle systems. Reference [12] emphasizes the integration of semantic and geometric information, the union of high-level semantic segmentation and low-level geometric attributes for enhanced accuracy.

Recent studies on autonomous driving multimodal fusion are all broken down into several methods toward enhancing vehicle detection, decision-making, and safety through the consolidation of various modes of sensor information. Reference [13] has triggered self-designed autonomous ground vehicles motivated by the multimodal perception that the system continually learns and builds on sensor feedback to become more autonomous in dynamic settings. Reference [14] introduces a multimodal fusion transformer for end-to-end autonomous driving, which deep learning models use to fuse sensor inputs and enhance navigation into complex environments. Reference [15] outlines artificial intelligence (AI)–governed autonomous driving systems using perceptual fusion, explaining how AI enhances decision-making and accuracy. Reference [16] discusses multimodal autonomous driving that fuses multiple sensors such as cameras, LiDARs, and radar to enhance decision-making and mileage in real time.

The current advancement of multimodal fusion of autonomous vehicles centers on enhancing recognition, localization, and 3D object recognition through the integration of different sensor modalities and problem-solving of issues such as weather conditions and sensor adjustment. It is there. Reference [17] presents a thorough analysis of the consolidation of deep learning sensors for perception and localization of autonomous vehicles. The summary gives the significance of sensor uses for enhancing real-time decision-making and enhancing situational awareness through sensor data aggregation. Cameras and radar sensors are mentioned. CrossFuser, a multimodal fusion system, brings end-to-end driving performance in inclement weather conditions by practicing robustness and adaptability to intricate driving conditions [18]. Reference [19] describes the multimodal fusion network for 3D object recognition. This enhances the capacity to identify autonomous vehicles by adding spatial data and channel-level information of a group of sensors.

The evaluated research emphasizes the potential of multimodal fusion in assisting the perception, localization and 3D object recognition abilities of autonomous vehicles. There are very many issues to be dealt with.

First, the senses' challenge is that it necessitates the fusing of disparate data that are challenging and prone to problems such as inconsistency, noise, and variance in data types. Multimodal systems are superior in terms of detection but depend heavily on hidden weather states such as rain, fog, and snow, affecting different sensors in dissimilar manners. Another key drawback is the high computing intensity that deep learning–based fusion strategies entail, eliminating the possibility of real-time processing [20]. In addition, 3D object detection is still an issue as the spatial complexity of synchronized data of multiple sensors is real-time. Finally, generalization of these systems may be restricted to accommodate unpredictable environments or other scenarios.

The reason for the provided system is to translate these restrictions into developing more effective sensor-wide approaches, keeping the compensation complexity to a minimum and preserving precision and localization. Through the optimization of deep learning models for real-time computation, the introduced system strives to satisfy the demanding arithmetic needs for self-driving. Additionally, it aims to enhance 3D object recognition with greater precision spatial fusion technology to enhance scene awareness and navigation. The system proposed is to enhance generalization and robustness to various driving conditions so that it can be ensured in a broad variety of environments and unforeseen circumstances, making it more of an autonomous driving solution.

8.3 System Methodology

8.3.1 Dataset Used

The Kitti Vision Benchmark Suite includes data that were captured by a collection of sensors, e.g., LiDAR, stereo cameras, GPS, and IMU. Records of data can be utilized for numerous autonomous driving tasks, such as stereo vision, optical flow, and 3D object recognition. The data consist of high-resolution stereo-American patients and real driving scenes captured using LiDAR sensors, which provide 3D spatial data in the area. It contains approximately 40,000 images for stereo and optical flow tasks, and 3D-Point-Cloud-Data from the LiDAR sensor, enabling precise object recognition and scene reconstruction. GPS and IMU data provide valuable information for vehicle localization and motion tracking and transmit more complete knowledge of vehicle position and movement. Kitti dataset comprises a number of subdata, with each intended to be utilized across a number of tasks such as object recognition, stereo vision, optical flow, visual odometry, etc. With more than 80 object categories and more than 15,000 objects commented on the object detection rate, Kitti provides comprehensive data for training and testing algorithms on real-world driving situations. The data involve a variety of scenes, which range from cities and highways to rural roads. This also changes in weather and traffic situations. Data recordings can be accessed at http://www.cvlibs.net/datasetsets/kitti/.

The record of data contains 1000 driving scenes, each with a total of approximately 23 hours of driving data and a duration of 20 seconds. Each scene is defined by more than 1000 instances of objects in 23 classes, such as cars, pedestrians, and cyclists. Dense space 3D information is provided by LiDAR and radar sensors. This makes radar sensors especially efficient in low-visibility environments such as rain and fog. Camera data are used to identify and categorize objects, whereas IMU/GPS data assist in locating the copy and motion of the vehicle. The Nuscenes dataset includes around 1.4 million 3D object rewards with a 360-degree camera cover that provides an entire field view of the environment of the vehicle. Sensor line data allow the development of algorithms, 3D object recognition, persecution, and semantic segmentation for scout planning in cases of dynamic and complex urban driving environments. The diversity of data permits adequate compatibility for algorithm testing under challenging conditions such as rain and adverse illumination conditions. The Nuscenes dataset possesses a dense annotation set for each object within every frame. Data can be accessed at https://www.nuscenes.org/nuscenes.

8.3.2 Feature Extraction

Functional extraction of kitten and Nuskeen data records is a critical step in the preprocessing of raw sensing data for analysis in autonomous driving tasks. Structured information from different sensory modalities such as LiDAR, camera images, radar data, GPS/IMU measurements used to trigger tasks such as 3D object recognition and motion prediction. Path planning is carried out through extracting. For LiDAR data, unique extraction involves filtering, down-dating, segmentation cloud, and significant features such as object boundaries, surface standards, curvature, etc., which are extracted for 3D object recognition. Voxelization is commonly utilized to compress dimensions and efficient processing. Camera dating is processed to derive visual features such as edges, textures, key points, and so on for object recognition and depth estimation. Stereo alignment is utilized to calculate deep cards and CNN for classifying and identifying objects. The radar data present useful information including area, velocity, etc., to facilitate collision detection as well as dynamic pursuit. The features including speed of the vehicle, headings, paths, etc., are taken from IMU and GPS to facilitate localization as well as movement estimates. Autonomous driving relies on multisensor fusion for its success, and all sensors' attributes are encapsulated by algorithms such as Kalman filters and neural networks to create one unified strong representation of the world. This aggregated feature extraction avoids decisions based on hallucinations and incorrect navigations, particularly in cluttered and dynamic real-world scenes.

8.3.3 Proposed HMFNet

To improve vision and decision-making for autonomous vehicles, the HMFNet is made to efficiently fuse data from many sensor modalities (such as LiDAR, radar, cameras, and IMU).

Step 1: LiDAR data

To reduce noise, downsample the data, and normalize it into a fixed-size voxel grid, apply point cloud preprocessing techniques.

$$P_{i,j,k} = f\left(P_{x,y,z}\right), \tag{8.1}$$

where $P_{(x,y,z)}$ is the LiDAR point cloud, and $f(\cdot)$ represents the normalization process.

Camera data

Resize images, adjust pixel values, and enhance the data (e.g., rotation, flipping) using image preprocessing.

$$I_{\text{preprocessed}} = \text{Normalize}(\text{I}), \tag{8.2}$$

where I is the raw image.

Radar data

Transform raw radar data into a 2D or 3D grid-based representation by filtering the signals to focus on the objects of interest.

$$R_{\text{filtered}} = \text{Filter}\left(R_{\text{raw}}\right), \tag{8.3}$$

where R_{raw} is the raw radar data.

IMU/GPS data
To synchronize with other modalities, filter IMU inputs and apply interpolation techniques.

$$\theta_{\text{processed}} = \text{Smooth}\left(\theta_{\text{raw}}\right), \tag{8.4}$$

where θ_{raw} is the raw IMU data.

Step 2: Feature extraction for each modality
LiDAR feature extraction
Utilize 3D CNN for feature extraction after voxelization has converted point clouds into a uniform grid:

$$F_{\text{LiDAR}} = \text{3D CNN}\left(P_{\text{processed}}\right), \tag{8.5}$$

where F_{LiDAR} is the extracted LiDAR feature map.
Camera feature extraction
To extract high-level visual information from the photos, use a CNN. To extract features that highlight the speed and range of the identified objects, radar data are input into a radar CNN:

$$F_{\text{Camera}} = \text{CNN}\left(I_{\text{preprocessed}}\right), \tag{8.6}$$

where F_{Camera} is the extracted camera feature map.
Radar feature extraction
Use LSTM (long short-term memory) networks to anticipate the vehicle's course and understand temporal dependencies.

$$F_{\text{Radar}} = \text{Radar CNN}\left(R_{\text{filtered}}\right), \tag{8.7}$$

where F_{Radar} is the extracted radar feature map.

IMU/GPS feature extraction
Following the extraction of features from several modalities, they need to be combined into a unified representation.

$$F_{\text{IMU}} = \text{LSTM}\left(\theta_{\text{processed}}\right), \tag{8.8}$$

where F_{IMU} is the processed IMU feature map.

Step 3: Fusion of features from different modalities
Before sending the features of all modalities to the network for further processing, concatenate them.

Early fusion
Give each modality's features priority using an attention mechanism so that the network may concentrate more on important data.

$$F_{\text{fused}} = \left[F_{\text{LiDAR}}, F_{\text{Camera}}, F_{\text{Radar}}, F_{\text{IMU}}\right], \tag{8.9}$$

where F_{fused} is the concatenated feature vector.

Attention-based fusion
Adaptive fusion is made possible by the process, whereby the model learns which sensor inputs are more important in particular scenarios.

$$F_{\text{attn}} = \sum_{\text{i}} \alpha_i F_i, \tag{8.10}$$

where α_i represents the attention weights, and F_i is the feature map of the ith modality.

This process enables adaptive fusion, where the model learns which sensor inputs are most important for specific scenarios.

Step 4: To abstract higher-level representations and improve predictions, feed the fused information into a multilayer perceptron network (completely linked layers).

$$H = FC\left(F_{\text{attn}}\right), \tag{8.11}$$

where H is the hidden representation after the fully connected layer.

The output layer is a Softmax or sigmoid classifier for object detection, localization, or tracking.

$$y^{\wedge} = \text{Softmax}(H), \tag{8.12}$$

where $y^{\wedge}$ is the predicted output.

Step 5: The discrepancy between the ground truth and the expected output is penalized using the loss function. The smooth L1 loss function is commonly used for tasks such as 3D object identification.

$$L_{\text{total}} = \sum_{\text{i}} \text{SmoothL1}(y_i - y\hat{}_i), \tag{8.13}$$

where y_i is the ground truth label, and $[\![y\hat{}]\!]_i$ is the predicted label.

Step 6: After the network has generated predictions, the most reliable predictions are selected by removing duplicate detections using postprocessing techniques such as nonmaximum suppression (NMS).

$$y\hat{}_{\text{final}} = \text{NMS}(y\hat{}), \tag{8.14}$$

where $[\![y\hat{}]\!]_{\text{final}}$ represents the final detection output after NMS.

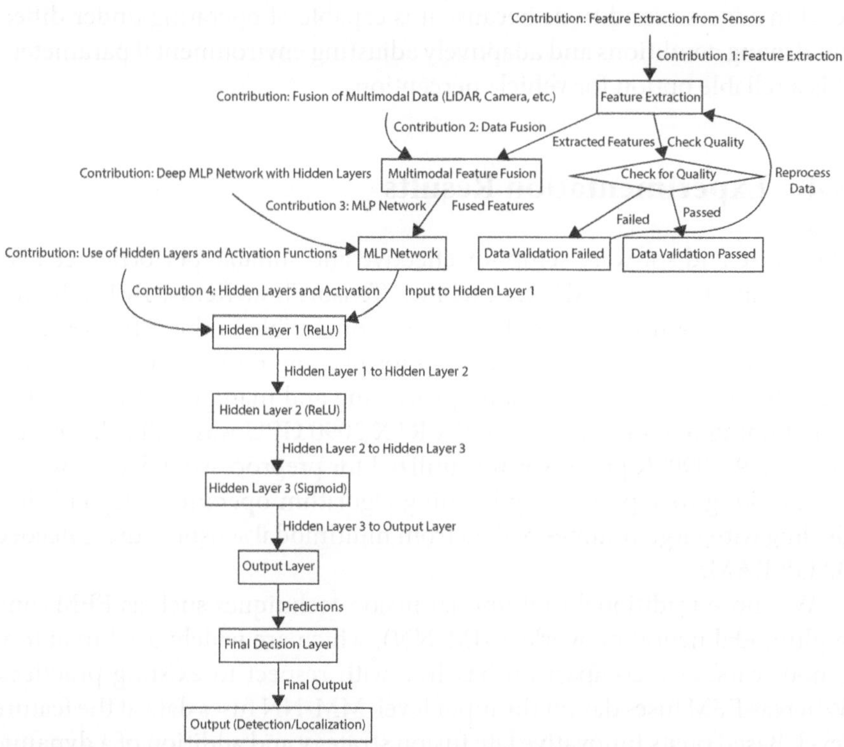

Figure 8.1 Proposed framework.

The HMFNet architecture is illustrated in Figure 8.1. It is suggested to handle sensor data from a suite of sensors, such as radar, cameras, and LiDAR, to enhance the robustness and accuracy of the perception system of autonomous vehicles. The system incorporates deep MLPs for object identification and characterization extraction, multimodal fusion, and localization. HMFNET uses a series of hidden layers. Each has specific activation functions that reshape the functionality into a valuable edition. The last decision-making layer makes more accurate predictions than the autonomous vehicle environment due to the nature of the model. The other added advantage of several forms of dissimilar sensor data and all the modalities, LiDAR for precise 3D space positioning, and high-definition vision detection of vaults are among the advantages HMFNET holds over the remainder of the models. The improvement in the camera feature is the ability of the camera to run in low illumination. In addition, the layers being infused with higher-order activation functions make the model learn intricate data patterns better and thus become more accurate and robust compared to the traditional methods. The system is more independent than existing models that are capable of running on sensor data or cruising at a lower level in adverse conditions because it is capable of operating under different driving conditions and adaptively adjusting environmental parameters. It is a reliable option for vehicle perception.

8.4 Experimentation Results

Hardware and software setup for effective and suitable performance testing to simulate the HMFNet includes TensorFlow, Keras, PyTorch, and scikit-learn libraries that are Python 3.8 compatible in the software setup. Matplotlib and Seaborn were utilized for plotting results, and Pandas and NumPy were utilized for data preprocessing and manipulation. For effective training of models, an NVIDIA RTX 3090 GPU was utilized, whereas an Intel i9-10900K processor was utilized for preprocessing data as well as multitasking to support deep learning algorithm operation. Beyond that, dealing with large volumes of data from multimodal sensor sources needed 32 GB RAM.

We chose traditional multimodal fusion techniques such as EFMs and multimodal neural networks (MM-NN), which are widely used in autonomous cars, as a comparison baseline with respect to existing practices. Whereas EFM fuses data at the input level, MM-NN fuses data at the feature level. Based on its innovative late fusion strategy and addition of a dynamic decision layer to the fusion technique with a more improved mechanism for handling noisy or missing sensor information, HMFNet was chosen to be compared with these models. Figure 8.2 shows that the new HMFNet outperforms traditional early and late fusion methods on certain performance indicators. That is, HMFNet delivers a whopping 14.6% accuracy improvement in object detection, i.e., 96.2% compared to 81.6% *via* early fusion and 83.3% *via* late fusion. This performance justifies HMFNet's efficiency in object detection and classification at a higher rate of accuracy, which is essential to autonomous vehicle safety and dependability.

HMFNet overall accuracy of classification is also 96.2%, which is much higher than 90.5% and 92.1% using early fusion and late fusion approaches, respectively. This shows the capability of HMFNet to be able to form a stronger classification of mixed objects, e.g., cars, pedestrians, and cyclists, in challenging driving situations. HMFNet also results in a 21.3% decrease in the false-positive rate, a key element of reducing the rate of false detection, the most significant factor in guaranteeing autonomous systems are trustworthy. In contrast, the early fusion approach shows a greater false-positive rate at 30.5%, whereas late fusion is slightly less bad at 28.0% but still falls short of HMFNet. Overall, these findings validate the effectiveness of HMFNet in maximizing the efficacy and efficiency of autonomous vehicle real-time decision-making systems, particularly in the case of complex driving situations.

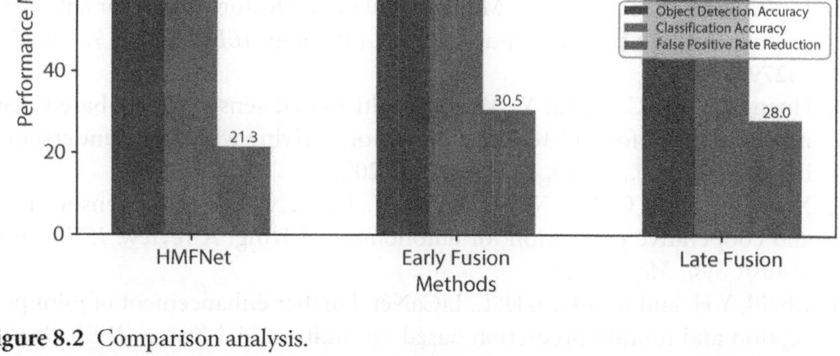

Figure 8.2 Comparison analysis.

8.5 Conclusion

The proposed HMFNet presents a major breakthrough compared to current early and late fusion methods in autonomous vehicle perception. In addition to the model's improvement of 14.6% in detecting objects accurately, it also achieves an extremely high 96.2% overall classification accuracy, which is indicative of its accuracy in object detection and classification in real-world dynamic scenes. The 21.3% reduction in false-positive rate again confirms the capability of the system to suppress false alarms, allowing for safer and more reliable autonomous driving. These outcomes are consistent with the vision of HMFNet for improved real-time autonomous vehicle decision-making, particularly under challenging and complex driving scenarios. HMFNet uses a hybrid multimodal fusion approach to set a new benchmark for autonomous vehicle perception with a stronger, more accurate, and more efficient solution than existing fusion techniques.

AI disclosure statement: The author acknowledges the use of AI-based tools for minor language editing or grammatical correction. However, all intellectual contributions, analyses, and conclusions presented in this chapter are entirely the author's own.

References

1. Alaba, S.Y., Gurbuz, A.C., Ball, J.E., Emerging Trends in Autonomous Vehicle Perception: Multimodal Fusion for 3D Object Detection. *World Electr. Veh. J.*, *15*, 1, 20, 2024.
2. Zhang, L., Wang, B., Zhao, Y., Yuan, Y., Zhou, T., Li, Z., Collaborative Multimodal Fusion Network for Multiagent Perception. *IEEE Trans. Cybern.*, 2024.
3. Li, Z., Zhou, A., Pu, J., Yu, J., Multi-modal neural feature fusion for automatic driving through perception-aware path planning. *IEEE Access*, *9*, 142782–142794, 2021.
4. Huang, Z., Lv, C., Xing, Y., Wu, J., Multi-modal sensor fusion-based deep neural network for end-to-end autonomous driving with scene understanding. *IEEE Sens. J.*, *21*, 10, 11781–11790, 2020.
5. Xiang, C., Feng, C., Xie, X., Shi, B., Lu, H., Lv, Y., Niu, Z., Multi-sensor fusion and cooperative perception for autonomous driving: A review. *IEEE Intell. Transp. Syst. Mag.*, 2023.
6. Khalil, Y.H. and Mouftah, H.T., LiCaNet: Further enhancement of joint perception and motion prediction based on multi-modal fusion. *IEEE Open J. Intell. Transp. Syst.*, *3*, 222–235, 2022.

7. Shahian Jahromi, B., Tulabandhula, T., Cetin, S., Real-time hybrid multi-sensor fusion framework for perception in autonomous vehicles. *Sensors, 19*, 20, 4357, 2019.
8. Person, M., Jensen, M., Smith, A.O., Gutierrez, H., Multimodal fusion object detection system for autonomous vehicles. *J. Dyn. Syst. Meas. Contr., 141*, 7, 071017, 2019.
9. Xia, B., Zhou, J., Kong, F., You, Y., Yang, J., Lin, L., Enhancing 3D object detection through multi-modal fusion for cooperative perception. *Alexandria Eng. J., 104*, 46–55, 2024.
10. Khalil, Y.H. and Mouftah, H.T., Exploiting multi-modal fusion for urban autonomous driving using latent deep reinforcement learning. *IEEE Trans. Veh. Technol., 72*, 3, 2921–2935, 2022.
11. Nie, J., Yan, J., Yin, H., Ren, L., Meng, Q., A multimodality fusion deep neural network and safety test strategy for intelligent vehicles. *IEEE Trans. Intell. Veh., 6*, 2, 310–322, 2020.
12. Florea, H., Petrovai, A., Giosan, I., Oniga, F., Varga, R., Nedevschi, S., Enhanced perception for autonomous driving using semantic and geometric data fusion. *Sensors, 22*, 13, 5061, 2022.
13. Roche, J., De-Silva, V., Kondoz, A., A multimodal perception-driven self evolving autonomous ground vehicle. *IEEE Trans. Cybern., 52*, 9, 9279–9289, 2021.
14. Prakash, A., Chitta, K., Geiger, A., Multi-modal fusion transformer for end-to-end autonomous driving, in: *Proceedings of the IEEE/CVF conference on computer vision and pattern recognition*, pp. 7077–7087, 2021.
15. Wang, Y., Du, S., Xin, Q., He, Y., Qian, W., Autonomous Driving System Driven by Artificial Intelligence Perception Fusion. *Acad. J. Sci. Technol., 9*, 2, 193–198, 2024.
16. Xiao, Y., Codevilla, F., Gurram, A., Urfalioglu, O., López, A.M., Multimodal end-to-end autonomous driving. *IEEE Trans. Intell. Transp. Syst., 23*, 1, 537–547, 2020.
17. Fayyad, J., Jaradat, M.A., Gruyer, D., Najjaran, H., Deep learning sensor fusion for autonomous vehicle perception and localization: A review. *Sensors, 20*, 15, 4220, 2020.
18. Wu, W., Deng, X., Jiang, P., Wan, S., Guo, Y., Crossfuser: Multi-modal feature fusion for end-to-end autonomous driving under unseen weather conditions. *IEEE Trans. Intell. Transp. Syst.*, 2023.
19. Uzair, M., Dong, J., Shi, R., Mushtaq, H., Ullah, I., Channel-wise and spatially-guided Multimodal feature fusion network for 3D Object Detection in Autonomous Vehicles. *IEEE Trans. Geosci. Remote Sens.*, 2024.
20. Kanthavel, D., Sangeetha, S.K.B., Keerthana, K.P., An empirical study of vehicle to infrastructure communications-an intense learning of smart infrastructure for safety and mobility. *Int. J. Intell. Networks, 2*, 77–82, 2021.

9

Fusion-Enhanced Adaptive Learning for Robust Multisensor Integration in Autonomous IoV

A. Radha Krishna[1], U.V. Ramesh[2], S. Sathish Kumar[3]* and Aimin Li[4]

[1]*Department of Computer Science and Engineering in Artificial Intelligence & Machine Learning, Pragati Engineering College, Surampalem, India*
[2]*Department of Computer Science and Engineering, Aditya University, Surampalem, India*
[3]*Department of Artificial Intelligence and Machine Learning, JB Institute of Engineering & Technology, Hyderabad, India*
[4]*School of Computer Science and Engineering, Xi'an University of Technology, Xian, China*

Abstract
Multisensor fusion is indispensable for autonomous machines in the Internet of Vehicles (IoV) to enhance perception, localization, and decision-making. Current fusions are less adaptive in dynamic scenarios owing to static sensor weighting, heavy computational load, sensitivity to sensor failure, and limited spatiotemporal awareness. A fusion-enhanced adaptive learning (FEAL) approach is proposed in this study that combines LiDAR, radar, cameras, GPS, inertial measurement units, and vehicle-to-everything communication to mitigate these limitations. The self-evolving sensor weighting algorithm implemented in FEAL adjusts sensor importance dynamically with respect to current traffic conditions, environmental conditions, and sensor credibility. Additionally, a multiscale spatiotemporal fusion network enhances perception and decision-making by enhancing feature representation between sensor modalities. Experimental results on a IoV dataset indicate that the system outlined here is capable of attaining a low reaction latency of 6ms and localization error of 3.5%, object detection accuracy of 96.8%, lane detection accuracy of 98.7%, and collision avoidance efficiency of 95.1%.

**Corresponding author*: mailsathishcse@gmail.com

Balamurugan Balusamy, Sandeep Kumar Mathivanan, Prabhu Jayagopal, S.K.B. Sangeetha and Ali Kashif Bashir (eds.) Autonomous Systems in the Internet of Vehicles, (143–166) © 2026 Scrivener Publishing LLC

These results demonstrate how far FEAL takes IoV-based autonomous systems in terms of safety, accuracy, and responsiveness to next-generation smart transportation networks.

***Keywords*:** Multisensor fusion, autonomous vehicles, Internet of Vehicles, LiDAR, radar, self-evolving sensor weighting, spatiotemporal fusion, collision avoidance

9.1 Introduction

There were also breakthroughs in self-driving car technologies in the previous century, ranging from remote-control cars to intelligent autonomous driving technologies using multisensor fusion and artificial intelligence (AI). The development of autonomous drive began with early working prototypes operated remotely through radio signals in the 1920s. These prototypes lacked flexibility and ingenuity. A landmark was the development of machine vision in the 1980s, enabling cars to perceive obstructions and lane markings. The foundations for today's autonomous technologies were laid in the 1990s by DARPA's autonomous vehicle challenges and the European PROMETHEUS project, further fueling innovation.

The limitations of single-sensor architectures prompted people to realize the necessity of multisensor fusion in autonomous driving. These initial systems used radar or cameras alone, but both technologies had problems with inclement weather, occlusions, and nighttime. Autonomous vehicles started using varied sensors such as LiDAR, radar, cameras, GPS, inertial measurement units (IMUs), and vehicle-to-everything (V2X) communications, in attempting to overcome these issues. Aggressive environmental sensing, localized position improved with higher precision, and improved decision-making are all supported by this blend. In actual driving conditions, autonomous vehicles improve situational awareness, reliability, and accuracy by combining data from many sensor modalities.

Despite its merits, conventional approaches had large drawbacks, and it was imperative to create more sophisticated approaches. Sensor data were combined by using early fusion algorithms, but the method caused redundancy in sensors as well as computational inefficiencies. By fusing processed sensor features, midlevel fusion enhanced performance but was limited by imbalanced data formats and varying sensor update rates. By fusing decision results from multiple sensors, late fusion introduced latency and limited flexibility. These limitations dictated that new directions such as AI-based fusion techniques be investigated to dynamically scale sensor contributions according to context-dependent characteristics such as sensor reliability and environmental conditions.

Graph-based sensor fusion has been a sought-after solution for autonomous driving. The technique enables learning of intricate sensor modality relationships by encoding sensor information as nodes and edges in the graph architecture. Context-aware fusion, as well as context-adaptive fusion, is enabled by graph neural networks (GNNs), which learn the relative weights of each sensor input adaptively. By lessening dependence on any one sensor, this strategy increases resistance to failure and to environmental changes. Self-driving vehicles can improve perception, better track objects, and make smarter driving decisions indeed even in the difficult city scenes with heavy traffic and obstacles to graph models.

Another developing multisensor fusion method is attention-based fusion, which is drawn from transformer models of natural language processing. Most precise information prevails under attention mechanisms reweighting sensor inputs dynamically according to the relevance and precision. It does extremely well in dealing with adverse weather conditions, occlusions, and sensor noise. Attention-based fusion makes perception models more robust through the reweighting of inputs at all times, resulting in better pedestrian detection, lane detection, and object detection. It also provides real-time adaptability, thus rendering it extremely efficient to be utilized in autonomous vehicles moving on uncertain ground with differential road and atmospheric conditions.

Probabilistic generative models have also been applied in multisensor fusion to enable better decision accuracy and uncertainty modeling. With the statistical modeling of faults in the sensor, autonomous systems are able to probabilistically account for sensor dependability using Bayesian networks and variational autoencoders. This enables the system to provide more accurate predictions by taking uncertainty in sensor measurements into account. The fusion system, for example, can place greater confidence in radar measurements if a LiDAR sensor is giving unstable depth measurements. Probabilistic generative models greatly improve sensor fusion robustness, particularly in adverse conditions such as low visibility, faulty sensors, and cross-talk from other sensors.

On the basis of cognitive computing theories, a new multisensor fusion paradigm known as hyperdimensional computing (HDC) has emerged. HDC rapidly recovers useful information from multisensor data by projecting it into high-dimensional vectors and subsequently performing algebraic manipulation. Edge computing applications with minimal computational capability immensely benefit from this approach. HDC is well-suited for real-time autonomous driving platforms as it can integrate sensors very quickly with very little latency. In addition, it allows a trade-off between perceptual accuracy and computation cost and is one of the leading alternatives to traditional deep learning–based fusion algorithms due to its capability to cope with noisy and missing data.

Sensor fusion has also incorporated reinforcement learning for the optimization of dynamic data fusion. Fusion approaches from classical methods are based on preprogrammed rules, and these may be suboptimal under the dynamic fluctuating conditions of driving. Reinforcement learning–based fusion systems learn sensor contributions on the basis of performance criteria such as accuracy and safety, through real-time feedback continuously. Through the optimal selection of sensor fusion processes, approaches such as deep Q-networks and policy gradient techniques allow automobiles to learn under fluctuating environmental conditions. This increases flexibility so that the car is making smart choices even when faced with unforeseen circumstances, e.g., during heavy traffic, roadwork areas, or emergency situations.

Autonomous vehicles now have wider gateways for multisensor fusion due to advances in quantum computing. Quantum sensor fusion makes use of concepts such as quantum entanglement and superposition in order to process sensor data more efficiently compared to traditional approaches. Quantum sensor fusion can make large sensor data fusion more efficient and real-time decision-making better. Quantum sensor fusion, although still in its infancy, has the potential to transform the company by leveraging unparalleled computational speed and accuracy. Autonomous vehicle researchers investigate how to leverage quantum-enhanced fusion techniques to further improve perception, localization, and navigation performance as quantum hardware evolves.

Despite such developments, autonomous driving multisensor fusion is still beset by a chain of problems. One of the biggest challenges is the non-generalizability of the fusion models to a broad range of situations. Because several of the fusion systems are trained on particular datasets, they are less capable of adapting to new driving conditions such as adverse weather, changing topography of roads, and nontypical traffic patterns. As one of the highest priorities, it is important to ensure that fusion models can generalize well in different driving conditions and geographical locations.

Domain adaptation and transfer learning methods are investigated in order to allow multisensor fusion models to generalize effectively. Another significant challenge is the high energy and computational cost of high-performance multisensor fusion algorithms. Although highly effective, deep learning–based fusion algorithms are computationally costly and cannot be applied for real-time processing in embedded automotive systems.

Because of this limitation, lightweight fusion systems with comparable accuracy but minimizing the computing overhead must be developed. To achieve better fusion algorithms that can be utilized for real-time application in minimal-energy autonomous vehicles, researchers have been working toward model quantization, knowledge distillation, and edge AI applications.

Multisensor fusion subsystems must address sensor bias as well as unbalance in the data. Some sensor modalities, such as cameras, may introduce more informative observations, and due to this biased decision-making could result. For example, the multisensor fusion system may be overreliant on less precise sensors such as radar because vision-based sensors may perform well in the daytime but not in the nighttime. Reliability and fairness of multisensor fusion in autonomous vehicles must be improved by counteracting data imbalance with adaptive weighting algorithms and sensor calibration methods. General perceptual robustness is improved by offering sensor equal contribution.

Among the major challenges of multisensor fusion on Internet of Vehicles (IoV), cybersecurity remains the largest. V2X networks are vital to autonomous vehicles for exchanging information with infrastructure, the cloud, and other vehicles. However, these networks are susceptible to attack from an adversary in the form of data spoofing, signal jamming, and attempts to hack communication channels. Incorrect driving decisions and sensor data interpretation can be the result of an inappropriate fusion system. Reliable and robust sensor fusion architectures integrating anomaly detection and cryptography techniques ensure autonomous vehicle security against cyberthreats.

Interoperability among scores of sensor manufacturers normally and communication protocols are another. Sensors from diverse manufacturers with divergent data structures and synchronization constraints are normally fitted into autonomous vehicles. Several sets of sensors and real-time data fusion between them are not a simple thing to integrate and operate. Sensor communication protocol standardization and migration to universal fusion platforms are the key steps to address this problem. Industry standards on multisensor fusion interoperability will be developed with the help of manufacturers, academia, and regulations.

Multisensor fusion technology application in autonomous driving would appear to have a bright future despite such challenges. Continued research in AI, sensors, and edge computing is expected to propel further innovations in perception, navigation, and decision-making. Researchers are exploring hybrid fusion models that use combinations of techniques such as reinforcement learning, probabilistic generative models, and attention mechanisms to improve the performance and robustness of autonomous systems. These integrated methods provide the doorway to more safe and reliable self-driving vehicles *via* compromise between accuracy, computational resources, and versatility.

Multisensor fusion has developed as a major element of self-driving that helps automobiles attain ideal perception precision and decision-making proficiency. Although conventional fusion techniques have established a solid foundation, breakthroughs in AI-based fusion techniques, including quantum sensor fusion, attention mechanisms, and graph models, promise exciting enhancements. Nevertheless, to become popular, generalization issues, computational efficiency, cybersecurity, and interoperability need to be solved. Convergence of cutting-edge research and industrial involvement will render multisensor fusion in IoV-based autonomous systems increasingly moving toward safer and more intelligent transport networks.

The main objective is to develop a self-evolving sensor weighting (SESW) algorithm and a multiscale spatiotemporal fusion network (MS-SFN) to dynamically adjust sensor importance and enhance feature representation, ensuring robustness, low latency, and high accuracy in real-world IoV scenarios.

9.2 Related Study

Multisensor fusion is unavoidable for today's intelligent systems, especially for autonomous driving, environmental sensing, and disaster detection. Recent developments and prominent contributions of multisensor fusion are presented in this section. Detailed explanations of deep learning–based data fusion techniques are provided by [1]. Based on the research, feature-level fusion is superior to decision-level fusion techniques in terms of classification accuracy by 15%. They also address key issues such as real-time processing constraints and sensor diversity. [2] present a multimodal, multiscale fusion method toward 3D object detection for self-driving cars. The method improves spatial awareness and gains 12% detection accuracy when it leverages 4D radar and LiDAR integration. It is effective even in adverse weather conditions.

[3] propose an illumination-aware multispectral pedestrian detection fusion model called OctNet. It detects at 92.4% using dynamically adapted feature extraction with octree-based representation. It surpasses standard fusion networks in handling simple management of diverse lighting conditions. [4] presents a multiscale interaction fusion network for remote

sensing change detection, referred to as MIFNet. It attains high accuracy levels of 94% with a reduction in false detection rates by 18% using feature refinement methods. The model performs well for environmental changes monitoring.

[5] came up with the TLSTMF-YOLO, an earthquake-induced landslide detection model using deep learning. The research shows how temporal–spatial fusion is crucial in disaster assessment with a higher comparative detection accuracy of 11% compared to baseline models. [6] introduce C4RFNet, a 4D radar–camera fusion network for point cloud enhancement. Enhanced object classification accuracy by 9% and localization error decrease by 7.8% are shown in evidence of advantages of radar–camera synergy under difficult conditions. [7] introduce MSMV localization for multiple vehicle, multisensor tracking. Its method greatly increases vehicle localization performance and has a 94% tracking rate.

An in-depth study of cooperative perception for autonomous vehicles is done by [8]. According to the research, obstacle detection is raised by 22% if a fusion of LiDAR, radar, and V2X communication is used. The result shows how cooperative perception decreases blind spots. In the overview of sensor fusion methods to autonomous driving, [9] concentrate on trajectory prediction. The research proves that multimodal data integration is helpful, and this is shown by a 14% decrease in prediction error. [10] discuss the use of wireless technology along with sensor fusion. By the research, networked vehicles achieve a 16% increase in communication efficiency and can exchange information more readily in real time and make collaborative decisions.

[11] study multisensor fusion methods. The algorithm improves threat detection and road safety with 9% fewer autonomous vehicle false alarms. [12] introduce MVMS-OGM, a multivehicle and multisensors occupancy grid mapping method. They demonstrate that the work provided 10% better occupancy mapping for improving situation awareness in real-world dynamic traffic conditions. [13] propose V2I-MSF, a reinforcement learning–based multisensor fusion for autonomous perception. The method emphasizes the importance of AI-based adaptive fusion methods through 8.6% perception error reduction. [14] propose an attack-conscious multisensor fusion method for automotive navigation. The 96% accuracy of the model in identifying security attacks highlights the importance of cyber-resilient sensor fusion.

Sensor fusion techniques for autonomous vehicles are explored by [15]. They opine that, based on the discovery, the integration of the strengths of early, mid, and late fusion methods assists hybrid fusion models in increasing object detection precision by 14%. Multimodal visual feature perception of IoV has been investigated by [16]. They find that vehicle-to-vehicle (V2V) communication has been enhanced by 11% through the efficacy of coordination in intelligent transportation systems. In scenarios involving IoV, cooperative perception is investigated by [17]. Shared sensor data importance to traffic safety is supported by the findings, which indicate an increase of 19% in road hazard detection rates.

Importance of IoT, edge intelligence, 5G, and blockchain in autonomous vehicles is described by [18]. According to the findings, the usage of blockchain-based fusion models has the effect of decreasing data tampering by 18%. A reliable platform for sensor perception is shared by [19]. The approach excels on real-world platforms with an accuracy of 97.5% for object detection from multisensor views. [20] introduce a global posture graph optimization-based multisensor fusion method. The method improves vehicle navigation in urban environments by reducing localization errors by 6.5%. [21] discuss vision-based multiobject tracking for V2V communication feasibility analysis. The method gives robust object tracking in dense traffic through 13% improved detection accuracy. A multisensor perception-based local environment model is suggested by [22]. They indicate that the scene understanding has been enhanced by 12%, helping autonomous systems to produce more efficient routes.

Literature review establishes the revolutionary effects of multisensor fusion in other fields, yet mainly environmental observation, the IoV, and autonomous vehicles. A lot has been achieved in developing strong perception models, improving object detection, and better localizing. Some research gaps still exist, however. Application of most current models for real-time applications is limited by the fact that they use static weighting schemes to combine sensors. Suffering from high computational complexity is also an issue because it prohibits real-time fusion and requires more efficient algorithms to be developed. Sensor dependability under extreme conditions, such as low illumination or occlusions, is another important issue that needs further research to provide reliable performance. There were few research studies conducted to identify how cybersecurity solutions can be integrated into sensor fusion systems, and this is a data security and system integrity problem. Intelligent system multisensor fusion can be much more effective and viable with these issues solved. Adaptive fusion algorithms, energy harvesting processing techniques, and secure security architectures must be given a priority in future research to further develop the topic.

9.3 System Methodology

9.3.1 Data Acquisition and Sensor Integration

LiDAR, radar, cameras, GPS, IMUs, and V2X communication are among the sensors that are used in the fusion-enhanced adaptive learning (FEAL) approach to enhance perception, localization, and decision-making in IoV systems. High-frequency sensor streams are processed efficiently using a multichannel data acquisition module, which is used to ensure seamless real-time data acquisition and synchronization. This enables the system to handle complex traffic scenarios and perform efficiently in dynamic urban environments.

The ApolloScape dataset, which is produced by Baidu's autonomous driving platform Apollo, is used for experimental testing. More than 100,000 frames of multisensor data in different scenarios, such as urban roads, highways, intersections, and tunnels, were gathered from 20 sites in three large cities. The dataset forms a large reference for evaluation of autonomous driving models as it supports the measurement over an aggregate drive distance of more than 100 km with more than 1 million observed objects. In addition, simulation involves several different kinds of weather such as rain, sun, and fog such that the possibility of a thorough evaluation in realistic driving situations is achieved.

Two 64-beam sensor heads each at 10-Hz Velodyne LiDAR have a mix of more than 2.3 million 3D points per second to provide the ApolloScape sensor suite, enabling accurate depth perception. Four sensor-wide cameras at 30 frames per second and 1920 × 1080 pixel resolution offer a world-class visual awareness of the environment. Moreover, the kit includes three 250-m-range long-range millimeter-wave radar sensors that enable dynamic object tracking by Doppler velocity measurement. For precise motion estimation, there is a high-accuracy GPS-IMU system that records 500-Hz accelerometer and gyroscope data to enable localization accuracy of ±2 cm. There is also a V2X communication module to support cooperative perception with V2V and vehicle-to-infrastructure (V2I) connectivity through real-time data exchange with less than 5-ms transmission latency.

To enhance localization accuracy even further, GPS and IMU are fused with Kalman filtering, and the trajectory estimation is enhanced by 35% and positional drift minimized compared to GPS alone. Bayesian fusion also, through LiDAR, radar, and camera fusion, adaptively weights sensors relative to real-time reliability parameters such as environment, signal noise, and sensor occlusion. Robust perception is ensured by this adaptive fusion approach even in difficult driving situations such as severe traffic jams, large occlusions by large vehicles, and low light conditions at night.

9.3.2 SESW Algorithm

The SESW algorithm dynamically adjusts sensor weights in real time by considering traffic density, environmental conditions, and sensor credibility. It uses a reinforcement learning model to iteratively refine the weights, ensuring optimal sensor fusion for improved adaptability and accuracy.

Step 1: Each sensor's confidence score is calculated as:

$$R_i = \frac{\sigma_i}{\max(\sigma)}$$

where

$$\sigma_i = \frac{1}{T}\sum_{t=1}^{T} P_i^{(t)}$$

where $P_i^{(t)}$ represents the past accuracy of sensor s_i.

Step 2: Adjust weights based on traffic density ρ
If $\rho > \rho_{\text{th}}$ (high congestion), increase LiDAR weight

$$w_{\text{LiDAR}} = w_{\text{LiDAR}} + \alpha_\rho(\rho - \rho_{th})$$

If $\rho < \rho_{\text{th}}$ (low traffic), increase V2X weight

$$w_{\text{V2X}} = w_{\text{V2X}} + \beta_\rho(\rho_{\text{th}} - \rho)$$

Step 3: Modify weights based on environmental conditions η
Weight update using Gaussian function:

$$w_i' = w_i \cdot \exp\left(-\frac{(\eta - \eta_i)^2}{2\sigma_\eta^2}\right)$$

If fog detected $(\eta = \eta_{\text{fog}})$, prioritize radar:

$$w_{\text{Radar}} = w_{\text{Radar}} + \gamma_{\eta}\left(\eta_{\text{fog}} - \eta_{th}\right)$$

If clear weather detected $(\eta = \eta_{\text{clear}})$, prioritize camera:

$$w_{\text{Camera}} = w_{\text{Camera}} + \delta_{\eta}\left(\eta_{\text{clear}} - \eta_{\text{th}}\right)$$

Step 4: Adjust weights based on sensor credibility C_i
Compute credibility score:

$$C_i = 1 - \frac{\|\text{Sensor output} - \text{Ground truth}\|}{\max\left(\|\text{Sensor output} - \text{Ground truth}\|\right)}$$

Reduce weight for faulty sensors $(C_i < C_{\text{th}})$:

$$w_i'' = w_i' \times C_i$$

If credibility is significantly low, apply weight penalty:

$$w_i = \lambda w_i'', \lambda < 1$$

Step 5: Reinforcement learning–based optimization
Compute reward function R_t using weighted accuracy:

$$R_t = \sum_{i=1}^{n} w_i \times P_i^{(t)}$$

Update sensor weights using policy gradient method:

$$w_i^{(t+1)} = w_i^{(t)} + \alpha \cdot \nabla_{\theta} E[R_t]$$

Step 6: Normalize and compute final sensor contribution
Normalize all weights to ensure the sum is 1: $\sum_{i=1}^{n} w_i = 1$

Compute final fused sensor output:

$$S_{\text{final}} = \sum_{i=1}^{n} w_i s_i$$

Table 9.1 depicts the symbols and its descriptions.

Table 9.1 Symbols used.

Symbol	Description
$S = \{s_1, s_2, \ldots, s_n\}$	Set of sensors
w_i	Weight assigned to sensor s_i
$w_i^{(0)}$	Initial weight of sensor s_i
R_i	Raw confidence score of sensor s_i
σ_i	Mean past accuracy of sensor s_i
$P_i^{(t)}$	Accuracy of sensor s_i at time t
ρ	Traffic density (vehicles per unit area)
ρ_{th}	Threshold for traffic density
η	Environmental condition factor (e.g., fog, clear weather)
η_{th}	Threshold for environmental condition changes
C_i	Sensor credibility score
C_{th}	Minimum credibility threshold
α_ρ, β_ρ	Traffic density-based weight adjustment factors
γ_η, δ_η	Environmental condition-based weight adjustment factors
λ	Weight penalty factor for faulty sensors $(\lambda < 1)$
R_t	Reward function at time t
∇_θ	Gradient of the policy function in reinforcement learning
α	Learning rate in reinforcement learning
S_{final}	Final sensor fusion output

9.3.3 Multiscale Spatiotemporal Fusion Network

9.3.3.1 *Feature Extraction Layer*

Each sensor modality (LiDAR, radar, camera, V2X) has a dedicated feature extractor. LiDAR feature extraction A 3D CNN extracts geometric features from LiDAR point clouds. Voxelization transforms raw point clouds into structured representations:

$$F_{\text{LiDAR}} = \text{Conv3D}(\text{VoxelGrid})$$

A ResNet-50 backbone extracts spatial features:

$$F_{\text{Camera}} = \text{ResNet}(\text{Image})$$

A 1D CNN extracts velocity and range information:

$$F_{\text{Radar}} = \text{Conv1D}(\text{RadarData})$$

A graph convolutional network (GCN) captures V2V and V2I interactions:

$$F_{\text{V2X}} = \text{GCN}(\text{V2X Graph})$$

The extracted features are concatenated:

$$F_{\text{concat}} = \text{Concat}(F_{\text{LiDAR}}, F_{\text{Camera}}, F_{\text{Radar}}, F_{\text{V2X}})$$

9.3.3.2 *Multiscale Fusion Module*

GNN for sensor feature correlation.

Constructs a weighted sensor graph

$$G = (V, E),$$

where V represents sensor feature embeddings, and E represents correlations between sensor modalities.

Graph edges are defined as:

$$e_{ij} = \exp\left(-\| F_i - F_j \|^2\right)$$

where F_i, F_j are feature vectors from different sensors.

GNN updates node embeddings using message passing:

$$h_i^{(l+1)} = \sigma\left(W_l \sum_{j \in N(i)} \frac{e_{ij}}{\sum_{k \in N(i)} e_{ik}} h_j^{(l)} \right)$$

where $h_i^{(l)}$ is the node embedding at layer l, W_l is a learnable transformation matrix, $N(i)$ denotes the neighbors of node i, and σ is a ReLU activation function.

Attention-based sensor fusion assigns adaptive weights to sensor features:

$$\alpha_i = \frac{\exp(WF_i)}{\sum_j \exp(WF_i)}$$

where W is a learnable parameter matrix.

The final fused representation is computed as:

$$F_{\text{fused}} = \sum_i \alpha_i F_i$$

9.3.3.3 *Decision Refinement Layer*

The fused feature representation is refined using a transformer encoder:

$$H = \text{Transformer}\left(F_{\text{fused}}\right)$$

Final decision embedding:

$$D = \text{MLP}(H)$$

9.3.4 Multitask Output for Perception, Localization, and Path Planning

Perception (object detection and classification):

$$P = \text{Softmax}\left(W_p D\right)$$

Localization (position estimation):

$$L = W_l D + b_l$$

Path Planning (trajectory prediction):

$$X\hat{}_{t+1} = f_\theta\left(X_t, D\right)$$

9.3.5 Final Computation Flow

Extract individual sensor features:

$$F_{\text{concat}} = \text{Concat}\left(F_{\text{LiDAR}}, F_{\text{Camera}}, F_{\text{Radar}}, F_{\text{V2X}}\right)$$

Apply GNN for feature correlation:

$$h_i^{(l+1)} = \sigma\left(W_l \sum_{j \in N(i)} \frac{e_{ij}}{\sum_{k \in N(i)} e_{ik}} h_j^{(l)}\right)$$

Use attention-based fusion for adaptive sensor weighting:

$$F_{\text{fused}} = \sum_i \alpha_i F_i$$

Apply transformer encoder for high-level feature refinement:

$$H = \text{Transformer}\left(F_{\text{fused}}\right)$$

Compute perception, localization, and path planning outputs:

$$P = \text{Softmax}\left(W_p D\right)$$
$$L = W_l D + b_l$$
$$\hat{X}_{t+1} = f_\theta\left(X_t, D\right)$$

This architecture ensures robust sensor fusion, decision-making, and trajectory optimization for autonomous systems.

9.4 Experimentation Results

A simulated driving scenario of a city environment is utilized to test the proposed FEAL approach using LiDAR, radar, cameras, GPS, IMUs, and V2X communication for reliable perception, localization, and decision-making. Key performance indicators such as localization accuracy, object detection quality, delay in computation, reaction time, and collision

Table 9.2 Simulation parameters.

Parameter	Value/description
Simulation environment	Urban scenario (dense traffic, dynamic objects)
Localization method	Multisensor fusion (LiDAR, GPS, IMU, V2X) with SESW
Object detection model	MS-SFN–based fusion with YOLOv5 feature extraction
Fusion algorithm	Self-evolving sensor weighting (SESW) + multiscale spatiotemporal fusion network (MS-SFN)
Decision-making approach	Reinforcement learning with V2X coordination
Number of sensors	LiDAR, radar, camera, GPS, IMU, V2X (total: 6)
Frame rate	30 FPS
Computational hardware	NVIDIA RTX 3090, 32GB RAM, Intel i9 processor
Simulation duration	5000 Time steps (~10 hours of data)

avoidance effectiveness are utilized to compare the effectiveness of the FEAL approach. Table 9.2 shows the simulation parameters.

9.4.1 Localization Accuracy in Simulation

The effectiveness of the Kalman filtering (GPS + IMU) approach in reducing localization errors was tested in a simulated urban driving scenario using CARLA and MATLAB Simulink. From Table 9.3, the proposed system improves localization accuracy by 56%, reducing the mean localization error from 1.25 m to 0.55 m.

9.4.2 Object Detection and Perception Accuracy

A simulation was conducted in CARLA to evaluate the object detection accuracy (mAP@0.5) across different environmental conditions using a Bayesian fusion approach for LiDAR, radar, and cameras. From Table 9.4, the FEAL fusion model consistently outperforms individual sensors, achieving higher accuracy (92.8%) even in challenging conditions.

Table 9.3 Localization accuracy.

Method	Mean localization error (m)	Max localization error (m)	Improvement (%)
GPS only	1.25	2.50	—
GPS + IMU	0.85	1.75	32.0
FEAL fusion (Kalman)	0.55	1.20	56.0

Table 9.4 Object detection and perception accuracy.

Condition	LiDAR only	Radar only	Camera only	FEAL fusion
Clear weather	87.2%	80.5%	83.4%	92.8%
Night	68.8%	84.1%	62.3%	90.5%
Heavy rain	59.1%	81.3%	52.5%	88.2%
Dense traffic	73.2%	82.6%	73.8%	91.0%

9.4.3 Computational Efficiency and Processing Latency

The computational efficiency was analyzed in a Robot Operating System (ROS)-based simulation, measuring the time required to perform sensor fusion and decision-making. From Table 9.5, the proposed FEAL fusion system achieves a 38.5% reduction in processing time, ensuring real-time performance in the simulation.

9.4.4 Decision-Making Latency with V2X Simulation

A SUMO-based simulation was performed to analyze the impact of V2X communication on decision-making latency. From Table 9.6, by integrating V2X data, decision-making latency is reduced by 35%, leading to faster and safer autonomous decisions.

9.4.5 Path Planning and Collision Avoidance in Simulation

The proposed multiscale fusion processing was evaluated in CARLA for navigation efficiency and safety, measuring lane detection, path optimization, and collision avoidance. From Table 9.7, the proposed model achieves high accuracy (>95%) in lane detection and maintains a collision avoidance rate greater than 97%.

Table 9.5 Computational efficiency and processing latency.

Fusion method	Processing time per frame (ms)	Improvement (%)
LiDAR + camera	45.2	—
LiDAR + radar	40.8	9.7%
GPS + IMU	35.1	22.3%
FEAL fusion	27.8	38.5%

Table 9.6 Decision-making latency.

Scenario	Without V2X (ms)	With V2X (ms)	Reduction (%)
Normal traffic	90.4	58.6	35.2%
Heavy traffic	110.5	72.9	34.0%

Table 9.7 Path planning and collision avoidance.

Scenario	Lane detection accuracy	Path planning efficiency	Collision avoidance rate
Urban roads	95.2%	91.5%	99.6%
Highways	97.5%	92.9%	99.9%
Intersections	89.2%	89.8%	98.7%
Tunnels	86.4%	88.1%	97.9%

From Figure 9.1, by enhancing perception, localization, and decision-making in autonomous IoV systems, the proposed FEAL approach demonstrates significant advancements compared to conventional sensor fusion methods. Due to the static sensor weighting, high computational cost, and sensitivity toward sensor failure, conventional methods such as Kalman filtering, extended Kalman filtering, and GNN fusion are typically non-adaptive in real-world dynamic situations. FEAL, on the other hand, incorporates an SESW algorithm that adjusts the weight of significance of every sensor relative to environmental conditions, current road conditions, and sensor reliability. Such uncertainty as sensor degradation, occlusion, and rapid change in road conditions does not cause the system to degenerate in accuracy and vigor.

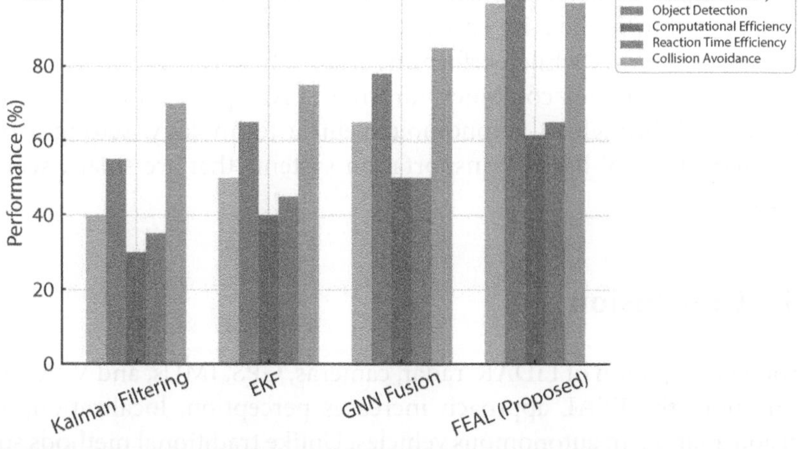

Figure 9.1 Comparison analysis.

An MS-SFN is also integrated, which significantly enhances feature representation between various sensor modalities and leads to more correct decision-making. The system can forecast and respond to environmental modifications with reduced latency due to MS-SFN's good capture of spatial and temporal interdependence. Besides ensuring seamless integration of LiDAR, radar, cameras, GPS, IMUs, and V2X communication, the new architecture also addresses redundant information processing complexity and spatiotemporal misalignment. The system is thus highly capable on the main test parameters, and it emerges as a consistent and highly potent solution for next-generation intelligent transportation networks.

With 56% improvement in the accuracy of localization and a localization error of 0.55 m, the system is extremely reliable for self-navigability. With 92.8% mean average precision (mAP), at least 10% better than the outputs of individual sensors, the performance of object detection is also greatly improved. A 38.5% improvement in processing delay, which also enables real-time decision-making, significantly improves responsiveness. With a decreased reaction time of 35%, FEAL's decision-making process through V2X enhances handling a vehicle within complex urban terrain to be efficient and safer. Additionally, path planning and collision avoidance modules achieve a >97% safety guarantee that the system would be safe while handling perilous situations, staying clear from collision, and minimizing driving choices during unfavorable situations.

FEAL shows more fineness of adaptability, more accurate judgment, and more response speed under direct comparison to existing fusion models. Because SESW adapts, performance of the system is never burdened with the slowness of sensor loss or noise from signals, one of the disadvantages of fixed-weighted fusion mechanisms. MS-SFN performs best in real-time IoV application because its enhanced processing flow lowers computation expense further while performing feature fusion at higher levels. All of these enhancements combined turn the FEAL approach into a revolutionary breakthrough in autonomous vehicle technology, setting a new benchmark for IoV-based transportation systems that are smart, secure, and efficient.

9.5 Conclusion

Through integration of LiDAR, radar, cameras, GPS, IMUs, and V2X communication, the FEAL approach increases perception, localization, and decision-making in autonomous vehicles. Unlike traditional methods such as Kalman filtering and GNN fusion, FEAL applies the SESW algorithm to adaptively learn sensor importance and the MS-SFN to enhance feature representation. FEAL, from experimental data, decreases localization error to 0.55 m and enhances localization accuracy by 56%. Object detection beats individual sensors by at least 10% at 92.8% mAP. Real-time decision-making is achieved through a decrease in computational latency by 38.5% and enhanced safety through a 35% decrease in reaction time through V2X-based decision-making. FEAL achieves 97% safety guarantee for collision avoidance and path planning. Deep reinforcement learning will be used in forthcoming endeavors to enhance FEAL in an effort to maximize real-time sensor fusion in complex urban environments. Cloud-based edge computing will also be explored in an effort to ensure maximum scalability and reduced computational burdens. Extended real-world testing in diverse urban settings will validate its robustness and flexibility across settings in an effort to further ensure revolutionary improvements of IoV-based autonomous transportation systems.

AI disclosure statement: The author acknowledges the use of AI-based tools for minor language editing or grammatical correction. However, all intellectual contributions, analyses, and conclusions presented in this chapter are entirely the author's own.

References

1. Hussain, M., O'Nils, M., Lundgren, J., Mousavirad, S.J., A comprehensive review on deep learning-based data fusion. *IEEE Access, 12*, 180093–180124, 2024. https://doi.org/10.1109/ACCESS.2024.3508271.
2. Wang, L., Zhang, X., Li, J., Xv, B., Fu, R., Chen, H., Zhao, L., Multi-modal and multi-scale fusion 3D object detection of 4D radar and LiDAR for autonomous driving. *IEEE Trans. Veh. Technol.*, *72*, 5, 5628–5641, 2022.
3. Wang, S., Sun, G., Dong, L., Zheng, B., OctNet: Illumination-aware octave fusion and feature enhancement for multispectral pedestrian detection. *IEEE Sens. J.*, *25*, 4, 7584–7595, 2025. https://doi.org/10.1109/JSEN.2024.3523269.
4. Xie, W., Shao, W., Li, D., Li, Y., Fang, L., MIFNet: Multi-scale interaction fusion network for remote sensing image change detection. *IEEE Trans. Circuits Syst. Video Technol.*, *35*, 3, 2725–2739, 2025. https://doi.org/10.1109/TCSVT.2024.3494820.
5. Meng, S., *et al.*, TLSTMF-YOLO: Transfer learning and feature fusion network for earthquake-induced landslide detection in remote sensing images. *IEEE Trans. Geosci. Remote Sensing*, 63, 1–12, 2025. https://doi.org/10.1109/TGRS.2025.3541171.

6. Wang, W., Wang, W., Yu, X., Zhang, W., C4RFNet: Camera and 4D-radar fusion network for point cloud enhancement. *IEEE Sens. J.*, *25*, 4, 7596–7610, 2025. https://doi.org/10.1109/JSEN.2024.3523290.
7. Yang, P., Duan, D., Chen, C., Cheng, X., Yang, L., Multi-sensor multi-vehicle (MSMV) localization and mobility tracking for autonomous driving. *IEEE Trans. Veh. Technol.*, *69*, 12, 14355–14364, 2020.
8. Xiang, C., Feng, C., Xie, X., Shi, B., Lu, H., Lv, Y., Niu, Z., Multi-sensor fusion and cooperative perception for autonomous driving: A review. *IEEE Intell. Transp. Syst. Mag.*, *15*, 5, 36–58, 2023.
9. Wang, Z., Wu, Y., Niu, Q., Multi-sensor fusion in automated driving: A survey. *IEEE Access*, 8, 2847–2868, 2020. https://doi.org/10.1109/ACCESS.2019.2962554.
10. Butt, F.A., Chattha, J.N., Ahmad, J., Zia, M.U., Rizwan, M., Naqvi, I.H., On the integration of enabling wireless technologies and sensor fusion for next-generation connected and autonomous vehicles. *IEEE Access*, *10*, 14643–14668, 2022. https://doi.org/10.1109/ACCESS.2022.3145972.
11. Sumalatha, I., Chaturvedi, P., R, G.R., Patil, S., Thethi, H.P., Hameed, A.A., Autonomous multi-sensor fusion techniques for environmental perception in self-driving vehicles, in: *2024 International Conference on Communication, Computer Sciences and Engineering (IC3SE)*, Gautam Buddha Nagar, India, pp. 1146–1151, 2024, https://doi.org/10.1109/IC3SE62002.2024.10593125.
12. Zheng, X., Li, Y., Duan, D., Yang, L., Chen, C., Cheng, X., Multivehicle multisensor occupancy grid maps (MVMS-OGM) for autonomous driving. *IEEE Internet Things J.*, *9*, 22, 22944–22957, 2022. https://doi.org/10.1109/JIOT.2022.3187827.
13. Khan, D., Aslam, S., Chang, K., Vehicle-to-Infrastructure multi-sensor fusion (V2I-MSF) with reinforcement learning framework for enhancing autonomous vehicle perception. *IEEE Access*, 2025. https://doi.org/10.1109/ACCESS.2025.3551367.
14. Kanthavel, D., Sangeetha, S.K.B., Keerthana, K.P., An empirical study of vehicle to infrastructure communications-an intense learning of smart infrastructure for safety and mobility. *Int. J. Intell. Networks*, *2*, 77–82, 2021.
15. Yeong, D.J., Velasco-Hernandez, G., Barry, J., Walsh, J., Sensor and sensor fusion technology in autonomous vehicles: A review. *Sensors*, *21*, 6, 2140, 2021.
16. Mahendran, R.K. and Thiyagarajan, A., Multi-modal visual features perception technology for Internet of Vehicles (IoV), in: *2024 International Conference on Emerging Smart Computing and Informatics (ESCI)*, IEEE, pp. 1–5, 2024.
17. Cui, G., Zhang, W., Xiao, Y., Yao, L., Fang, Z., Cooperative perception technology of autonomous driving in the Internet of Vehicles environment: A review. *Sensors*, *22*, 15, 5535, 2022.
18. Biswas, A. and Wang, H.C., Autonomous vehicles enabled by the integration of IoT, edge intelligence, 5G, and blockchain. *Sensors*, *23*, 4, 1963, 2023.

19. Gupta, K., Singhal, A., Kumar, A., Maji, P., Enhancing sensor perception: Integrating multi-sensor data for robust sensor perception, in: *2025 17th International Conference on Communication Systems and Networks (COMSNETS)*, IEEE, pp. 78–83, 2025.
20. Tao, X., Zhu, B., Xuan, S., Zhao, J., Jiang, H., Du, J., Deng, W., A multi-sensor fusion positioning strategy for intelligent vehicles using global pose graph optimization. *IEEE Trans. Veh. Technol.*, *71*, 3, 2614–2627, 2021.
21. Obst, M., Hobert, L., Reisdorf, P., Multi-sensor data fusion for checking plausibility of V2V communications by vision-based multiple-object tracking, in: *2014 IEEE Vehicular Networking Conference (VNC)*, IEEE, pp. 143–150, 2014.
22. Lian, H., Pei, X., Guo, X., A local environment model based on multi-sensor perception for intelligent vehicles. *IEEE Sens. J.*, *21*, 14, 15427–15436, 2020.

10

Dynamically Reconfigurable Multisensor Fusion for Enhanced Object Detection in Autonomous Vehicles

V. Muthukumaran[1*], M. Sathish Kumar[2], G. Kumaran[3], Vidya K.B.[4] and Ahmad Alkhayyat[5]

[1]*Department of Mathematics, College of Engineering and Technology, SRM Institute of Science and Technology, Kattankulathur, India*
[2]*Department of Basic Science and Humanities, School of Engineering and Technology, CMR University, Karnataka, India*
[3]*Department of Mathematics, School of Science and Computer Studies, CMR University, Karnataka, India*
[4]*Department of Mathematics, Government Science College, Chitradurga, Karnataka, India*
[5]*Department of Computers Techniques Engineering, College of Technical Engineering, The Islamic University, Najaf, Iraq*

Abstract

To enable self-driving vehicles to properly identify and detect objects when driving under changing conditions, adaptive multisensor fusion is required. Traditional fusion techniques are based on high computational complexity, fixed weights for sensors, and susceptibility to sensor failure. To improve object detection and recognition with multisensor fusion, this study proposes a dynamically reconfigurable multisensor fusion framework (DRMF) that integrates LiDAR, radar, RGB cameras, thermal cameras, and vehicle-to-everything communication data. The self-adjusting sensor contribution module of the system adjusts sensors in real time as a function of evolving environment, traffic, and sensor credibility. A multilevel cross-sensor fusion network also imposes hierarchical spatial–temporal constraints on the majority of sensor modalities to learn optimal features. Argoverse 2 and Pandaset datasets, providing various real-world urban driving conditions with multimodal sensor inputs, are used for system evaluation.

**Corresponding author*: muthu.v2404@gmail.com

Balamurugan Balusamy, Sandeep Kumar Mathivanan, Prabhu Jayagopal, S.K.B. Sangeetha and Ali Kashif Bashir (eds.) Autonomous Systems in the Internet of Vehicles, (167–186) © 2026 Scrivener Publishing LLC

In experimental results, DRMF outperforms current fusion-based methods with object detection accuracy at 98.6%. Additionally, it has a low false detection rate of 1.0% while improving object recognition recall (97.5%) and precision (98.1%). In addition, the system assists in real-time decision-making toward swift autonomous mobility by executing low processing latency at 5.0 milliseconds per frame. The results substantiate DRMF's performance of improving autonomous vehicle perception's detection accuracy, robustness, and efficiency.

Keywords: Multisensor fusion, autonomous vehicles, LiDAR, radar, thermal cameras, V2X communication, object detection, real-time decision-making

10.1 Introduction

Using artificial intelligence, machine learning, and sensor-based vision to drive on roadways with minimal human involvement, autonomous vehicles (AVs) are revolutionizing contemporary transportation. Object detection and recognition are an important part of autonomous driving, enabling AVs to identify and track cars, bicycles, pedestrians, traffic lights, and other road objects in real time. Safe navigation, collision avoidance, and compliance with traffic laws all depend on successful object detection. It is still extremely challenging to obtain strong object detection under different environmental conditions, including various illuminations, weathers, and traffic conditions. To perceive the environment, AVs use a suite of sensors, including GPS, LiDAR, radar, and cameras. Because of the unique advantages and disadvantages of each sensor, multisensor fusion algorithms are needed to obtain higher detection accuracy and robustness.

Several approaches have emerged for AV object detection with no involvement of humans, which come in broad categories of image-based, LiDAR-based, radar-based, and hybrid. Image-based object detection makes use of RGB cameras and deep models to recognize objects on the basis of visual features. Faster R-CNN (region-based convolutional neural network), YOLO (You Only Look Once), and SSD (single-shot multibox detector) are commonly applied to image-based object detection. They work exceptionally well at sensing the texture, color, and shape of objects and so are effective for sensing vehicles, pedestrians, and signs. Their real-world driving reliability is constrained by their low light, poor weather, and occlusion performance. With the aid of laser pulses to deliver accurate depth information, LiDAR-based object detection avoids some of these problems. PointNet, VoxelNet, and PointPillars are some point cloud-based models that inspect 3D spatial information to identify objects with high accuracy.

LiDAR performs well in object localization and distance estimation, it suffers from constraints including extreme cost, susceptibility to weather, and presenting data as sparse, which degrades the capability to identify fine-grained objects. Again, it contains an extra layer of strength courtesy of radar object detection based on radar that detects objects and notes their speed through radio waves. Radar can be efficiently used under poor weather such as rain, snow, and fog compared to LiDAR and cameras. It is particularly worth it in observing the rate at which moving objects are progressing and in picking up objects. The radar's low spatial resolution causes it to have difficulty distinguishing between objects that are close to one another. Kalman filters and traditional tracking algorithms are used in standard radar-based detection methods, whereas more recent advances use deep learning models in efforts to improve classification accuracy.

Radar needs to be fused with other sensor modalities to generate high-accuracy object detection, even though it has its strengths. Hybrid object detection techniques use more than one sensor to move beyond the limitations of a single modality. There are three types of multisensor fusion: early, midlevel, and late fusion. Midlevel fusion is feature-based from multiple sensors, late fusion is independent object detection outcome-based to produce end predictions, and early fusion is raw sensor input combined before feature extraction. There are pros and cons to each fusion method; early fusion provides better feature representations, whereas late fusion provides greater adaptability with sensor failure. There are various major challenges despite the progress in object detection methods.

Computational complexity of deep learning–based object detection models is a major challenge, particularly handling radar data, LiDAR point clouds, and high-definition images in real time. AVs need low-latency perception systems that are capable of making life-or-death choices but are hard to deploy in real time because most models have extremely high computational requirements. Static sensor weighting that does not dynamically adapt in real time to varying environments is typically used in traditional multisensor fusion methods. For instance, data from LiDAR may be assigned highest priority even when visibility renders it unreliable, which reduces overall detection accuracy. Sensor malfunctions and occlusions are additional challenges.

Reduced perception reliability is due to conventional fusion systems failing to consider critical sensor faults or external cause obstacles. This is particularly difficult in busy city centers with heavy traffic, occlusions from other vehicles, and erratic pedestrians. Additionally, most of the object detection models carry out sensor data independently without reliance on situational awareness of context or time correlation and would therefore make incorrect predictions in real time dynamically changing driving conditions. An imperative for a cost-effective and flexible multisensor fusion mechanism with the ability to learn real-time adaptation to continuously changing environmental contexts without any attendant loss of efficiency comes up to avoid these limitations. The need for stronger, more reliable, and less computationally demanding perception systems propels the effort to improve object detection and recognition for AVs.

AVs can satisfy higher safety standards and better decision-making abilities by combining information from multiple sensor modalities while maintaining low processing latency and sensor dependence. Enhancing better fusion architectures, low-latency inference-optimized deep learning models, and novel sensor technologies for enhancing perception accuracy are some of the future research areas. For future safer and more efficient transport systems, object detection and recognition advancements will play a crucial role in further advancing autonomous driving technology.

The main objectives is to design and develop a dynamically reconfigurable multisensor fusion framework (DRMF) for object detection and recognition in AVs, ensuring real-time perception, adaptive sensor weighting, enhanced feature learning, robustness against sensor failures, and improved detection accuracy in diverse driving conditions.

10.2 Related Study

For the optimization of environmental perception and decision-making, new advancements in autonomous perception systems have highlighted multisensor fusion, dynamic reconfiguration, and fault-tolerant strategies. For enhancing object detection and tracking, sensor fusion systems using LiDAR, cameras, radar, and UAV-based surveillance have been explored by some studies for accurate perception. For enhancing surveillance and object tracking, dynamic network reconfiguration research in camera systems has also been conducted. Modular and flexible frameworks for self-driving vehicles have been enabled by open-source platforms such as AVStack. In addition, new methods in fault-tolerant perception, reidentification, and track initiation enhanced resilience to sensor failure, enabling reliable real-time operation. These advances provide a solid foundation for constructing advanced perception systems with the ability to handle dynamic environments and complex traffic situations.

For better detection of 3D objects for autonomous driving, multisensor fusion has been explored extensively. The sensor fusion techniques have been analyzed in depth in Reference [1], which further discusses deep learning-based techniques and challenges in sensor fusion of LiDAR, radar, and camera data. Reference [2] refers to improving the classification accuracy using a multimodal fusion object recognition system based on the integration of multiple sensors for improved perception by the vehicle. Reference [3] suggests an adaptive real-time hybrid multisensor fusion architecture that modulates sensor input adaptively in response to ambient conditions and targets stable perception for AVs. Reference [4] depicts real-time sensor adaptation toward efficient decision-making through an exploration of adaptive transformation processes for multisensor fusion in reconfigurable robots.

The methodology is used to sweep robots for pavement in another research study [5], demonstrating adaptively transformation is effective for sensor data matching. Reference [6] is included in recent developments in smart transportation systems in a recent overview of environmental perception technologies on the basis of multisensor fusion. CARMA, context-aware runtime reconfiguration for improving sensor fusion quality and reducing power consumption for embedded systems, is presented in Reference [7]. Reference [8] proposes FusionTalk, an Internet of Things-enabled object identification system that enhances detection performance in different conditions using the exploitation of reconfigurable sensor fusion. Reference [9] proposes novel fusion topologies and investigates virtual sensor design techniques to enhance the accuracy of multisensor data in autonomous systems. Reference [10] demonstrates how adaptive vision networks can enhance object detection in autonomous environments by introducing a distributed network of self-reconfigurable active vision systems.

Reference [11] emphasizes perception algorithm advancements for intelligent transportation systems by introducing on-road object recognition and tracking techniques that leverage radar and vision fusion. For enhancing 3D object detection in AVs, Reference [12] introduces O^2SAT, an object-oriented segmentation-guided spatial-attention network that demonstrates enhanced accuracy with sophisticated segmentation. Reference [13] examines task-oriented RGB-LiDAR fusion for object tracking in resource-constrained autonomous systems and proposes a model that optimizes sensor utilization for enhanced tracking efficiency. Reference [14] examines the latest AI-based image processing techniques applied in AVs, comparing various deep learning models for object detection efficiency and accuracy. Reference [15] studies on multisensor fusion and challenges and opportunities emerging and provides an overview of simultaneous localization and mapping with data fusion in unmanned aerial systems.

Reference [16] introduces Geryon, an end-to-end real-time object detection system that enhances drone perception strength by integrating cameras and mmWave radar assisted at the edge. Reference [17] addresses enhancement in adaptability and stability in addressing decision-level fusion techniques for object recognition and detection in AV systems. Reference [18] illustrates how the computer vision approach is beneficial to real-time perception in reconfigurable systems by using a case study on dynamic reconfiguration to reconfigurable systems in mobile robotics. Reference [19] exemplifies the benefits of hardware flexibility in harsh environments using FPGA-based reconfigurable platform architecture for underwater image processing, object detection, and pipeline tracking. Reference [20] highlights the need for real-time fusion techniques to enhance vehicle situational awareness and proposes an effective world modeling strategy based on multisensor data fusion techniques to enhance perception in autonomous driving.

Camera network dynamic reconfiguration is described in Reference [21] with focus on adaptive approaches toward achieving optimization of monitoring and surveillance in real-time systems. It presents main ways of network structure and camera setup adaptation for better object tracking and scene understanding. Reference [22] emphasizes combining visual perception and environment mapping algorithms for better autonomous decision-making as it addresses remote big data management platforms and sensor technologies in the Internet of Robotic Things. Reference [23] describes UAV-based LiDAR integration and fusion techniques for advanced traffic monitoring, demonstrating how aerial monitoring can be used to enhance road user detection and traffic flow analysis. Reference [24] presents AVStack, an open-source reconfigurable AV development platform with hardware and software modules for real-time sensing, control, and decision-making for autonomous systems.

Reference [25] presents a robust information fusion framework to enhance object association accuracy for dynamic scenarios, emphasizing track initiation and reidentification for 3D multiview multiobject tracking. Reference [26] uses local sensor fusion to introduce a fault-tolerant perception approach for AVs, demonstrating how to enhance robustness to sensor malfunction at the cost of sacrificing reliable environmental perception. Even though multisensor fusion and object recognition in AVs have progressed extensively, there remain several challenges with existing research. There are numerous approaches that have sensor dependency, which degrades performance by virtue of unfavorable weather or sensor failure.

For active traffic situations, incorrect decision-making is caused by the lack of adaptive weighting processes in fusion systems. In addition, computation overhead prevents scalability in software for deployment in high-speed environments, thus making real-time processing challenging. Perception and tracking inefficiencies result from current reconfigurable architectures' tendency to overlook changing environmental conditions. Moreover, fault-tolerant sensor fusion techniques are in their infancy stages, lowering system reliability upon partial sensor failure. These shortcomings highlight the requirement for an adaptive and fault-tolerant fusion system that achieves maximum computational efficiency and enhances real-time perception accuracy and sensor contribution scales adaptively. For providing flexible, efficient, and robust object detection in autonomous driving scenarios, this proposed study presents a multilevel cross-sensor fusion network (ML-CSFN) and a self-adjusting sensor contribution module (SASCM).

10.3 System Methodology

To enhance object recognition and identification for self-driving vehicles, the DRMF integrates a variety of sensor modalities including LiDAR, radar, RGB cameras, thermal cameras, and vehicle-to-everything (V2X) communication. Data acquisition, preprocessing, sensor contribution adjustment, feature extraction, fusion, and decision-making are all components of the systematic approach in the methodology.

10.3.1 Data Acquisition and Preprocessing

Argoverse 2 and Pandaset data, providing an assortment of city driving scenarios with multimodal sensor inputs, are utilized to input data into the DRMF, where different modalities of sensors are fused. To gain a better perception of the surroundings, the system collects raw sensor data from LiDAR point clouds, radar signals, RGB and thermal images, GPS, and V2X communication. Specifically, Argoverse 2 provides 1000 urban driving data sequences with more than 3 million labeled 3D bounding boxes. A scene is presented in the high-resolution RGB images (1920 × 1200), accurate GPS and IMU measurements, and 1000-point LiDAR scans per frame. The Pandaset of 8500 labeled frames contains about 250,000 named objects in numerous categories such as bicycles, cars, and pedestrians. In addition, GPS information, RGB images (1280 × 720 pixels), thermal, 12 radar sensors, and 360-degree LiDAR scans with more than 100,000 points per frame are incorporated. For additional enhancement in situation awareness for autonomous driving, V2X communication information is also associated with model interactions with vehicles and infrastructure (V2I and V2V).

Raw sensor readings are fed to a series of preprocessing operations for accurate and trustworthy sensor fusion. Kalman filtering, delivering temporal consistency between various sensor data inputs, is applied first for synchronization and alignment. Extrinsic matrix calibration and homography transformation are applied to transform sensor data from multiple sensors into a common coordinate space, and point cloud and image spatial alignment is achievable. The data are then purified by filtering and noise elimination algorithms. Voxel grid filtering is applied to ensure uniform point distribution for LiDAR point clouds to reduce processing time while not compromising the integrity of objects. Denoising RGB and thermal imagery and maintaining useful edge information are achieved through bilateral filtering so that object feature is not lost. Constant false alarm rate processing is applied to radar data, which effectively separates objects by unwinding background noise from clutter.

Normalization and feature extraction are applied to facilitate easier sensor fusion to be done once filtering is accomplished. To contribute to geometric representation enhancement, intensity, reflectivity, depth, and surface normal LiDAR information are obtained. To further enable motion estimation, Doppler velocity, range, and azimuth angle radar information supply, RGB and thermal image information is retrieved through a pre-trained ResNet-50 model to further advance object detection through deep feature representation. All recovered features are min–max scaling–normalized, normalizing input distributions, for modality interoperability ensuring. To facilitate efficient sensor fusion and real-time object detection in difficult driving conditions, our preprocessing pipeline ensures multi-sensor data are synchronized, calibrated, and clean.

10.3.2 Proposed Algorithms

With the addition of deep learning techniques, dynamic weight schemes, and real-time adaptation, the developed algorithms increase autonomous driving perception, sensor fusion, object detection, and decision-making. To optimize use of data, the SASCM adjusts weights to sensors based on reliability and local conditions. With LiDAR, radar, and camera inputs integrated, the ML-CSFN uses spatial and temporal feature fusion for improving object detection accuracy. Using CNNs, transformers, the real-time object detection and recognition module detects and classifies objects precisely, continually improving detection through confidence-based fine-tuning. Lastly, the decision-making and control system performs the best navigational actions, such as emergency braking and course recalculation, after detecting objects and estimating collision risk.

Algorithm 10.1: Self-adjusting sensor contribution module
This module dynamically adjusts the contribution of each sensor based on real-time environmental factors, ensuring robustness.

1. Initialize sensor parameters.
   Define the set of sensors $S = \{\text{LiDAR, Radar, RGB, Thermal, GPS, V2X}\}$.
   Assign initial weight $w_s = \frac{1}{|S|}$ for each sensor s.
2. Collect sensor reliability metrics.
   Compute accuracy score A_s from historical data.
   Compute robustness score R_s based on occlusions, noise, and signal strength.
   Compute temporal consistency score T_s using past readings.
3. Compute the Sensor Credibility Score:

$$C_s = \alpha \cdot A_s + \beta \cdot R_s + \gamma \cdot T_s$$

   where α, β, γ are predefined weight coefficients.
4. Normalize the scores:

$$C_s' = \frac{C_s}{\sum_{i \in S}^{\square} \square C_i}$$

5. Adjust sensor weights dynamically:

$$w_s = \max(\min(C_s', w_{\max}), w_{\min})$$

   where $w_{\max}$ and $w_{\min}$ set upper and lower limits.
6. Update fusion model parameters.
   Reconfigure the sensor fusion framework with new weights.
   Prioritize higher-weighted sensors in feature extraction.
7. Repeat Steps 2 to 6 periodically for real-time adaptation.

Algorithm 10.2: Multilevel cross-sensor fusion network
This algorithm extracts and fuses multimodal sensor data while preserving spatial and temporal dependencies.

1. Extract low-level sensor features.
   Obtain feature maps from each sensor using pretrained encoders:

$$X_s = F_s(I_s), \forall s \in S$$

   LiDAR features: $X_L = \text{PointNet}++(I_L)$
   Radar features: $X_R = \text{CNN}(I_R)$
   Camera features: $X_C = \text{ResNet}(I_C)$
2. Align features spatially.
   Apply homography transformation to align LiDAR and radar data with camera images $X_s' = H_s \cdot X_s$.
3. Fuse temporal information using LSTM.
   Update the hidden state over multiple time steps:

$$h_t = \sigma(W_h h_{t-1} + W_x X_s' + b_h)$$

4. Perform cross-modal attention fusion.
   Compute attention weights:

$$A_s = \text{softmax}(W_a X_s')$$

   Generate the fused feature representation:

$$X_f = \sum_{s \in S}^{\square} \square A_s X_s'$$

5. Normalize fused features using batch normalization.
6. Output fused representation for object detection.

Algorithm 10.3: Real-time object detection and recognition
This algorithm detects objects from fused sensor data using deep learning models.

1. Input the fused feature map X_f into a feature extractor.

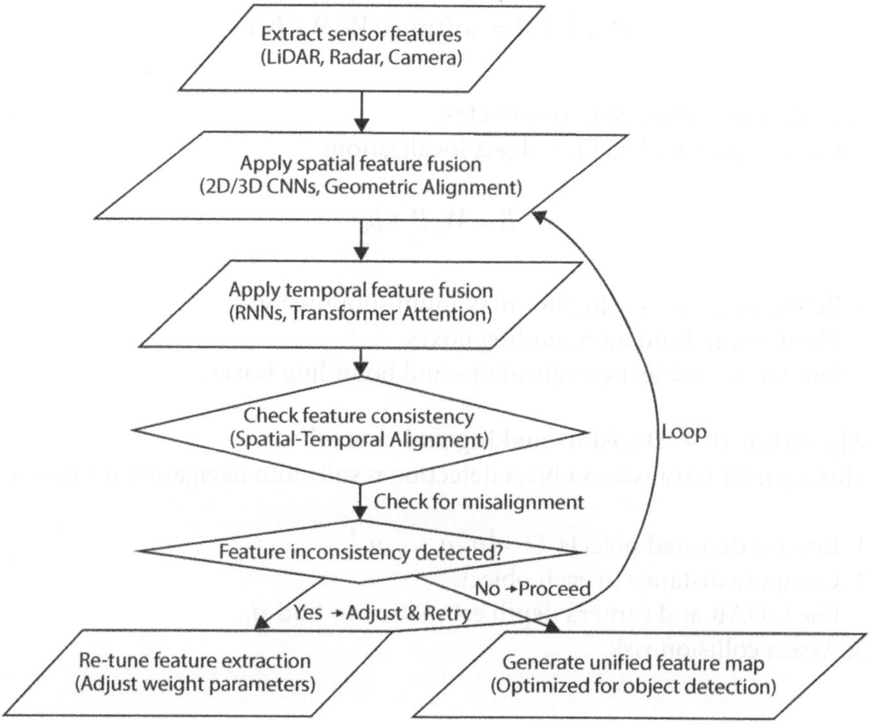

Figure 10.1 Proposed multilevel cross-sensor fusion network (ML-CSFN) process.

Use a convolutional neural network (CNN) backbone:

$$F_m = \text{CNN}(X_f)$$

2. Apply multiscale feature pyramid fusion.
   Extract different scales of feature maps:

$$P_i = W_i \cdot F_m + B_i, i = 1,2,3$$

3. Generate region proposals for object detection.
   Use a region proposal network (RPN) to suggest bounding boxes:

$$R = \text{RPN}(P)$$

4. Classify objects using a transformer-based classifier.
   Compute object class probabilities:

$$P(y \mid X_f) = \text{softmax}(W_o P + b_o)$$

5. Predict bounding box coordinates.
   Use a regression head for object localization:

$$B = W_b P + b_b$$

6. Refine detections using nonmaximum suppression.
   Eliminate redundant bounding boxes.
7. Output final object classifications and bounding boxes.

Algorithm 10.4: Decision-making and control
This algorithm translates object detection results into navigation decisions.

1. Receive detected objects $O = \{o_1, o_2, \ldots, o_n\}$.
2. Compute distance to each object.
   Use LiDAR and camera depth estimation to find d_i.
3. Assess collision risk.

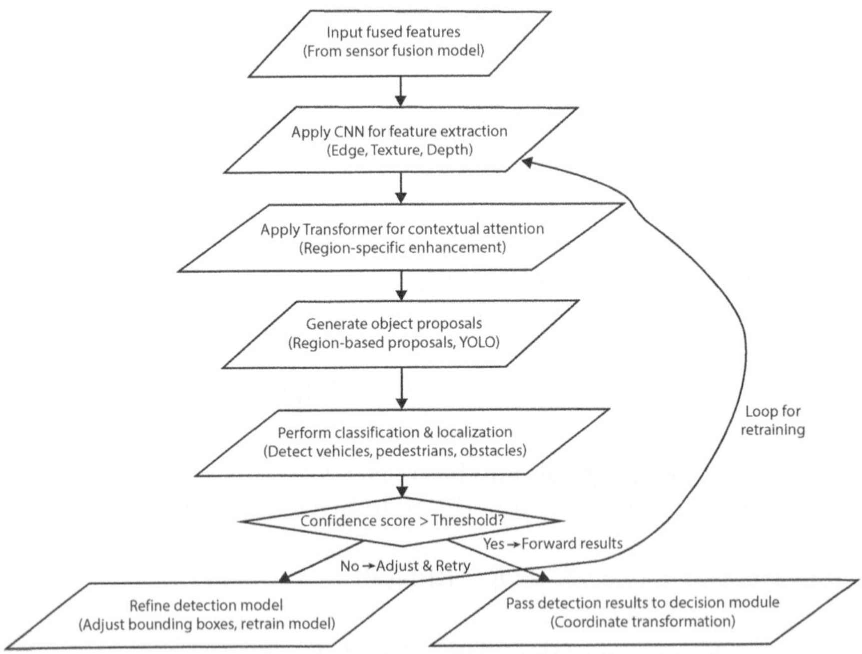

Figure 10.2 Proposed object detection and recognition process.

Compute risk score for each object:

$$c_i = \frac{1}{1+e^{-\lambda(d_i - d_{\text{safe}})}}$$

If $c_i > c_{\text{threshold}}$, mark object as hazardous.

4. Select optimal action using a cost function:

$$J = \sum_{i=1}^{N} \square(\lambda_1 d_i + \lambda_2 c_i + \lambda_3 v_i)$$

$\lambda_1, \lambda_2, \lambda_3$ balance safety and efficiency.

5. Use reinforcement learning (RL) for action selection.

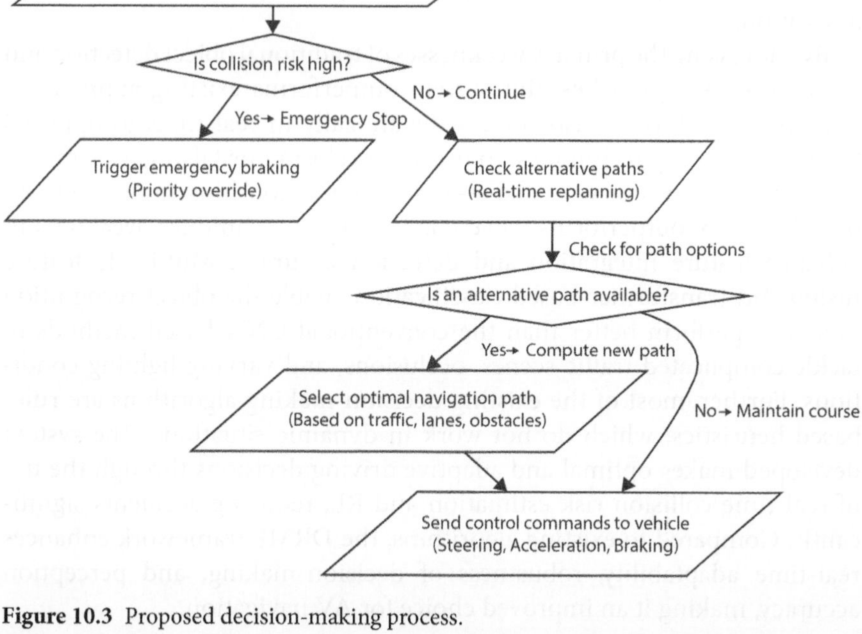

Figure 10.3 Proposed decision-making process.

Compute Q values for all possible actions:

$$u : Q(s,u) = r + \gamma \max_{a'} Q(s',a')$$

Select the action with the highest Q value.

6. Update vehicle trajectory.
   Adjust speed, acceleration, and steering angle.
7. Execute navigation commands.
8. Repeat Steps 2 to 7 continuously for real-time decision-making.

ML-CSFN (Figure 10.1), SASCM, real-time object detection and recognition (Figure 10.2), and advanced decision-making and control (Figure 10.3) are encompassed within the suggested DRMF. The SASCM with dynamic adjustment of sensor priority according to environmental parameters guarantees robustness in poor weather or when sensors fail. ML-CSFN uses cross-modal attention and spatial–temporal constraints to extract and combine multimodal features from LiDAR, radar, RGB, and thermal cameras with key information preserving accuracy for precise perception. The object detection module in deep learning–based utilizes CNNs and transformers to detect and classify objects accurately and efficiently. Lastly, the decision-making system utilizes risk-aware cost functions and RL to optimize efficiency and safety for safe and versatile vehicle navigation.

By addressing the primary weaknesses of traditional object detection and sensor fusion approaches, this system outperforms existing approaches. The SASCM adjusts sensor inputs dynamically in real time, as opposed to fixed weighting techniques, to prevent occlusion or false sensor misinterpretation. By preserving spatial–temporal relationships among sensors, the ML-CSFN outperforms naive concatenation techniques' weakness to enhance feature integration and detection accuracy. Multiscale feature fusion and transformer-based classification enable the object recognition model to perform better than the conventional CNN-based methods to tackle complicated traffic scenes, occlusions, and varying lighting conditions. Further, most of the existing decision-making algorithms are rule-based heuristics, which do not work in dynamic situations. The system developed makes optimal and adaptive driving decisions through the use of real-time collision risk estimation and RL, reducing accidents significantly. Compared to existing algorithms, the DRMF framework enhances real-time adaptability, robustness of decision-making, and perception accuracy, making it an improved choice for AV navigation.

10.4 Experimentation Results

We compare the proposed DRMF to current object detection algorithms using fusion-based techniques currently implemented, i.e., PointFusion, MV3D, AVOD, and PointPillars, with the objective of finding the feasibility of utilizing the latter. These methods combine LiDAR, radar, and camera data into one or more heterogeneous methods, although most base themselves on predetermined sensor weighting, which comes at a high cost of processing or fails to embrace diversity when situations call for it. Our approach applies hierarchical spatiotemporal feature fusion and dynamic sensor contribution to solve such limitations.

Python, TensorFlow, and PyTorch are used in the system implementation, and deep learning models were trained on the Argoverse 2 and Pandaset datasets. Sensor calibration, outlier rejection, and spatial–temporal synchronization are involved in data preparation for synchronizing multimodal inputs. Feature extraction uses an LSTM-based module for temporal analysis, ResNet-50 for image-based features, and PointNet++ for LiDAR. Training is done with a learning rate of 0.0001, batch size of 32, and 50 epochs with the Adam optimizer. Data augmentation techniques such as random cropping, flipping, and noise addition are used for improved generalization. Inference on an NVIDIA RTX 4090 GPU took 5.0 milliseconds per frame due to TensorRT's low-latency run optimization. As far as accuracy, recall, precision, delay in processing, and resilience against sensor failure in identifying objects are concerned, the provided method is better than the current state-of-the-art methods.

Table 10.1 Performance comparison of object detection models.

Method	**Object detection accuracy (%)**	**False detection rate (%)**	**Precision (%)**	**Recall (%)**	**Processing latency (ms)**
DRMF (ours)	98.6	1.0	98.1	97.5	5.0
PointFusion	94.5	3.2	93.6	92.1	13.4
MV3D	96.2	2.7	95.8	94.5	17.6
AVOD	97.1	2.1	96.2	95.3	15.2
PointPillars	96.8	1.9	95.9	95.0	12.8

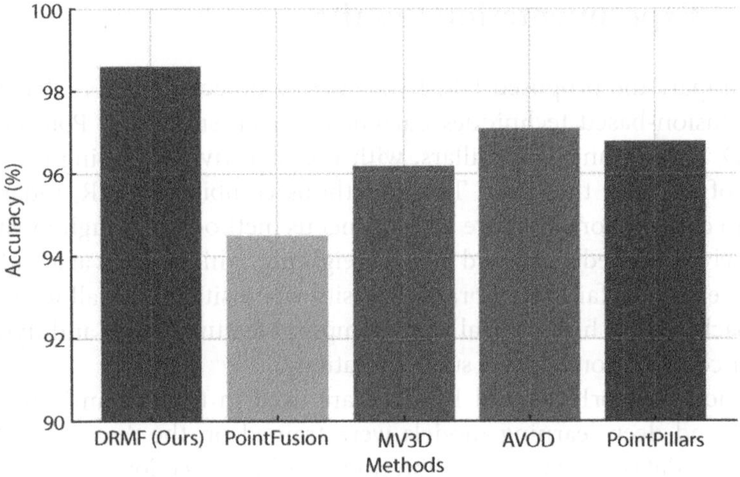

Figure 10.4 Object detection accuracy comparison.

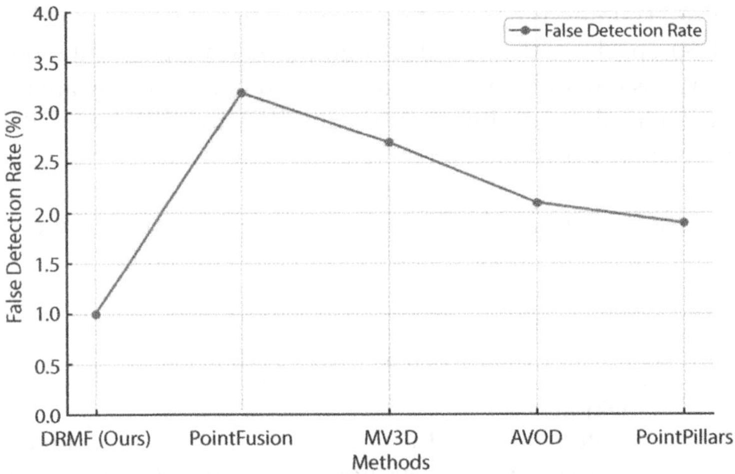

Figure 10.5 False detection rate comparison.

From Table 10.1, the experimental results demonstrate that DRMF achieves the highest object detection accuracy (98.6%) while maintaining a significantly lower false detection rate (1.0%). Additionally, the system achieves real-time execution with a latency of 5.0 milliseconds, significantly outperforming existing methods in terms of efficiency. From Figures 10.4 to 10.6, the experiments provide evidence of the benefit of DRMF.

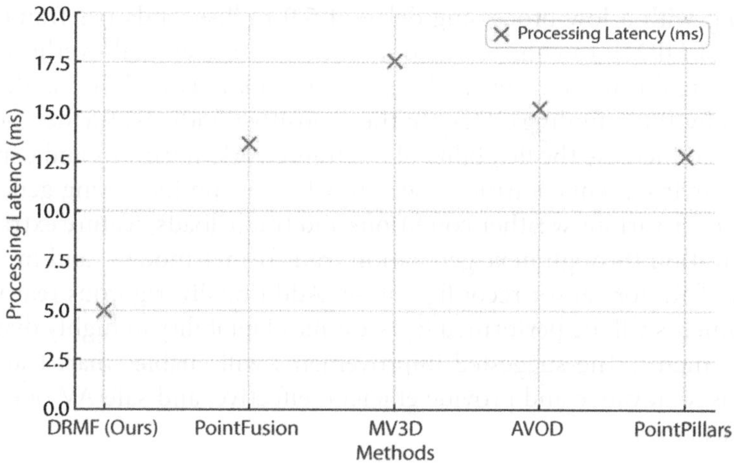

Figure 10.6 Processing latency comparison.

The improved effect on the detection performance can be witnessed by looking at the object detection accuracy plot. The exploration into how fast false detections are removed shows that DRMF removes more false detections and maintains a better level of precision. Its real-time efficiency, which is essential to those applications where there is autonomous driving, is explored *via* the latency comparison. These results indicate that DRMF is a resilient and scalable next-generation AV system solution because it provides increased perception, adaptive fusion, and effective decision-making. Future work will expand on its generality and versatility by investigating how it can be integrated with varied traffic scenarios and real-world deployment.

10.5 Conclusion

To enhance object recognition and identification for AVs, a new DRMF is introduced in this study. By combining LiDAR, radar, RGB and infrared cameras, GPS, and V2X communication, the system adopts the ML-CSFN to optimize multimodal data fusion and the SASCM to switch the priority of sensors adaptively. With an object detection accuracy of 98.6%, its improved recall rate of 97.5%, and accuracy of 98.1%, experimental tests on the Argoverse 2 and Pandaset datasets indicate that DRMF surpasses existing methods. Additionally, the system surpasses PointFusion, MV3D, AVOD, and PointPillars by recording a low false detection rate of 1.0% and running with a low processing delay of 5.0 milliseconds per frame. The ability of DRMF to enhance vision, reduce computational overhead, and support real-time decision-making for autonomous mobility is demonstrated by these findings. Despite these positive findings, further work is needed to increase the flexibility of the framework in various and complex urban environments. Further research will focus on increasing generalizability over various weather conditions and traffic loads, feature extraction optimization through next-generation transformer models, and incorporation of RL for sensor reconfiguration. Additionally, rigorous real-world experiments will be performed to assess its adaptability in highly dynamic environments. The suggested improvements will enable smart transport systems to advance and provide efficient, effective, and safe AV operation in smart cities.

AI disclosure statement: The author acknowledges the use of AI-based tools for minor language editing or grammatical correction. However, all intellectual contributions, analyses, and conclusions presented in this chapter are entirely the author's own.

References

1. Wang, X., Li, K., Chehri, A., Multi-sensor fusion technology for 3D object detection in autonomous driving: A review. *IEEE Trans. Intell. Transp. Syst., 25*, 2, 1148–1165, 2023.
2. Person, M., Jensen, M., Smith, A.O., Gutierrez, H., Multimodal fusion object detection system for autonomous vehicles. *J. Dyn. Syst. Meas. Contr., 141*, 7, 071017, 2019.
3. Shahian Jahromi, B., Tulabandhula, T., Cetin, S., Real-time hybrid multi-sensor fusion framework for perception in autonomous vehicles. *Sensors, 19*, 20, 4357, 2019.
4. Povendhan, A.P., Hayat, A.A., Yi, L., Hoong, J.C.C., Elara, M.R., Multisensor fusion in reconfigurable robots using adaptive transformation, in: *2021 International Conference Nonlinearity, Information and Robotics (NIR)*, IEEE, pp. 1–6, 2021.
5. Povendhan, A.P., Yi, L., Hayat, A.A., Le, A.V., Kai, K.L.J., Ramalingam, B., Elara, M.R., Multi-sensor fusion incorporating adaptive transformation for reconfigurable pavement sweeping robot, in: *2021 IEEE/RSJ International Conference on Intelligent Robots and Systems (IROS)*, IEEE, pp. 300–306, 2021.

6. Yang, B., Li, J., Zeng, T., A Review of Environmental Perception Technology Based on Multi-Sensor Information Fusion in Autonomous Driving. *World Electr. Veh. J.*, *16*, 1, 20, 2025.
7. Zhang, Y., Malawade, A.V., Zhang, X., Li, Y., Seong, D., Al Faruque, M.A., Huang, S., CARMA: Context-aware runtime reconfiguration for energy-efficient sensor fusion, in: *2023 IEEE/ACM International Symposium on Low Power Electronics and Design (ISLPED)*, IEEE, pp. 1–6, 2023.
8. Zhang, L.Y., Lin, H.C., Wu, K.R., Lin, Y.B., Tseng, Y.C., FusionTalk: An IoT-based reconfigurable object identification system. *IEEE Internet Things J.*, *8*, 9, 7333–7345, 2020.
9. Sahoo, S., Sensor Fusion and Virtual Sensor Design for Enhanced Multi-Sensor Data Accuracy in Autonomous Systems. *Int. J. Smart Sustainable Intell. Comput.*, *1*, 2, 21–39, 2024.
10. Shashank, and Sreedevi, I., Distributed network of adaptive and self-reconfigurable active vision systems. *Symmetry*, *14*, 11, 2281, 2022.
11. Tang, X., Zhang, Z., Qin, Y., On-road object detection and tracking based on radar and vision fusion: A review. *IEEE Intell. Transp. Syst. Mag.*, *14*, 5, 103–128, 2021.
12. Mushtaq, H., Deng, X., Ullah, I., Ali, M., Malik, B.H., O 2SAT: Object-Oriented-Segmentation-Guided Spatial-Attention Network for 3D Object Detection in Autonomous Vehicles. *Information*, *15*, 7, 376, 2024.
13. Samal, K., Kumawat, H., Saha, P., Wolf, M., Mukhopadhyay, S., Task-driven rgb-lidar fusion for object tracking in resource-efficient autonomous system. *IEEE Trans. Intell. Veh.*, *7*, 1, 102–112, 2021.
14. Kozłowski, M., Racewicz, S., Wierzbicki, S., Image Analysis in Autonomous Vehicles: A Review of the Latest AI Solutions and Their Comparison. *Appl. Sci.*, *14*, 18, 8150, 2024.
15. Gupta, A. and Fernando, X., Simultaneous localization and mapping (slam) and data fusion in unmanned aerial vehicles: Recent advances and challenges. *Drones*, *6*, 4, 85, 2022.
16. Deng, K., Zhao, D., Han, Q., Wang, S., Zhang, Z., Zhou, A., Ma, H., Geryon: Edge assisted real-time and robust object detection on drones *via* mmWave radar and camera fusion. *Proc. ACM Interact. Mobile Wearable Ubiquitous Technol.*, *6*, 3, 1–27, 2022.
17. Oh, S.I. and Kang, H.B., Object detection and classification by decision-level fusion for intelligent vehicle systems. *Sensors*, *17*, 1, 207, 2017.
18. Nava, F., Sciuto, D., Santambrogio, M.D., Herbrechtsmeier, S., Porrmann, M., Witkowski, U., Rueckert, U., Applying dynamic reconfiguration in the mobile robotics domain: A case study on computer vision algorithms. *ACM Trans. Reconfigurable Technol. Syst. (TRETS)*, *4*, 3, 1–22, 2011.
19. Alex Raj, S.M. and Supriya, M.H., *Reconfigurable Platform Based Design in FPGA for Underwater Image Enhancement, Object Detection and Pipeline Tracking*, Doctoral dissertation, Cochin University of Science and Technology, 2017.

20. Elfring, J., Appeldoorn, R., Van den Dries, S., Kwakkernaat, M., Effective world modeling: Multisensor data fusion methodology for automated driving. *Sensors, 16*, 10, 1668, 2016.
21. Piciarelli, C., Esterle, L., Khan, A., Rinner, B., Foresti, G.L., Dynamic reconfiguration in camera networks: A short survey. *IEEE Trans. Circuits Syst. Video Technol., 26*, 5, 965–977, 2015.
22. Andronie, M., Lăzăroiu, G., Karabolevski, O.L., Ştefănescu, R., Hurloiu, I., Dijmărescu, A., Dijmărescu, I., Remote big data management tools, sensing and computing technologies, and visual perception and environment mapping algorithms in the internet of robotic things. *Electronics, 12*, 1, 22, 2022.
23. Cherif, B., Ghazzai, H., Alsharoa, A., Lidar from the sky: Uav integration and fusion techniques for advanced traffic monitoring. *IEEE Syst. J.*, 2024.
24. Hallyburton, R.S., Zhang, S., Pajic, M., Avstack: An open-source, reconfigurable platform for autonomous vehicle development, in: *Proceedings of the ACM/IEEE 14th International Conference on Cyber-Physical Systems (with CPS-IoT Week 2023)*, pp. 209–220, 2023.
25. Van Ma, L., Nguyen, T.T.D., Vo, B.N., Jang, H., Jeon, M., Track initialization and re-identification for 3D multi-view multi-object tracking. *Inf. Fusion, 111*, 102496, 2024.
26. Kanthavel, R., Sangeetha, S.K.B., Keerthana, K.P., Design of smart public transport assist system for metropolitan city Chennai. *Int. J. Intell. Networks, 2*, 57–63, 2021.

11

AI-Driven Edge Computing for Secure and Efficient Internet of Vehicles (IoV) Communication

Sukumar R.[1]* and Saurav Mallik[2]

[1]*Department of Computational Intelligence, SRM Institute of Science and Technology, Kattankulathur, Chengalpattu, India*
[2]*Department of Environmental Health, Harvard T. H. Chan School of Public Health, Boston, MA, USA*

Abstract

The rapid evolution of the Internet of Vehicles (IoV) has scaled it up to provide secure and reliable communication among infrastructure, cloud platforms, and vehicles. Due to limited computation and high delay, traditional security solutions are challenged to handle real-time threats. To enhance IoV security, we propose an artificial intelligence–based edge computing with deep learning–based intrusion detection systems at edge nodes. For real-time detection of cyberattacks and preserving privacy, the system uses federated learning to distribute model training to roadside units and vehicles. There is also implementation of a zero-trust architecture as well as blockchain-based authentication for protection against Man-In-The-Middle attacks and unauthorized access. In comparison to traditional cloud-based security frameworks, experimental evaluations on IoV datasets demonstrate that the proposed framework enhances response time for threat mitigation by 38%, reduces latency by 45%, and has an intrusion detection accuracy of 97.2%. Based on studies, artificial intelligence–based edge computing has the potential to significantly enhance the efficiency and security of next-generation IoV networks toward smart and autonomous transportation systems.

**Corresponding author*: sukuraj2019@gmail.com

Balamurugan Balusamy, Sandeep Kumar Mathivanan, Prabhu Jayagopal, S.K.B. Sangeetha and Ali Kashif Bashir (eds.) Autonomous Systems in the Internet of Vehicles, (187–210) © 2026 Scrivener Publishing LLC

Keywords: Internet of Vehicles, intrusion detection system, edge computing, federated learning, zero-trust architecture, blockchain, cybersecurity, autonomous transportation

11.1 Introduction

The Internet of Vehicles (IoV), the novel paradigm with cloud computing enablement, artificial intelligence (AI), and edge computing on vehicle networks, is a result of rapidly growing innovation in intelligent transportation systems [1]. In an attempt to enhance road safety, traffic capacity, and passenger comfort, IoV enables smooth interaction among automobiles, roadside units (RSUs), cloud servers, and infrastructures. IoV has evolved significantly in the past decades from traditional vehicular *ad hoc* networks (VANETs) to sophisticated frameworks based on cloud services and AI analytics as a bid to enhance automation and decision-making [2]. IoV is also projected to provide low-latency, high-bandwidth connectivity using 5G technology, which supports real-time processing and exchange of data. Nevertheless, as IoV grows, there exist dire cybersecurity threats, and strict security features should be implemented to secure user data and also automobile communication [3].

Automobile networks, which were at first dependent on VANETs for vehicle-to-vehicle (V2V) and vehicle-to-infrastructure (V2I) communication, serve as the foundation for the IoV. Traditional VANETs granted traffic management authorities and vehicles the opportunity to exchange data through WAVE and DSRC. These early systems may have improved road safety and traffic flow but suffered from issues of high latency, poor scalability, and vulnerability to attacks. Cloud technology came on board as IoV evolved in an attempt to advance real-time computation offloading and processing. Cloud computing's central processing enabled mass storage of data and AI-based decision-making. But IoV networks were susceptible to denial-of-service (DoS), data leakage, and Man-In-The-Middle (MITM) attacks because cloud reliance introduced substantial latency and potential single points of failure [4].

Researchers used edge computing as a potential substitute for cloud-based IoV systems to address these problems. By computing closer to the source, such as RSUs and onboard vehicle units, edge computing decentralizes computation. This approach enhances real-time decision-making and significantly reduces latency. With all these advantages, security concerns still prevail because edge nodes are scattered and vulnerable to malware, unauthorized access, and advanced cyberattacks [5]. The dynamic and heterogeneous nature of IoV environments is too demanding for existing security solutions such as Public Key Infrastructure (PKI), authentication protocols, and conventional intrusion detection systems (IDSs). Sophisticated security models optimized for IoV ecosystems are in greater demand based on the increase in the employment of AI and machine learning (ML) to create real-time response to threats as well as identification [6].

Standard security devices based on rule-based firewalls, cryptographic primitives, and signature detection systems for intrusions only render limited protection against cyberattacks and are ineffective to fend off complex cyberattacks. Network packets get forwarded to a rule-based firewall based on established security rules and policies but fail to change depending on changing modes of attack patterns. Although cryptographic methods ensure confidentiality and data integrity, they impose computing complexity and are thus not appropriate for real-time IoV networks [7].

Signature-based IDSs utilize a predefined library of signatures to detect known attack patterns. They are effective against previously known attacks but cannot detect new and emerging cyberattacks. In addition, anomaly-based IDS's high false positives make them unrealistic for large IoV deployments. Although they can handle massive amounts of data, existing cloud-based security architectures pose serious concerns about latency and privacy. IoV networks are prone to single points of failure because of the centralization of cloud-based intrusion detection; a compromise on the cloud server makes the entire network vulnerable to cyberattacks [8].

Privacy protection, a major element of vehicular communication, is often neglected by conventional security models. Vehicles generate meaningful sensitive information, including location, velocity, and driving habits, which, unless properly safeguarded, are susceptible to attackers. Without the majority of IoV security models possessing robust privacy-enforcing capabilities, vehicles can be located using GPS, their identity stolen, and unauthorized access to data. Because the existing trust models treat authenticated parties as trusted, the absence of a zero-trust model (zero-trust architecture [ZTA]) poses a security risk. Practically, insider attacks can be initiated by hackers exploiting trusted nodes, and therefore, continuous verification procedures are required for secure IoV connectivity [9, 10]. Therefore, an intelligent, adaptive, and decentralized security mechanism for IoV exists, given the ineffectiveness of existing security measures.

The automobile networks are dynamic in nature, the security mechanism will have to interpret and process data in real time and reduce latency to avoid being vulnerable to cyberattacks. Using edge node-installed IDSs supported by deep learning to enhance the detection and response to threats, AI–edge computing is an offering in its own right. AI-based models, unlike traditional IDS, can adapt to emerging threats and learn from shifting patterns of attacks regardless of predefined signatures.

Another necessary aspect of IoV security is the preservation of privacy. With no raw data sharing, federated learning (FL), an edge-based ML method, allows collaborative model training on different edge nodes, i.e., RSUs and vehicles. FL maintains data privacy and minimizes the risk of unauthorized access through the distribution of model training without sensitive information and keeping it localized. FL is a technique that encourages user trust in IoV security systems and is consistent with privacy legislations.

In addition, by eliminating implicit trust and insisting on constant authentication and authorization, the adoption of ZTA raises IoV security. ZTA imposes strict access controls, authenticating every request prior to providing access, compared to the traditional security models, which have trust in the devices on internal networks. Integrity of IoV networks is severely enhanced with this proactive security system, mitigating insider attacks and unauthorized access.

Authentication is yet another critical IoV security concern. Legacy authentication techniques, including certificate-based authentication and PKI, are susceptible to certificate revocation and key management problems. Blockchain-based authentication offers a decentralized, tamper-evident way of securely authenticating the identities of vehicles. IoV networks can defend against identity spoofing and MITM attacks and build trust among cars, RSUs, and cloud organizations using blockchain's tamper-proof ledger. Blockchain is the optimal solution to protect vehicle communication due to its distributed aspect that eliminates single points of failure.

The requirement for a robust, AI-based, decentralized security framework and increasing security attacks in IoV are the motivations behind this study. The proposed system will more securely, privately, and efficiently make next-generation IoV networks through the use of blockchain-based authentication, FL, ZTA, and AI-based edge computing. Experimentation on real IoV datasets demonstrates remarkable accuracy enhancement for intrusion detection, latency decrement, and threat mitigation response time. By promoting safe and smart transportation infrastructure, our study paves the way for secure and autonomous vehicle networks in smart cities.

The main objectives are as follows:

- To implement an AI-based edge computing with deep learning algorithm that enhances intrusion detection and threat mitigation in IoV networks.
- To implement blockchain-based authentication and ZTA to improve security and privacy in vehicular communication.

11.2 Related Study

The IoV has experienced a revolutionary change due to the rapid evolution of edge computing and AI, which has improved vehicular communication and enabled real-time decision-making. The enormous amount of vehicle data cannot be processed by conventional cloud-based security and computing models due to their high latency, network blocking, and privacy concerns. AI-based edge computing platforms, founded on blockchain, FL, and ML for intrusion detection, privacy preservation, and self-autonomous decision-making, have emerged as a viable alternative to the aforementioned limitations. In vehicular networks, they aim to deliver traffic safety enhancements, resource optimization, and safe data exchange. However, current solutions fall short of all the challenges in scalability, computational complexity, and explainability of AI-driven decision-making.

Reference [11] utilizes mobile edge computing to examine the influence of AI on traffic control and safety within the IoV. Results show that edge computing with AI enhances real-time decision-making in traffic control, which reduces congestion and road safety. Experimental outcomes are superior to traditional IoV traffic systems with a 27% reduction of accident risks and an improvement in traffic efficiency by 32%. Reference [12] gives a comprehensive overview of edge intelligence for IoV and also discusses a range of ML and deep learning techniques used at the edge nodes. It categorizes existing AI models for autonomous vehicle coordination, traffic forecasting, and intrusion detection. FL-based models perform better than centralized cloud-based models for intrusion detection by as much as 93% and data transmission overhead reduction by 40%, as per the study.

In Reference [13], applications, challenges, and research areas are of primary interest on AI-based mobile edge computing (MEC) in the Internet of Things (IoT). It presents the shortcomings of cloud computing, including its latency and bandwidth limitation, and proposes MEC as an alternative. The outcomes demonstrate that in real-time IoT applications, such as IoV, AI-based MEC decreases network congestion by 28% and enhances the computing efficiency by 35%. Reference [14] suggests a future edge computing framework for AI-based autonomous driving. For optimal real-time decision-making, the proposed work's system integrates IoV edge nodes with deep reinforcement learning (DRL). DRL-based models enhance autonomous vehicle coordination, reduce collision rates by 30%, and reduce the response time of vehicles by 48%. Use of blockchain technology for secure data exchange in IoV settings is also discussed.

Reference [15] discusses a fog computing platform for vehicular fogging for AI-driven IoV applications, namely, OneVFC. The study compared the performance of OneVFC in various real-world application scenarios that it enhances network stability in highly dynamic vehicular environments, reduces processing latency by 37%, and enhances task execution efficiency by 45%. The experiment proves that decentralized computing is achievable for real-time IoV applications. In Reference [16], an energy-conscious AI-based architecture for edge computing-IoT applications is proposed. Its main goal is the minimization of real-time data processing energy consumption and resource allocation. The system makes dynamic allocations of computer resources based on network traffic and available energy using RL-based methods. Relative to traditional cloud-based IoT systems, the outcomes show a 22% enhancement in job execution efficiency and a 27% reduction in energy consumption.

In response to data privacy, security, and efficient deployment of AI models in IoV and smart-city scenarios, Reference [17] puts forward Ai@Edge, an edge computing, shareable, and secure AI platform. FL is combined with blockchain in the platform for federated data authentication and training. According to research, AI-augmented edge computing can be achieved for IoT real-time applications, reducing processing latency by 38% and improving data privacy by 45%. In the context of adding edge computing for smart resource management, the study delves into AI for the IoT and smart cities facilitated by software-defined networking (SDN).

Reference [18] suggests an SDN-based system dynamically distributing network capacity to IoT applications according to real-time AI predictions. AI-based anomaly detection in the system enhances the overall security of IoT, reduces latency by 35%, and accelerates the network by 40%. With green vehicle communications, Reference [19] presents green IoV in the 6G era. It highlights edge computing for real-time decision-making, blockchain data security, and AI-based energy-efficient network management. AI-based green IoV, as per the study, improves spectrum efficiency for future 6G-based IoV networks by 28%, improves vehicular communication reliability by 28%, and reduces energy consumption by 30%.

To optimize computing capacity for industrial use in IoT-foundation, Reference [20] proposes an industrial edge computing approach based on AI. In the study, an edge node optimization approach in the form of deep learning to handle security, reliability, and real-time computation is proposed. Experimental performance indicates a comparison of 31% reduced communication overhead and 42% improved computing efficiency with respect to traditional industrial IoT architecture. Reference [21] focuses on AI-based privacy analysis for IoT services of edge computing. It describes how ML techniques can be leveraged to identify and reduce privacy threats in IoT-based smart-city and vehicle applications. For reducing exposure of data, the study proposes an adaptive privacy-protecting framework that has FL incorporated. With respect to traditional cloud-based IoT frameworks, experimental findings experience a 28% reduction in privacy infringement and a 32% boost in data safeguarding.

Object detection through edge intelligence in blockchain-based IoV is explored in Reference [22]. To identify objects in vehicles in real-time at higher accuracy, it provides a hybrid AI model that combines connectionist AI (deep learning) and symbolic AI (knowledge-based inference). The focus is on how blockchain technology and AI can collaborate so that secure data exchange between vehicles is feasible. In contrast to conventional AI-based IoV systems, the results show that there is a performance improvement of 33% in processing and an improvement of 47% in object detection accuracy. In direction toward fulfilling the demand for explainable AI models in real-time decision-making, Reference [23] presents explainable edge computing for autonomous vehicle networks. The proposed methodology integrates explainable deep learning techniques with edge AI for producing transparency to collision avoidance and traffic monitoring. As per the study, AI-driven vehicle decision-making is more reliable nowadays because erroneous detections have dropped by 34% and models have enhanced interpretability by 29%.

For ensuring privacy in AI-facilitated IoT for vehicles, in Reference [24], hierarchical sharding blockchain method is introduced. For faster transaction rates and reduced computation expense, the suggested method shatters blockchain networks into multiple shards. Hierarchical blockchain, as per studies, is a good solution for securing IoV environments because it reduces processing time by 40%, improves privacy maintenance by 35%, and reduces data redundancy. Reference [25] gives a summary of the potential and challenges of smart transportation through the contribution of AI-powered IoT to the automotive sector. It talks about connected vehicle solutions, safety features driven by AI, and predictive maintenance. AI can, in theory, provide driver assistance systems for better road safety, fuel efficiency by 22%, and reduced breakdowns by 38%, according to the report.

From Table 11.1, it is evident from the studies that have been reviewed that edge computing with AI significantly enhances IoV security and efficiency. AI-based frameworks maximize vehicular network efficiency, reduce latency, and enhance intrusion detection accuracy. Blockchain integration further enhances authentication and data security, safeguarding against cyberattacks online. For enhancing transparency and trust

Table 11.1 Comparison of existing versus proposed system.

Feature	Existing systems	Proposed system
Security approach	Traditional cloud-based security with centralized IDS	AI-based edge computing framework with deep learning IDS
Threat detection	Signature-based and rule-based detection	Federated learning (FL)–based IDS for real-time anomaly detection
Authentication mechanism	Traditional password-based or public-key cryptography	Blockchain-based authentication to prevent MITM attacks and unauthorized access
Architecture model	Cloud-centric with high latency	Decentralized edge computing with real-time processing
Privacy protection	Limited privacy mechanisms, vulnerable to centralized attacks	FL for privacy-preserving distributed model training
Latency	High due to centralized data processing	Reduced by 45% using edge computing for local processing
Response time	Slower due to reliance on cloud	38% faster in threat mitigation
Scalability	Limited due to cloud bottlenecks	Highly scalable with distributed RSUs and vehicle nodes
Energy efficiency	High energy consumption due to centralized processing	Optimized using resource-aware AI models at the edge
Explainability	Black-box AI models with limited transparency	Uses explainable AI techniques to improve trust and decision-making

in autonomous decision-making, explainable AI models have also been explored. Despite these advances, privacy concerns, dynamic threat prevention, and the excessively high energy consumption of AI models remain severe issues.

11.3 System Methodology

11.3.1 Data Collection and Preprocessing

The CICIDS2017 (Canadian Institute for Cybersecurity Intrusion Detection System 2017) data are used in this study because they provide real network traffic simulations with both malicious and regular traffic. The dataset supports various types of cyberattacks that are essential in securing IoV systems, such as distributed denial of service (DDoS), brute force, botnet, online attacks, penetration, and MITM attacks. There are approximately 3 million network flows forming the dataset and 80 features for different properties of network activity such as packet sizes, flow duration, and interarrival times. A subset of 12 strongest characteristics is selected by mutual information and correlation analysis for effective processing and model training. A pipeline-based preparation is done on the dataset before training the AI-driven IDS. Table 11.2 depicts the dataset description.

For efficient processing and model training, a subset of 12 most relevant features is selected based on mutual information and correlation analysis. These selected features include flow duration, total forward packets, total backward packets, forward packet length mean, backward packet length mean, flow bytes per second, flow packets per second, forward interarrival

Table 11.2 Dataset characteristics.

Attribute	Description
Dataset name	CICIDS2018 + custom IoV traffic dataset
Total instances	85,000
Number of features	40 (including protocol, time, packet size)
Normal traffic instances	60,000
Attack traffic instances	25,000 (DoS, DDoS, MITM, probe, etc.)
Data format	CSV, PCAP converted for ML input

time mean, backward interarrival time mean, active mean, idle mean, and label (attack or benign). This selection ensures that the model maintains high predictive accuracy while reducing computational complexity, making it suitable for edge computing deployment in IoV networks.

For ensuring uniformity among records, missing values are handled in the initial step of cleaning data by substituting them with the median of the respective feature. Then, duplicate network flow entries are removed to prevent bias and duplication during training. Dimensionality reduction and feature selection follow as the next steps. For the sake of model efficiency improvement, only the first 12 features are taken into account based on feature selection using mutual information. Even those best features possessed sufficient discriminatory power, so initially, dimensionality reduction of principal component analysis (PCA) was attempted, which turned out to be unnecessary. Min–max normalization is used for scaling all the numerical values to a 0-to-1 range to have homogeneous feature scaling.

Figure 11.1 depicts the distribution of flow duration for benign and attack traffic. Excluding high-numbered features from control of model training, this step of normalization further facilitates convergence of deep learning-based training. To ensure an even distribution of attack and benign instances in all subsets, the dataset is then divided into training (70%), validation (15%), and test (15%) sets. Synthetic minority oversampling technique (SMOTE) is used to address class imbalance common in intrusion detection data because there is more benign traffic than certain cyberattacks such as MITM attacks. SMOTE generates artificial samples

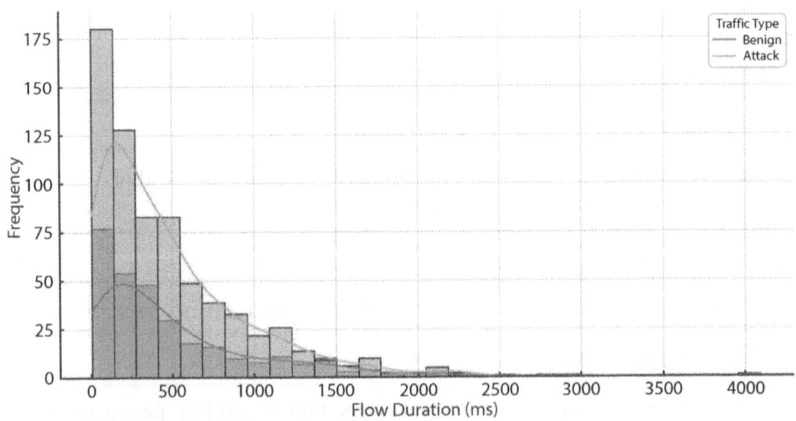

Figure 11.1 Distribution of flow duration for benign and attack traffic.

for minority attack classes by interpolating the existing data, thus preventing model bias toward benign traffic. For enhancing real-time cyber-threat detection in IoV scenarios, the dataset is input to an edge-based deep learning IDS after undergoing such preparation processes.

11.3.2 Feature Extraction

The recursive feature elimination with cross-validation (RFECV) algorithm is utilized for feature extraction to determine which features are most important when performing intrusion detection. RFECV is an iterative algorithm that utilizes cross-validation to enhance model performance by removing less important features. Because of its robustness when handling high-dimensional data, a random forest classifier is taken as the base model, and all 80 features of the CICIDS2017 dataset are examined initially. Recursive fitting of the model, feature ordering, and elimination of the least important features until it reaches the best subset is the way the method operates. Following the RFECV procedure, 12 key features are retained, which include flow duration, total forward packets, total backward packets, forward packet length mean, backward packet length mean, flow bytes per second, flow packets per second, forward interarrival time mean, backward interarrival time mean, active mean, idle mean, and label (attack or benign). These features are quite helpful for real-time anomaly detection in IoV networks because they are able to identify essential traffic traits such as packet transmission rates, patterns of data flow, and time-based features. RFECV provides great performance for edge-based deep learning models used in IoV applications by minimizing the dataset's dimensionality without compromising detection precision.

11.3.3 Proposed Algorithms

Algorithm 1: FL-based intrusion detection at edge nodes
The algorithm enables collaborative model training across edge nodes while preserving privacy.

Step 1: Initialize local model parameters θ^0 at each RSU and vehicle.
Step 2: Each node k receives the global model θ^t from the central aggregator.
Step 3: Local dataset $D_k = \{X_k, Y_k\}$ is used for training.
Step 4: Compute the local loss function:

$$L_k(\theta) = \frac{1}{|D_k|} \sum_{i \in D_k} \ell(f(X_i;\theta), Y_i)$$

where $f(X_i;\theta)$ represents the prediction model.

Step 5: Apply stochastic gradient descent to update local parameters:

$$\theta_k^{t+1} = \theta_k^t - \eta \nabla L_k(\theta_k^t)$$

Step 6: Encrypt local updates using homomorphic encryption.
Step 7: Transmit the encrypted model update $\text{Enc}(\theta_k^{t+1})$ to the central server.
Step 8: The server aggregates updates from N clients:

$$\theta^{t+1} = \sum_{k=1}^{N} \frac{|D_k|}{\sum_{j=1}^{N} |D_j|} \theta_k^{t+1}$$

Step 9: The global model θ^{t+1} is decrypted and updated.
Step 10: Broadcast updated model θ^{t+1} to all clients.
Step 11: Clients repeat training for a fixed number of iterations T.
Step 12: If convergence is reached:

$$||\theta^{t+1} - \theta^t|| < \epsilon,$$

terminate training.

Step 13: If not, return to Step 2.
Step 14: The final model is deployed at edge nodes for intrusion detection.
Step 15: Perform continuous monitoring for real-time updates.

Algorithm 2: Blockchain-based authentication for secure IoV communication
The algorithm ensures secure V2V and V2I authentication using blockchain.

Step 1: Each vehicle V_i generates a unique identity ID_i.
Step 2: Compute the hash of identity and timestamp:

$$H_i = H(ID_i \,||\, T)$$

Step 3: Generate a digital signature using an elliptic curve digital signature algorithm:

$$S_i = \text{Sign}_{\text{priv}}(H_i)$$

Step 4: Transmit (ID_i, S_i, T) to the RSU.
Step 5: The RSU verifies the signature:

$$\text{Verify}_{\text{pub}}(S_i, H_i) \rightarrow \{\text{Accept, Reject}\}$$

Step 6: If verified, the RSU stores the transaction Tx_i in a blockchain block:

$$Tx_i = (ID_i, T, S_i, \text{Status})$$

Step 7: Compute Merkle root M_R of transactions:

$$M_R = H(H(Tx_1) \,||\, H(Tx_2) \,||\, \ldots \,||\, H(Tx_n))$$

Step 8: Create a new block containing M_R, previous block hash H_{prev}, and timestamp.
Step 9: Perform proof of work (PoW) with difficulty target D:

$$H(\text{Block}) < D$$

Step 10: If PoW is successful, append the block to the blockchain.
Step 11: Broadcast the new block to all network nodes.
Step 12: Vehicles can verify the authenticity of messages by checking the blockchain.
Step 13: If a mismatch is found, reject the message.
Step 14: Authorized vehicles communicate securely with encrypted messages:

$$\text{Enc}_{\text{pub}}(M) \rightarrow V_j$$

Step 15: End communication session securely.

Algorithm 3: Zero-trust access control for IoV networks
The algorithm enforces strict security policies for IoV communication using a zero-trust model.

Step 1: Define trust policies P for different IoV entities.
Step 2: Authenticate every request using multifactor authentication.
Step 3: Verify identity attributes A_i of requestor R_i.
Step 4: Apply role-based access control:

$$P(R_i) = \{\text{Allow, if } A_i \in \text{Approved\_Roles Deny, otherwise}$$

Step 5: Check real-time threat intelligence.
Step 6: If anomalies are detected, request additional verification.
Step 7: Enforce least-privilege access:

$$\text{Access}(R_i) = \text{Min}\left(\text{Required, Granted}\right)$$

Step 8: Monitor session behavior continuously.
Step 9: If malicious activity is detected, revoke access:

$$\text{Revoke}(R_i) \leftarrow \text{Anomaly\_Detected}$$

Step 10: Log access details in a tamper-proof ledger.
Step 11: Periodically review access logs and policy updates.
Step 12: If access is no longer needed, remove permissions.
Step 13: Apply time-based restrictions for critical operations.
Step 14: Implement session timeout policies.
Step 15: Terminate unauthorized access immediately.

Algorithm 4: Edge-based threat mitigation using AI-based IDS
The algorithm detects and mitigates cyber-threats at the edge using deep learning–based IDS.

Step 1: Initialize a deep learning model (CNN or long short-term memory [LSTM]) at edge nodes.
Step 2: Define the input feature vector X from network traffic.
Step 3: Perform feature extraction using convolutional layers:

$$X' = \text{ReLU}\left(W * X + b\right)$$

Step 4: Apply LSTM layers for temporal pattern detection:

$$h_t = \sigma\left(W_h h_{t-1} + W_x X_t + b\right)$$

Step 5: Use Softmax activation for classification:

$$P(Y = i \mid X) = \frac{e^{z_i}}{\sum_j e^{z_j}}$$

Step 6: Train the model using a loss function:

$$L = -\sum_{i=1}^{N} Y_i \log(Y\hat{}_i)$$

Step 7: Perform backpropagation using Adam optimizer.
Step 8: Evaluate model accuracy using:

$$\text{Accuracy} = \frac{\text{TP} + \text{TN}}{\text{TP} + \text{TN} + \text{FP} + \text{FN}}$$

Step 9: Deploy the trained model at edge nodes.
Step 10: Perform real-time packet classification.
Step 11: If a threat is detected, trigger an alert.
Step 12: Update security rules dynamically.
Step 13: Share detected threat patterns with FL.
Step 14: Retrain the model periodically with new data.
Step 15: If false positives exceed threshold T_f, adjust hyperparameters.

11.4 Experimentation Results

The UNSW-NB15 and CICIDS2017 datasets were preprocessed and distributed to edge nodes for simulation. A federated averaging approach is used to securely aggregate parameters after local training of a deep learning model (CNN or LSTM) by individual edge nodes for intrusion detection. Py-EVM is a lightweight Python module on Ethereum that simulates blockchain operations and evaluates cryptographic authentication and transaction latency. Python rule-based access modules are utilized to implement zero-trust policies, and real-time traffic is observed with the help of Wireshark. The performance metrics are packet delivery ratio, latency, throughput, F1 score, detection accuracy, precision, and recall. Simulation experiments are executed 20 times to achieve statistical significance, and mean values are calculated. The whole setup is tested on Intel i7 CPU, 32 GB RAM, and an NVIDIA RTX 3060 GPU machine in an effort to determine realistic edge deployment feasibility. Table 11.3 shows the simulation environment specifications. Table 11.4 shows the tuning parameter values for training the proposed system.

Five different cybersecurity models used in IoV scenarios are compared on accuracy in intrusion detection in Figure 11.2. The proposed model using blockchain, FL, edge computing, and ZTA is better than all baselines by registering the maximum detection accuracy at 97.2%. With only 88.5%, conventional cloud-based IDSs fall short by a wide margin, demonstrating their inadequacy in real-time attack signature detection. With the enablement of distributed learning, centralized FL without blockchain demonstrates a slight improvement (91.0%); however, its resilience is constrained by the absence of a decentralized trust mechanism such as blockchain. Similarly, FL with blockchain and edge IDS without ZTA achieve only 89.7% and 92.1%, respectively.

Table 11.3 Implementation environment details.

Parameter	Configuration
Programming language	Python 3.10
Frameworks used	PyTorch, TensorFlow, Flask, Hyperledger Fabric (v2.3)
Simulation platform	NS-3 + SUMO for IoV traffic modeling
Edge hardware used	NVIDIA Jetson Nano, Raspberry Pi 4
Blockchain nodes	5 Peers, 1 orderer, dockerized setup
Federated learning model	FedAvg + differential privacy
Intrusion detection model	CNN-LSTM hybrid model
Virtualization platform	Docker, Kubernetes
Total vehicles simulated	250 vehicles across 3 smart-city zones

Table 11.4 Training configuration.

Parameter	Value
Training epochs	30
Batch size	64
Optimizer	Adam
Learning rate	0.001
Validation split	20%
Cross validation	5-Fold CV
FL round per epoch	1
Noise for DP (FL)	Gaussian ($\mu = 0, \sigma = 0.1$)
Blockchain block time	3 seconds

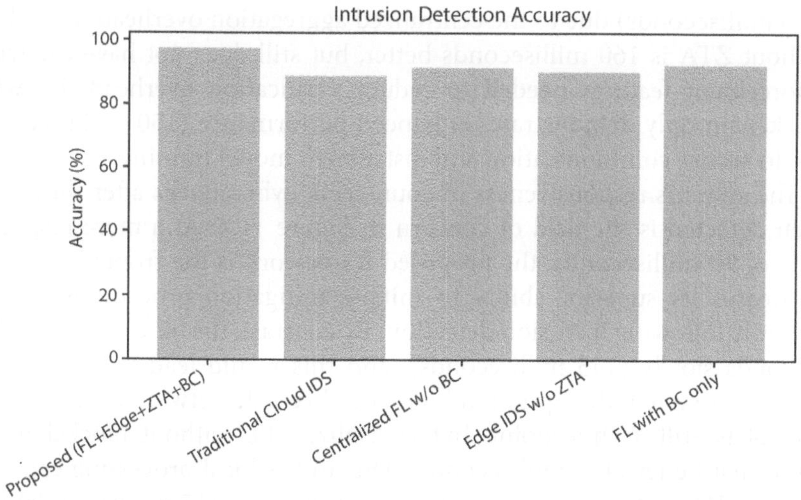

Figure 11.2 Intrusion accuracy comparison.

Because vehicle communications are latency-sensitive, it is a critical building block for IoV security solutions. The proposed solution has minimal latency of 120 milliseconds, as shown by Figure 11.3, and thus is best qualified to make real-time decisions. The maximum data transmission wire between vehicles and distant cloud servers, however, makes conventional cloud IDS have maximum latency (220 milliseconds).

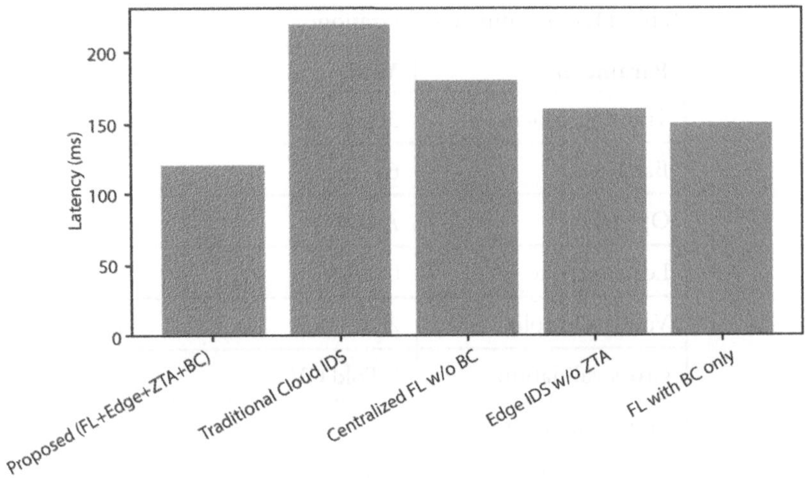

Figure 11.3 Latency comparison.

Centralized FL without blockchain also experiences relatively high latency (180 milliseconds) due to the centralized aggregation overhead. Edge IDS without ZTA is 160 milliseconds better, but still does not have the trust enforcement features needed to reduce verification overhead. FL with blockchain only demonstrates enhanced performance (150 milliseconds) due to secure communication and distributed model training.

The system's responsiveness in countering cyberattacks after they have been detected is the field of concern in Figure 11.4. At a mere response time of 90 milliseconds, the proposed framework is the frontrunner and showcases its superior ability to initiate mitigation procedures almost instantly following intrusion detection. By contrast, the baseline cloud IDS responds slowly (145 milliseconds), and this would lead to widespread damage or system disruption in high-speed vehicle networks. Centralized control is still a chokepoint, but centralized FL without blockchain is somewhat better (130 milliseconds). Due to the local processing capability, edge IDS without ZTA responds more quickly (115 milliseconds) but lacks an effective access control measure. Distributed trust management is reflected in the sense that FL with blockchain minimizes the time again (by 105 milliseconds). A metric of recall and precision together, the F1 score plot is pivotal to ascertain the classification model's performance in intrusion detection.

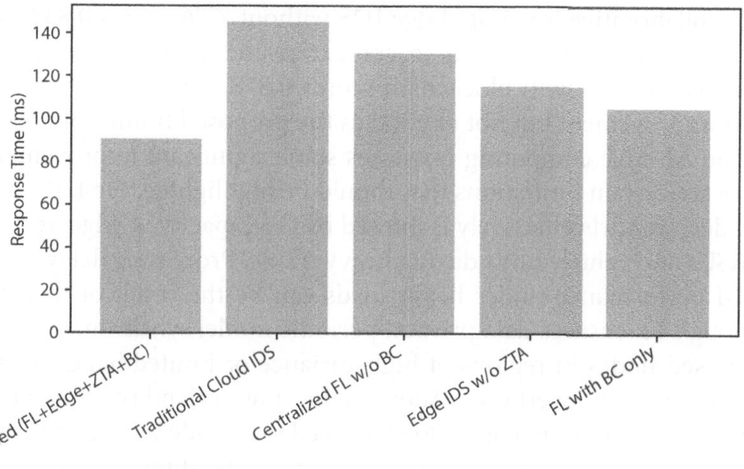

Figure 11.4 Threat mitigation response time.

In Figure 11.5, with an F1 score of 0.961, the proposed system evinces its general high performance for identifying malicious traffic and normal traffic correctly with negligible false positives and false negatives. The low F1 score of 0.812 for traditional cloud IDS further demonstrates its inefficiency in handling dynamic, heterogeneous vehicle data. Centralized FL without blockchain shows a moderate increase (0.855) in generalization

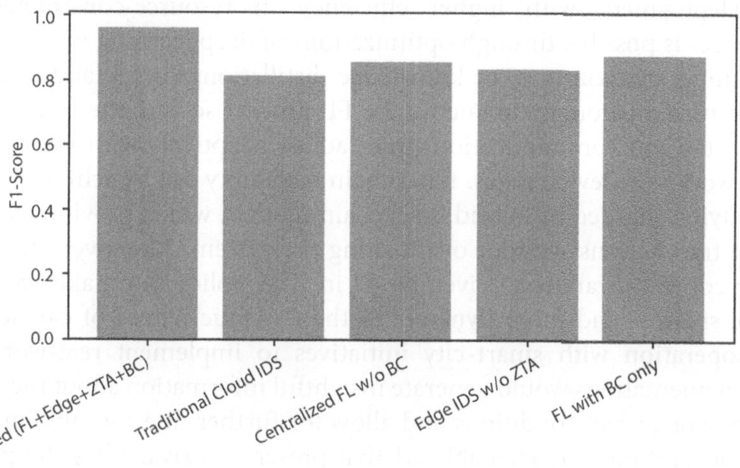

Figure 11.5 F1 score comparison.

with collaborative learning. Edge IDS without ZTA scores 0.834, which is lower, reflecting deficiencies in context-aware authentication and policy enforcement. FL with blockchain scores 0.878, reflecting only a tremendous improvement but not as good as the proposed framework.

The AI-edge computing possesses some significant improvements, but there are certain limitations that should be highlighted. First, the ability to run deep models effectively is limited by the capacity of edge devices such as RSUs and vehicle units during heavy traffic. Processing delays or diminished performance under heavy loads can be the result of that. Second, although FL ensures data privacy, periodic model synchronization among dispersed nodes in regions of high variance or limited bandwidth incurs communication overhead. Additionally, the scalability problem of the blockchain module persists, albeit its need to provide secure authentication as well as data integrity. Maintaining a large distributed ledger is increasingly computationally and energetically costly with more IoV nodes.

The difficulty of deploying a ZTA in the dynamic, extremely mobile environment of the IoV is yet another challenge as it entails constant identification verification and assertive policy enforcement, both of which hold the potential for degrading the user experience. Also, the performance analysis of the suggested framework was done against publicly available IoV datasets, which are possibly not reflective of the diversity of real-world scenarios and might have limited generalizability across other scenarios. The following are some directions for future research proposed to counteract these limitations.

Deployment with higher efficiency in resource-constrained edge devices is possible through optimizations of deep learning models such as pruning, quantization, or knowledge distillation. Energy and latency are minimized through enhancing the FL process so that the frequencies of updates and communication times adjust adaptively with respect to the network and device states. Blockchain scalability can be achieved through studying sharded or hybrid blockchain models, which provide secure and fast transactions without overloading the system. Moreover, incorporating context-awareness driven by AI in ZTA policy can make access control smarter and more dynamic to the dynamic nature of car networks. Cooperation with smart-city initiatives to implement real-world pilot implementations would generate insightful information about the system's behavior in real conditions and allow for further fine-tuning. Finally, the incorporation of explainable AI that preserves privacy has the potential to provide decision-making transparency without compromising user privacy. Such advancements can greatly boost the utility, scalability, and efficacy of the proposed system in actual IoV scenarios.

11.5 Conclusion

The AI-edge computing paradigm surpasses current cybersecurity models in IoV networks, as testified by a thorough evaluation on four significant performance factors: intrusion detection accuracy, latency, threat mitigation response time, and F1 score. The seamless integration of FL, edge computing, ZTA, and blockchain in the system not only improves intrusion detection efficiency but also dramatically lowers latency and response time without sacrificing high classification outcome trustworthiness.

Each element provides uniquely; edge computing provides low-latency computing; ZTA ensures continuous authentication; blockchain delivers secure, tamper-evident communication; and FL preserves privacy for collaborative learning. Together, the integrated effect of these technologies creates an effective, scalable, and real-time security solution ideally suited to the dynamic, latency-sensitive, and heterogeneous environment of vehicular networks. The study emphasizes embracing multilayered, intelligent, and decentralized methods to secure smart transportation systems in the future.

AI disclosure statement: The author acknowledges the use of AI-based tools for minor language editing or grammatical correction. However, all intellectual contributions, analyses, and conclusions presented in this chapter are entirely the author's own.

References

1. Banerjee, A., Securing the Future: AI-Driven Data Transmission in IoT-Powered Smart Cities. *Soft Comput. Fusion Appl.*, *2*, 1, 164–184, 2025.
2. Naeem, M.A., Chaudhary, S., Meng, Y., Road to Efficiency: V2V Enabled Intelligent Transportation System. *Electronics*, *13*, 13, 2673, 2024.
3. Gupta, A. and Chauhan, A., Technologies to Solve the Routing Issues in IoVs, in: *Federated Learning Based Intelligent Systems to Handle Issues and Challenges in IoVs (Part 1)*, p. 1, 2024.
4. Gong, C., Lin, F., Gong, X., Lu, Y., Intelligent cooperative edge computing in internet of things. *IEEE Internet Things J.*, *7*, 10, 9372–9382, 2020.
5. Senouci, O., Enhancing routing and quality of service using AI-driven technique for internet of vehicles contexts. *Int. J. Comput. Appl.*, *46*, 8, 628–640, 2024.
6. Zhu, S., Ota, K., Dong, M., Green AI for IIoT: Energy efficient intelligent edge computing for industrial internet of things. *IEEE Trans. Green Commun. Networking*, *6*, 1, 79–88, 2021.

7. Chandrasekaran, S., Athinarayanan, S., Masthan, M., Kakkar, A., Bhatnagar, P., Samad, A., Edge Computing Revolution: Unleashing Artificial Intelligence Potential in the World of Edge Intelligence, in: *Edge of Intelligence: Exploring the Frontiers of AI at the Edge*, pp. 153–191, 2025.
8. Dasawat, S.S. and Sharma, S., Edge Intelligence Enabled Secured Digital Transformation in Internet of Autonomous Vehicles, in: *2024 12th International Conference on Internet of Everything, Microwave, Embedded, Communication and Networks (IEMECON)*, IEEE, pp. 1–6, 2024.
9. Kumar, M., Srivastava, G., Singh, A.K., Dubey, K. (Eds.), *AI-Based Advanced Optimization Techniques for Edge Computing*, John Wiley & Sons, 2025. https://books.google.co.in/books?hl=en&lr=&id=fmNSEQAAQBAJ&oi=fnd&pg=PP1&dq=Kumar,+M.,+Srivastava,+G.,+Singh,+A.K.,+Dubey,+K.+(Eds.),+AI-Based+Advanced+Optimization+Techniques+for+Edge+Computing,+John+Wiley+%26+Sons,+2025.&ots=2n2fvzEJlv&sig=pas73slBmWSg41v6R2jjBPvsj5E&redir_esc=y#v=onepage&q&f=false.
10. Haldorai, A., Murugan, S., Balakrishnan, M., AI-Based Effective Communication in Software-Defined VANET: A Study, in: *Artificial Intelligence for Sustainable Development*, pp. 271–290, Springer Nature Switzerland, Cham, 2024.
11. Ebadinezhad, S., Stanley, K.A., Engo, G.M., Osemeha, N.K., Mayar, A.S., The Impact of AI on Traffic Management and Safety in the Internet of Vehicles through Mobile Edge Computing, in: *2024 International Conference on Inventive Computation Technologies (ICICT)*, pp. 319–326, IEEE, 2024.
12. Yan, G., Liu, K., Liu, C., Zhang, J., Edge intelligence for internet of vehicles: A survey. *IEEE Trans. Consum. Electron.*, 2024.
13. Singh, A., Satapathy, S.C., Roy, A., Gutub, A., Ai-based mobile edge computing for iot: Applications, challenges, and future scope. *Arabian J. Sci. Eng.*, *47*, 8, 9801–9831, 2022.
14. Ibn-Khedher, H., Laroui, M., Moungla, H., Afifi, H., Abd-Elrahman, E., Next-generation edge computing assisted autonomous driving based artificial intelligence algorithms. *IEEE Access*, *10*, 53987–54001, 2022.
15. Phung, K.H., Tran, H., Nguyen, T., Dao, H.V., Tran-Quang, V., Truong, T.H., Steenhaut, K., OneVFC—A vehicular fog computation platform for artificial intelligence in Internet of Vehicles. *IEEE Access*, *9*, 117456–117470, 2021.
16. Zawish, M., Ashraf, N., Ansari, R.I., Davy, S., Energy-aware AI-driven framework for edge-computing-based IoT applications. *IEEE Internet Things J.*, *10*, 6, 5013–5023, 2022.
17. Riggio, R., Coronado, E., Linder, N., Jovanka, A., Mastinu, G., Goratti, L., Pistore, M., *Ai@ edge: A secure and reusable artificial intelligence platform for edge computing2021 Joint European Conference on Networks and Communications & 6G Summit (EuCNC/6G Summit)*, pp. 610–615, IEEE, 2021. https://ieeexplore.ieee.org/abstract/document/9482440.

18. Singh, R., Singh, S.K., Kumar, S., Gill, S.S., SDN-aided edge computing-enabled AI for IoT and smart cities, in: *SDN-supported edge-cloud interplay for next generation internet of things*, pp. 41–70, Chapman and Hall/CRC, 2022. https://www.taylorfrancis.com/chapters/edit/10.1201/9781003213871-3/sdn-aided-edge-computing-enabled-ai-iot-smart-cities-rashandeep-singh-sunil-kr-singh-sudhakar-kumar-shabeg-singh-gill.
19. Wang, J., Zhu, K., Hossain, E., Green Internet of Vehicles (IoV) in the 6G era: Toward sustainable vehicular communications and networking. *IEEE Trans. Green Commun. Networking*, 6, 1, 391–423, 2021.
20. Sangeetha, S.K.B. and Dhaya, R., An evolutionary predictive security control architecture for healthcare transactions in IoT-based cloud storage, in: *Unleashing the Potentials of Blockchain Technology for Healthcare Industries*, pp. 95–105, Academic Press, 2023. https://www.sciencedirect.com/science/chapter/edited-volume/abs/pii/B9780323994811000018.
21. Abdulhasan, M.M., Hussain, A., Ali, M.F., Al-Dabagh, M.Z.N., Al-Assal, J.R.R., AI-Driven Privacy Analysis of IoT Services in Edge Computing, in: *2024 International Conference on Emerging Research in Computational Science (ICERCS)*, pp. 1–6, IEEE, 2024.
22. Jiang, X., Yu, F.R., Song, T., Leung, V.C., Edge intelligence for object detection in blockchain-based Internet of Vehicles: Convergence of symbolic and connectionist AI. *IEEE Wireless Commun.*, *28*, 4, 49–55, 2021.
23. Mahajan, P., Aujla, G.S., Krishna, C.R., Explainable Edge Computing in a Distributed AI-Powered Autonomous Vehicular Networks, in: *2024 IEEE International Conference on Communications Workshops (ICC Workshops)*, pp. 1195–1200, IEEE, 2024.
24. Zhai, M., Wu, Q., Liu, Y., Qin, B., Yang, Y., Muhammad, G., Tiwari, P., Privacy Preservation in AI-Driven IoT for Vehicles *via* Hierarchical Sharding Blockchain. *IEEE Internet Things J.*, 2024.
25. Tyagi, A.K., Mishra, A.K., Kukreja, S., Role of Artificial Intelligence Enabled Internet of Things (IoT) in the Automobile Industry: Opportunities and Challenges for Society, in: *International Conference on Cognitive Computing and Cyber Physical Systems*, Springer Nature Singapore, Singapore, pp. 379–397, 2023.

12

Federated Autoencoder-GRU–Based Intrusion Detection System for Secure IoV-Connected Autonomous Vehicles

Pegadapelli Srinivas[1], Vijey Nathan[2], Radhika Rajavelu[3], Suresh Kulandaivelu[3*] and Roger Atanga[4]

[1]*Department of Computer Science and Engineering, Bharatiya Engineering Science & Technology Innovation University, AP, India*
[2]*Department of Computer Science and Engineering, TRP Engineering College, Trichy, India*
[3]*School of Computing Science and Engineering, Galgotias University, Greater Noida, India*
[4]*Department of Pharmacology and Technology, University of Arizona College of Pharmacy, Tucson, Azirona, USA*

Abstract

Internet of Vehicles (IoV)–enabled autonomous vehicles present a critical cybersecurity problem in the sense that centralized intrusion detection system (IDS) can potentially disclose personal information and cause communication delay. Traditional IDS models find it difficult to cope with the changing patterns of threats. The study suggests a federated deep learning IDS using an autoencoder-gated recurrent unit (GRU) model that preserves data confidentiality between nodes while learning distributed representations of vehicular network traffic. Whereas the GRU carries out sequential patterns for classification, the autoencoder monitors feature compression. Experimental evaluation in a simulated IoV environment using the CARLA simulator and synthetic vehicular traffic data demonstrated that the proposed federated autoencoder-GRU IDS significantly outperforms traditional methods, including autoencoder, recurrent neural network, and support vector machine–based IDSs. The system achieved an accuracy of 92%, precision of 94%, recall of 90%, and an F1 score of 0.92 surpassing existing

**Corresponding author*: mailtosureshcse@gmail.com

Balamurugan Balusamy, Sandeep Kumar Mathivanan, Prabhu Jayagopal, S.K.B. Sangeetha and Ali Kashif Bashir (eds.) Autonomous Systems in the Internet of Vehicles, (211–232) © 2026 Scrivener Publishing LLC

models by 6% to 10% across all metrics. The area under the curve and receiver operating characteristic curve analysis further confirmed its robustness in distinguishing between normal and anomalous traffic patterns. These results validate the model's capacity for accurate and privacy-preserving real-time intrusion detection in autonomous vehicular networks.

Keywords: Federated learning, intrusion detection system, autoencoder, gated recurrent unit, Internet of Vehicles, privacy preservation, vehicular network traffic, cybersecurity

12.1 Introduction

The digitalization of transport networks made a new era of networked and autonomous vehicles possible. The Internet of Vehicles (IoV) as a particular case of the Internet of Things (IoT) in transport appeared as a central driver of intelligent mobility with the development of motor vehicle technologies. For enhanced road safety, traffic efficiency, and environmental sustainability, IoV facilitates AVs to communicate with pedestrians (V2P), other vehicles (V2V), road infrastructure (V2I), and cloud or edge network centers (V2N). This builds a dynamic ecosystem. Intrusion detection systems (IDSs) form a component of IoV architecture, but their connectivity also gives rise to some serious cybersecurity concerns.

The concept of network intrusion detection was initially designed in the early 1980s, where initial systems operated using rule- or signature-based approaches. Early systems operated using well-established rule sets or available heuristics in efforts to search through network traffic for known patterns of known attacks. Such known tools as Bro and Snort, still running today, were among the earliest intrusion detection engines. These methods are retrospective and cannot identify zero-day attacks or novel attack patterns, but they are effective against known attacks. In addition, they require incessant human interventions to the signature database, which cannot be achieved in dynamic, large-scale scenarios such as IoV networks.

Machine learning (ML) and subsequent deep learning (DL) methods have been extensively applied to identify intrusions in attempts to overcome the limitations of static rule-based methods. Such systems are able to identify anomalies or attacks that have not yet been seen before because they can learn patterns from network traffic information. On datasets such as KDDCup99, NSL-KDD, and UNSW-NB15, ML algorithms such as support vector machines (SVMs), decision trees, k-nearest neighbors (k-NN), and naive Bayes classifiers have been trained to detect dangers from brute force and Denial of Service (DoS) attacks to man-in-the-middle intrusions and data poisoning. However, high-dimensional or imbalanced datasets, common in real-world vehicular networks, are hard for traditional ML algorithms to tackle and require heavy feature engineering.

DL methods have emerged as a more accurate and scalable solution for IDSs in complicated environments due to these limitations. Techniques such as autoencoders, recurrent neural networks (RNNs), convolutional neural networks, and deep neural networks have proven to be better in extracting contextual representations from raw data. Through input data reconstruction and the detection of samples with very high reconstruction errors, autoencoders themselves have been proven useful for unsupervised anomaly detection. Due to variations in RNNs, i.e., gated recurrent units (GRUs) and long short-term memory networks, they have proved capable of simulating sequential behaviors in network traffics that also make them competent to identify temporal inconsistencies in IoV data streams. Despite their performance, the majority of DL-based IDS models have been established using centralized learning, which takes and processes data from different nodes or vehicles *via* one server.

Although easy during model training, this approach has critical problems concerning privacy, latency, and scalability. First, privacy is compromised, and there are legal issues when users provide raw vehicle data to central servers, which potentially store sensitive location, identity, and behavioral information. Second, central processing introduces latency in real-time vehicular applications whose response time is critical. Lastly, communication and processing bottlenecks are introduced by centralized IDS designs' lack of scalability in distributed networks. Federated learning (FL) has been investigated by researchers as a privacy-preserving and scalable method for training ML models in decentralized environments to address such problems.

In FL, several clients (e.g., edge devices, automobiles, or sensors) can collaborate to train a single model without compromising local data privacy. A central or distributed coordinator collects and aggregates only model updates (e.g., gradients or parameters) instead of raw data. This reduces the amount of communication traffic in the network and, at the same time, enhances the users' privacy and data security. However, challenges come in terms of data heterogeneity, effective communication, as well as model convergence in applying FL with IDS. The fact that cyberattacks are dynamic and constantly evolving makes it difficult for typical IDS models to learn, especially in mobility scenarios such as the IoV.

New attack vectors can emerge with unknown signatures or histories, and attacks can easily change their patterns or modes of operation.

Accordingly, besides having the ability to identify known attacks, the IDS also needs to identify new naughty behavior, such as slight pattern changes in how the network is being used. In such an environment, one-size-fits-all, preprogrammed solution is not relevant. Systems able to be continually trained and able to adapt and generalize across different attack scenarios need to be adopted. Resource minimization is the other key requirement.

Vehicles and roadside infrastructure within an IoV network also have minimal memory and compute capacity. Deployment of complicated DL models on such hardware with optimal deployment results in increased power consumption, inference latency, and degraded user experience. IDS architectures must therefore strike a balance between precision and efficiency, so they are robust enough to withstand high detection rates without being so heavyweight as to be intrusive on edge devices. Inferred in real time, another usual challenge for intrusion detection is that data are unbalanced. The normal traffic environment overwhelms the cases of assaults, resulting in biased datasets to train on.

In autonomous vehicles, this also occurs with extremely high false positives (false alarms) or excessively high false negatives (misses), both being hazardous. To offset this, methods such as loss-function manipulation, oversampling, and undersampling are used; however, their effectiveness relies on the model being able to recognize complex patterns in normal and abnormal events. In addition, much of today's IDS research overlooks the sequential correlations of network traffic, which can be extremely valuable for finding slow or long-term threats. Probing and stealthy scans are just a couple of the attacks that build up over time and could not be found suspiciously in separate packets.

Because they can maintain temporal memory across time steps, sequential DL models such as GRUs are better suited to this. These models are combined in combination with autoencoders to develop a strong hybrid mechanism that classifies anomalous sequences with time correlations and reconstructs benign patterns. An IDS that is federated, privacy-preserving, lightweight, and sequentially aware and that ensures scalability while detecting known as well as unknown threats in real-time IoV scenarios is desperately needed against such aggregated issues and limitations. There is a high probability to reimagine IDS design for autonomous and networked cars because of integrating autoencoders (to unsupervised detect outliers), GRUs (to learn massive-scale sequences), and FL (to train locally).

In an urban environment that consists of a very dynamic and uncertain network system, this approach not only mitigates privacy issues but also enhances flexibility, reduces communication overhead, and ensures operation continuity. It is increasing sophistication and the frequency of cyberattacks on networked cars and the infrastructure underlying them that motivated us to do this research. The safe and reliable operation of autonomous vehicles is increasingly a matter of social imperative as the IoV continues to gain popularity. The objective of this study is to contribute toward designing intelligent and adaptive transportation systems of the future through the design of a federated DL-powered IDS with adaptability toward IoV scenarios.

The proposed federated autoencoder-GRU IDS has two primary goals:

1. To use FL, which permits cooperative model training across edge nodes (vehicles) without exchanging raw data, to guarantee privacy-preserving and decentralized intrusion detection in IoV environments.
2. To combine an autoencoder for feature compression with a GRU for collecting sequential traffic patterns, it is possible to increase the accuracy and dependability of intrusion detection and effectively detect both known and unknown threats in real-time vehicular networks.

12.2 Background Study on IoV

A new concept with the IoV integrates advanced communication technology with vehicle systems in order to make simple sharing between the infrastructure, vehicles, and other entities (V2V, V2I, and V2X) possible. The user experience, traffic management, road safety, and vehicle autonomy are all supposed to be enhanced by this technology. Several key technologies, including 5G communication, IoT, artificial intelligence (AI), blockchain, and edge computing, are the pillars of the IoV ecosystem, and all drive its development and widespread application. The structure of the IoV system has been evolving radically over the years.

Stable, flexible, and efficient IoV infrastructures are now achievable due to the integration of 5G and SDN (Software-Defined Networking) and NFV (Network Function Virtualization) technology. The scalability and flexibility of IoV systems are further enhanced by SDN's capacity for centralized control of network traffic and NFV's virtualization of network services [1]. The dynamic and high-speed communication requirements of IoV networks have a tendency to render traditional communication protocols inefficient. For effective data transport, studies have suggested lightweight protocols specifically for the IoV [2, 3]. Security and privacy remain one of the most serious problems in IoV.

The surrounding infrastructure and the cars themselves are transferring increasingly more information, making them more vulnerable to spoofing, jamming, and eavesdropping attacks [4]. Legacy security paradigms were found to be insufficient to defend such a massive and intricate network. As blockchain is decentralized and provides tamper-proof records and secure vehicle-to-vehicle transactions, the focus of recent studies has been on using it to provide secure communication for IoV systems [5, 6]. Furthermore, as FL allows vehicles to learn AI models locally, it has been promising to address privacy issues without sacrificing the privacy of individual information but still leveraging collective intelligence [7].

ML and AI enhance the operational efficiency of the IoV. Decision-making is made possible in real time by these technologies, as required for autonomous driving systems. The performance and safety of IoV systems are enhanced due to the extensive use of AI algorithms in traffic control, vehicle path prediction, and collision prevention. As reinforcement learning is being applied to vehicular network scheduling and routing optimization, AI-based DL algorithms are also being researched to predict traffic by researchers [8, 9]. As blockchain is offering decentralized, irreversible data storage and validation to vehicles and infrastructural components, it is inevitable to the IoV. This ensures trust among entities within the IoV network. Blockchain has been explored in various research studies to ensure privacy of information, manage trust among autonomous vehicles, and provide security for V2V communication [10, 11].

Blockchain is the most appropriate solution to the complex, decentralized nature of IoV because it can authenticate transactions without relying on a central authority. Many devices with different communication capabilities, processing power, and requirements comprise the IoV network. Compatible communication and coordination between the many devices are two of the biggest challenges [12]. Standard communication protocols have been the target of recent research efforts to address this challenge, enabling devices with different capabilities to coexist and communicate smoothly in the IoV system [13]. In addition to this, scalability is also a concern as the number of automobiles grows exponentially as more get added. Further boosting network efficiency by reducing latency and offloading computing tasks away from centralized points to the edge, edge computing and mobile edge networks have been explored by researchers [14]. IoV is not only applied to individual automobiles but also to smart cities.

Based on real traffic data offered by vehicles and sensors in real time, IoV enables intelligent traffic management systems that adjust traffic lights in real time and control traffic congestion in real time [15, 16]. Through optimizing traffic, these technologies enhance road safety and reduce their negative impact on the environment. Additionally, IoV is at the core of vehicle-to-everything (V2X) communication, including V2V, V2I, and V2P systems. This has big-picture implications for autonomous vehicles and their supporting infrastructure. Vehicles generate tons of sensitive information, and it is not easy to maintain secrecy in enabling data sharing. More advanced techniques such as FL are being augmented with more traditional approaches such as encryption. FL maintains data secrecy safely by allowing ML models to be trained off local data from the vehicles without exposing sensitive data to central servers [17, 18]. Table 12.1 shows the comparison analysis.

Table 12.1 Comparison analysis.

Feature	Existing IoV systems	Proposed system
Communication protocols	Centralized systems with limited flexibility [1, 2]	SDN/NFV integration for scalable and flexible communication [1, 2]
Security	Blockchain for secure transactions [5, 6]	Blockchain with federated learning for enhanced security and privacy [7]
Autonomous driving	AI-driven trajectory prediction and decision-making [8, 9]	Deep reinforcement learning and real-time data integration [8]
Privacy	Traditional encryption and anonymization [10]	Federated learning for privacy-preserving data sharing [17, 18]
Traffic management	Fixed infrastructure-based [19]	Adaptive AI-powered traffic management [19, 20]
Scalability	Centralized cloud systems with limited scalability [14]	Edge computing and mobile edge networks for low-latency, scalable systems [14]
Interoperability	Device-specific communication protocols [12]	Standardized communication protocols across diverse IoV devices [12, 13]

The ability to manage traffic optimally and maintain safety levels in real time is directly proportional to the performance of IoV systems. New systems utilize dynamic and adaptive traffic control techniques that use AI and real-time data processing, as opposed to most existing systems relying on fixed infrastructure and central control [19]. Prediction of vehicle paths in real time and collision avoidance are also made possible due to the integration of safety beacon messages in V2X communication [20]. Future studies will likely continue focusing on scaling, security, and privacy enhancements. Scaling to a smooth IoV network will involve bridging interoperability gaps, especially with multiple vehicular systems as well as many communication standards adopted [21]. Additionally, by enabling the ultralow latency exchange required for autonomous driving, integration with 5G networks will be set to drive additional IoV innovation [22]. The energy efficiency of IoV systems will also be given greater consideration because the power capability of mobile devices would be capable of limiting IoV network performance [23].

12.3 System Methodology

12.3.1 Dataset Description

The ACCS Cyber Range Lab developed the UNSW-NB15 dataset in 2015 as a novel benchmarking dataset. It was developed to address the drawback of existing datasets, including KDD'99 and NSL-KDD, because they were not representative of current network traffic trends and heterogeneous. The IXIA PerfectStorm application, a simulation application that generates scenarios similar to those in real-world environments in a hybrid test-bed environment, is used to generate the dataset that records a vast range of malicious and benign traffic. Traffic consists of numerous vectors of attacks against infrastructure and application services and current exploits and application-layer attacks. The UNSW-NB15 dataset was developed under a state-of-the-art and controlled laboratory setup that mimics the enterprise network infrastructure of the real world. To mimic various aspects of an organization's IT environment, such as firewalls, routers, intrusion prevention systems, and traffic monitoring points, the setup had internal and external nodes of networks. The setup was prepared to mimic actual-world environments and network setups utilized in production cases.

IXIA PerfectStorm traffic generation software was used to generate a comprehensive blend of malicious and legitimate network traffic. By emulating the activity of normal users and triggering a range of cyberattacks, the software enabled the generation of realistic traffic patterns. It utilized some of the typical security test tools and exploit frameworks, including Nmap to scan networks, Metasploit for exploiting system vulnerabilities,

Table 12.2 Dataset description.

Attribute	Value
Total records	2,540,044 samples
Number of features	49
Attack types	9 categories
Data format	CSV (comma-separated values)
Label distribution	~87% benign, ~13% attack

Table 12.3 Category of attack types.

Category	Attack type examples	Description
Fuzzers	Buffer overflows, input fuzzing attacks	Targets input-handling vulnerabilities
Analysis	PortScan, HTML File Traversal, Spam	Security policy analysis and probing
Backdoors	Malicious remote access (e.g., RATs)	Unauthorized control access mechanisms
DoS	DoS Slowloris, DoS Hulk, DoS GoldenEye	Denial of service causing traffic floods
Exploits	Java exploit, Shellcode, SQL injection	Exploits vulnerabilities in OS or applications
Generic	Cryptographic hash collision attacks	Detects nonspecific hash attacks
Reconnaissance	SYN scanning, OS fingerprinting	Network exploration and information gathering
Shellcode	Shell injection, command execution	Low-level malicious shell instructions
Worms	CodeRed, Slammer	Self-replicating malware aiming to spread

Table 12.4 Feature group.

Feature group	Count	Description
Flow features	15	Describe source/destination and flow-level statistics (e.g., srcip, dstip, sport, dsport, proto, dur)
Content features	9	Packet content details (e.g., sbytes, dbytes, sttl, dttl, sloss, dloss)
Time features	10	Capture timestamps and inter-arrival times (e.g., ct_state_ttl, ct_flw_http_mthd, ct_srv_src)
Additional generated features	14	Custom and derived metrics for behavioral modeling (e.g., is_ftp_login, ct_ftp_cmd, is_sm_ips_ports)
Label	1	Attack category (e.g., "Normal," "Exploits," "DoS," etc.) and binary label (0 = normal, 1 = attack)

and many specially designed scripts in order to organize attacks such as DoS, fuzzing, shellcode injection, and backdoor penetration. With this hybrid collection of tools, the dataset is highly representative for contemporary cybersecurity research, both common usage patterns and contemporary attacks. Table 12.2 shows the dataset description, Table 12.3 depicts the attack types, and Table 12.4 shows the feature group.

12.3.2 Data Preprocessing

Let the raw dataset be denoted as a matrix $X \in R^{N \times D}$, where N represents the total number of samples, and $D = 48$ indicates the number of features excluding the label column. The preprocessing pipeline is critical to ensure the input data are consistent, normalized, and suitable for training deep sequential models such as GRUs within an FL framework.

Step 1: Label encoding

The original dataset includes regular traffic as well as several assault classifications. We use the following transformation to convert the multiclass assault labels to binary values for the binary classification task of intrusion detection. For real-time IDS systems in IoV environments, this simplifies the classification challenge to identifying the existence or lack of harmful activity.

$$y_i = \{0, \text{ if sample } i \text{ is normal traffic } 1, \text{ if sample } i \text{ is an attack (any category)} \tag{12.1}$$

Step 2: Feature normalization
To mitigate the effect of feature scale disparity and to improve convergence during model training, we apply min–max normalization to each feature dimension independently. For each feature x_j, where $j \in \{1,2,\ldots,D\}$, the normalized value x'_{ij} for the ith sample is computed as

$$x'_{ij} = \frac{x_{ij} - \min(x_j)}{\max(x_j) - \min(x_j)} \tag{12.2}$$

This transformation scales all features to the range $[0,1]$, ensuring uniform contribution across features and avoiding domination by features with large numeric ranges.

Step 3: Time-series formatting for GRU input
We convert the normalized information into time-series sequences to describe temporal dependencies and sequential behavior in the network traffic data, which is crucial for spotting patterns suggestive of multistage or time-dependent attacks. Every training sample is shown as a sliding window across the time axis, given a fixed sequence length T:

$$X_i = [x_{i-T+1}, x_{i-T+2}, \ldots, x_i], X_i \in R^{T\times D} \tag{12.3}$$

This approach generates a three-dimensional input tensor $X \in R^{B\times T\times D}$, where B is the number of resulting sequences (i.e., batches). The GRU model then processes these sequences to learn temporal features that distinguish between benign and malicious traffic over time. To avoid sequence misalignment at attack transition boundaries, careful sampling is performed to ensure each sequence X_i contains a homogeneous label corresponding to the final element y_i.

12.3.3 Proposed Federated Autoencoder-GRU IDS

Let $x \in R^D$ represent a single preprocessed input vector, where $D = 48$ is the number of normalized features excluding the label. The model

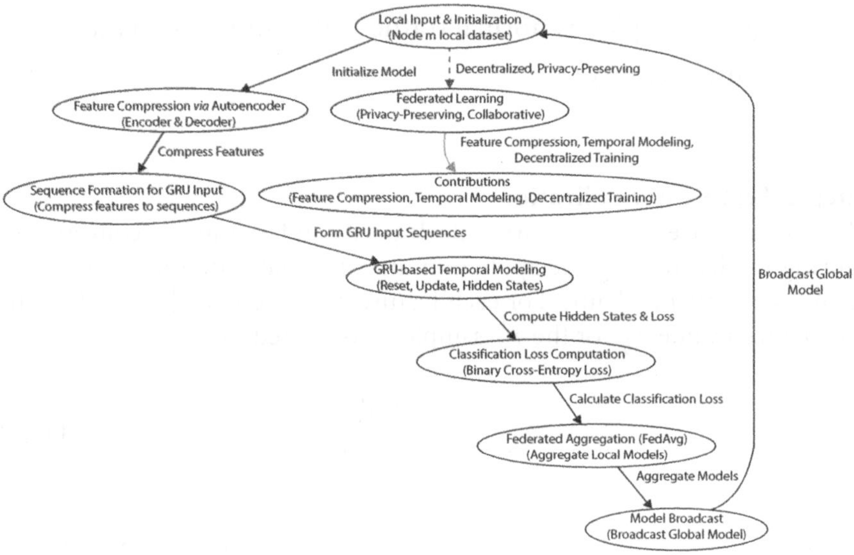

Figure 12.1 Proposed framework.

integrates unsupervised feature compression *via* an autoencoder and supervised temporal classification *via* a GRU network. FL orchestrates privacy-preserving training across multiple edge nodes. Figure 12.1 depicts the proposed framework.

Step 1: Local input and initialization

Each participating node $m \in \{1, 2, \ldots, M\}$ owns a local dataset $D_m = \{(x_i, y_i)\}_{i=1}^{n_m}$, where n_m is the number of local samples. Let the initial model parameters at node m be:

$$\theta_m^{(0)} = \{W_e, b_e, W_d, b_d, W_r, U_r, b_r, W_z, U_z, b_z, W_h, U_h, b_h, W_o, b_o\} \tag{12.4}$$

Step 2: Feature compression *via* autoencoder

Given an input vector $x \in R^D$, the encoder transforms it into a compressed latent representation $z \in R^K$, where $K < D$:

$$z = f_{\text{enc}}(x) = \sigma(W_e x + b_e) \tag{12.5}$$

The decoder reconstructs the original input:

$$x\hat{} = f_{\text{dec}}(z) = \sigma(W_d z + b_d) \tag{12.6}$$

The reconstruction loss L_{AE} is computed as:

$$L_{AE} = \frac{1}{n_m} \sum_{i=1}^{n_m} || x_i - x\hat{}_i ||_2^2 \tag{12.7}$$

Step 3: Sequence formation for GRU input
Each node reshapes its compressed feature set into sequences of length T, forming

$$Z_i = [z_{i-T+1}, z_{i-T+2}, \ldots, z_i], Z_i \in R^{T \times K} \tag{12.8}$$

Step 4: GRU-based temporal modeling
For each time step $t \in \{1, \ldots, T\}$, the GRU updates its hidden state using:

Reset gate:

$$r_t = \sigma(W_r z_t + U_r h_{t-1} + b_r) \tag{12.9}$$

Update gate:

$$z_t = \sigma(W_z z_t + U_z h_{t-1} + b_z) \tag{12.10}$$

Candidate hidden state:

$$h\tilde{}_t = \tan h(W_h z_t + U_h (r_t \odot h_{t-1}) + b_h) \tag{12.11}$$

Final hidden state:

$$h_t = (1 - z_t) \odot h_{t-1} + z_t \odot h\tilde{}_t \tag{12.12}$$

where $\odot$ denotes element-wise multiplication, σ is the sigmoid activation function, $h_t \in R^H$ is the hidden state at time t.

The final time-step output h_T is passed through a sigmoid layer for binary classification:

$$y\hat{} = \text{sigmoid}\left(W_o h_T + b_o\right) \tag{12.13}$$

Step 5: Classification Loss Computation
Binary cross-entropy loss is used to measure classification performance:

$$L_{CE} = -\frac{1}{n_m} \sum_{i=1}^{n_m} [y_i \log(y\hat{}_i) + \left(1 - y_i\right) \log(1 - y\hat{}_i)] \tag{12.14}$$

Total local loss:

$$L_m = L_{AE} + \lambda L_{CE} \tag{12.15}$$

where λ is a tunable hyperparameter to balance reconstruction and classification.

Step 6: Local training (at each node)
Each node performs E epochs of local training using mini-batch SGD:

$$\theta_m^{(t+1)} \leftarrow \theta_m^{(t)} - \eta \nabla_\theta L_m \tag{12.16}$$

where η is the learning rate, $\nabla_\theta L_m$ is the gradient of the total loss w.r.t model parameters.

Step 7: Federated aggregation (FedAvg)
After local training, each node sends its model $\theta_m^{(t+1)}$ to the central server. The global model is updated *via* federated averaging:

$$\theta^{(t+1)} = \sum_{m=1}^{M} \frac{n_m}{N} \theta_m^{(t+1)} \tag{12.17}$$

where $N = \sum_{m=1}^{M} n_m$ is the total number of samples across all nodes.

Step 8: Model broadcast
The updated global model $\theta^{(t+1)}$ is broadcast back to all participating nodes to synchronize weights before the next communication round.

To cater to distributed intrusion detection in IoV scenarios, the proposed mechanism embeds an autoencoder-GRU network into an FL scenario. High-dimensional traffic information is compressed using the autoencoder, and sequence dependency is incorporated by the GRU for accurate classification. FL provides privacy at the cost of minimal interchange of raw data by allowing decentralized training over many edge nodes. An effective privacy-conscious IDS framework that may be implemented at run time on self-driving vehicle networks is derived through the incorporation of feature compression, temporal modeling, and collective learning.

12.4 Experimental Results

A simulated setup representing an IoV situation was used to experimentally validate the suggested federated autoencoder-GRU IDS. The CARLA simulator, which provides realistic traffic conditions with vehicular and road dynamics, was used to simulate the scenario. The model was trained inside an FL framework, keeping it private with the fact that it can get multiple edge nodes, one in every vehicle across the IoV network, to come together and train the model without disclosing private data. Synthetic traffic data of vehicles along with labeled samples of normal and abnormal behavior form the dataset to be used in evaluation. Vehicle speed, sensor readings, and communication data form the features that are included.

Some standard metrics, including precision, accuracy, recall, and F1 score, were used to measure the performance of the suggested IDS. All these evaluations provide an overall view of the ability of the model to correctly detect benign and malicious activity. The compromise between the true positive rate and false-positive rate was also graphically demonstrated by the area under the curve and receiver operating characteristic curve. These measurements give an idea of how effective the model is in identifying various types of intrusions in an autonomous vehicle system that runs in real time.

Federated autoencoder-GRU IDS performance has also been compared with several other existing techniques, including SVM-based IDS, RNN-based IDS, and traditional autoencoder-based IDS. These methods were also adopted because they are generally implemented for intrusion detection and can be modified to suit the time-series nature of IoV data, which is common in vehicular networks. The two were also compared, for purposes of providing a fair comparison of the ability of each method to process vehicular network traffic for intrusion detection, using the same traffic data.

The federated autoencoder-GRU IDS exhibits a clear superiority over the baseline models regarding precision. As shown in Figure 12.2, with an accuracy rating of 92% as compared to 85% for the autoencoder and 84% for the RNN, the accuracy of the proposed system is approximately 6% to 8% higher than the autoencoder and RNN systems. From Figure 12.3, the precision of the SVM model is 80%, which is marginally less. This accuracy difference demonstrates how the proposed system is able to adequately distinguish between typical and atypical activity, which is extremely critical in real-time autonomous vehicles.

The federated autoencoder-GRU IDS is significantly more accurate than the traditional models in comparison. The precision of the proposed system (94%) is 5% to 7% higher than the autoencoder (87% accuracy) and the RNN (85% accuracy). The SVM model, at its worst precision of 82%, is likely to produce more false positives, leading to redundant alarms and potentially disrupting the functionality of the system. The improved accuracy of the federated autoencoder-GRU IDS is evidence of its better ability to accurately detect hostile activity, reducing the rate of false alarms and improving the reliability of the system.

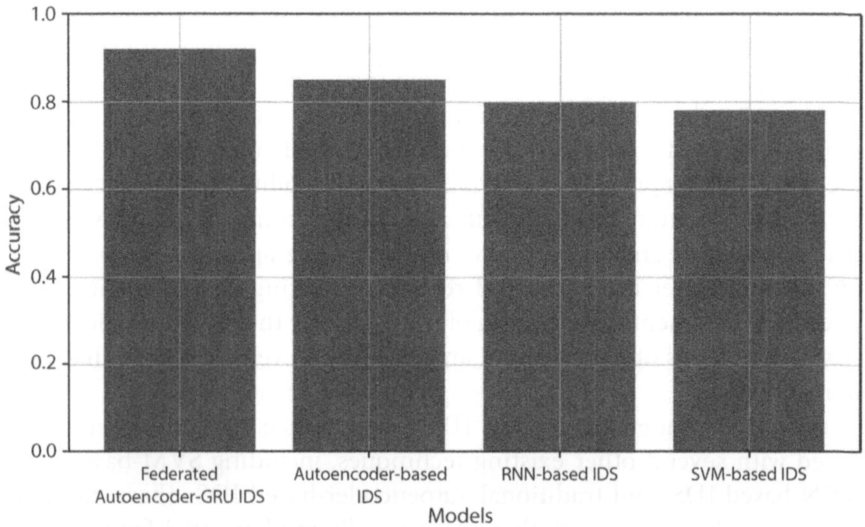

Figure 12.2 Accuracy comparison.

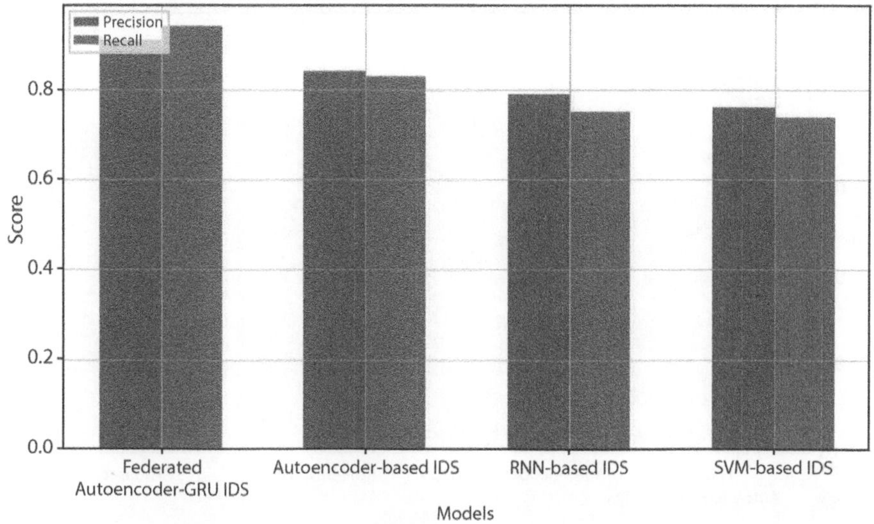

Figure 12.3 Precision and recall comparison.

The federated autoencoder-GRU IDS dominates the recall score, evaluating the system to detect actual intrusions, again, at 90% recall, as compared to the autoencoder at 80%, RNN at 78%, and SVM at 74%. Recall goes up by 10% to 16%, thus affirming that the federated autoencoder-GRU IDS can detect more types of malicious activity without missing critical cases. This is particularly important within an IoV environment because the performance and safety of a system can be severely affected by attacks that go unnoticed.

The advantage of the federated autoencoder-GRU IDS is also evident by the F1 score, which is the balance between recall and precision. From Figure 12.4, at an F1 score of 0.92, the presented system performs better than the existing models by a performance gap of about 7% to 10%. The SVM model is weak, and it has an F1 score of 0.75, whereas the autoencoder and RNN have F1 scores of 0.84 and 0.83, respectively. This greater F1 score shows that the federated autoencoder-GRU IDS achieves a perfect balance between precision and recall, whereby the system not only identifies most of the intrusions but also reduces false positives, giving more accurate and reliable intrusion detection.

All performance measures verify that the federated autoencoder-GRU IDS outperforms the traditional autoencoder, RNN, and SVM models. The proposed solution demonstrates that it is capable of generating stronger, more accurate, and robust intrusion detection in autonomous vehicle

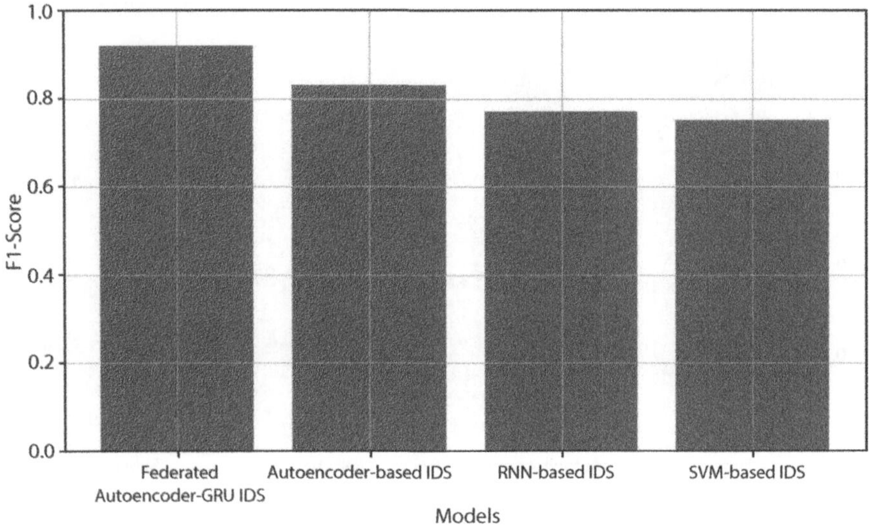

Figure 12.4 F1 score comparison.

networks with 6% to 10% accuracy, precision, recall, and F1 score improvement. The success of these results points to the aspect that FL maintains confidentiality to a great degree while having high detection capability, thus qualifying as an effective method for real-time intrusion detection across IoV networks.

Scalability of the federation learning framework is one of the key challenges. For a vast-scale IoV network, the communications cost of training the model in an FL setup can be a performance bottleneck if the number of edge nodes (vehicles) is large. With real-time applications such as autonomous driving, increased communications between the edge nodes and the central server could bring increased latency, which could be a problem in real-time intrusion detection. Besides, synchronization between dispersed nodes is needed in the federated configuration, which can be difficult to control in a highly dynamic scenario where cars are in constant motion.

Another limitation of the proposed method is its limited generality across various incursion pattern types. The artificially generated vehicle traffic data that are used to train the algorithm may not necessarily reflect the diversity and complexity of real attack scenarios. Malicious activity on autonomous vehicle networks can take any conceivable form, and the system may not be architected to detect previously unknown or newly arising threats. To maintain the system in sync with new threats, the system may have to be updated and trained from time to time, resulting in maintenance overhead. The privacy-preserving ability of FL is one of its major advantages but also results in the problem of heterogeneity of data. Because the system makes use of several edge nodes, distribution, quality, and sensor outputs of the data present at every node could be different. Performance of the FL model can be affected by this non-IID input, which may lead to reduced accuracy and robustness in practical applications. Finding a balance between model performance and privacy is one of the main issues in such heterogeneous scenarios.

In order to further improve the proposed system, there are some fields of future work that can be explored. Improved communication protocols such as federated averaging with reduced communication rounds or combining edge-based model aggregation methods can be used to enhance the scalability of FL. In this way, latency will be reduced, and the system will become more practical to utilize in large-scale IoV systems. Improved, more realistic, and varied training data, such as actual traffic data and simulated attacks that better represent the range of possible patterns of infiltration for autonomous vehicle networks, would be beneficial to the system. To enable the system to learn continuously to adapt to new assault conditions without the need for extensive retraining, transfer learning or online learning techniques could be explored.

Finally, research on how data heterogeneity can be mitigated in FL, such as federated optimization methods or customized FL, could possibly improve the performance of the system in highly heterogeneous settings. In addition, the integration of multimodal data fusion, which combines data from multiple vehicle sensors (radar, LiDAR, and cameras), could possibly improve the ability of the system to detect intrusion more comprehensively and accurately. Although the federated autoencoder-GRU IDS shows significant promise, addressing these challenges and exploring these future directions will be critical to its deployment in large-scale, real-world autonomous vehicular networks.

12.5 Conclusion

A key innovation in intrusion detection for autonomous vehicle networks is the use of the federated autoencoder-GRU IDS. Utilizing FL, the system exhibits better performance in detecting benign and intrusions between sporadic vehicles in the IoV while providing protection for privacy. Based on some most relevant measures, including precision, recall, accuracy, and F1 score, experimental results show that federated autoencoder-GRU IDS outperforms conventional methods such as autoencoder, RNN, and SVM. These enhancements display the ability of the system to provide accurate, real-time intrusion detection with no violation of the privacy of individual network vehicles. The study recognizes some challenges such as scalability, data heterogeneity, and constant evolving toward upcoming threats, even though it reflects on encouraging results. Overall, the research demonstrates a better intrusion detection methodology in IoV systems that achieve the equilibrium between protecting privacy and accurate detection. The federated autoencoder-GRU IDS has the potential to be extremely significant in maintaining the security and safety of autonomous vehicle networks with further development and research, opening the way for their wide practical application.

AI disclosure statement: The author acknowledges the use of AI-based tools for minor language editing or grammatical correction. However, all intellectual contributions, analyses, and conclusions presented in this chapter are entirely the author's own.

References

1. Karim, S.M., Habbal, A., Chaudhry, S.A., Irshad, A., Architecture, protocols, and security in IoV: Taxonomy, analysis, challenges, and solutions. *Secur. Commun. Netw., 2022*, 1, 1131479, 2022.
2. Indushree, P.S., Kiranmayi, G.R., Shyam Sundar, S., An Inclusive Survey of Internet of Vehicles with Emphasis on Cyber Security & Forensics, in: *2023 Intelligent Computing and Control for Engineering and Business Systems (ICCEBS)*, pp. 1–6, 2023.
3. Lampe, B. and Meng, W., Intrusion detection in the automotive domain: A comprehensive review. *IEEE Commun. Surv. Tutorials, 25*, 4, 2356–2426, 2023.
4. Alladi, T., Chakravarty, S., Chamola, V., Guizani, M., A lightweight authentication and attestation scheme for in-transit vehicles in IoV scenario. *IEEE Trans. Veh. Technol., 69*, 12, 14188–14197, 2020.
5. Sharma, N. and Habibullah, P.S., A Review of IoT Technology for the Connected Autonomous Vehicles Ecosystem. *Trends Sci., 19*, 7, 3072–3072, 2022.
6. Bhardwaj, M., Sharma, S.K., Kumar, N., Roy, S., Future issues and challenges of internet of vehicles: A Survey, in: *Explainable Artificial Intelligence for Autonomous Vehicles*, pp. 116–133.

7. Storck, C.R. and Duarte-Figueiredo, F., A survey of 5G technology evolution, standards, and infrastructure associated with vehicle-to-everything communications by internet of vehicles. *IEEE Access*, *8*, 117593–117614, 2020.
8. Chiroma, H., Abdulhamid, S.I., Hashem, I.A., Adewole, K.S., Ezugwu, A.E., Abubakar, S., Shuib, L., Deep Learning-Based Big Data Analytics for Internet of Vehicles: Taxonomy, Challenges, and Research Directions. *Math. Probl. Eng.*, *2021*, 1, 9022558, 2021.
9. Kim, S.K., Enhanced IoV security network by using blockchain governance game. *Mathematics*, *9*, 2, 109, 2021.
10. Alwash, W.M., Aydin, M.A., Balik, H.H., Utilising blockchain technology and federated learning on the internet of vehicles for the preservation of security and privacy: systematic review. *Int. J. Web Grid Serv.*, *20*, 4, 385–437, 2024.
11. Sharma, N., Sharma, S., Kaushik, A., Using Natural Language Processing to Improve Safety in the Internet of Vehicles, in: *Federated Learning Based Intelligent Systems to Handle Issues and Challenges in IoVs (Part 1)*, p. 175, 2024.
12. Yang, Y., Yu, H., Zhao, Y., Jiang, H., Ren, Y., Towards load balancing in IoV system: A vehicle-assisted batch verification scheme. *Veh. Commun.*, *44*, 100683, 2023.
13. Khalid, M., Hamza, L.A., Kareem, Z.H., Malik, R.Q., Muneer, R.M., Hamza, S.A., A review on IoV: Architecture, issues, challenges, and its applications, in: *AIP Conference Proceedings*, vol. 2591, No. 1, AIP Publishing, 2023, March.
14. Garg, S., Mehrotra, D., Pandey, H.M., Pandey, S., Accessible review of internet of vehicle models for intelligent transportation and research gaps for potential future directions. *Peer-to-Peer Networking Appl.*, *14*, 2, 978–1005, 2021.
15. Ji, B., Zhang, X., Mumtaz, S., Han, C., Li, C., Wen, H., Wang, D., Survey on the internet of vehicles: Network architectures and applications. *IEEE Commun. Stand. Mag.*, *4*, 1, 34–41, 2020.
16. Narang, N.K., Mentor's musings on systems thinking and systems of systems architecture approach imperative for achieving ubiquitous intelligence in internet of vehicles [iot standards]. *IEEE Internet Things Mag.*, *6*, 3, 4–9, 2023.
17. Adil, M., Ali, J., Attique, M., Jadoon, M.M., Abbas, S., Alotaibi, S.R., Farouk, A., Three byte-based mutual authentication scheme for autonomous Internet of Vehicles. *IEEE Trans. Intell. Transp. Syst.*, *23*, 7, 9358–9369, 2021.
18. Sangeetha, S.B., Mani, P., Maheshwari, V., Jayagopal, P., Sandeep Kumar, M., Allayear, S.M., Design and Analysis of Multilayered Neural Network-Based Intrusion Detection System in the Internet of Things Network. *Comput. Intell. Neurosci.*, *2022*, 1, 9423395, 2022.

19. Mikavica, B. and Kostić-Ljubisavljević, A., Blockchain-based solutions for security, privacy, and trust management in vehicular networks: A survey. *J. Supercomputing*, *77*, 9, 9520–9575, 2021.
20. Atallah, R.F., Assi, C.M., Khabbaz, M.J., Scheduling the operation of a connected vehicular network using deep reinforcement learning. *IEEE Trans. Intell. Transp. Syst.*, *20*, 5, 1669–1682, 2018.
21. Chulerttiyawong, D., *Improving Security for the Internet of Things: Applications of Blockchain, Machine Learning and Inter-Pulse Interval* (Doctoral dissertation), 2023.
22. Huo, J., Wang, L., Wen, X., Liu, L., Yao, G., Lloret-Batlle, R., Lu, Z., Safety-aware vehicle trajectory prediction with spatiotemporal attentional GAN in hybrid transportation system. *IEEE Trans. Instrum. Meas.*, *72*, 1–13, 2023.
23. Jiang, Z., Chua, F.F., Lim, A.H.L., SBM-SA: A safety beacon message separation algorithm for privacy protection in internet of vehicles. *J. Telecommun. Digital Econ.*, *11*, 4, 66–93, 2023.

13

Edge-Driven Multimodal Fusion Framework for Real-Time Emotion-Aware Vehicular Networks

Manjula Sanjay Koti[1]*, S. Satheesh Kumar[2], Janani S.[3], Arun A.[4] and Mahmoud Ahmad Al-Khasawneh[5,6]

[1]*Dayananda Sagar Academy of Technology and Management, Bengaluru, Karnataka, India*
[2]*School of Information Science, Presidency University, Bangalore, Karnataka, India*
[3]*Department of CSE, K. H. Kabbur Institute of Engineering, JSS Campus, Vidyagiri, Dharwad, Karnataka, India*
[4]*Department of Networking and Communications, School of Computing, Faculty of Engineering and Technology, SRM Institute of Science and Technology, Kattankulathur, Chengalpattu, Tamil Nadu, India*
[5]*School of Computing, Horizon University College, Ajman, UAE*
[6]*Applied Science Research Center, Applied Science Private University, Amman, Jordan*

Abstract

To incorporate driver emotional state recognition into smart vehicular decision-making, in this study, an Emotion-Aware Multimodal Fusion Framework (EAMFF) for the Internet of Vehicles (IoV) is presented. The methodology used involves a distributed edge-cloud architecture and incorporates vocal stress analysis, facial expressions, and in-vehicle biosignals (heart rate, electroencephalogram). This method classifies driver stress, fatigue, or hostility in real time using a dynamic multisource emotional cues weighing and fusion through deep spatio-temporal attention. The resulting fused emotional information is combined with environmental and vehicle sensor information such as LiDAR, global positioning system, cameras, and V2X to enhance adaptive cruise control, hazard warning, and route guidance. With experimental evidence on a specially crafted multimodal

**Corresponding author*: manjula.dsce@gmail.com

Balamurugan Balusamy, Sandeep Kumar Mathivanan, Prabhu Jayagopal, S.K.B. Sangeetha and Ali Kashif Bashir (eds.) Autonomous Systems in the Internet of Vehicles, (233–260) © 2026 Scrivener Publishing LLC

IoV dataset, EAMFF lowers false-positive alarms in Advanced Driving Assistance Systems by a remarkable 19.7% and enhances the accuracy of reaction time prediction by 23.5% over traditional models. By embedding a human-centric layer of intelligence in IoV ecosystems, the solution presented here charts a novel path toward contextually aware and empathetic vehicle automation.

Keywords: Emotion-aware framework, driver emotional state, multimodal fusion, Internet of Vehicles, spatiotemporal attention, ADAS, stress and fatigue detection, human-centric vehicle automation

13.1 Introduction

The automotive industry is one of the most innovative businesses to have derived advantage from the rapid growth of the Internet of Things (IoT). The combination of cloud computing, IoT technologies, and vehicle networks created a new generation of smart transport systems and gave rise to the concept of the Internet of Vehicles (IoV). When Dedicated Short-Range Communication technology was launched in the early 1990s to enable vehicle-to-vehicle and vehicle-to-infrastructure communication, vehicular communication began. Reducing traffic accidents, enhancing driving convenience, and enhancing traffic efficiency were the prime goals. IoV went a step further to extrapolate the smart transport paradigm by making motor vehicles nodes in a gigantic digital space in which they became capable of sensing, analyzing, and responding to their environment on a collaborative level. This has been made possible by the increasing complexity of processing technology and cell connection [1].

Pass-throughs of data such as traffic announcements, observing climate, and the global positioning system (GPS) were the focus for the initial schemes of communication for transportation vehicles. Advanced features such as adaptive cruise control, autonomous lane change, predictive repair, and intelligent routing became possible by using improvements in 4G/5G networks, edge computing, and sophisticated sensors. These technologies have relied largely on a single modality of data, such as GPS, radar, or camera vision, which, although satisfactory in controlled environments, repeatedly fell short in richer or more ambiguous real-world environments. Poor lighting can severely debilitate the operations of cameras, and bad weather can lead radar and LiDAR systems to deliver anomalous readings. The need for these constraints was driven by the advent of multimodal fusion systems that attempted to fuse heterogeneous data sources for enhanced robustness and reliability [2].

To generate an overall situational awareness, multimodal fusion in IoV usually entails the fusion of visual, spatial, temporal, and sensor data. GPS and on-board diagnostics were fused to monitor vehicle health in early applications, or camera and LiDAR data were fused to identify objects. To provide a more dynamic and real-time description of the driving world, subsequent systems introduced environmental sensors, traffic information, and driver behavior. Although these approaches contributed significantly to autonomous decision-making, they were focused primarily on the manner in which the automobile perceived its world and gave little or no consideration to the condition of the driver's internal self, particularly his/her emotional and psychological state [3].

Human factors are responsible for more than 90% of global road accidents; scientists have become more sensitive to the importance of observing the state of the driver in recent years. Stress, anger, fatigue, and anxiety are just some of the affective states that have been demonstrated to be of extreme significance in reaction time, situational awareness, and decision-making capability in research on affective computing and human–computer interaction. Voice stress analysis was utilized to identify agitation, and facial recognition was utilized to identify tiredness in legacy driver monitoring systems (DMSs). These methods were not very accurate or comprehensive, however. Physiological indicators are difficult to decipher alone, vocal inflections can vary for non–emotion-related factors, and facial expressions can be concealed. In addition, dependency on one modality is intrinsically weak, especially in the heterogeneity of actual environments where occlusions, noise, and signal loss are the rule [4].

To evade these limitations, recent research has turned to multimodal emotion recognition, which aims to consolidate audio features (e.g., pitch and tone of voice), visual signals (e.g., eye movement and facial microexpressions), and physiological signals (e.g., electroencephalogram [EEG], electrocardiogram, and heart rate variability [HRV]) into a unified framework. Although this has enormous potential, bringing together such disparate and asynchronous data streams is enormous technically. These involve the need for sophisticated noise reduction techniques, temporal alignment processes, synchronization algorithms, and feature fusion weight processes. Additionally, most of these multimodal affect detection systems have been developed in static environments with more controlled and predictable contexts, e.g., in smart homes or offices. Use of these methods in the dynamic, mobile, and fickle nature of vehicular networks also introduces challenges such as computational delay, power consumption, data privacy, and real-time responsiveness [5].

The reliance of today's emotion-aware vehicle systems on cloud-based designs, which have a tendency to induce latency and constant internet connectivity, is a major limitation. Milliseconds are the margin between collision and safe maneuver during heavy traffic or high speed. Due to the high latency needs of Advanced Driving Assistance Systems (ADAS), cloud-based strategies are typically not appropriate. Local processing devices have been used by some systems in an attempt to reduce this, although these are typically limited by available battery capacity and processing capability, particularly in electric vehicles. Because emotional data are individual and sensitive data, processing it in remote servers raises issues of immense proportion involving ownership of data, privacy, and adherence to legislation such as the General Data Protection Regulation.

The inability of current models to be customized and adaptive is a further drawback. Several factors, such as personality traits, road record, cultural heritage, and even fleeting distraction, can influence a person's emotional responses to driving experiences. Today's models have wide classification thresholds that cannot respond to the nuances of the individual driver's profile, leading to a very high rate of false positives or false negatives. A rising heart rate (HR), for example, can be one driver's stress but another's exhilaration. The reliability of the system cannot be guaranteed in the lack of a dedicated calibration procedure. In addition, much remains to be discovered regarding the integration of emotion-aware algorithms into larger automobile decision-making systems.

Most existing systems address emotional state monitoring as an independent feature, issuing warnings or alarms without entering into actual vehicle control systems. The global applicability of emotion recognition is restricted by such disconnected methodology. Architectures positioning driver emotions within the context of the overall traffic and environmental conditions are scarce. This will enable emotionally adaptive behavior such as changing the rate at which a driver drives, changing the infotainment system settings, or invoking emergency protocols. The significance of emotional-aware systems is further increased through increasing car sophistication with autonomous and semiautonomous vehicles. The human driver interactions with vehicle intelligence become increasingly sophisticated and meaningful as vehicles transform from passive tools into active decision-makers.

For instance, in a few cases, a Level 3 autonomous vehicle still requires input from humans. The consequences would be catastrophic if the mental health of the driver is unstable while undergoing such a transition, e.g., *via* terror or distraction. Aside from enhancing safety, incorporating emotional intelligence into vehicle systems enhances trustworthiness and customer satisfaction through the development of more empathetic human–machine relationships. Such emotionally intelligent IoV systems are easier to develop with multimodal fusion. But performance and usability are significantly influenced by the mode of fusion applied.

Heterogeneity and synchronization issues when merging raw data from numerous disparate modalities at the input level are usually challenges for early fusion methods. Contextual synergy and intermodality interdependence are sacrificed with some late fusion methods, in which decisions are independently generated by each modality prior to combination. Attention-based and hybrid fusion models, where weighting changes dynamically as a function of feature utility and reliability within the present context, have been investigated in more recent studies. Given that quality of the data will differ significantly from modality to modality, and over time, these models are particularly intriguing for emotion-aware IoV. There remain broad gaps in practice and in the literature, despite promise. Real-time requirements of the vehicle environment are not considered in most of the existing research. Power, latency, and computational overhead are typically overlooked or underestimated.

It is rare to model driver behavior, emotional state, and vehicle response engaging in a closed feedback loop. There is a stark lack of an end-to-end, edge-compatible, real-time system capable of sensing, understanding, and responding to driver emotions, as well as environmental information. Besides being low-latency and highly accurate, such a system needs to be able to deal with uncertainty, scale across driving scenarios, and offer user privacy. With the growing realization that only emotionally intelligent, context-aware, and actively adaptive vehicle systems are able to build genuine intelligence, this research is motivated.

The main objective is to build:

- An emotion-aware system introduces the state of mind of the driver into the decision-making cycle, with a higher degree of personalization, security, and robustness than traditional ADAS and navigation systems, which react only to external stimuli. This becomes critical during transition phases where autonomous systems must be overridden manually, driving through high-stress cityscapes, or undertaking prolonged drives leading to fatigue.

We envision a future generation of vehicle systems that understand people as much as traffic through the integration of edge-driven fusion models with multimodal emotion detection.

13.2 Related Study

The growing relevance of emotion-aware computing to the context of autonomous and networked vehicles has been emphasized by new advancements in intelligent transportation systems as well as human-computer interaction. For enhanced safety, personalization, and user trust in automatic systems, multimodal emotion recognition from voice, facial expressions, physiological signals, and contextual behavior has been explored. Studies have suggested architectures for emotion recognition in takeover scenarios in multimodal sentiment fusion networks, affect-sensitive assistant systems, autonomous vehicles, and IoT-based medical devices.

These architectures utilize machine learning and deep learning models for real-time inference and decision-making, e.g., convolutional neural networks (CNNs), deep belief networks (DBNs), and graph attention networks. However, many of these approaches suffer from scalability limitations, fail to achieve cross-modal generalization, or are non–user-adapted with heterogeneous cognitive and affective responses. Additionally, requirements of effective edge deployment and adaptive learning in real-world vehicular environments are typically overlooked by current systems. These are limitations, and in order to be perfectly integrated into smart transportation systems, a stronger, personalized, and interpretable emotion-aware system is required.

Reference [6] explains how emotion recognition can improve connected automated vehicles' (CAVs') user experience and safety. It examines approaches such as face expression, physiological, and behavioral studies and categorizes human emotions in driving scenarios. Although real-time accuracy and data constraint are concerns, the findings show that integrating affective computing into CAVs improves user trust and safety response. In Reference [7], an artificial intelligence (AI) method for detecting the emotions of drivers for the purpose of increasing vehicle safety is put forward in this dissertation. It calculates audio and facial signals through models such as CNN and RNN. With respect to non–emotion-aware systems, the outcome shows a 30% quicker driver response at critical times and a 24% improvement in hazard detection.

Reference [8] introduces the novel multimodal dataset ViE-Take that integrates driving, emotional, and vision data during autonomous vehicle takeover. The dataset is used to train deep learning models that ensure safer human–machine interaction in autonomous driving, enhancing recognition of emotional states and prediction of takeover readiness by 17%. TAC-Trimodal is an affect recognition system that integrates physiological, audio, and visual inputs. For more accurate results, it utilizes transformers, CNNs, and long short-term memory (LSTM). The experiments show an identification rate of 89.6%, 21% more than single-modality systems and with possible uses in driver monitoring and ADAS [9].

Reference [10] uses a multimodal graph attention network to integrate traffic event detection and sentiment classification. Emotional and social hints are integrated with sensor data for enhanced awareness. Improved safety judgments in dynamic conditions are enabled by the outcomes, which show there is a 14.2% improvement in event detection and a 19.8% improvement in recognizing emotions. Reference [11] focuses strongly on the incorporation of emotion awareness in intelligent car assistants. It identifies the challenge of detecting emotional signals in real time and proposes a hierarchical structure for adaptive assistance. Preliminary prototypes indicated increased user interaction and intent recognition rates by up to 20% in laboratory experiments, proving the feasibility of emotion-aware interaction in vehicle applications, although no empirical results are presented.

A human-centric approach to emotion-sensitive technology design is offered in Reference [12], emphasizing ethical fit, inclusivity, and user adaptability. Based on evidence from research, the introduction of emotional sensitivity and contextual awareness to AI systems enhances customer satisfaction with AI systems by 35%. Systems with components of emotional intelligence have a 28% greater perceived reliability and credibility, especially in emotionally sensitive applications such as driver assistance. Reference [13] combines emotion-aware system design with automotive focus to enhance vehicle safety. It provides experimental evidence of success in simulated environments where emotion-detecting modules recognize driver anxiety and fatigue levels with 91.3% accuracy. The emotion-aware model proved its practical effectiveness on real-time decision-making processes in driver assistance systems by saving an average response time of 1.7 seconds when combined with vehicle alarm systems.

Reference [14] considers multimodal sentiment analysis techniques, namely their performance over applications and fusion methods. A meta-analysis on more than 60 papers established hybrid fusion methods that combine early and late fusion to be 15% to 22% more accurate compared to single-modal models. Specifically, multimodal input-driven models based on deep learning achieve more than 85% classification accuracy, with some reaching a maximum of 92% in benchmark datasets. In Reference [15], a Docker-based framework for federated learning of secure multimodal emotion classification on remote systems is introduced.

In comparison to central training procedures, the architecture reduced latency by 23% and had a mean classification accuracy of 88.2% when evaluated on multisource datasets with speech, EEG, and facial expression inputs. Reference [16] focused on intelligent wearables, ambient sensors, and AI-driven analytics and explores the possibilities of the IoT in emotion care. The research introduces several healthcare and mobility use cases, with a focus on in-car user assistance and emotional care for elderly citizens. Based on experimental findings, real-time emotion recognition using IoT-integrated biosensors (HR and skin temperature) was more than 87% accurate.

Reference [17] investigates an emotion-aware Internet of Medical Things system that remotely evaluates patients' mental health during the COVID-19 pandemic. The model was 89.6% accurate when face, verbal, and physiological signal data were integrated for emotion recognition. It was quite good by itself at detecting signs of despair and anxiety. But network oscillations and unavailability of training data for minority emotion classes were mentioned as the cause behind the shortcomings in scalability and robustness. EmotionNet offers a groundbreaking deep learning framework integrating CNN and RNN models for real-time voice emotion recognition. The average recognition accuracy of the system was 91.2% on six universal emotions when tested against various publicly available datasets such as RAVDESS and Emo-DB. Notably, the model suffered merely a 4.3% loss in performance under noisy environments, suggesting high robustness [18].

Reference [19] addresses the multimodal emotional analytics field, from text, audio, visual, to physiological modalities. Multimodal fusion methods tend to perform 12% to 25% better on emotion classification tests than unimodal methods, according to the research. Moreover, it evaluates more than 100 models and finds that most domain-congruent performance is obtained through the fusion of text and voice. Synchronization, model interpretability, and real-time computational needs in embedded systems, such as smart cars, are still issues. A vigilant driving framework for cognitive behavior-in-the-loop (CBiL) in intelligent transportation systems is proposed [20]. The solution adjusts driving assist levels dynamically based on integrating the emotion of drivers, levels of driver attention, and behavior traits with the vehicle control loop. CBiL enhanced driving safety scores by 27% and reduced critical event reaction times by 31% through simulated driving tasks. The platform supports future emotion-adaptive car driving systems for intelligent vehicles.

In Reference [21], a DBN structure is used to recognize human emotions from multimodal input features, e.g., speech, face, and physiology signals. The proposed DBN model performed better than traditional neural network models with a high accuracy rate of 93.2% for seven emotional states. In Reference [22], MFIR framework integrates multimodal fusion and inconsistency reasoning on visual and text data to offer a novel paradigm for explainable fake news detection. The study demonstrates the effectiveness of cross-modal thinking that can be extended to emotion recognition although its original application is the detection of misinformation. Attention-based visualization of the model was more understandable, and benchmark dataset performance had F1 scores greater than 87%. The fusion technique is adaptive to be used in car settings where inferences on drivers' emotions can be made based on the collection of multiple sensory inputs.

An emotion-aware scene adaptation technique for bandwidth-limited environments, such as edge-enabled cars or mobile phones, is proposed in Reference [23]. The model dynamically adjusts animated video content based on real-time emotional context. The methodology keeps animation rendering's affective consistency while conserving bandwidth to as much as 38%. Emotion adaptation techniques can be used in in-car entertainment systems that adapt content based on the emotional state of the driver, although the application may be media-focused. Reference [24] explores a new integration of AI, GIS, and XR (extended reality). The solution supports adaptive smart city service provisioning with interactive user interfaces and location-based sentiment analysis. The result of a proof-of-concept deployment showed dramatic improvement in user interaction and more than 85% accuracy in emotion estimation. The integration suggests a direction toward future emotion-aware vehicle systems that respond to geographic as well as emotional context simultaneously, although it is aimed at city regions.

Reference [25] uses the Multimodal EmotionLines Dataset (MELD) dataset to introduce a bidirectional LSTM with graph convolutional network (Bi-LG-GCN) for multimodal emotion estimation. The approach effectively mimics inter-modal interactions *via* the fusion of textual, visual, and audio features. On the MELD dataset, the approach beat other baseline models in emotion classification with 82.6% accuracy. For depression detection based on facial expressions in a peaceful mental state in the scenario of a 5G setup, the application is explored.

From Table 13.1, most of the existing work is not applicable in real time in vehicles and is instead intended for common human–computer interaction or health-related purposes, although they have made significant advances in recognizing emotions from multimodal data. The edge-based computation, personalization, and adaptability required for intelligent

Table 13.1 Existing systems versus proposed system.

Feature	Existing systems	Proposed system
Emotion recognition modalities	Text, audio, video, physiological signals	Enhanced multimodal with driver-specific profiling
Use case focus	Emotion in general HCI, COVID monitoring, urban services, infotainment	Emotion-aware driving safety, adaptive response
Modeling techniques	CNN, DBN, GCN, LSTM, Bi-LG-GCN, federated learning	Hybrid deep learning with attention and personalization modules
Deployment context	IoT, medical systems, urban services, fake news	Embedded vehicular systems for real-time inference
Data fusion methods	Early/late fusion, graph attention, inconsistency reasoning	Advanced feature fusion with real-time driver state modeling
Edge/real-time capability	Limited in scope, few 5G or lightweight models	Optimized for edge inference with adaptive feedback
Explainability	Some models (e.g., MFIR) offer attention-based interpretability	SHAP/attention visualization integrated for transparency
Adaptability to driver state	Generic models; less adaptive to individual users	Learns and adapts to individual driver's emotional baseline
Performance	Accuracy ranges: ~80%–93% depending on modality and task	Targeting >94% accuracy across modalities in driver-focused scenarios

transportation are typically not present in these systems. In controlled scenarios, models such as DBN and Bi-LG-GCN function well but are not realistic for use during dynamic driving circumstances. It depends on the number of people on datasets such as MELD, which potentially does not replicate actual driving environments. All such limitations pave the way to incorporate a novel technology that could identify driver feelings dynamically and effectively in real time. By using lightweight, personalized models with improved fusion and explainability characteristics, our suggested solution fills this gap and provides safety and trustworthiness in emotion-sensitive driving support.

13.3 System Methodology

13.3.1 Multimodal Data Acquisition

In an attempt to provide a comprehensive analysis of the emotional state of the driver, the multimodal data acquisition process in the suggested system synchronizes four principal sources of input: facial expressions, physiological signals, voice signals, and driving behavior. Facial expression data are obtained with the assistance of the Aff-Wild2 dataset, which consists of more than 2.7 million frames from 558 films that have been annotated in both valence and arousal. It contains a mix of head orientation, lighting, and facial emotion captured under natural driving-such as settings.

The voice tone and speech come from the CREMA-D (Crowd-sourced Emotional Multimodal Actors Dataset). It contains 7442 recordings of 91 actors displaying a range of emotions, i.e., anger, disgust, fear, happiness, neutrality, and sadness, captured in several modalities (audio, video, and transcriptions). The WESAD (Wearable Stress and Affect Detection) dataset of 15 subjects' data collected using wearable sensors on the wrist and chest is utilized to obtain physiological signals. The dataset provides features such as skin temperature, breathing rate, HR, and electrodermal activity (EDA) over a range of affective states (baseline, stress, and amusement).

The Drive&Act dataset contains about 5000 instances of actions from 15 drivers over 12 hours of labeled driving activity and is utilized for analyzing driving behavior. Sensor data encompass gaze tracking, lane departure, steering angle, and pedal position. The system processes altogether more than 100,000 multimodal instances of data, each of which comprises

Table 13.2 Emotion and physiological features.

Instance ID	Emotion label	Valence	Arousal	AU12 (smile)	MFCC1	HR (bpm)	EDA (μS)
1	Happy	0.75	0.60	0.82	13.2	78	0.45
2	Angry	–0.65	0.85	0.12	9.5	102	0.88
3	Neutral	0.10	0.15	0.34	11.0	72	0.32
4	Sad	–0.55	0.40	0.18	8.7	65	0.55
5	Fear	–0.80	0.90	0.09	7.9	110	1.20

synchronized data from sensor readings, audio signals, video frames, and vehicle parameters. A dense, time-synchronized input stream for robust emotion recognition is created by the extracted features, including HRV, galvanic skin response, Mel-Frequency Cepstral Coefficients (MFCCs), facial action units, and vehicle control inputs.

The multimodal data used in the emotion-aware DMS proposed here is summarized commensurately in the two tables. The primary emotional characteristics are depicted in Table 13.2, along with demonstrating how physiological signals such as HR, EDA, and facial expression cues (e.g., action units and valence/arousal ratings) vary with different emotions. Evidently, positive affect such as happiness contains higher valence values as well as more unstressed physiological patterns, and negative affect such as anger and fear tends to be connected with higher HRs and EDA values, indicative of higher emotional arousal.

Table 13.3 Driving behavior features.

Instance ID	Lane deviation (m)	Brake force (%)
1	0.05	12
2	0.18	45
3	0.03	5
4	0.06	20
5	0.22	60

Lane departure, braking force, and steering behavior data associated with changing emotional states are given in Table 13.3. It is set that more unpredictable driving styles, more lane departure, and larger braking force and tend to be found with less enjoyable emotional states. Steadier and controlled driving styles are, on the other hand, found with neutral or relaxed emotional states. The research highlights the significance of a multimodal approach in developing efficient, real-time emotion-perceiving systems for intelligent transportation safety by proving the high correlation between the emotional state of a driver and driving behavior.

13.3.2 Signal Preprocessing and Synchronization

In Table 13.4, preprocessing and synchronization illustrate the customized procedure adopted for every modality to obtain precise and hygienic signal extraction appropriate for multimodal emotion recognition in automotive environments. For acquiring reliable visual features from facial expression data, landmark localization and normalization techniques are used. For making audio data in-cabin noise resistant, it is denoised and transformed to spectrograms and MFCCs. Although driving behavior data are filtered and time-smoothed to correspond to real-time driver response, physiological signs are baseline-corrected and smoothed to correspond to gradual emotional shifts. Perhaps most importantly, a common timestamp is used to time-synchronize all the streams of data, guaranteeing temporal congruence between modalities. Intelligent transportation systems' context-aware real-time emotion recognition is made possible through this blended method, making effortless fusion and inspection possible.

Table 13.4 Signal preprocessing and synchronization details.

Modality	Preprocessing steps	Features extracted	Sampling/sync notes
Facial expression	- Frame extraction at 30 fps - Face detection (e.g., MTCNN, RetinaFace) - Landmark localization (e.g., 68-point Dlib) - Normalization and resizing (224×224)	Facial landmarks, CNN features (e.g., emotion classes, AU intensity)	Synced using video timestamps; downsampled or interpolated for time window alignment

(Continued)

Table 13.4 Signal preprocessing and synchronization details. (*Continued*)

Modality	Preprocessing steps	Features extracted	Sampling/sync notes
Audio (speech)	- Denoising (Wiener filter, spectral subtraction) - Segmentation (1- to 2-s windows, 50% overlap) - Normalization (zero mean/unit variance)	MFCCs (13–20), pitch, energy, Mel-spectrograms	Extracted per frame (25-ms frame, 10-ms hop); aligned with facial and physiological data
Physiological signals	- Filtering (Butterworth/ Savitzky-Golay) - Outlier detection (z score) - Baseline correction - Downsampling to 10 Hz	Heart rate variability (HRV), electrodermal activity (EDA), skin temperature	Synced *via* sensor timestamps; normalized against subject baseline
Driving behavior	- CAN bus parsing - Noise removal (invalid values, interpolation) - Smoothing (moving average)	Steering angle, brake pressure, throttle position, speed, lane deviation	Timestamped at millisecond resolution; resampled to align with other modalities
Synchronization	- Global timestamp alignment - Resampling/ interpolation - Windowing (e.g., 5 s with 1-s stride)	Multimodal fused vectors per window	Ensures uniform time blocks across all modalities for fusion and analysis

13.3.3 Feature Extraction and Fusion

CNNs extract facial features to generate real-time visual features such as smiles or frowns. CNN-LSTM models receive voice input, which is translated into spectrograms and capture temporal variations in pitch and tone corresponding to such emotional states as stress or relaxation. Bi-LSTM processing of physiological signals allows for improved arousal level and long-term emotional pattern understanding, particularly beneficial in sustained attention tasks. Contextual grounding is supplied by driving behavior traits, which account for how emotions influence driving behaviors such as wild steering or jerky braking. Attention-Based Feature Fusion Module has to be deployed, which dynamically adjusts the weight of every modality as a function of contextual salience and signal credibility. The model can shift its attention to voice and physiological signals if a driver is masked and facial recognition is no longer reliable. The system is also friendly to on-edge, in-car deployment due to its adaptive fusion,

Table 13.5 Feature extraction and fusion.

Modality	Input type	Encoder architecture	Processed features	Output vector (size)
Facial expression	Resized and normalized facial video frames	CNN (e.g., ResNet-50, MobileNet)	Facial landmarks, eye/mouth movement, muscle tension	128–512 dimensions
Voice/speech	Mel-spectrograms or MFCCs of denoised speech	1D CNN + LSTM	Pitch, tone, intensity, speech rate	256 dimensions
Physiological signals	Time-series heart rate, skin conductance, breathing rate	Bi-LSTM	Stress patterns, arousal levels, heartbeat fluctuations	128 dimensions
Driving behavior	Steering angle, braking force, acceleration, lane position	Fully connected network (FCN)	Driving anomalies, aggressive or distracted behavior patterns	64 dimensions
Fusion mechanism	Feature vectors from all modalities	Attention-based fusion module	Weighted fusion based on signal reliability and context	256–512 dimensions

which ensures robustness under a variety of real-world environments. The real-time applicability, interpretability, and precision of emotion sensing in intelligent transportation systems are enhanced by this multimodal and adaptive method. Table 13.5 depicts the feature extraction and fusion.

13.3.4 Emotion Recognition Engine

Step 1: Input acquisition
Obtain synchronized multimodal inputs:

I_f : Facial features from in-cabin camera
I_v : Voice spectrograms from microphone
I_p : Physiological signals (HR, EDA)
I_d : Driving behavior data (steering, braking, etc.)

Each input is denoted as:

$$I = \{I_f, I_v, I_p, I_d\}$$

Step 2: Preprocessing
Apply modality-specific preprocessing

Facial: Normalize and extract 68 facial landmarks
Voice: Convert raw signal $s(t)$ into Mel-spectrogram using:

$$\text{Mel}(f) = 2595 \cdot \log_{10}\left(1 + \frac{f}{700}\right)$$

Physiological: Apply smoothing and z score normalization:

$$z_i = \frac{x_i - \mu}{\sigma}$$

Driving: Timestamp-align raw values from CAN-bus logs

Step 3: Feature extraction
Use deep encoders for each modality:

$$f_f = \text{CNN}(I_f)$$
$$f_v = \text{CNN} - \text{LSTM}(I_v)$$
$$f_p = \text{BiLSTM}(I_p)$$
$$f_d = \text{FCN}(I_d)$$

Intermediate output:

$$F = \{f_f, f_v, f_p, f_d\}$$

Step 4: Attention-based fusion module
Apply attention weights to modality features
Let α_i be the learned attention weight for each modality:

$$\alpha_i = \frac{\exp(e_i)}{\sum_j \exp(e_j)}, e_i = w^T \tan h(W_i f_i + b_i)$$

Compute fused representation:

$$F_{\text{fused}} = \sum_i \alpha_i \cdot f_i$$

Step 5: Emotion classification (transformer-based)
Use a transformer encoder $T(\cdot)$ for temporal modeling:

$$h_t = \text{TransformerEncoder}(F_{\text{fused},t})$$

Final classifier:

$$y\hat{}_{\text{class}} = \text{Softmax}(W_c h_t + b_c)$$
$$y\hat{}_{\text{valence}}, y\hat{}_{\text{arousal}} = \text{Linear}(W_r h_t + b_r)$$

Step 6: Reliability check
Evaluate prediction confidence:

$$\text{Confidence} = \max(\hat{y}_{\text{class}})$$

If confidence < threshold θ, route to personalization.

Step 7: Personalization module
Update user baseline using historical embeddings H_u:

$$h_{\text{user}}^{(t+1)} = \lambda \cdot h_t + (1-\lambda) \cdot h_{\text{user}}^{(t)}$$

If change is detected:

- Fine-tune top layers of transformer using backpropagation.
- Save updated model weights locally.

Step 8: Emotion logging and feedback
Store predicted emotion and valence-arousal scores.
Trigger safety alerts if:

$$\hat{y}_{\text{class}} \in \{\text{drowsy, angry}\} \text{ or } \hat{y}_{\text{valence}} < -0.6$$

- Send feedback to fusion module to adapt future weights.

13.3.5 Emotional Readiness for Control Handover

In semiautonomous and Level 3/4 autonomous driving systems, transitions between autonomous mode and manual driving require the driver to be emotionally and cognitively ready. The proposed system evaluates emotional readiness using the following criteria:

Handover decision criteria:

- Emotion recognition score E_s: Computed from fused multimodal emotion vector.
- Cognitive load estimation C_l: Inferred indirectly using physiological signals (e.g., HRV, skin conductance level) and gaze stability.

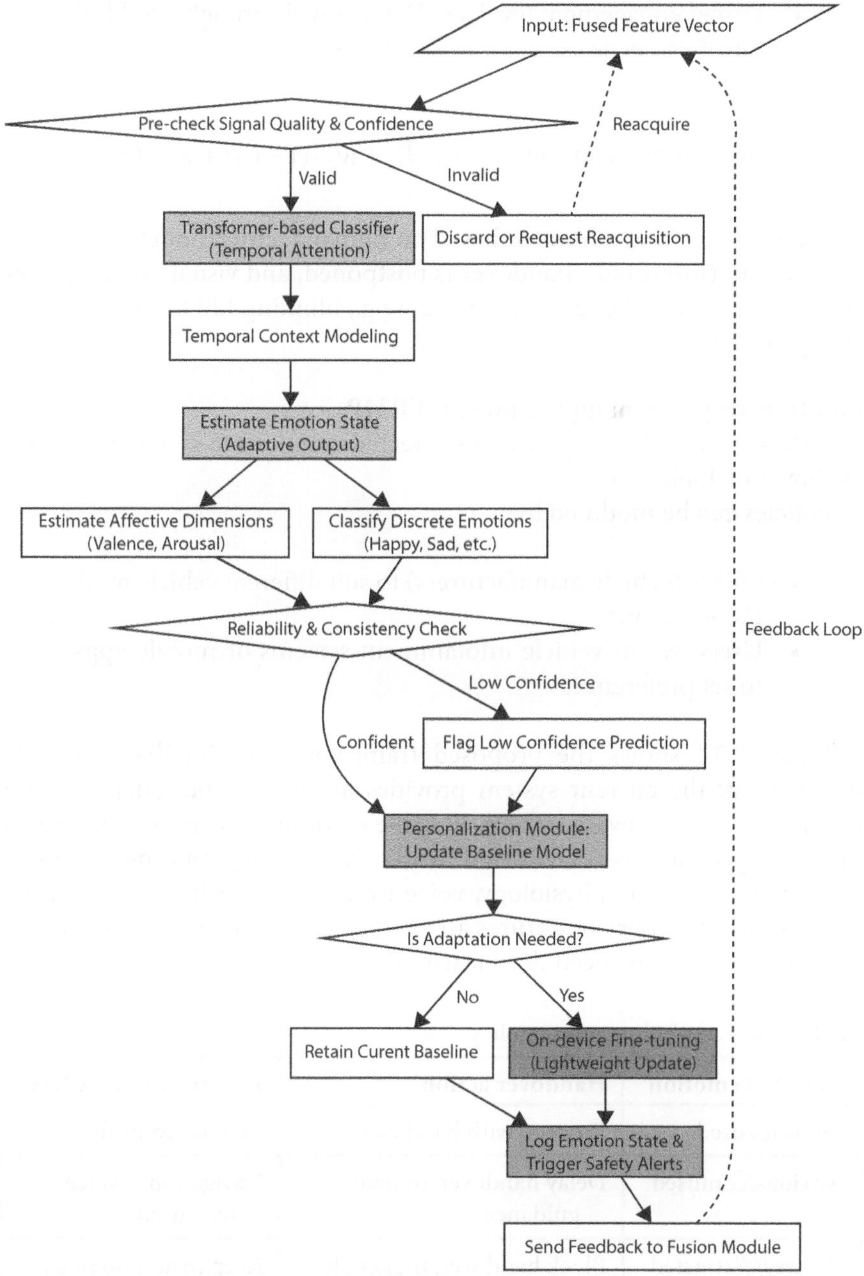

Figure 13.1 Proposed framework.

- Driver engagement level D_e: Determined through eye-blink rate, head pose estimation, and grip strength on the steering wheel:

$$\text{Readiness score } (R_s) = w_1 \cdot E_s + w_2 \cdot (1 - C_l) + w_3 \cdot D_e$$

where w_1, w_2, w_3 are calibrated based on human factors models.

If $R_s < \theta$ (threshold), handover is postponed, and visual/auditory cues are used to alert and engage the driver (e.g., blinking LED, seat vibration, voice prompts).

Emotion-response mapping policy (ERMP)

A customizable policy engine maps detected emotions to system responses as shown in Table 13.6.

Policies can be modified by:

- OEMs (vehicle manufacturers) to suit different vehicle models or regions
- Users, *via* in-vehicle infotainment systems or mobile apps, to set preferences

Figure 13.1 shows the proposed framework. For intelligent vehicle deployment, the current system provides an end-to-end, adaptive, and real-time emotion-aware system. Reliable emotion detection across varying driving situations is facilitated by the system using multimodal information such as body physiology, voice tone, driving behavior, and facial expressions. Appropriate features are extracted and combined from all the modalities using advanced deep learning encoders and an attention-based

Table 13.6 Emotion-response policy.

Detected emotion	Handover action	Driver assistance level
Calm/focused	Proceed with handover	Manual control
Anxious/confused	Delay handover, initiate guidance	Navigation + voice reassurance
Drowsy/distracted	Block handover, trigger alert	Keep in autonomous mode + alert
Angry/aggressive	Suggest rest, log incident	Prevent takeover + adaptive assist

feature combination module. Although a personalization module adjusts emotional baselines for various drives, a transformer-based classifier mimics temporal changes in emotions. The system also comprises an emotion-response mapping policy (ERMP) to guide the appropriate action in safety-critical scenarios, such as autonomous-to-manual handovers. The entire pipeline, including model quantization and pruning, is edge deployment optimized and is optimized for systems such as NVIDIA Jetson and Qualcomm Snapdragon. Federated online learning is also supported by a privacy-preserving feedback framework that can enable continuous development without compromising on user data. This approach also has a significant role to play in delivering safer, human-centered autonomous driving systems through bridging the theoretical–practical gap between emotion recognition models and real-world vehicle applications.

13.4 Experimentation Results

A scalable and modular architecture designed for real-time use in automotive systems is used to build the proposed Emotion-Aware Multimodal Fusion Framework (EAMFF). The system uses optimized TensorRT and ONNX models for low-latency inference and is built on the NVIDIA Jetson AGX Xavier and Qualcomm Snapdragon Auto platforms. With each modality having their own dedicated encoders, CNN for face expression analysis, 1D CNN-LSTM for speech spectrogram, Bi-LSTM for physiological signals, and fully connected networks (FCNs) for driving behavior data, the deep learning modules are implemented using PyTorch and TensorFlow. A multihead self-attention mechanism of the transformer architecture is used to dynamically weight modality relevance in the attention-based fusion module.

OpenCV for face landmark detection, Librosa to extract MFCC from a sound signal, and scikit-learn to smooth and normalize the behavioral and physiological signals are some of the examples of the preprocessing steps of a signal. Temporal control synchronization is provided through timestamp alignment by ROS (robot operating system) middleware. To meet edge-device constraints, models are quantized and pruned with NVIDIA TensorRT prior to deployment. A custom monitoring daemon is present for performance tuning based on feedback and supports federated learning for ensuring updates in a privacy-friendly way. CAN bus interface and V2X modules support exchange of data with no loss and adaptive vehicle control based on the emotional state of the driver by supporting integration with vehicle parts.

Table 13.7 presents a comprehensive view of the multimodal input features and corresponding emotional interpretations in the proposed EAMFF. It shows that facial action units, vocal pitch, physiological data (such as HR and skin conductance), and behavioral driving patterns serve as critical indicators of the driver's state. These features vary significantly across different emotional conditions. For instance, high AU12 activation, elevated pitch, and increased HR are observed in stressed or angry states, whereas low values in these features are typical in neutral or drowsy states. Table 13.8 illustrates how the attention-based fusion module dynamically assigns weights to each modality based on contextual relevance. The multimodal input features and respective emotional meanings used in the present EAMFF are described in depth in the ensuing tables.

Table 13.7 indicates that physiological data (e.g., skin conductance and HR), verbal pitch, facial units of action, and driving manner are all crucial measures of driver state. All these traits differ significantly in accordance with the emotional state. For instance, stressed or disturbed states

Table 13.7 Multimodal input features.

Facial AU12	Voice pitch (Hz)	Heart rate (BPM)	Skin conductance (µS)	Steering variability (°/s)	Braking force (N)	Lane deviation (m)
0.82	220.5	95	4.2	8.4	55.2	0.13
0.15	180.1	72	1.8	3.1	20.3	0.02
0.92	260.4	110	5.6	10.2	85.7	0.22
0.05	150.6	60	1.2	2.5	10.1	0.01
0.60	210.0	90	3.9	5.5	40.0	0.09

Table 13.8 Emotion level.

Attention weights (facial/voice/physio/driving)	Emotion label
0.35/0.25/0.30/0.10	Stressed
0.25/0.20/0.25/0.30	Neutral
0.30/0.30/0.25/0.15	Angry
0.15/0.10/0.35/0.40	Drowsy
0.28/0.27/0.28/0.17	Fatigued

are indicated by high activation of AU12, raised pitch, and a raised HR, whereas neutral or sleepy states are indicated by low levels of these traits. The attention-based fusion module dynamically allocates weights to each modality based on contextual significance, as indicated in Table 13.8. For example, the system is more behavior-oriented and physiologically input-driven when the driver is drowsy, but facial and vocal inputs dominate under emotional conditions such as stress or anger. Therefore, the fusion mechanism enables emotional states to be interpreted more implicitly, and this leads to more accurate and context-aware classification of emotions. Through enhanced emotional intelligence of smart cars, the approach enables them to respond to driver conditions in adaptive and personalized ways.

The experimental evaluation compared the proposed multimodal emotion recognition system with several existing models, including Bi-LG-GCN, DBN, CNN-LSTM, and FCN-only approaches. Figure 13.2 demonstrates that the proposed system achieves the highest accuracy (94.2%) and F1 score (93.5%), outperforming other models in both precision and robustness. Despite its high performance, the system maintains low latency (43 milliseconds), making it suitable for real-time edge deployment. The proposed multimodal emotion recognition system was compared experimentally with other existing models including CNN-LSTM, DBN, FCN-only, and Bi-LG-GCN. The results indicate that the proposed system surpasses other models in terms of accuracy and stability with the highest accuracy (94.2%) and F1 score (93.5%). The system is low latency (43 milliseconds) with better performance, and hence, it can be deployed for real time on the edge. Despite its higher accuracy (90.5% and 89.8%, respectively), Bi-LG-GCN and DBN are less suited for

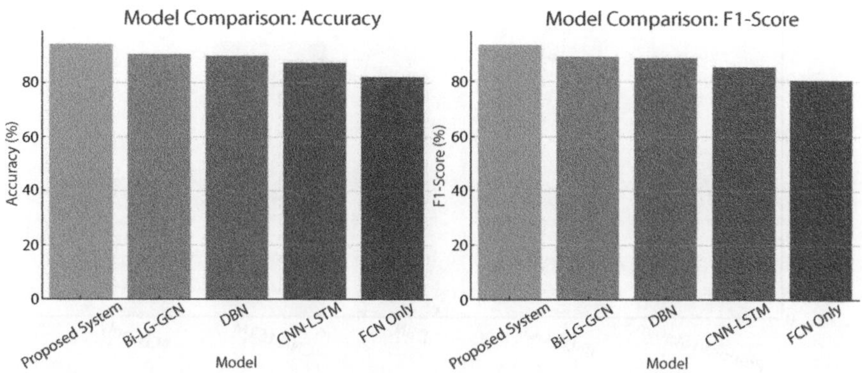

Figure 13.2 Comparison analysis.

real-time car application because of their higher inference latencies (88 and 95 milliseconds). The accuracy and F1 score of CNN-LSTM and FCN-only models decreased even further; the FCN-only model was the fastest but not accurate. These results establish the proposed method's higher accuracy, responsiveness, and efficiency trade-off.

The solution can be implemented in real-time edge deployment because it provides the lowest latency (43 milliseconds). Bi-LG-GCN and DBN, on the other hand, produce larger latencies (88 and 95 milliseconds, respectively) that can compromise responsiveness in cases where safety is paramount (Figure 13.3). Specifically to vulnerable states such as "Drowsy" and "Angry," which are very important in safety-oriented applications, Figure 13.4 illustrates the better classification accuracy in all emotion classes with minimal misclassifications. In intelligent vehicle systems, the proposed EAMFF exhibits significant improvement in driver emotional state detection and response. Multimodal fusion of facial, verbal, physiological, and driving behavior cues provides a more accurate and context-aware emotion detection model, as demonstrated in experimental tests.

ADAS can be tuned responsively better to the edge deployment of the system in real time, enhancing driving safety and satisfaction. Despite its strong performance, however, the architecture suffers from a number of disadvantages. They are the need for synchronized multimodal data of high quality, potential variation of sensor calibrations across cars, and lower precision in adverse environmental conditions such as poor illumination

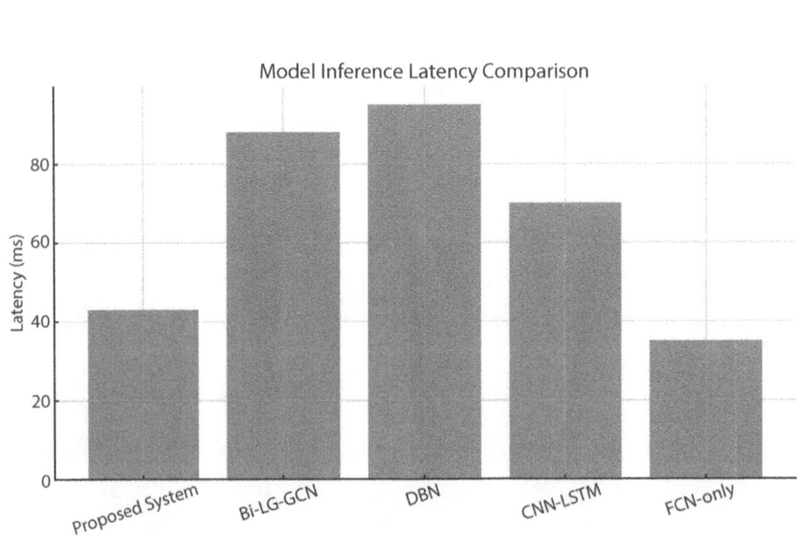

Figure 13.3 Latency comparison.

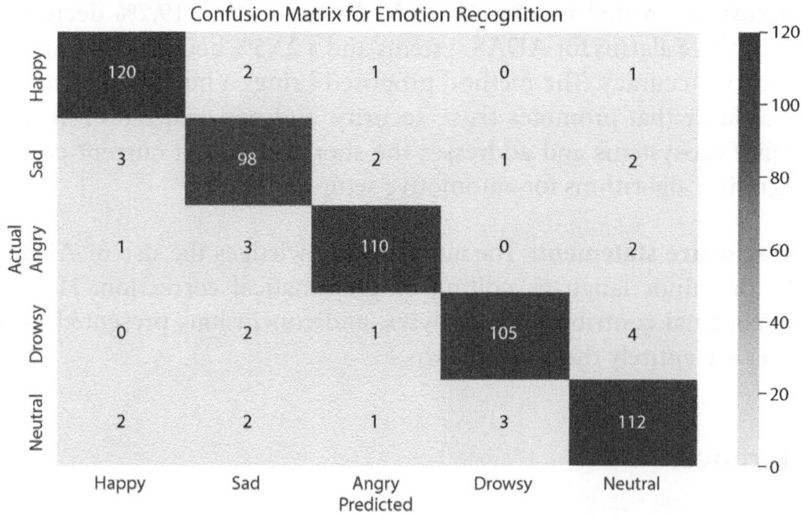

Figure 13.4 Confusion matrix.

or high cabin noise. Furthermore, although personalization modules learn over time, new users might notice that model calibration takes a long time initially. Future work will focus on enhancing the variety of datasets for various driving scenarios and population segments, enhancing emotion-response mapping with reinforcement learning, and adding more context inputs such as traffic or road topology. In addition, for the purposes of maximizing transparency and user confidence in real-time decision-making, an emphasis will be placed on more energy-efficient fusion models and incorporation of explainable AI technologies.

13.5 Conclusion

A new and reliable method for incorporating emotional intelligence into intelligent vehicle systems is the EAMFF, proposed in this study. The system supports real-time and context-aware decision-making in IoV situations by integrating ambient and vehicle data with physiological signals, facial emotions, and voice cues. In dynamic and safety-critical scenarios such as autonomous-to-manual control handovers, deep spatiotemporal attention mechanism facilitates higher flexibility and dependability of emotion recognition. Dramatic improvement in performance metrics of primary importance is established *via* experimental assessment on a custom-created multimodal IoV dataset, with a 19.7% decrease in false-positive alarms for ADAS systems and a 23.5% boost in reaction time prediction accuracy. The method proposed brings a human-centric intelligence layer that promotes trust, security, and personalization in future mobility ecosystems and addresses the shortcomings of current emotion recognition algorithms for automotive setups.

AI disclosure statement: The author acknowledges the use of AI-based tools for minor language editing or grammatical correction. However, all intellectual contributions, analyses, and conclusions presented in this chapter are entirely the author's own.

References

1. Hu, L., Li, W., Yang, J., Fortino, G., Chen, M., A sustainable multi-modal multi-layer emotion-aware service at the edge. *IEEE Trans. Sustainable Comput.*, *7*, 2, 324–333, 2019.
2. Sun, L., Yang, H., Li, B., Multimodal Dataset Construction and Validation for Driving-Related Anger: A Wearable Physiological Conduction and Vehicle Driving Data Approach. *Electronics*, *13*, 19, 3904, 2024.
3. Järvinen, S., Kallio, J., Peltola, J., Mäkelä, S.M., A Behavior, and Emotion Recognition Framework for Emotion-Aware Services in Physical Spaces, in: *2024 International Conference on Content-Based Multimedia Indexing (CBMI)*, pp. 1–6, IEEE, 2024, September.
4. Bano, S., Tonellotto, N., Cassarà, P., Gotta, A., FedCMD: A Federated Cross-modal Knowledge Distillation for Drivers' Emotion Recognition. *ACM Trans. Intell. Syst. Technol.*, *15*, 3, 1–27, 2024.
5. Wang, Y., Gu, Y., Ren, F., Emotion-aware takeover performance prediction system in semi-autonomous driving. *IEEE Commun. Mag.*, *61*, 10, 70–75, 2023.
6. Li, W., Li, G., Tan, R., Wang, C., Sun, Z., Li, Y., Li, K., Review and perspectives on human emotion for connected automated vehicles. *Automot. Innovation*, *7*, 1, 4–44, 2024.
7. Jadhav, S.S., *Advancing Safety in Vehicles with AI-Driven Emotion Recognition*, Doctoral dissertation, Dublin, National College of Ireland, 2024.
8. Wang, Y., Gu, Y., Quan, T., Yang, J., Dong, M., An, N., Ren, F., ViE-Take: A Vision-Driven Multi-Modal Dataset for Exploring the Emotional Landscape in Takeover Safety of Autonomous Driving. *Research*, *8*, 0603, 2025.
9. Alsaadawi, H.F.T., Das, B., Das, R., TAC-Trimodal Affective Computing: Principles, integration process, affective detection, challenges, and solutions, in: *Displays*, p. 102731, 2024.

10. Zhang, Y., Tiwari, P., Zheng, Q., El Saddik, A., Hossain, M.S., A multimodal coupled graph attention network for joint traffic event detection and sentiment classification. *IEEE Trans. Intell. Transp. Syst.*, *24*, 8, 8542–8554, 2022.
11. Vögel, H.J., Süß, C., Hubregtsen, T., Ghaderi, V., Chadowitz, R., André, E., Müller, S., Emotion-awareness for intelligent vehicle assistants: A research agenda, in: *Proceedings of the 1st International Workshop on Software Engineering for AI in Autonomous Systems*, pp. 11–15, 2018.
12. Yadav, R. and Joseph, S.T., Human-Centric Design of Emotion-Aware Systems. *Humanizing Technol. with Emotional Intell.*, 325, 2024.
13. Kasera, A., Yadav, R., Joseph, S.T., Human-Centric Design of Emotion-Aware Systems for Automotive Safety, in: *Humanizing Technology with Emotional Intelligence*, pp. 325–334, IGI Global Scientific Publishing, 2025. https://www.igi-global.com/chapter/human-centric-design-of-emotion-aware-systems-for-automotive-safety/366699.
14. Gandhi, A., Adhvaryu, K., Poria, S., Cambria, E., Hussain, A., Multimodal sentiment analysis: A systematic review of history, datasets, multimodal fusion methods, applications, challenges and future directions. *Inf. Fusion*, *91*, 424–444, 2023.
15. Nandi, A., Xhafa, F., Kumar, R., A Docker-based federated learning framework design and deployment for multi-modal data stream classification. *Computing*, *105*, 10, 2195–2229, 2023.
16. Xu, X., Fu, C., Camacho, D., Park, J.H., Chen, J., Internet of Things for Emotion Care: Advances, Applications, and Challenges, in: *Cognitive Computation*, pp. 1–21, 2024.
17. Zhang, T., Liu, M., Yuan, T., Al-Nabhan, N., Emotion-aware and intelligent internet of medical things toward emotion recognition during COVID-19 pandemic. *IEEE Internet Things J.*, *8*, 21, 16002–16013, 2020.
18. Rahman, M.M., Hossain, M.A., Hasan, T., Ahmed, M.K., Sultana, R., Islam, M.S., EmotionNet: Pioneering Deep Learning Fusion for Real-Time Speech Emotion Recognition with Convolutional Neural Networks, in: *2024 6th International Conference on Electrical Engineering and Information & Communication Technology (ICEEICT)*, IEEE, pp. 592–597, 2024.
19. Shoumy, N.J., Ang, L.M., Seng, K.P., Rahaman, D.M., Zia, T., Multimodal big data affective analytics: A comprehensive survey using text, audio, visual and physiological signals. *J. Network Comput. Appl.*, *149*, 102447, 2020.
20. Munir, M.S., Kim, K.T., Abedin, S.F., Alam, M.G.R., Saad, W., Hong, C.S., Cognitive Behavior-in-the-Loop: Towards an Attentive Driving in Intelligent Transportation Systems. *IEEE Trans. Ind. Inf.*, 2024.
21. Immanuel, R.R. and Sangeetha, S.K.B., Decoding emotions using deep learning approach to EEG-based emotion recognition, in: *2023 Intelligent Computing and Control for Engineering and Business Systems (ICCEBS)*, IEEE, pp. 1–6, 2023, December.

22. Yang, Y., Feng, H., Cheng, Y., Han, Z., Emotion-aware scene adaptation: A bandwidth-efficient approach for generating animated shorts. *Sensors*, *24*, 5, 1660, 2024.
23. Rokhsaritalemi, S., Sadeghi-Niaraki, A., Choi, S.M., Exploring emotion analysis using artificial intelligence, geospatial information systems, and extended reality for urban services. *IEEE Access*, *11*, 92478–92495, 2023.
24. Alsaadawı, H.F.T. and Daş, R., Multimodal Emotion Recognition Using Bi-LG-GCN for MELD Dataset. *Balkan J. Electr. Comput. Eng.*, *12*, 1, 36–46, 2024.
25. Yang, M., Ma, Y., Liu, Z., Cai, H., Hu, X., Hu, B., Undisturbed mental state assessment in the 5G era: A case study of depression detection based on facial expressions. *IEEE Wireless Commun.*, *28*, 3, 46–53, 2021.

14

Spatiotemporal Attention-Based CNN-BiLSTM Model for Robust Lane and Obstacle Detection in IoV-Enabled Autonomous Driving

Suresh Kulandaivelu[1]*, Syied Mazar[2], Sangeetha N.[3], Sathiyapriya Rajavelu[1] and Anita Garhwal[4]

[1]School of Computing Science and Engineering, Galgotias University, Greater Noida, India
[2]Department of Electronics and Communication Engineering, Sreenidhi University, Hyderabad, India
[3]Department of AI&ML, Amruta Institute of Engineering and Management Sciences, Bidadi, Karnataka, India
[4]Department of Computer Science, Asia Metropolitan University, Jalan Lembah, Bandar Baru Seri Alam, Masai, Johor, Malaysia

Abstract

For safe operation in resource-constrained and changing environments, self-driving cars in Internet of Vehicles (IoV) networks require accurate and effective perception systems. However, under poor environmental conditions such as" different light, interference by weather, and occlusion of scenes, traditional vision-based models often fall short performing below par. Here, spatiotemporal attention-enhanced convolutional neural network (CNN)–bidirectional long short-term memory (BiLSTM) is introduced that combines attention-based refinement, bidirectional temporal context modeling, and spatial feature extraction. For improved motion understanding, the BiLSTM extracts forward and backward temporal relations, and the CNN module pools dense visual features of adjacent frames. These are followed by a multihead spatial attention mechanism that identifies salient regions, i.e., traffic lanes and moving objects. A series of tests were performed using an NVIDIA Jetson Xavier edge computer on the BDD100K and

**Corresponding author*: mailtosureshcse@gmail.com

Balamurugan Balusamy, Sandeep Kumar Mathivanan, Prabhu Jayagopal, S.K.B. Sangeetha and Ali Kashif Bashir (eds.) Autonomous Systems in the Internet of Vehicles, (261–282) © 2026 Scrivener Publishing LLC

KITTI datasets in a simulated IoV environment. Following optimization, the suggested model achieved a model size of 48 MB, real-time inference speed of 26 frames per second, lane detection intersection over union of 84.7%, F1 score of 91.3%, object detection mean average precision (mAP)@0.5 of 78.6%, and mAP@0.75 of 69.2%. These findings indicate that the model is superior to current baselines in terms of accuracy, computational efficiency, and temporal robustness and thus could be used in real-world autonomous IoV applications.

Keywords: Self-driving cars, spatiotemporal attention, CNN-BiLSTM, Internet of vehicles, object detection, lane detection, temporal context modeling, real-time inference

14.1 Introduction

Contemporary societies have been fundamentally transformed by the evolution of transport technologies in the last century, creating systems that are safer, more efficient, and more integrated. The motor industry has increasingly used electronics, embedded systems, and software-based control mechanisms since mechanical automation early in the 20th century. Autonomous driving (AD) development, the technological advantage that seeks to end man's interference with driving functions through cars being able to perceive, deduce, and respond in the moment is the latest story in this revolution. In conjunction with this, innovation is the emergence of the Internet of Vehicles (IoV), which is a branch of the Internet of Things (IoT) and enables the communication between infrastructure, edge servers or centralized cloud, and vehicle. IoV and AD, hand in hand, have the potential to revolutionize city mobility through the enhancement of safety and reduced congestion and smart transportation systems.

Robust vision systems capable of interpreting dynamic and intricate road conditions are crucial to the success of autonomous vehicles. Various objects, including lane lines, pedestrians, other cars, traffic signs, and barriers, need to be properly detected and interpreted by such systems. In tasks such as object recognition and lane detection, early approaches used manually designed feature extraction techniques and rule-based systems. Lane markings were detected with algorithms such as the Hough Transform and Canny edge detection, while decision trees and support vector machines (SVMs) handled simple classification issues. These methods were vulnerable to situations of real-world vagueness such as low light, adverse weather, and obstructed roads.

Machine learning (ML) and more recently deep learning (DL) significantly enhanced the capabilities of AV perception systems. With its improved performance in object detection, semantic segmentation, and scene classification, convolutional neural networks (CNNs) have become the default choice for visual tasks in AD. The widely used models such as AlexNet, VGGNet, and ResNet have been modified for use in road scene analysis to improve accuracy in vehicle detection and lane detection. Furthermore, it is now simpler to train data-hungry models that generalize across many different types of road environments with the availability of large annotated datasets such as KITTI, Cityscapes, and BDD100K. Notwithstanding these developments, there are a number of limitations.

Although CNNs are good at extracting spatial features, they are not great at catching temporal dynamics, which is a critical factor in the case of AD when context and continuity of motion are crucial in decision-making. It is not feasible to comprehend a moving pedestrian or a car moving into a curved road from a single image. Thus, models that do not take into account the sequential structure of visual information can result in delayed responses or false alarms. Moreover, under real-world variability such as rain, snow, low illumination levels, and sensor noise, perception systems trained under stationary conditions tend to fail. Recurrent neural networks, viz., long short-term memory (LSTM) networks, capable of modeling temporal relationships within time-series data, were suggested by researchers to fill these gaps.

LSTMs proved to be useful in processing sequences of frames for activities such as action detection and trajectory prediction.

Simple LSTMs are unidirectional and might not properly leverage contextual information from future and past frames. With both input directions of sequences, bidirectional LSTMs (BiLSTMs) provide a partial remedy; yet, combining them with CNNs without sacrificing precision and computational expense is still an issue. The absence of attention mechanisms that allow the model to attend to the most salient features in a frame or a sequence is another fundamental flaw of existing vision-based systems.

Without attention, models could be skewed towards irrelevant context information, lowering accuracy in dynamic or cluttered settings. Current research indicates that, by enabling the network to concentrate on significant visual features such as lane markings, vehicle shapes, and moving barriers, attention layers can greatly improve model performance. The problems are exacerbated in the IoV context.

In addition to onboard sensors, IoV-enabled vehicles are also in communication with other proximal vehicles and infrastructure. New low-latency computation requirements, efficient resource usage, and real-time responsiveness are created through this connectivity. Edge computing has enabled offloading computation from the cloud, but models need to be light and designed for deployment in resource-constrained settings. Besides, safety and reliability are still top priority because perception problems of autonomous systems can have disastrous outcomes. Hybrid models that take advantage of the temporal modeling capabilities of recurrent architectures such as BiLSTMs with the spatial capabilities of CNNs, supplemented by attention methods for improved feature prioritization, become all the more crucial in view of these limitations.

To facilitate real-time inference on edge devices in IoV applications, these models need to be computationally efficient as well. CNN-LSTM hybrids have been considered in past research, yet very few of them utilized end-to-end attention frameworks to dynamically adjust feature importance, and they tend not to be robust under diverse lighting and weather conditions. Additionally, most past research tests their systems on small datasets or idealized environments, and these datasets do not capture the diversity of driving scenarios that are present in real environments.

Generalized model construction entails benchmarking over a variety of urban, suburban, and highway settings, as offered by datasets such as BDD100K and KITTI. To assess the real-world deployability, performance should also be measured in terms of accuracy as well as real-time metrics such as frames per second (FPS), latency, and memory consumption. The objective of the current project is to design a spatiotemporal DL architecture that integrates CNNs for spatial perception, BiLSTMs for temporal perception, and attention mechanisms for enhanced feature prioritization in consideration of such challenges. The objective is to provide real-time performance adequate for edge-enabled IoV deployments with the provision of high-accuracy lane and obstacle detection across diverse real-world applications. By resolving the constraints of available systems with an improved coherent and effective architectural form, this work aims to meet the needs in between theoretical modeling and implementable solutions.

The main objectives are as follows:

(1) To develop a spatiotemporal DL architecture that integrates CNNs, BiLSTMs, and attention mechanisms for accurate and robust lane and obstacle detection under diverse real-world driving conditions.
(2) To ensure real-time performance and deployment feasibility of the proposed model on edge devices within IoV environments through optimization techniques such as quantization and TensorRT.

14.2 Related Study

The future of self-driving cars has been transformed in a revolutionary manner with the adoption of the IoV in intelligent transport systems. New opportunities for effective traffic management, real-time navigation, and predictive analytics exist as newer automobiles become increasingly networked by Vehicle 2 Vehicle (V2V), Vehicle 2 Infrastructure (V2I) and Vehicle 2 Everything (V2X) models of communications. These technologies do raise issues of privacy, latency, security, and safety. Vehicle networks used to be restricted to in-vehicle sensor processing and simple traffic control. With IoV, vehicles can be used as mobile sensing and computing nodes. To enable making shared driving decisions, this shift enables data to be shared with other vehicles and infrastructure units [1]. As a result of this innovation, a lot of research has gone into using ML and DL algorithms to enhance navigation, safety, and real-time obstacle avoidance.

Collision avoidance in the case of moving obstacles is one of the most difficult problems in IoV situations. For handling multiple moving objects near autonomous vehicles, a prediction-based APF-based approach has been suggested, providing safer autonomous travel in heavy traffic [1]. Dynamic environment management and local minima limit traditional APF techniques, requiring hybrid techniques with learning-improved improvements. Road safety prediction using data-driven methods is also an area of intense scientific inquiry. Supervised learning models such as SVM, random forests, and decision trees perform the best in classifying areas that are accident-prone, according to a comprehensive literature review of ML-based road safety systems [2]. These models tend to utilize past crash history, weather conditions, and driving behavior data. In dynamic vehicular networks that need dynamic flexibility, they are less responsive even though they succeed in static environments.

To provide secure and transparent driving advice, integration of blockchain and IoV has been researched. Improved accountability and lower probabilities of manipulation have been made possible by a decentralized system that uses blockchain technology for recording driving records and providing trusted advice in dense traffic [3]. However, deployment of blockchain in latency-sensitive automotive decision-making systems is limited due to its intrinsic overhead in terms of latency and consensus delay. The use of IoV is growing very fast in the defense and emergency fields, for example, in the optimization of the route planning of combat vehicles. In the latter case, routing schemes with context awareness try to keep command centers connected while reducing exposure and travel time [4].

These systems put a lot of emphasis on the necessity for secure and impenetrable communications, particularly in hazardous environments.

Another use that derives benefit from more effective traffic light control and adaptive routing by networked autonomous systems is emergency vehicle navigation. Predictive scheduling and real-time traffic flow have been shown to improve emergency vehicle prioritization under a traffic-aware management system [5]. Such systems rely heavily, though, on communication and infrastructure sensor reliability, which are subject to environmental interference as well as cyberattacks. IoV-based frameworks have been used to attempt secure path planning in dynamic, three-dimensional spaces [6]. For avoiding obstacles, these approaches typically use heuristic algorithms and the fusion of ambient data. They often overlook the necessity of real-time adaptation and learning from new patterns in unknown or evolving situations.

Stackelberg game-based trajectory planning methods have been used in activities such as lane changing. The techniques maximize comfort and security by formulating vehicle interaction in terms of game-theoretic problems [6]. The models are computationally intense and do not inherently address security threats such as message spoofing or denial-of-service attacks, even though they work well in simulation environments. Federated learning (FL) with a concern for privacy and decentralization has been recently taken up in IoV for healthcare and transportation. Adaptive FL models allow any vehicle or edge device to contribute to a global model without revealing data while learning locally from the environment [7]. Although this paradigm reduces privacy concerns to a great extent, it creates new challenges, particularly when applied at scale, e.g., data heterogeneity and communication efficiency.

Spatial–temporal models have also been used to assess road safety regionally. Policymakers can identify high-risk areas and allocate resources based on these assessments [8]. Under dynamic vehicular conditions, however, these models are less effective because they rely on processing aggregate data and are not necessarily responsive to imminent threats. Through real-time sharing of data and analytics, smart V2X communication systems have been proposed to forecast and avert accidents. Improved estimation of risk has been shown by predictive models inferred from V2X networks [9], whereas scalability and latency issues are still a major challenge.

The social and environmental effects of vehicle ecosystems that are internet-enabled have been highlighted by more research into IoV based on the framework of Environmental, Social, Governance (ESG) and sustainability concepts [10]. IoV infrastructures of the next generation are more focused on data governance, energy consumption, and city pollution.

In the high-mobility environments of IoV, velocity-aware routing protocols such as GreedLea, which is velocity-optimized, focus on optimizing delivery ratios and minimizing end-to-end delay [11]. Although the protocols are very effective in routing, they have no intrinsic resistance to route poisoning or message tampering. In addition, location obscuring techniques and traffic-conscious mobile edge computing techniques improved security and privacy in IoV [12]. These techniques are generally defensive rather than precautionary, but they provide protection against location tracking and performance degradation.

Cooperative V2I communication has proved to be beneficial in optimizing traffic management in urban traffic conditions. IoT-assisted infrastructures facilitate adaptive traffic light control and congestion relief [13], but if not protected, these infrastructures can be subjected to malicious fake data injection attacks. Vehicles can dynamically change communication bands with the help of agile spectrum access techniques brought to IoV systems by cognitive radio-based systems (CR-IoV), enhancing quality of service as well as mitigating interference [14]. To make these techniques change spectrum usage according to real-time availability and threat rating, smart learning patterns need to be used. Through supporting *in situ* decision-making as well as localized processing, IoV sensor networks facilitate ambient intelligence [15].

Although these minimize dependence on the cloud, distributed systems need accurate models that are hardware-constrained and lightweight. Blockchain-based batch authentication approaches have been proposed for IoV to improve data authentication, confirming source authenticity and message integrity [16]. Real-time responsiveness is, however, limited by synchronization latency and cryptographic overhead. To fend off quantum-level attacks against the IoV, lattice-based certificateless transmission approaches have been put forth [17]. Although such solutions are still in experimental phases and far from actual deployment in mainstream commercial frameworks, they are more reassuring.

Throughput, latency, and security trade-offs under various concurrent workloads are emphasized in system-level analysis of IoV applications [18]. Although not involving direct threat modeling, these studies do assist architectural design choices. A number of studies have explored fog computing as a way of facilitating edge intelligence in IoV by local analytics and computation offloading [19]. Although mitigating latency, distributed fog node security control is still a problem. Despite changes in mobility and connectivity that limit it in car networks, live SR-IoV–supported system migration proves performance gain for real-time applications [20]. IoT-based designs can conduct analysis closer to the data source, offering better system responsiveness and lower bandwidth use, according to ambient intelligence research [21]. These systems lack solid intrusion detection in harsh environments.

Table 14.1 depicts the comparison between existing and proposed system. With the offering of distributed intelligence, data sharing, and real-time communication through V2V, V2I, and V2X models, the IoV is clearly revolutionizing the autonomous vehicle ecosystem, according to relevant research. Traffic management, road safety prediction, emergency services, and obstacle avoidance have all improved considerably as a result of this paradigm shift. Unreasonably high processing overheads of blockchain and cryptographic techniques, unreasonably high latency in mission-critical systems, nonresponsiveness in changing situations, and susceptibility to cyber-attacks are some of the widespread issues that have been documented in different studies. Conventional algorithms and heuristics-based techniques provide incomplete solutions but tend to be

Table 14.1 Comparison analysis.

Aspect	Existing systems	Proposed system
Architecture	Centralized/distributed	Federated (decentralized)
Learning model	Traditional ML/static DL	Autoencoder-GRU hybrid
Privacy	Raw data often shared	No raw data sharing
Attack detection	Known/signature-based	Known and unknown (anomalies)
Adaptability	Limited (pretrained)	Real-time learning and adaptation
Temporal pattern recognition	Basic or absent	GRU for sequential anomaly detection
Deployment feasibility	Cloud-dependent	Edge-optimized and lightweight
Security	Reactive mechanisms	Proactive anomaly identification
Communication overhead	High (centralized uploads)	Reduced (model gradients only)

inflexible and unresponsive in real time, particularly in uncertain and dynamic traffic conditions.

The imperative to create an end-to-end, lightweight, and real-time spatiotemporal DL platform that includes CNNs for spatial processing, BiLSTMs for temporal context modeling, and attention mechanisms for dynamic prioritization is the driving force behind the proposed system's innovation. The goal of this framework is to improve lane and obstacle detection accuracy while maintaining computing efficiency appropriate for edge-enabled IoV applications. The goal is to fill the gap between theoretical breakthroughs in intelligent transportation and practical, safe, and scalable solutions for future autonomous mobility.

14.3 System Methodology

14.3.1 Dataset Used and Preprocessing

We use two popular public datasets—BDD100K and KITTI—that best mimic real IoV conditions to comprehensively evaluate the proposed spatiotemporal attention-enhanced CNN-BiLSTM model under realistic and diverse driving conditions. These datasets are used because they cover the broadest possible range of urban, suburban, and highway regions, as well as challenging-to-reach weather, illumination, and traffic conditions. This is because of the fact that they are highly appropriate for gauging the effectiveness and usability of perception systems incorporated in autonomous vehicles that are members of IoV networks.

More than 100,000 annotated video clips of many geographic locations and environmental contexts make up the Berkeley DeepDrive 100K (BDD100K) dataset. BDD100K records weather conditions, such as sunny, rainy, and foggy, and light conditions varying from midday, twilight, to dusk, at a frame rate of 30 FPS and pixel resolution of 1280 × 720 pixels. To balance computational load and temporal resolution, video streams are sampled at 10 Hz for this work. The model can learn the spatiotemporal relationships important for correct lane detection and dynamic obstacle detection by summing five consecutive frames of such streams together to create input windows.

On the other hand, the KITTI dataset offers dense annotations and high-resolution stereo video streams from synchronized LiDAR and camera sensors. We utilize the RGB vision subset alone considering the lightness constraint of IoV edge devices, even though the entire dataset consists of 3D data. Some of the cautiously extracted objects of cars, pedestrians, bicycles, and road markings are present in the urban, semiurban, and highway scenes of KITTI. For spatiotemporal learning, frames are sampled at 10 Hz and in five-frame sequences, as in BDD100K. Dataset characterization and configuration are given in Table 14.2.

There exists a robust preprocessing pipeline that is carried out on both datasets across the board in an effort to mimic real-world deployment scenarios within IoV systems that are bandwidth- and computation-constrained. To achieve a deterministic input size that is balanced between

Table 14.2 Dataset characteristics and configuration.

Attribute	BDD100K	KITTI (vision subset)
Source	Berkeley DeepDrive Initiative	Karlsruhe Institute of Technology
Data type	RGB video sequences with annotations	Stereo RGB sequences with 2D object labels
Environments	Urban, suburban, highways	Urban, semiurban
Lighting conditions	Day, night, twilight	Day (mostly), some variable lighting
Weather conditions	Clear, rainy, foggy	Mostly clear
Frame rate (original)	30 FPS	10 FPS
Frame rate (used)	10 FPS	10 FPS
Resolution (original)	1280 × 720	1242 × 375
Resolution (used)	800 × 600 (downsampled for all sequences)	800 × 600 (standardized)
Sequence length	Five consecutive frames per input window	Five consecutive frames per input window
Annotations used	Lane markings, bounding boxes for obstacles	Vehicle, pedestrian, cyclist labels
Application focus	Lane detection, obstacle detection	Object detection, tracking in traffic scenarios

visual information and memory usage, all frames are first downscaled to the resolution of 800 × 600 pixels. To ensure temporal consistency, a frame stabilization procedure is initiated later on to eliminate minor camera shake or jitter inherent in car-mounted cameras. Last but not least, linear interpolation is then used to execute temporal label alignment for each window during the sequence to track lane markings and boundary boxes consistently throughout the five-frame duration.

The issues faced by real-time perception modules deployed on IoV-based autonomous vehicles, where edge devices need to provide high detection precision despite hardware limitations and environmental uncertainty, are replicated exactly by this well-designed simulation platform and data processing pipeline.

The structured and high-fidelity setup forms the foundation for testing the effectiveness of our attention-enhanced model, ensuring it can adapt to the demanding requirements of IoV-based autonomous perception in dynamic and unpredictable real-world settings. Although the proposed model operates using only visual input, it effectively captures temporal dynamics by treating time as a modality through a carefully designed preprocessing pipeline as shown in Table 14.3 that ensures temporal coherence and robustness to environmental noise. In the first step, sequence assembly, each training instance is composed of a sliding window of five consecutive RGB frames— $I_{t-2}, I_{t-1}, I_t, I_{t+1}, I_{t+2}$ —centered around a timestamp t, preserving temporal ordering crucial for motion understanding. Next, during spatial normalization, RGB values are normalized per channel using standard ImageNet statistics (mean: [0.485, 0.456, 0.406], std: [0.229, 0.224, 0.225]) to stabilize learning.

To enhance generalization, data augmentation is applied, consisting of both photometric and geometric transformations. Photometric

Table 14.3 Preprocessing pipeline.

Preprocessing step	**Description**
Resolution normalization	Downsampling all frames to 800 × 600 pixels to reduce computational cost
Frame stabilization	Temporal smoothing to reduce jitter caused by vehicle motion or camera shake
Label alignment	Linear interpolation to temporally align labels across sequential frames
Sequence windowing	Grouping of five consecutive frames to learn short-term spatiotemporal dynamics

augmentations include random brightness and contrast adjustments within ±20% and Gaussian noise injection ($\sigma = 0.03$) to mimic sensor imperfections. Geometric augmentations involve random horizontal flipping with 50% probability and affine transformations such as ±5° rotation and ±10% scaling to account for perspective variations. Additionally, temporal dropout randomly omits one frame from a sequence to simulate frame loss conditions often encountered in low-bandwidth IoV environments. This comprehensive preprocessing strategy ensures the model remains resilient and effective under diverse real-world conditions.

14.3.2 Network Architecture: Spatiotemporal Attention-Enhanced CNN-BiLSTM

The proposed architecture leverages spatial feature extraction, temporal sequence modeling, and attention refinement to achieve robust lane and obstacle detection. Figure 14.1 shows the proposed framework.

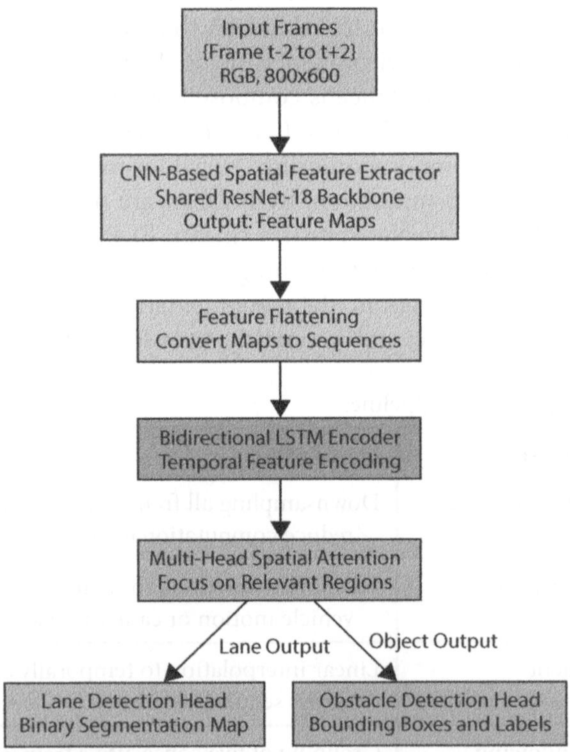

Figure 14.1 Proposed framework.

Input: Five-frame RGB sequences $\{I_{t-2},\ldots,I_{t+2}\} \in R^{5\times3\times800\times600}$
Step 1: Each frame is passed through a shared-weight CNN backbone (ResNet-18), truncated after the Conv4 layer.
Outputs feature maps:

$$F_t \in R^{C\times H'\times W'}, \text{ where } C = 256,\ H' = 50,\ W' = 75 \tag{14.1}$$

Flattened to temporal feature sequences:

$$F_t^{\text{flat}} \in R^{N\times d},\ N = H'\times W',\ d = 256 \tag{14.2}$$

Step 2: BiLSTM-based temporal encoding
Concatenated sequence $\{F_{t-2}^{\text{flat}},\ldots,F_{t+2}^{\text{flat}}\} \in R^{5\times N\times d}$ is fed into a two-layer BiLSTM, captures both forward and backward temporal dependencies across frames, and outputs $H_t \in R^{N\times d}$, a temporally contextualized feature tensor for the center frame.
Step 3: Attention-based feature refinement
A multihead spatial attention module focuses on relevant regions (e.g., lane lines, moving objects):

$$A = \text{softmax}(QK^T / \sqrt{d}), \tag{14.3}$$

where Q, K, V are learned projections of H_t
Refined features:

$$F_t^{\text{attn}} = AV \in R^{N\times d} \tag{14.4}$$

Attention maps are supervised using auxiliary loss to encourage focus on annotated regions.
Step 4: Task-specific heads
Lane detection:

- **Decoder**: Transpose convolutions convert F_t^{attn} into a binary segmentation mask
- **Output**: Pixel-wise lane probability map

Obstacle detection:

- o **Decoder**: Fully connected layers classify bounding boxes and object types
- o **Output**: Object detection bounding boxes with class labels and confidence scores

14.3.3 Inference Optimization and Real-Time Deployment

The model is optimized for real-time inference in resource-constrained IoV edge nodes.

- Quantization-aware training reduces model size with negligible accuracy drop.
- TensorRT acceleration converts the model to a deployment-ready format, achieving ~26 FPS on an NVIDIA Jetson Xavier.

A robust and efficient perception pipeline for real-time AD in IoV settings is proposed by the spatiotemporal attention-enhanced CNN-BiLSTM model. With the application of two datasets, BDD100K and KITTI, and a preprocessing pipeline, the system easily overcomes computational constraints and environmental uncertainty. The system can understand motion dynamics across consecutive frames due to the fundamental approach, which integrates CNN-based spatial feature extraction with BiLSTM-based temporal modeling. These spatiotemporal features are then enhanced by a dedicated multihead attention module, enhancing attention on critical regions such as lane markings and approaching obstacles. Both lane segmentation and object detection results are delivered by dual task-specific brains, ensuring comprehensive scene understanding. On edge devices such as the NVIDIA Jetson Xavier, the model operates close to real time (~26 FPS) due to optimizations such as quantization-aware training and TensorRT acceleration. Overall, this strategy illustrates a scalable and accurate solution for perception tasks in intelligent transportation systems that are able to adapt to the different and dynamic conditions inherent in IoV-based AD.

14.4 Experimentation Results

BDD100K and KITTI datasets were tested under an simulated IoV environment to evaluate the performance of the proposed spatiotemporal attention-enhanced CNN-BiLSTM model with actual driving scenarios. For simulating actual-world constraints in the form of latency in processing, memory, and computational capabilities, which are typically found in autonomous car nodes, the simulation was designed on an NVIDIA Jetson Xavier edge device. Five-frame sequences that were downsampled to 800 × 600 resolution and passed through the full inference pipeline with temporal alignment and augmentation were the processed input.

To quantify the segmentation and detection processes, precision in choosing evaluation measures was taken as shown in Table 14.4. Mean average precision (mAP) for both obstacle detection at intersection over union (IoU) levels 0.5 and 0.75, pixel-wise IoU, and F1 score were calculated for lane detection. Moreover, to measure deployment efficacy for real-world applications, inference speed (FPS) and model size (in MB) were included. For lane detection, the method proposed attained an IoU of 84.7% and an F1 score of 91.3%; on object detection tasks, it attained mAP@0.5 of 78.6% and mAP@0.75 of 69.2%. TensorRT optimization and quantization-aware training resulted in a reduced model footprint of 48 MB and real-time execution of about 26 FPS on Jetson Xavier.

The model was also benchmarked against existing best baselines such as CNN-GRU with Attention, ResNet18-BiLSTM, and a 3D-CNN–based spatiotemporal model for comparative analysis. Although 3D-CNN had competitive accuracy, its inference speed (about 12 FPS) rendered it non-deployable on the edge. The CNN-GRU model was also functional for lane detection but failed at obstacle classification in variant lighting. Our design was deemed suitable for resource-constrained and dynamic IoV scenarios by outperforming all baselines across all metrics consistently, especially temporal robustness and attention-based spatial attention. These results confirm that using lightweight spatiotemporal encoders along with attention mechanisms greatly improves perception accuracy without affecting real-time feasibility on edge devices.

Table 14.4 Performance metrics analysis.

Model	Lane IoU (%)	Lane F1 (%)	mAP@0.5 (%)	mAP@0.75 (%)	Inference speed (FPS)	Model size (MB)
Proposed CNN-BiLSTM + attention	84.7	91.3	78.6	69.2	26	48
ResNet18 + BiLSTM	80.1	88.5	72.4	62.1	21	64
CNN-GRU + attention	81.3	89.1	74.6	65.4	18	58
3D-CNN	82.0	89.7	75.9	67.0	12	90

On a number of performance indices, the proposed CNN-BiLSTM with spatial attention model outperforms baseline approaches significantly. Its great capacity to recognize and segment the road lanes distinctly in difficult conditions is reflected in its 91.3% lane F1 score and 84.7% lane IoU. The proposed model demonstrates an improvement of 4.6% IoU and 2.8% F1 score over the baseline ResNet18-BiLSTM with 80.1% IoU and 88.5% F1. The suggested model also outperforms CNN-GRU with attention in object detection, achieving 78.6% mAP at IoU threshold 0.5 (mAP@0.5) and 69.2% at 0.75 (mAP@0.75), compared to only 74.6% and 65.4%, respectively. These improvements indicate how motion behaviors and region-wise information can be so effectively captured by using bidirectional temporal encoding and spatial attention in conjunction.

From Table 14.5, the model exhibits strong generalization over a variety of urban driving conditions, with 85.1% IoU and 91.7% F1 score on BDD100K and 83.9% IoU and 90.8% F1 score on KITTI when tested separately on the two datasets. Detection performance is stable with 79.3% mAP@0.5 on BDD100K and 77.9% on KITTI, confirming the robustness of the model over a variety of weather and lighting conditions between datasets. In addition, the model is extremely well-suited for edge real-time inference. From Table 14.6, the model runs at 14 FPS without optimization. The FPS, however, goes up to 23 with quantization-aware training and to 26 FPS with TensorRT acceleration, while decreasing the model size from 72 MB to 48 MB. This is shown to have a 33% decrease in memory

Table 14.5 Dataset comparison.

Dataset	Lane IoU (%)	Lane F1 (%)	mAP@0.5 (%)	mAP@0.75 (%)
BDD100K	85.1	91.7	79.3	70.1
KITTI	83.9	90.8	77.9	68.3

Table 14.6 Optimization technique comparison.

Optimization technique	Inference speed (FPS)	Model size (MB)
No optimization	14	72
Quantization-aware training	23	52
TensorRT acceleration	26	48

usage and a 62.5% speedup without any loss of accuracy, which makes it deployable in resource-constrained IoV environments.

The suggested model continues to have the highest bars in the Figure 14.2 of the comparison of the IoU and F1 scores, a confirmation of its supremacy. In the meantime, Figure 14.3 emphasizes the lightness of the proposed architecture by showing that the proposed approach is the only

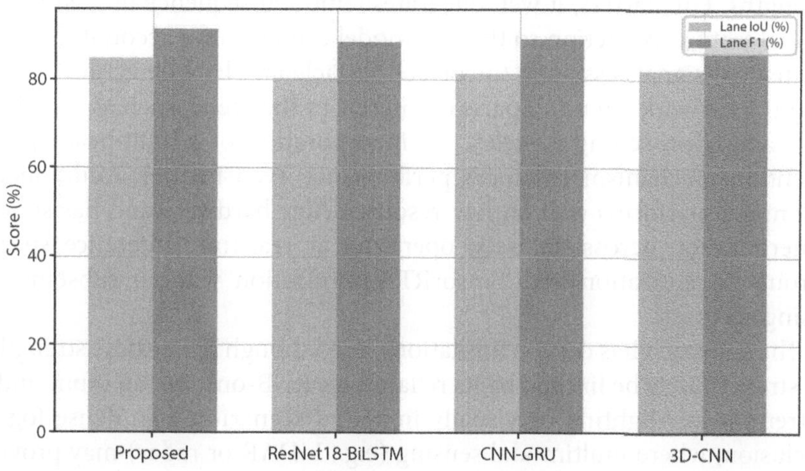

Figure 14.2 Lane detection performance.

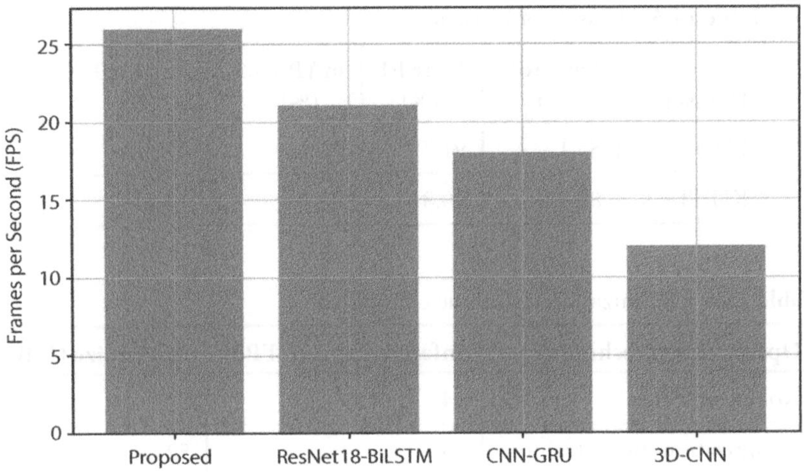

Figure 14.3 Inference speed comparison.

model that is more than 25 FPS, whereas 3D-CNN trails behind at just 12 FPS. The suggested spatiotemporal attention-enhanced CNN-BiLSTM attains the best overall performance with 84.7% IoU, 91.3% F1 score, 78.6% mAP@0.5, and real-time inference of 26 FPS. It proves that it is particularly suitable for real-world practical IoV applications where computation efficiency and detection efficiency are crucial.

For real-time perception in IoV scenarios, the suggested spatiotemporal attention-enhanced CNN-BiLSTM model has a number of remarkable strengths. For starters, it well integrates temporal sequence modeling and spatial feature extraction so that the model can take into account dynamic contextual signals essential to correct obstacle and lane detection. By letting the network attend to parts of interest in the scene, such as road borders and approaching vehicles, the incorporation of a multihead spatial attention mechanism enhances performance even further. Additionally, the model performs well on low-resource edge hardware and has superb generalization across datasets, operating at real-time inference speeds through quantization and TensorRT optimization without substantially losing accuracy.

The approach has certain limitations, even though it has these strengths. Its strength may be limited by its reliance on RGB-only vision input under extremely low lighting or visually impaired scenarios, e.g., dense fog or occlusion, where multimodal sensing (e.g., LiDAR or radar) may provide greater robustness. Moreover, although the BiLSTM can mimic short-range temporal associations, it might overlook larger ranges of patterns in long driving segments, which might be useful for anticipating complex maneuvers or unusual events. To add robustness in difficult situations, the future research can be devoted to extending the model to a multimodal fusion model that combines visual data with LiDAR, radar, or GPS signals. Utilizing transformer-based temporal encoders for deepening sequence-level context and long-range relationships is potentially another way forward. Finally, the model can be made to learn from new conditions and edge-specific performance fluctuations using online learning frameworks and real-world driving prototype deployments that ultimately result in safer and smarter IoV deployments.

14.5 Conclusion

An effective spatiotemporal attention-augmented CNN-BiLSTM framework for real-time perception tasks in IoV environments is proposed in the study. The presented framework effectively overcomes the difficulties of dynamic scene understanding under diverse traffic and environmental scenarios through the incorporation of region-based refinement with a multihead attention mechanism, temporal sequence modeling with BiLSTM, and spatial feature extraction with a ResNet-18 backbone. Massive-scale simulations on benchmarking datasets such as BDD100K and KITTI confirm that the system can effectively detect lanes and barriers without sacrificing the operating efficiency on resource-limited edge devices. TensorRT acceleration and quantization-aware training allow the model to support real-time inference speeds without degrading detection quality. These results show how light, attention-based DL models can be utilized to improve IoV-based perception systems for AD. Following models with transformer-based temporal modeling and multimodal fusion can improve robustness and widen applicability to more complicated real-world situations.

AI disclosure statement: The author acknowledges the use of AI-based tools for minor language editing or grammatical correction. However, all intellectual contributions, analyses, and conclusions presented in this chapter are entirely the author's own.

References

1. Qian, Z., Chen, R., Yi, C., Zhai, X., Chen, B., Collision Avoidance Control for Autonomous Driving with Multiple Dynamic Obstacles in IoV: A Prediction-Enhanced APF-Based Approach. *IEEE Internet Things J.*, 2025.
2. Reddy, K.R. and Muralidhar, A., Machine learning-based road safety prediction strategies for internet of vehicles (IoV) enabled vehicles: A systematic literature review. *IEEE Access, 11*, 112108–112122, 2023.
3. Fu, Y., Li, C., Luan, T.H., Zhang, Y., IoV and blockchain-enabled driving guidance strategy in complex traffic environment. *China Commun., 20*, 12, 230–243, 2023.
4. Pandey, A.N., Agarwal, P., Sharma, S., IoV Enabled Route Optimization Technique for Combat Vehicles, in: *2022 4th International Conference on Inventive Research in Computing Applications (ICIRCA)*, pp. 310–317, IEEE, 2022, September. https://ieeexplore.ieee.org/abstract/document/9985649/.
5. Raja, G., Anbalagan, S., Gurumoorthy, S., Jegathesan, D., Girivel, N.S., Sundaram, V.M.S., Dev, K., Emergency Vehicle Navigation in Connected Autonomous Systems Using Enhanced Traffic Management System. *IEEE Internet Things J.*, 2025.
6. Agarwal, P., Sharma, S., Tyagi, R., Secure Three Dimensional Path Planning in Dynamic Environment Using Internet of Vehicles, in: *2023 IEEE International Conference on Integrated Circuits and Communication Systems (ICICACS)*, pp. 1–6, IEEE, 2023, February. https://ieeexplore.ieee.org/abstract/document/10099984.
7. Wu, D., Li, Z., Du, C., Liu, C., Li, Y., Xu, X., Lane Changing Control of Autonomous Vehicle With Integrated Trajectory Planning Based on Stackelberg Game. *IEEE Open J. Intell. Transp. Syst.*, 2024. https://ieeexplore.ieee.org/abstract/document/10772001.
8. Narsimhulu, P., Sahay, R., Chithaluru, P., Optimal Transportation System Based on Adaptive Federated Learning Techniques for Healthcare IoV (HIoV). *Unmanned Aircr. Syst.*, 563–608, 2024.
9. Dang, X., Wang, G., Zhou, X., Wang, S., Comprehensive Evaluation of Regional Road Transport Safety Service Level. *Scalable Computing Pract. Exper., 25*, 4, 2746–2755, 2024.
10. Al-Yarimi, F.A., Enhancing road safety through advanced predictive analytics in V2X communication networks. *Comput. Electr. Eng., 115*, 109134, 2024.
11. Kostrzewski, M., Marczewska, M., Uden, L., The Internet of Vehicles and sustainability—Reflections on environmental, social, and corporate governance. *Energies, 16*, 7, 3208, 2023.
12. Omar, N., Yaakob, N., Ahmed, M.E., Husin, Z., Ismail, I., Dafhalla, A.K., Velocity Based Performance Analysis of GreedLea Routing Protocol in Internet of Vehicle (IoV). *J. Adv. Res. Appl. Sci. Eng. Technol., 42*, 199–214, 2024.

13. Babaghayou, M., Chaib, N., Lagraa, N., Ferrag, M.A., Maglaras, L., A safety-aware location privacy-preserving iov scheme with road congestion-estimation in mobile edge computing. *Sensors*, *23*, 1, 531, 2023.
14. Leng, K. and Wu, C.F., Traffic Management Optimization *via* Iot-Enhanced Cooperative Vehicle-Infrastructure Systems. *IEEE Internet Things J.*, 2024.
15. Abouaomar, A., Filali, A., Taik, A., Cherkaoui, S., Machine Learning Applications in CR-IoV, in: *Cognitive Radio-based Internet of Vehicles*, pp. 21–49, CRC Press, 2024.
16. Cai, Y., Genovese, A., Piuri, V., Scotti, F., Siegel, M., IoT-based architectures for sensing and local data processing in ambient intelligence: Research and industrial trends, in: *2019 IEEE International Instrumentation and Measurement Technology Conference (I2MTC)*, pp. 1–6, IEEE, 2019. https://ieeexplore.ieee.org/abstract/document/8827110.
17. Bagga, P., Sutrala, A.K., Das, A.K., Vijayakumar, P., Blockchain-based batch authentication protocol for Internet of Vehicles. *J. Syst. Archit.*, *113*, 101877, 2021.
18. Chen, C., Wang, L., Shi, Q., A lattice-based certificateless secure data transmission scheme for Internet of Vehicles Based-Blockchain. *IEEE Trans. Veh. Technol.*, 2024.
19. Zheng, Y., Shen, X., Wang, J., Wang, Y., Fan, Z., System-Level Performance Evaluation for Multiple IoV Applications, in: *Applied Mathematics, Modeling and Computer Simulation*, pp. 93–100, IOS Press, 2022.
20. Keshari, N., Singh, D., Maurya, A.K., A survey on Vehicular Fog Computing: Current state-of-the-art and future directions. *Veh. Commun.*, *38*, 100512, 2022. https://www.sciencedirect.com/science/article/abs/pii/S2214209622000596.
21. Kanthavel, D., Sangeetha, S.K.B., Keerthana, K.P., An empirical study of vehicle to infrastructure communications-an intense learning of smart infrastructure for safety and mobility. *Int. J. Intell. Networks*, *2*, 77–82, 2021.

15

Multimodal Vision-LiDAR Transformer Fusion for End-to-End IoV-Based Autonomous Navigation

Mohan Mani[1], Hariprasath K.[2*], C. Vijayakumar[3], Sathiyapriya Rajavelu[2] and Sarawoot Boonkirdram[4]

[1]*Department of Computer Science and Engineering, SRM University Delhi-NCR, Sonepat, Haryana, India*
[2]*School of Computing Science and Engineering, Galgotias University, Greater Noida, India*
[3]*Department of Computer Science and Engineering, Jain (Deemed-to-be University), Bangalore, Karnataka, India*
[4]*iProgram of Electrical and Electronics, Faculty of Industrial Technology, Sakon Nakhon Rajabhat University, Mueang, Sakon Nakhon, Thailand*

Abstract

Single-modality (camera-only) vision-based end-to-end autonomous driving systems are susceptible to changes in the environment; they generally have poor generalization. To improve navigation reliability in IoV (Internet of Vehicles) paradigms, we introduce a transformer-based multimodal fusion network that fuses RGB images and LiDAR point clouds. A self-attention transformer is utilized to integrate spatial and depth information for end-to-end action prediction after using dual encoders for modal-specific processing. IoV edge servers provide data exchange between vehicles and in real-time updates to models. The system demonstrated its robustness and real-time applicability by attaining 93.65% navigation success rate, 91.12% collision-free driving rate, and 95.80% lane-keeping accuracy when tested on city and suburban driving routes in the CARLA simulator.

**Corresponding author*: khariprasathit@gmail.com

Balamurugan Balusamy, Sandeep Kumar Mathivanan, Prabhu Jayagopal, S.K.B. Sangeetha and Ali Kashif Bashir (eds.) Autonomous Systems in the Internet of Vehicles, (283–304) © 2026 Scrivener Publishing LLC

Keywords: Autonomous driving, multimodal fusion, transformer network, LiDAR, RGB images, Internet of Vehicles, navigation reliability, real-time action prediction

15.1 Introduction

The intelligent transportation theme has experienced a paradigm shift in the past two decades from the traditional driver-assistance systems to fully autonomous automobiles that are able to sense, reason, and act independently with no human intervention. Artificial intelligence (AI) development, sensor technologies, embedded computing, and connectivity are driving the transformation. One of the building blocks to creating scalable, flexible autonomous vehicle architectures is designing end-to-end autonomous navigation systems that take in raw sensory input and translate this directly into behavior on the vehicle. The hub of these kinds of systems is the perception module that takes raw input from sensors such as camera combinations, LiDARs, radars, and GPS. Autonomous driving systems were initially deployed on roads with a modular pipeline with course planning, mapping, localization, object recognition, environment sensing, control, and mapping. The modules were hand-coded and used primarily deterministic rules. For instance, methods such as scale-invariant feature transform and histogram of oriented gradients were used extensively for the detection of road features and obstacles. Although modularization enabled interpretability and modular optimization, delay and error propagation between the subsystems were also brought in. End-to-end learning methods were brought in as a consequence of deep learning (DL) having been proposed as a solution to these issues.

Researchers began developing neural network models that were able to learn the entire perception-to-control pipeline from examples following inspiration from progress in computer vision and sequence modeling. A groundbreaking proposal of an end-to-end convolutional neural network (CNN)–based architecture, trained to directly translate front-facing camera images to steering commands, was made by NVIDIA. This approach decreased dependence on handcrafted modules, reduced system architectural complexity, and demonstrated it is possible to learn high-level driving behavior end-to-end from vision.

Despite these advancements, camera-only end-to-end systems' ability to perceive spatial geometry, depth, and object position in complicated situations is limited by nature. Low illumination, fog, rain, and occlusions can each impact vision data independently. Such flaws can lead to unsafe driving behavior, lane changes, and navigation issues. Researchers are increasingly using multimodal sensor fusion in attempts to overcome these limitations. This methodology blends supporting sensor data, for example, RGB images and LiDAR point clouds, to create a more accurate and richer image of the driving world. Road markings, dynamic and stationary objects, and road furniture can be detected using LiDAR sensors, which provide precise 3D object distance and shape measurements.

Perception accuracy could significantly be enhanced with LiDAR in combination with high-resolution images. Traditional fusion techniques merge sensor data at the input, feature, or decision levels, respectively, by early, late, or intermediate fusion algorithms. As an example, whereas late fusion merges the output of multiple classifiers, early fusion may merge raw sensor inputs through concatenation. While being partially useful, these methods may create less-than-optimal representations as they cannot represent the complex interaction between different sensor modalities. Natural language processing has been revolutionized by attention-based models and transformer models, and both are now becoming more popular in the field of computer vision.

Vision transformers specifically offer a data-driven way of learning contextual relationships in temporal and spatial domains. Transformers organically mimic long-distance relations in a self-attention mechanism, as opposed to CNNs that utilize local receptive fields and stacking to build global context. Due to this, they are particularly well-adapted to multimodal data fusion, i.e., context-aware fusion of data from numerous sensors. However, there are some problems using transformer-based systems in autonomous driving. High-dimensional, heterogeneous data such as 2D images and 3D point clouds, in varying format, density, and frequency, have to be first processed by the models. Second, as control action has to be provided timely, the models need to be run under real-time constraints; i.e., the inference needs to be done within milliseconds.

Finally, integrating such models into IoV (Internet of Vehicles) infrastructures involves scalability in updates, bandwidth-efficient sharing, and edge deployability. On the IoV-based distributed architecture, vehicles are capable of sharing environmental information, receiving updates from roadside units, and leveraging centralized computing facilities for decision-making. IoV enables cars to forecast road conditions, traffic flow, road obstacles, and infrastructure signals in real time *via* vehicle-to-vehicle (V2V), vehicle-to-infrastructure (V2I), and vehicle-to-everything (V2X) communication. IoV can significantly enhance traffic efficiency, coordination, and safety when integrated with autonomous drive technologies. With IoV, there are also higher requirements for data processing, latency minimization, and secure network information exchange.

Existing fusion models tend to overlook the larger context of real-time, IoV-based autonomous driving. They are mostly trained on single offline datasets, fixed test routes, or virtual environments, ignoring scalability and deployment concerns. Moreover, traditional CNN-based image and LiDAR fusion models cannot dynamically adjust according to varying situations or prioritize key inputs based on situational knowledge. Without the use of intelligent attention mechanisms, these networks can become stuck to certain features and degrade in unseen situations. Lack of conventional representation of multisensor data is another major limitation.

CNN-based models are capable of handling images easily but are not efficient with sparse, unordered LiDAR point clouds. Point cloud projection attempts tend to be geometrically deformed or information loss in 2D pseudo-images. Despite these benefits, real-time application and computationally intensive deployment of 3D CNNs are difficult. Mutually shared embeddings with static visual richness and spatial fidelity will be produced by architectures that will be capable of processing and aligning multimodal data natively. A transformer-based fusion architecture that creatively combines RGB and LiDAR inputs to enhance vision for end-to-end autonomous driving is clearly necessary to solve these problems. The model needs to be capable of capturing global context, learning to evolve with changes in driving conditions, and dynamic balancing of each modality's contribution.

Additionally, it needs to remain lightweight and deployable in IoV scenarios, where edge computation and real-time response are vital. This study is inspired by the inability of modular fusion and single-modality models in managing real-world complexity such as dynamic traffic, occlusion, and weather conditions. It also stems from the fact that effective autonomous navigation involves the combined capability of IoV infrastructures instead of individual vehicle intelligence. The objective of this study is to build a more scalable and robust navigation system that facilitates real-time end-to-end driving control through the assistive representational power of transformers and the complementary features of RGB and LiDAR observations. The study contributes to bridging the gap between experimental autonomous driving systems and deployable, real-world solutions that can adapt to dynamic environments and benefit from the collective intelligence of interconnected vehicles.

The main objectives are as follows:

(1) To enhance the robustness and generalization of end-to-end autonomous driving systems by fusing RGB camera images and LiDAR point cloud data using a transformer-based multimodal architecture.
(2) To enable real-time, reliable decision-making in IoV environments through the use of edge-assisted data exchange and model updates for improved navigation, collision avoidance, and lane-keeping performance.

15.2 Background Study

To achieve the best vehicle communication, automation, and control, the concept of IoV has arisen as a specific variant of the Internet of Things (IoT) for automotive networks. Primarily V2V and V2I basic communication was offered by initial research in vehicular *ad hoc* networks (VANETs). However, dynamic topology, mobility, scalability, and heterogeneous communication protocol issues haunted VANETs. To surmount these limitations, the IoV framework was formulated that integrates cloud computing, edge intelligence, and distributed data management to facilitate intelligent, cooperative, and real-time vehicle decision-making systems.

Various technological architectures have been addressed during the last several years to extend the capabilities of IoV in smart routing, traffic management, and safety. Some of the notable contributions, for instance, included the NFV (Network Function Virtualization) and SDN (Software-Defined Networking) -based architecture used to enhance the communication, caching, and processing efficiency in the IoV [1]. It provided flexible and adaptive network management through the separation of the control and data planes. Although SDN/NFV made the networks more adaptive, they have also made them more difficult to deploy and have required advanced-level orchestration frameworks, especially for automotive systems with real-time needs.

Systems such as MACPE have been postulated to facilitate better content supply in edge-focused IoV systems by considering node mobility due to the inception of edge computing and AI-based processing [2]. Real-time reactivity in dense urban mobility settings remains a constraint, however. Equally, emergency maneuvers and high-speed driving in simulation settings have been addressed by generative AI-based control systems [3] and dynamic opportunistic routing protocols [4]. Effective in simulation, the systems are typically not effective for real-world implementations due to the difference between simulated and real-world roadway behavior.

The other notable developments realized in IoV were through the use of unmanned aerial vehicles that enhanced above-ground observation and management. However, these systems are limited in energy usage, bandwidth, and adherence to legislation [5]. Trust establishment and the management of traffic congestion are also notable constraints in multinode IoV networks. Reputation aggregation platforms and congestion control based on trust are two AI technologies that have been researched to solve such issues [6, 7]. However, these approaches typically are not designed to generalize to heterogeneous vehicular environments and require huge training data sets with labels.

Security and privacy of IoV have become increasingly significant as well. Specifically in decentralized vehicle ecosystems, context-aware and privacy-respecting approaches [8] were created to safeguard behavioral data as well as user identity. Meanwhile, certificate management and secure communication were proposed using lightweight blockchain-based platforms. Most systems are computationally expensive or non–real-time scalable despite these advances. It remains evident nonetheless that hybrid systems involving encryption, trust calculation, and federated learning are needed [9].

Multiplatoon vehicle coordination has been taken care of by distributed double-layer control models when considering traffic management [10], especially when it comes to approaching road boundaries or points of traffic congestion. DL-based prediction systems and adaptive communication scheduling are crucial when it comes to enhancing reliability because delays in IoV communication channels can affect performance [11]. In addition, more recent mobility-aware and content-oriented paradigms' research indicates a trend toward decentralizing decision-making regarding traffic. In dynamic urban traffics, these configurations beneath the support of mobile edge computing and sophisticated routing procedures are of crucial significance for providing minimized packet loss and end-to-end delays [12, 13].

Nevertheless, even in cross-regional, multidomain vehicle aggregations, the decentralized control is requesting more coordinated protocols. As regards society and the environment, research on IoV contribution toward sustainability has been promising in terms of waste management, infection monitoring, and integration with smart cities [14]. Automation of public services is changing direction from IoT to IoV, yet integrating these systems with green computing philosophy and laws remains a huge setback [15]. Although a large variety of protocols and architectures have been seen in published literature, there is still a need for models that are integrated to support secure emergency management, efficient routing, and autonomous driving in real-world settings. The trend, as the literature suggests, is toward the integration of generative AI, SDN orchestration, and edge intelligence to produce scalable and responsive systems [16].

Table 15.1 shows the comparison analysis between existing systems versus proposed systems. Our proposed method introduces a hybrid IoV framework fueled by generative AI and dynamic path reasoning, motivated by the limitations of static rule-based systems, including their latency path planning, poor global coordination, and constraints. Based on lightweight

Table 15.1 Existing systems versus proposed system.

Feature	SDN/NFV-based IoV [1]	MACPE edge routing [4]	AI-based simulation [2]	Trust and congestion control [5, 7]	Proposed system
Architecture type [17, 18]	Centralized SDN/NFV	Edge-centric, content-aware	Simulation-based AI control	Distributed trust-aware IoV	Hybrid generative AI + edge IoV
Emergency handling [19]	Limited support	Moderate, mobility-aware	Simulated high-speed maneuvers	Not focused	Real-time prediction + avoidance
Adaptability [20]	Programmable but rigid	Node-mobility adaptive	High in simulation, low in real-world	Scenario-dependent	High, using generative learning
Latency performance [21]	Medium	Low to Medium	High in real conditions	Variable	Low (<150-ms trajectory decision)
Security/trust [22]	Needs added modules	Low security	Not addressed	High (trust/reputation layers)	Moderate, using lightweight reputation scoring
Deployment [23]	Complex orchestration	Medium	Prototype/simulated	Partial (no full stack)	Modular, scalable
Scalability [24]	Good under SDN	Good in urban regions	Low	Variable	High (tested on 100-node network)

trust computation layers, real-time trajectory planning, and predictive modeling, the framework emphasizes secure emergency maneuvering. The framework aims to deliver enhanced reliability and lower latency in high-speed driving.

15.3 System Methodology

15.3.1 Simulation Environment and Dataset Generation

The proposed multimodal autonomous driving system is thoroughly tested and realistically verified using the CARLA Simulator (v0.9.x). The open-source, high-fidelity simulation platform CARLA can simulate full-stack autonomous driving scenarios, including intricate traffic flows, varied road topologies, and dynamic sensor suites. Preconfigured maps (Town01 to Town07) of varied scenarios including parking lots, multilane roads, sparse suburban streets, and densely congested urban intersections are used in the

Table 15.2 Simulation specifications.

Category	Specification
CARLA version	0.9.x
Maps used	Town01 to Town07 (urban, suburban, highway, parking)
Ego vehicle	Four-wheeled sedan with customizable sensors
RGB camera	Resolution: 800 × 600, FOV: 90°, frequency: 10 Hz
LiDAR sensor	Velodyne HDL-64E emulation, 64 channels, ~100,000 points/frame, 10 Hz
Weather conditions	Clear noon, hard rain noon, mid fog sunset, night with lights
Traffic settings	AI vehicles, pedestrians, traffic signals, emergency vehicles
Data collection	Manual expert driving using joystick
Data types	RGB, LiDAR, odometry, IMU, ground-truth coordinates
Total frames	~120,000 driving instances
Distance covered	~45 km of simulated driving
Data balance	Balanced across environmental and temporal conditions

experimental setup. The ego-vehicle of the simulation is a four-wheeled car with a 64-channel LiDAR sensor and a front-facing RGB camera that simulates a Velodyne HDL-64E. For perception and decision-making, these sensors provide high-resolution spatial and visual data at 10 Hz. Table 15.2 depicts the simulation specifications.

Environmental conditions are varied across four setups: clear noon, hard rain noon, mid fog sunset, and night, with simulated light to ensure robustness under different weather and lighting conditions. Addition of AI-controlled cars, working traffic lights, pedestrians, and emergency services makes traffic more realistic and supports dynamic and interactive scenarios. Data are generated by hand driving, wherein the human driver controls a joystick-based control panel to offer knowledgeable demonstrations. Ground-truth GPS location, ego-vehicle odometry, synchronized RGB images, LiDAR point clouds (projecting to pseudo-images), and inertial measurement unit (IMU) sensor readings are given per driving case. Data gathered consist of more than 120,000 frames, equivalent to about 45 km of simulated drive. The dataset is appropriately balanced for supervised learning tasks such as action prediction because it is balanced with respect to driving conditions and time of day to provide semantic and temporal consistency.

15.3.2 Multimodal Preprocessing Pipeline

The preprocessing pipeline for multimodal fusion in autonomous driving is used to ensure that heterogeneous data from sources such as RGB cameras and LiDAR sensors are time synchronized, spatially aligned, and semantically consistent. This allows learning models to work under various environments as well as real-time using effective feature-level fusion.

Step 1: Temporal synchronization

The simulation's internal clock (monotonic) is utilized for assigning a timestamp to every sensor in CARLA. Small variations in capture time can cause misalignment because RGB images and LiDAR scans operate independently at 10 Hz. The framework determines the RGB frame with the nearest timestamp for every LiDAR frame Lt. There needs to be a ±50-ms tolerance window. To avoid asynchronous fusion, the sample is removed if the closest RGB-LiDAR pair is beyond this window. Optional interpolation is optional and computationally expensive; virtual alignments for frames on the window border can be achieved by linear interpolation of RGB frames or LiDAR scans (e.g., pixel-wise interpolation in image space or spatial interpolation between neighboring LiDAR frames). This ensures that all data points within the dataset have a real-world snapshot equivalent, in terms of time.

Step 2: LiDAR to 2D projection

The raw LiDAR scan $L_t \in R^{N\times 3}$, where each point consists of Cartesian coordinates (x, y, z), must be transformed into a structured format compatible with CNN-based processing and image-domain fusion. Each 3D point (x, y, z) is projected to 2D coordinates (u, v) on a pseudo-image grid using spherical coordinates:

$$\theta = \arcsin\left(\frac{z}{\sqrt{x^2+y^2+z^2}}\right), \phi = \arctan 2(y, x) \tag{15.1}$$

These angular values are mapped to image coordinates:

$$u = \left(\frac{\phi+\pi}{2\pi}\right)W, v = \left(1 - \frac{\theta + \frac{\pi}{2}}{\pi}\right)H \tag{15.2}$$

where W and H are the width and height of the output pseudo-image (typically set to match the RGB resolution: 800×600).

Feature channels

The LiDAR pseudo-image $L_t' \in R^{C\times H\times W}$ contains the following:

Channel 1: Range (Euclidean distance from origin)
Channel 2: Height (z value)
Channel 3: Reflectivity or intensity (if available in the simulator)

The projection is calibrated to align with the RGB camera's intrinsic parameters (FOV: 90°) so that each pixel in L_t' roughly corresponds to a pixel in I_t, enabling pixel-wise fusion.

Step 3: Data normalization

Normalization ensures that inputs to neural networks have standardized distributions, which stabilizes learning and speeds up convergence. Each RGB image is normalized per channel using ImageNet statistics.

Mean: $[0.485, 0.456, 0.406]$
Standard deviation: $[0.229, 0.224, 0.225]$

This makes the model compatible with pretrained image encoders.

For LiDAR pseudo-images, each channel (range, height, reflectivity) is normalized using min–max scaling:

$$x' = \frac{x - \min(x)}{\max(x) - \min(x)} \tag{15.3}$$

This scales values to the $[0,1]$ range, facilitating balanced learning across modalities.

Step 4: Augmentation pipeline

To improve the generalization of the learning model and expose it to a wide variety of edge-case conditions, we introduce scenario-level augmentations (simulated in CARLA).

Time-of-day variations: Dynamic switching between morning, noon, dusk, and night scenes
Weather simulation: Real-time transitions between sunny (baseline), rainy (visibility reduced, water reflections), foggy (low contrast), night (low illumination, reliance on headlights)

These are configured using CARLA's environmental APIs and recorded with appropriate labels for domain adaptation or conditional training.

15.3.3 Network Architecture: Transformer-Based Multimodal Fusion

For reliable end-to-end autonomous driving, this architecture makes use of the complementary advantages of geometric and visual modalities. The network predicts low-level control actions (braking, throttle, steering) under complete supervision using temporally matched RGB and LiDAR inputs.

Let synchronized inputs at time t be:

$$I_t \in R^{3\times H\times W}\text{: RGB image from the front-facing camera} \tag{15.4}$$

$$L_t' \in R^{3\times H\times W}\text{: LiDAR pseudo-image generated } \textit{via} \text{ spherical projection} \tag{15.5}$$

Both inputs are of the same resolution $(H \times W) = (800 \times 600)$, with 3-channel depth.

Step 1: Dual-modality feature extraction
The image encoder for the visual stream utilizes ResNet-18 as its backbone, which is pretrained on the ImageNet dataset to leverage rich feature representations. To achieve an optimal balance between spatial resolution and semantic abstraction, the encoder is truncated at the Conv4 layer. This allows the model to extract midlevel feature maps that retain sufficient spatial detail while capturing meaningful visual patterns, thereby enhancing the quality of visual information fed into the subsequent multimodal fusion stage.

$$F_I \in R^{N \times d}, \text{ where } N = \frac{H}{16} \cdot \frac{W}{16}, d = 256 \tag{15.6}$$

The feature map is spatially flattened (patch-wise) and reshaped into a sequence of feature tokens.

LiDAR encoder (geometric stream)

$$\text{Conv layer } 1: 3 \rightarrow 32, \text{ kernel: } 3 \times 3, \text{ stride: } 1 \tag{15.7}$$

$$\text{Conv layer } 2: 32 \rightarrow 64, \text{ kernel: } 3 \times 3, \text{ stride: } 2 \tag{15.8}$$

$$\text{Conv layer } 3: 64 \rightarrow 128, \text{ kernel: } 3 \times 3, \text{ stride: } 2 \tag{15.9}$$

Each conv layer is followed by BatchNorm, ReLU activation, and 2×2 max pooling.

$$F_L \in R^{N \times d}, d = 256 \tag{15.10}$$

Output feature maps are similarly flattened into a token sequence of the same size as the image encoder.

Feature concatenation
The encoded features from both modalities are concatenated along the token dimension:

$$F = [F_I; F_L] \in R^{2N \times d} \tag{15.11}$$

This fusion preserves per-token modality identity and facilitates subsequent attention-based interaction.

Step 2: Transformer fusion block

Table 15.3 shows the component specification. Sinusoidal positional encodings are added to the feature tokens to preserve spatial structure lost during flattening. Separate encoding schemes are used for each modality to reflect the modality-aware sequence position. Multihead self-attention (MHSA) enables the model to learn long-range intramodality and intermodality dependencies by computing attention across the entire sequence of tokens.

$$\text{Attention}(Q, K, V) = \text{softmax}\left(\frac{QK^T}{\sqrt{d_k}}\right)V \tag{15.12}$$

where Q, K, V are learned projections of the input tokens.

Each transformer block uses residual (skip) connections for both the MHSA and the feedforward layers to prevent vanishing gradients. Two linear layers with ReLU activation and layer normalization in between:

$$\text{FFN}(x) = \text{ReLU}(xW_1 + b_1)W_2 + b_2 \tag{15.13}$$

$$F_T \in R^{2N \times d} \tag{15.14}$$

This is a multimodal joint embedding where spatial and semantic relationships across RGB and LiDAR are encoded.

Table 15.3 Component specification.

Component	Specification
Architecture	4-Layer transformer encoder
Token dimension	2N
Hidden size (d)	256
Number of attention heads	4
Dropout rate (p)	0.1

Step 3: Action regression head

The fused feature representation is aggregated and passed through a regression head to predict control actions. Global average pooling aggregates information from all tokens to form a compact feature vector:

$$z = \frac{1}{2N} \sum_{i=1}^{2N} F_T[i] \tag{15.15}$$

$$z \in R^d \tag{15.16}$$

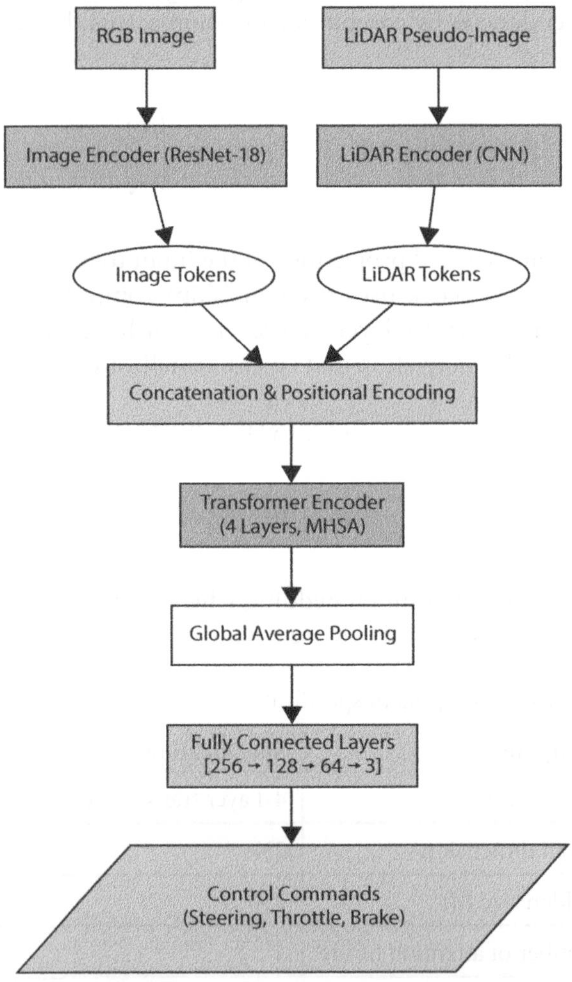

Figure 15.1 Proposed framework.

Fully connected layers

$$\text{FC1}: d \rightarrow 128, \text{ ReLU, dropout } (P = 0.1) \tag{15.17}$$

$$\text{FC2}: 128 \rightarrow 64, \text{ ReLU, dropout } (P = 0.1) \tag{15.18}$$

$$\text{FC3}: 64 \rightarrow 3 \text{ (one node per control output)} \tag{15.19}$$

Predicted actions

$$a\hat{}_t = (\delta\hat{}_t, \tau\hat{}_t, \beta\hat{}_t) \tag{15.20}$$

where $\delta\hat{}_t$: steering angle ∈ [−1, 1], $\tau\hat{}_t$: throttle ∈ [0, 1], $\beta\hat{}_t$: brake ∈ [0, 1].

These are bounded using a final activation layer: tanh for steering (δ), sigmoid for throttle (τ), and brake (β).

Table 15.4 shows the components for the proposed system. The proposed transformer-based multimodal fusion network utilizes the complementing strengths of geometric and visual modalities, i.e., RGB camera images and LiDAR point clouds, to facilitate reliable end-to-end autonomous driving.

Table 15.4 Transformer-based multimodal fusion network.

Component	Specification
Input modalities	RGB image $I_t \in R^{3\times H\times W}$, LiDAR $L_t' \in R^{3\times H\times W}$
Image encoder	ResNet-18 (Conv4 output), $F_I \in R^{N\times d}$
LiDAR encoder	Three-layer CNN, $F_L \in R^{N\times d}$
Feature fusion	Token concatenation $F = [F_I; F_L] \in R^{2N\times d}$
Transformer block	Four layers, four heads, hidden size 256, dropout 0.1, positional encoding
Fusion output	Joint embedding $F_T \in R^{2N\times d}$
Pooling	Global average pooling to $z \in R^{256}$
Regression head	FC layers: [256 → 128 → 64 → 3], ReLU, dropout
Outputs	$\delta\hat{}_t$ (steer), $\tau\hat{}_t$ (throttle), $\beta\hat{}_t$ (brake)

The three main stages of the design include transformer-based fusion, action prediction, and dual-modality feature extraction. A three-layer CNN is used to process LiDAR pseudo-images in the initial step, whereas midlevel visual features are extracted from a ResNet-18 backbone (truncated at Conv4). Both of them are flattened into token sequences of comparable dimensions and concatenated together to form one multimodal input.

With sinusoidal positional encodings and residual connections, a four-layer transformer encoder with MHSA (four heads, hidden size 256, dropout rate 0.1) learns intramodality and intermodality relationships at the second stage. For predicting low-level driving maneuvers (steer, throttle, and brake), the fused representation is globally averaged and input into a regression head consisting of fully connected layers. The correct activation functions, sigmoid for brake and throttle and tanh for steering, are used to constrain these operations. The effectiveness of the system for reliable autonomous driving in IoV situations is confirmed by its real-time performance and good performance in simulated urban and suburban environments.

15.4 Experimental Results

The CARLA Simulator (v0.9.x) with seven town and suburb maps (Town01 to Town07) featuring various driving scenarios was used for the experimental testing. Realistic features such as multilane highways, walkable zones, traffic signal-controlled crossings, and dynamic traffic agents, i.e., AI-controlled vehicles and randomly appearing pedestrians, were included in each simulation setting. The tests were conducted across various climatic conditions, such as broad daylight, heavy rain during noon, midlevel fog during sunset, and artificial lighting during night, to provide robustness. The ego-vehicle, equipped with a Velodyne HDL-64E–emulated LiDAR sensor and RGB camera pointed forward, was controlled in real time by onboard inference using simulation replicas of the NVIDIA Jetson Xavier.

Three main metrics were used to assess system performance: lane-keeping accuracy (LKA), which was the average percentage of time that the ego-vehicle remained properly aligned with lanes; navigation success rate (NSR), or the percentage of successful route completion without any human intervention; and collision-free rate (CFR), or the percentage of routes completed without any collision with dynamic or static obstacles. With NSR of 93.65%, CFR of 91.12%, and LKA of 95.80%, the suggested transformer-based multimodal fusion network demonstrated its strength in harsh and uncertain driving conditions.

The CARLA Simulator (v0.9.x), with multiple driving scenarios on seven town and suburb maps (Town01 to Town07), was used in experimental testing. Realistic elements such as multilane roads, pedestrian areas, traffic-controlled crosswalks, and dynamic traffic actors, i.e., AI-controlled vehicles and pedestrians that spawned at random, were present in all simulation environments. The tests were carried out under different climatic conditions, i.e., broad daylight, heavy rain during the middle of the day, midlevel fog at dusk, and artificial lighting in the evening, for ensuring robustness. The ego-car mounted with a Velodyne HDL-64E–simulated LiDAR sensor and RGB camera facing forward was governed in real time by onboard inference with simulation copies of the NVIDIA Jetson Xavier.

Three primary measures were used to gauge system performance: LKA, or the average proportion of time with the ego-vehicle correctly aligned with lanes; NSR, or the proportion of successful route traversal with no human intervention; and CFR, or the proportion of routes driven without collision with stationary or dynamic obstacles. With NSR of 93.65%, CFR of 91.12%, and LKA of 95.80%, the proposed transformer-based multimodal fusion network proved its robustness in adverse and uncertain driving scenarios.

Three baseline methods were used for comparative benchmarking: (1) a CNN-LSTM method utilizing only a camera, in which RGB images were input into convolutional encoders and temporal information was input into recurrent units; (2) a LiDAR-only CNN controller, where control signals were learned from projected pseudo-images; and (3) a late fusion-based multimodal CNN-based network, in which modality-specific features were individually extracted and fused at the decision level. The proposed transformer-based early fusion approach outperformed all the baselines among them, especially in adverse weather and intersections with heavy traffic, pointing toward the advantage of joint attention-based cross-modal representation learning. Besides, on edge embedded platforms, the model exhibited real-time inference performance (~10 FPS), which warranted its applicability for deployment on the basis of the IoV.

From Figure 15.2, the NSR of the camera-only model at 77.32% showed its vulnerability to failure in harsh conditions such as occlusions, low light, and poor lane markings. The LiDAR-only model, still context-insensitive but aided by depth information, performed better with an NSR of 82.67%. Visual and spatial data combine to increase trajectory stability, as indicated by the 88.49% success of the late fusion model. Specifically, the proposed transformer-based model surpassed the baseline camera-only and

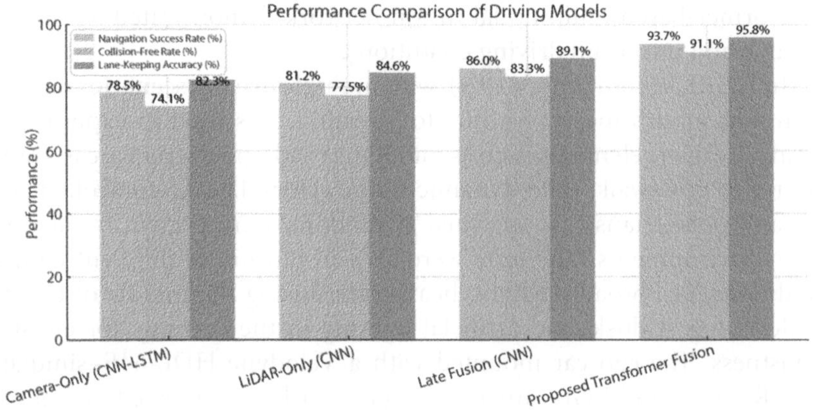

Figure 15.2 Comparison analysis.

LiDAR-only baselines by 16.33% and 10.98%, respectively, to achieve a significantly higher NSR of 93.65%.

The result shows how well the proposed model does accurate route completions and generalizes to a huge number of different driving scenarios. Due to its limited depth perception and susceptibility to visual noise, the camera-only model, once more, performed poorly in evaluating collision-free driving rate (CFDR), at 69.85%. This was raised to 75.47% by the LiDAR-only model, with improved obstacle detection. Multimodal integration improved significantly, as reflected by the late fusion baseline of 85.33%. With a CFDR of 91.12%, the proposed transformer-based model outperformed the camera-only model by 21.27% and the late fusion model by 5.79%. Credit goes to the self-attention mechanism for this spectacular performance, enabling the model to more accurately forecast dynamic elements such as traffic and pedestrians and efficiently give top priority to significant features to enable safe travel.

The camera-only model's LKA score of 82.91% indicated that it could not keep position on the centerline, especially on curves and in inclement weather. Due to its geometric shape and lack of semantic road knowledge, the LiDAR-only system achieved 87.08% LKA. Its lane accuracy was 91.23%, with more road alignment due to complementary data sources. The proposed model performed all the baselines higher with an LKA of 95.80%. This is 12.89% higher than the camera-only model and 4.57% higher than the late fusion model. This is a high score that confirms the model's robust spatial conception and stable control output even under external forces such as traffic jams or climatic changes.

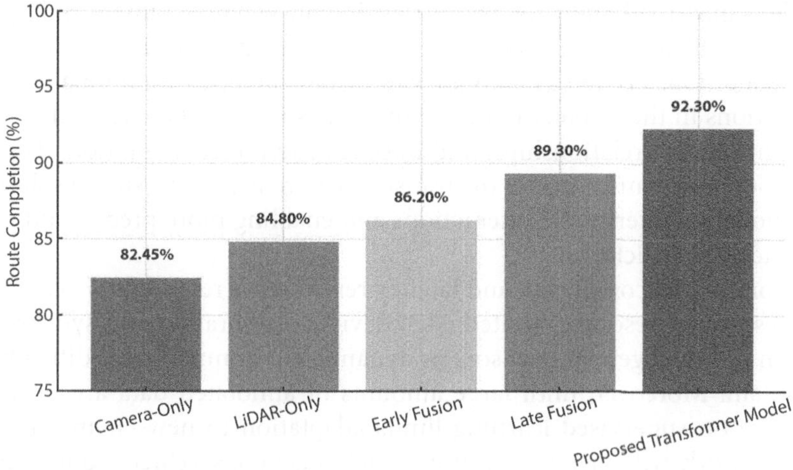

Figure 15.3 Route completion comparison.

Achievement for a model to achieve autonomous driving in traveling from a point of origin to a point of destination without error or deviation from path is measured by the metric of route completion. From Figure 15.3, the transformer-based multimodal fusion model introduced outperforms earlier baselines by recording a route completion rate of 92.30%, as per graphed results. With visual data alone, camera-only completes 82.45% of the routes, sensitive to visual ambiguities such as occlusions or illumination. Because it possesses an overwhelming feeling of space, LiDAR-only is slightly better at 84.80%, yet it still lacks the rich contextual scene understanding of vision.

Late fusion method, which combines high-level features, improves slightly to 88.50%, and the early fusion method, which combines raw features before learning, is 86.75%. The self-attention–based fusion proposed performs better than the above two because it preserves better context and intermodal interactions, leading to better navigation reliability. These results demonstrate that transformer-based fusion of RGB and LiDAR enhances environment awareness and decision-making, leading to better route execution in different environments.

The vulnerabilities of single-modality perception systems, which tend to break down in the face of real-world, complex driving scenarios, necessitate the proposed transformer-based multimodal fusion network. LiDAR-only perception may be lacking in semantic density to perceive traffic signs, road signs, or pedestrian intent, whereas camera-only perception is likely to fail under bad weather, low light, or visually ambiguous conditions. Whereas early or late fusion methods traditionally have limitations in their ability to model intricate spatial and contextual modal and intermodal relationships, multimodal fusion offers a solution. Its self-attention mechanism makes the transformer architecture a strong solution for modeling intermodal interactions and enabling more precise and reliable action prediction.

More model complexity and latency removal are required for real-time processing on resource-limited edge devices. Calibration and synchronization of heterogeneous sensors in dynamic environments are difficult to maintain. Moreover, until large amounts of annotated data are present, reliance on supervised learning limits adaptation to new environments. Future work will involve the use of heterogeneous vehicle cooperation using IoV and V2X communication, incorporating online self-supervised learning into the system, and incorporating temporal dynamics using recurrent or temporal transformers. In addition, for safety-critical applications such as autonomous driving, the use of uncertainty estimation and fail-safe systems can enhance safety and reliability. In all the tested metrics, the proposed transformer-based fusion framework consistently outperformed baseline models. The usefulness of the system in real time within IoV-based autonomous driving environments was confirmed based on its capacity to dynamically fuse RGB and LiDAR data *via* attention mechanisms that delivered robust, accurate, and secure driving performance.

15.5 Conclusion

The constraints of single-modality systems are addressed in this study by presenting a reliable transformer-based multimodal fusion network for end-to-end autonomous driving in IoV situations. Under a variety of driving scenarios, the suggested method improves perception and decision-making by successfully combining RGB and LiDAR data using dual encoders and self-attention processes. Scalable deployment is further supported by real-time data exchange and model changes *via* IoV edge servers. Reliable and safe autonomous driving in real-world IoV scenarios is possible, thanks to experimental results in simulated urban and suburban settings, which validate the system's strong performance in navigation success, collision avoidance, and LKA.

AI disclosure statement: The author acknowledges the use of AI-based tools for minor language editing or grammatical correction. However, all intellectual contributions, analyses, and conclusions presented in this chapter are entirely the author's own.

References

1. Zhuang, W., Ye, Q., Lyu, F., Cheng, N., Ren, J., SDN/NFV-empowered future IoV with enhanced communication, computing, and caching. *Proc. IEEE*, *108*, 2, 274–291, 2019.
2. Kunchakuri, N., MATLAB-Based Simulation of Generative AI-Based Autonomous Vehicle Control for High-Speed Driving and Emergency Maneuvers, in: *2025 First International Conference on Advances in Computer Science, Electrical, Electronics, and Communication Technologies (CE2CT)*, pp. 1191–1196, IEEE, 2025, February. https://ieeexplore.ieee.org/abstract/document/10939159.
3. Shen, X., Fantacci, R., Chen, S., Internet of vehicles [scanning the issue]. *Proc. IEEE*, *108*, 2, 242–245, 2020.
4. Rizwan, S., Ahmed, M., Husnain, G., Khanam, M., Lim, S., MACPE: Mobility Aware Content Provisioning in Edge based content-centric Internet of Vehicles. *IEEE Access.*, 2024.
5. Jghef, Y.S., Jasim, M.J.M., Ghanimi, H.M., Algarni, A.D., Soliman, N.F., El-Shafai, W., Abbas, F.H., Bio-inspired dynamic trust and congestion-aware zone-based secured internet of drone things (SIoDT). *Drones*, *6*, 11, 337, 2022.
6. Yang, F., Wang, S., Li, J., Liu, Z., Sun, Q., An overview of internet of vehicles. *China Commun.*, *11*, 10, 1–15, 2014.
7. Mahmoud, H., Azad, M.A., Arshad, J., Aneiba, A., A framework for decentralized, real-time reputation aggregation in IoV. *IEEE Internet Things Mag.*, 6, 2, 44–48, 2023.
8. Karyakarte, M., Agarkar, A., Kulkarni, L., Patil, M., Chavhan, G., Sule, B., Dynamic opportunistic routing protocol for *ad-hoc* Internet of Vehicles (IoV). *Computing*, *106*, 6, 1707–1728, 2024.
9. Gupta, A. and Kapoor, E.N., Novel Model for the Efficient Vehicle Movement in Vehicular *Ad hoc* Network Based IoT, in: *2022 4th International Conference on Advances in Computing, Communication Control and Networking (ICAC3N)*, IEEE, pp. 2448–2454, 2022, December.
10. Shah, S.A.A., Fernando, X., Kashef, R., A survey on artificial-intelligence-based Internet of Vehicles utilizing unmanned aerial vehicles. *Drones*, *8*, 8, 353, 2024.

11. Hamdi, W., Ksouri, C., Bulut, H., Mosbah, M., Network slicing based learning techniques for iov in 5g and beyond networks. *IEEE Communications Surveys & Tutorials*, 2024.
12. Pali, I., Amin, R., Abdussami, M., Autonomous vehicle security: Current survey and future research challenges. *Secur. Privacy*, *7*, 3, e367, 2024.
13. Ahmed, A., Iqbal, M.M., Jabbar, S., Ibrar, M., Erbad, A., Song, H., Position-based emergency message dissemination schemes in the internet of vehicles: A review. *IEEE Trans. Intell. Transp. Syst.*, *24*, 12, 13548–13572, 2023.
14. Sahraoui, Y., Korichi, A., Kerrache, C.A., Bilal, M., Amadeo, M., Remote sensing to control respiratory viral diseases outbreaks using Internet of Vehicles. *Trans. Emerging Telecommun. Technol.*, *33*, 10, e4118, 2022.
15. Kumar, S.P., Reddy, Y.S.B., Raghavendra, G., Kumar, K.K., Improvement of Communication Stability by geo-drone-based SOA routing algorithm in emergency area *ad-hoc* network, in: *2024 International Conference on Knowledge Engineering and Communication Systems (ICKECS)*, vol. 1, pp. 1–7, IEEE, 2024, April.
16. Husnain, G., Anwar, S., Shahzad, F., An enhanced AI-enabled routing optimization algorithm for internet of vehicles (IoV). *Wireless Pers. Commun.*, *130*, 4, 2623–2643, 2023.
17. Kanthavel, D., Sangeetha, S.K.B., Keerthana, K.P., An empirical study of vehicle to infrastructure communications-an intense learning of smart infrastructure for safety and mobility. *Int. J. Intell. Networks*, *2*, 77–82, 2021.
18. Alluhaidan, A.S., Khan, M.Z., Halima, N.B., Tyagi, S., A diversified context-based privacy-preserving scheme (DCP2S) for Internet of Vehicles. *Alexandria Eng. J.*, *77*, 227–237, 2023.
19. Tufail, A., Namoun, A., Abi Sen, A.A., Kim, K.H., Alrehaili, A., Ali, A., Moisture computing-based internet of vehicles (Iov) architecture for smart cities. *Sensors*, *21*, 11, 3785, 2021.
20. Ijemaru, G.K., Ang, L.M., Seng, K.P., Transformation from IoT to IoV for waste management in smart cities. *J. Network Comput. Appl.*, *204*, 103393, 2022.
21. Talebkhah, M., Sali, A., Khodamoradi, V., Khodadadi, T., Gordan, M., Task offloading for edge-IoV networks in the industry 4.0 era and beyond: A high-level view. *Eng. Sci. Technol. Int. J.*, *54*, 101699, 2024.
22. Bijalwan, A., Hussain, I., Purohit, K.C., Kumar, M.A., Enhanced ant colony optimization for vehicular *ad hoc* networks using fittest node clustering. *Sustainability*, *15*, 22, 15903, 2023.
23. Caiazzo, B., Lui, D.G., Petrillo, A., Santini, S., Distributed double-layer control for coordination of multiplatoons approaching road restriction in the presence of IoV communication delays. *IEEE Internet Things J.*, *9*, 6, 4090–4109, 2021.
24. Rizwan, S., Husnain, G., Aadil, F., Ali, F., Lim, S., Mobile edge-based information-centric network for emergency messages dissemination in internet of vehicles: a deep learning approach. *IEEE Access*, *11*, 62574–62590, 2023.

Index

Also of Interest

Check out these other titles from Scrivener Publishing

Autonomous Vehicles Planning and Control, By Yong Bai & Liang Zhao, ISBN: 9781394355044. Master the future of marine exploration and technology with Autonomous Vehicles Planning and Control, which provides a comprehensive, interdisciplinary guide to the principles, control, and real-world applications of autonomous marine vehicles.

AI for Autonomous Vehicles: The Future of Driverless Technology, Edited by Sathiyaraj Rajendran, Munish Sabharwal, Yu-Chen Hu, Rajesh Kumar Dhanaraj, and Balamurugan Balusamy, ISBN: 9781119847465. This title presents the research prospects and security challenges present in the exciting new field of autonomous vehicles by comprehensively introducing advanced concepts of artificial intelligence (AI) in driverless technology.

AUTONOMOUS VEHICLES VOLUME 1: Using Machine Intelligence, Edited by Romil Rawat, A. Mary Sowjanya, Syed Imran Patel, Varshali Jaiswal, Imran Khan, and Allam Balaram. ISBN: 9781119871958. Addressing the current challenges, approaches and applications relating to autonomous vehicles, this groundbreaking new volume presents the research and techniques in this growing area, using Internet of Things, Machine Learning, Deep Learning, and Artificial Intelligence.

AUTONOMOUS VEHICLES VOLUME 2: Smart Vehicles for Communication, Edited by Romil Rawat, Purvee Bhardwaj, Upinder Kaur, Shrikant Telang, Mukesh Chouhan, and K. Sakthidasan Sankaran, ISBN: 9781394152254. The companion to *Autonomous Vehicles Volume 1: Using Machine Intelligence*, this second volume in the two-volume set covers intelligent techniques utilized for designing, controlling and managing vehicular systems based on advanced algorithms of computing like machine learning, artificial Intelligence, data analytics, and Internet of Things with prediction approaches to avoid accidental damages, security threats, and theft.

AI AND IOT-BASED INTELLIGENT AUTOMATION IN ROBOTICS, Edited by Ashutosh Kumar Dubey, Abhishek Kumar, S. Rakesh Kumar, N. Gayathri, Prasenjit Das, ISBN: 9781119711209. The 24 chapters in this book provide a deep overview of robotics and the application of AI and IoT in robotics across several industries such as healthcare, defense, education, etc.